ENGLISH RECUSANT LITERATURE
1558–1640

Selected and Edited by
D. M. ROGERS

Volume 223

THOMAS PRESTON
A Cleare, Sincere, and
Modest Confutation
1616

THOMAS PRESTON

A Cleare, Sincere, and
Modest Confutation
1616

The Scolar Press

1974

ISBN 0 85967 207 7

*Published and printed in Great Britain by
The Scolar Press Limited, 59-61 East Parade,
Ilkley, Yorkshire and
39 Great Russell Street,
London WC1*

NOTE

Reproduced (original size) from a copy in Cambridge University Library, by permission of the Syndics.

References: Allison and Rogers 664; STC 25598.

A
CLEARE, SIN-
CERE, AND MODEST
confutation *of the vnsound, fraudu-*
lent, and intemperate *Reply* of T. F. who is
knowne to be M^r. *Thomas Fitzherbert*
now an Englifh IESVITE.

Wherein
ALSO ARE CONFVTED THE
chiefeft obiections which D. *Schulckenius*, who
is commonly faid to be Card. Bellarmine, *hath made*
againft WIDDRINTONS *Apologie* for the
right, or *Soueraigntie* of temporall PRINCES.

BY
Roger Widdrington an Englifh Catholike.

LVK. 6.
Benedicite maledicentibus vobis, & orate pro calumniantibus vos.
Bleffe them that curfe you, and pray for them that calumniate you.

Permiffu Superiorum 1 6 1 6.

THE
CONTENTS
of this Treatife.

The Contents.

The Preface to the Reader.

Wherein

M.ʳ Fitzherberts Preface *is confuted , the matter,* which Widdrington *handleth , and the manner how he proceedeth therein is declared , and his doctrine proued to be* truly probable, *and to be neither preiudiciall to his* Maieſties *ſeruice, nor to the conſciences of Catholikes, and the exceptions of* D. Schulckenius *againſt that rule of the Law brought by* Widdrington , In dubijs melior eſt conditio poſſidentis , In doubts, *or diſputable cauſes,* the condition of him who hath poſſeſſion , is to be preferred, *are confuted.*

The firſt Part.

wherein

The authorities, and teſtimonies of thoſe learned Catholikes

The Contents.

A 3

verbatim *in my* Appendix *to* Suarez, *must needes suppose, that the Pope hath no power to depofe Princes, as out of* Suarez *I conuince in this chapter.*

Chap. 6.

Wherein the authority of the Kingdome *and* State *of* France *is largely debated, the exceptions which D.* Schulckenius *taketh against* Petrus Pithæus *and* Bochellus *are confuted, and* Sigebert *is defended from Schifme, of which he is wrongfully taxed by Card.* Baronius *and D.* Schulckenius.

The fecond part.

wherein

All the principall arguments, which Card. Bellarmine *bringeth to prooue the vnion and fubordination of the temporall and fpirituall power among Chriftians, wheron Mr.* Fitzherbert, *and all the other vehement maintainers of the* Popes *power to depofe* Princes, *doe chiefely ground that doctrine, together with the* Replies, *which are brought by D.* Schulckenius *to confirme the fame vnion and fubordination, are exactly examined.*

Chap. 1.

Wherein the true ftate of the queftion concerning the vnion *of the temporall and fpirituall power among Chriftians is declared.*

Chap. 2.

Wherein the argument of Card. Bellarmine *taken from thofe words of S.* Paul, Wee being many are one body in Chrift, *to prooue, that the temporall & fpirituall power among Chriftians doe make one totall body, or commonwealth, whereof the* Pope *is head, is anfwered, and Card.* Bellarmine *conuinced of manifeft contradiction.*

Chap. 3.

Wherein the authoritie of S. Gregory Nazianzene *comparing the temporall and fpirituall power among Chriftians to the body and foule in man (which is fo often vrged*

The Contents.

The Contents.

The Contents.

The Adioynder.

B   6 Laſtly,

The Contents.

6 Laſtly, Widdrington *from the premiſes draweth foure concluſions cleane oppoſite to the foure concluſions, which* Mr. Fitzherbert *from his premiſes collecteth: and finally he concludeth, that neither this clauſe, nor any other is ſufficient to make the* oath *vnlawfull, or to moue any Catholike to refuſe the ſame, adding withall, what little hope of ſinceritie, and ſufficiencie the Reader may expect from the reſt of* Mr Fitzherberts *Replyes, ſeeing that in this (of which neuertheleſſe hee and his fauourers doe ſo greatly bragge) hee hath ſhewed ſuch great want of learning, and ſinceritie.*

TO

TO ALL ENGLISH
Catholikes, who are
of opinion, that the Pope *hath power*
to depofe temporal Princes,
Roger Widdrington
their Brother and Seruant in
CHRIST wiſheth *true* zeale,
knovvledge, and felicitie.

I *Haue written here a* Treatife *in*
anfwere to M^r. Fitzherberts
Reply, touching the Popes
power to depoſe Princes,
and the new oath *of* Allegiance, *which* I *thought fit to*
Dedicate to you, Deare Countrimen, *thofe efpeci-*
ally, who haue taken vpon you a charge to teach, and
inftruct others, for that the matter, which here is
handled, doth as much concerne your foules, and con-
fciences, or rather much more, then my owne. Doe
not you imagine, that when there is a controuerfie be-
twixt his Holineffe, *and your* Soueraigne, *concer-*
ning your fpirituall, and temporall allegiance, you may
fafely, and without danger of deadly finne adhere to
his

his Holineffe, *and forfake your* Soueraigne, *vnleffe you duly examine the right*, *and title which either haue* : *for that by the law of* G o d , *and Nature you are bound to giue to* G o d, *and* Cæfar *that which is their due* ; *that is, fpirituall obedience to your fpirituall* Paftours, *and temporall allegiance to your temporall* Prince. *Wherefore if the* Pope *fhould challenge, and exact from you not onely fpirituall obedience, which is due to him*, *but vnder colour of fpirituall obedience* , *fhould demand alfo temporall allegiance, which is not due to him*, *but onely to your temporall* Prince, *you fhould in obeying the* Pope *therein yeeld him that obedience* , *which is due only to your temporall* Prince, *and fo tranfgreffe the law of* G o d *and nature, and confequently it being a matter of fo great moment, you fhould* , *according to the approued doctrine of all* Diuines, *by yeelding fuch obedience incurre a moft heinous deadly finne.*

2. *For as there are but two only fupreme powers on earth, to which all Chriftian fubiects doe owe obedience and fubiection, to wit,* fpirituall , *which doth refide fpeciallie in the chiefe fpirituall* Paftour, *who in things fpirituall is* fupreme , *and* temporall *power, which doth refide in temporall* Princes, *who in things temporal are* fupreme, *and fubiect to none but* God; *So alfo there be only two fubiections* , *and obediences anfwerable thereunto, to wit,* fpirituall *and* temporall : *So that if fuch a power*, *or obedience be not fpirituall, it muft of neceffitie be temporall, and with the fame certaintie or probabilitie, that one is perfwaded fuch an authoritie not to be fpirituall* , *he muft be perfwaded that it is temporall. That authoritie is fpirituall,*

all, and due onely to the Pope, *which* Chriſt *hath giuen to his* Church, *and the ſpirituall* Paſtours *thereof;* All *other ſupreme authoritie is temporall, and due only to* temporall Princes. *And therefore if it be probable, as in very deede it is, and as you may ſee it in this* Treatiſe *clearely conuinced ſo to be, that the* Pope *hath no authority giuen him by* Chriſt *to depoſe* Princes, *it is conſequently* probable, *that the aforeſaid authoritie (if there be any ſuch authoritie on earth to depoſe Princes) is not ſpirituall but temporall, and that therfore, who ſoeuer granteth it to the* Pope, *doth giue to him that obedience, which is due to temporall* Princes, *and conſequently he doth againſt the expreſſe command of* Chriſt, *not render to* God *and* Cæſar, *that which is their due.*

3. *Well then thus you ſee, that if the* Pope *ſhould challenge that obedience as due to him by the inſtitution of* Chriſt, *which* Chriſt *hath not giuen him, and which conſequently is due only to* temporall Princes, *he ſhould vſurpe that authority, which he hath not, & in ſo doing he ſhould tranſgreſſe the law of* God *and* Nature, *and thoſe ſubiects, who ſhould adhere to him, and yeeld him that pretended ſpirituall obedience, ſhould alſo tranſgreſſe the law of* Chriſt, *and be not only pretended, but true* Traitors *both to* God *and their* Prince, *in not acknowledging their* Prince *to be their true* Soueraigne, *by yeelding that obedience, which is due to him to an other, and ſo by taking from him his* ſupreme *power, or* ſoueraingtie, *and giuing it to an other* Prince, *which in very deed is to take the* Diademe, *which doth ſignifie his ſupreme authoritie, off from his head, and place it vpon the head of an* other. B 3 4. *Now*

4. *Now there is none of you, as I ſuppoſe , of ſo meane vnderſtanding , that can imagine, that the Pope is ſo infallible in his opinion, iudgement, or any declaratiue command grounded thereon, as that he can not* poſſibly *erre therein, and challenge that authority as due to him by the inſtitution of* Chriſt, *which neuertheleſſe* Chriſt *hath not giuen him, but it belongeth only to temporall Princes. This you may ſee by experience in Pope* Boniface *the eight , who pretended, that* Philip *the* faire *the moſt Chriſtian* K I N G *of* France, was ſubiect *to him in ſpiritualls and* temporalls, *and declared them to be* heretikes, *who ſhould beleeue the contrarie : and that he was a temporall* Monarch *of the Chriſtiam world, and therefore that the* kingdome *of* France *by reaſon of the diſobedience, and rebellion of* Philip *their King, was falne into the handes of the* See Apoſtolike *: for which cauſe Pope* Boniface *was taxed by many learned* Catholikes *of great* impudencie, pride, *and* arrogancie: *and his* extrauagant, Vnam Sanctam, *which he made to curbe the ſaid* K ing *of* France, *declaring* that the temporall ſword is ſubiect to the ſpirituall , and temporall power to ſpirituall authoritie, *was reuerſed by Pope* Clement *the fift, the next Succeſſour but one to Pope* Boniface , *who declared,* that by the definition, and declaration of Pope *Boniface in his extrauagant, Vnam Sanctā,* no preiudice ſhould ariſe to the *King , and kingdome of France :* and that by it neither the *King,* kingdom, *or inhabitants* of *France* ſhould be more ſubiect to the Church of Rome, then they were before, but that all things ſhould be vnderſtood

to

to be in the ſame ſtate, wherin they were before the ſaid definition , as well concerning the *Church*, as concerning the *King* , *Kingdome* , and *Inhabitants* of *France*. *The like temporall authoritie Pope* Sixtus *the fift, if he had liued, would alſo haue challenged, for that as I haue been credibly informed by diuers* Ieſuites *of good account, who then liued at* Rome, *hee did intend to ſuppreſſe* Card. Bellarmines *firſt Tome of Controuerſies, becauſe he did not with the* Canoniſts *grant to the* Pope *this direct temporall Monarchie ouer the whole Chriſtian world.*

¶ *So that the onely controuerſie now is, whether the* Pope *hath* de facto *erred or no, in declaring the* oath *of* allegiance *to be vnlawful, and* to containe in it many things flat contrarie to faith and ſaluation, *vpon this ſuppoſall , that it is a* point of Faith, *that the* Pope *hath authoritie giuen him by* Chriſt, *to depoſe Princes , which is the ſubſtance of the oath, as Fa :* Suarez [a] *acknowledgeth , and the maine queſtion betwixt my* Aduerſaries *and mee , as* M.r. Fitzherbert [b] *in expreſſe words confeſſeth. Now you may ſee, if you pleaſe to reade, that I haue cleerely proued in this* Treatiſe, *that it is* probable, *that the authoritie, which the* Pope *claimeth to depoſe Princes, is not true, but vſurped, not granted him by* Chriſt, *but giuen him by men contrarie to thoſe expreſſe words of* Chriſt, [c] Render the things that are *Cæſars* to *Cæſar*, and the things that are *Gods*, to God. *And therefore conſider, I pray you, in what danger you ſtand , of doing great iniury to your Soueraigne, and committing flat treaſon*

a *Lib* 6 Defenſ. Fidei *fere ter totum.*
b *In the end of his* Preface.

c *Math.*22.

treaſon againſt his Royall perſon and Crowne, if you rashly, and without due examination follow the Popes *opinion, iudgement, or alſo declaratiue command grounded thereon, who, vnder pretence of demanding of you a profeſsion of his ſpirituall authoritie, and your ſpirituall obedience, exacteth in very deede not ſpirituall allegiance, but that obedience which is* probably *thought by many learned Catholikes to be a meere temporall allegiance, and due onely to your temporall Prince.*

6 *But obſerue,* deare Countrimen, *a more manifeſt, and dangerous gulfe, into which for want of due conſideration you may eaſily caſt your ſelues. For if once you grant, that it is* probable, *that it is a* controuerſie, *that it is a* diſputable *queſtion, as in very deed it is, and as I thinke very few of you, who haue ſtudied this queſtion, are perſwaded to the contrarie, that the right, title, power, and authoritie, which the* Pope *challengeth to depoſe Princes, is no true title, but pretended, a meere temporall, and not a true ſpirituall authoritie, although I ſhould grant you alſo for Diſputation ſake, of which as yet I doe not diſpute, that it is alſo* probable, *that the ſaid title is good, and that the* Pope *hath ſuch an authoritie to depoſe Princes giuen him by* Chriſt, *yet there is none of you ſo ſimple, but if you will duely conſider, will preſently perceiue, that this title, (ſo long as it is in controuerſie, is* titulus ſine re, *a meere title, which ſo long as it is diſputable, and debated on either ſide, can neuer be put in* practiſe *by any man, what opinion ſo euer he follow in* ſpeculation, *without doing the* Prince, *who is depoſed by the* Pope, *manifeſt wrong, and*

and if he be a fubiect, by committing that deteftable crime of treafon in a moft high degree.

7 *For if any one of you fhould be in lawfull poffefsion of a houfe, iewell, or any other thing, whereunto an other man pretendeth a title, and claimeth a power to difpofe thereof, and perchance it is alfo* probable, *that his title is in very deede the better, and his* Lawiers *doe bring ftrong reafons, and euidences to confirme the fame, would not you thinke, that it were a manifeft wrong, as in deed it were, and againft the knowne rules of iuftice grounded vpon the light of reafon, that your* Aduerfarie, *or any other in his behalfe, notwithftanding the* probabilitie *of his title, fhould put you out of poffefsion, and take it away from you by violence, before the* Iudge *had decided the controuerfie?*

8 *And if any one fhould* Reply *and fay, that the* Pope *is our* Soueraignes *Iudge; to whom alfo all* Chriftian Princes *are fubiect, and that hee hath decided this controuerfie betwixt him and our Prince, and defined, that this his title to depofe our Prince and all other Chriftian Princes, is a true and not onely pretended, a fpirituall, and not a temporall title, he is manifeftly deceiued. For neither is the* Pope *the Iudge of temporall Princes in temporall caufes, wherin they are fupreme, and fubiect to none but God; neither hath the* Pope *as yet decided this controuerfie, or defined by any Generall Councell, or any other authenticall inftrument (for I will not at this time contend what authority the* Pope *hath to define matters of faith without a* Generall Councell) *that this title, and authoritie which hee challengeth to depofe*

Princes,

Princes, *is a true ſpirituall title, and an authoritie granted him by the inſtitution of Chriſt. For concerning this point* Popes, *and* Emperours haue euer beene at great variance, *as well ſaid Fa:* Azor, [d] *and it is in controuerſie among* Catholike Doct ors, *as I haue conuinced in this* Treatiſe, *and as yet the controuerſie is not decided by the Iudge, as* Abbot Trithemius [e] *doth well affirme.*

9   *And if any one ſhould perchance imagine, that his* Holineſſe *that now is, hath by his late* Breues *decided the controuerſie, and defined, that hee hath authoritie to depoſe Princes, hee is alſo moſt groſely miſtaken; both for that there is not ſo much as one word mentioned in any of his* Breues *concerning his authoritie to depoſe Princes, but onely in generall words he declareth, that* Catholikes *ought not to take the oath,* for that it containeth many things flat contrarie to faith and ſaluation, *but what thoſe many things be he doth not expreſſe (and perchance he might imagine at the firſt ſight, as* Card. Bellarmine *did, that the* Popes *power to excommunicate, to binde and looſe, to diſpence in oathes is denyed in the oath, and that it was framed to make a diſtinction betwixt* Proteſtants *and* Catholikes *touching points of Religion, al which how vntrue they are I haue cleerely ſhewed in my* Theologicall Diſputation) *but eſpecially for this reaſon hee is fowly miſtaken, becauſe here is not in the* Breues *any one of thoſe words, which, according to the doctrine of* Card. Bellarmine, *and other Diuines related by me in the aforeſaid* Diſputation [f], *are required to make an infallible definition, and finall deciſion of a point of faith.*
Neither

d *Tom.* 2. *lib.* 11 *cap.q.*5.8.

e *See beneath part.*1.*cap.*1.

f *Cap.*10.*ſec.*2. *nn.*32.*& ſeq.*

Neither is euery Breue , *or* Apoftolicall *letter of the* Pope, *although it be regiftred in the body of the* Canon Law *among the* Popes Decretall *letters, a fufficient inftrument to define matters of faith, for that in them is commonly contained onely the* Popes *opinion concerning fome doubtfull cafe, or queftion, and not a finall decifion or definition, which all Ca-tholikes are bound to follow. Otherwife it muft needes be granted, that* Popes *haue defined in their* Breues *falfe doctrine, and alfo* herefie, *as may bee feene in the* Decretall *letters, and* Breues *of* Pope Celeftine *the firft,* Pope Nicolas *the third, and* Pope Boniface *the eight, as alfo I obferued in the aforefaid* Difputation ⁸ :

10. *Yea both the very manner of his* Holineffe *proceeding in condemning the* oath *in fuch gene-rall words,* for that it containeth many things flat contrary to faith and faluation, *not declaring any one of thofe many things, although he hath been in fome fort vrged therunto by his* Maiefty, ʰ *& we alfo his Catholike fubiects, whom it moft concernes, haue moft humbly and moft earneftly requefted it at his hands,* ⁱ *and the forbidding of my bookes alfo in fuch generall words, not declaring whether they are forbidden, for the matter which they handle, or for the manner, or in refpect of the perfons againft whom they are written, or for fome other caufe, but efpeci-ally, and which is more ftrange, and contrary to the practife of all tribunals, the commanding of mee to purge my felfe* forthwith, *and that vnder paine of* Ecclefiafticall Cenfures , *without fignifying any crime at all, either in generall or particular, whereof*

I fhould

g *Cap:* 10. *fec.* 2 *nu.* 47. 48.

h In his Apo-logic pag. 7. num. 5.

i Difput. The-olog. in the Epiftle to his Holineffe.

*I ſhould purge my ſelfe, are manifeſt ſignes to a pru-
dent man, that* latet anguis in herba, *and that they
themſelues doe diſtruſt their owne cauſe.* Can any
prudent man imagine, that if his Holineſſe, *or the
moſt Illuſtrious* Cardinals *of the Inquiſition, were
fully perſwaded, that the* Popes *power to depoſe
Princes is a point of faith, & defined by the Church
ſo to be, as Card.* Bellarmine, *and ſome few other
eſpecially Ieſuits would enforce the Chriſtian world
to beleeue, and that they were able to conuince the
ſame either by holy Scriptures, Apoſtolicall tradi-
tions, decrees of ſacred Councels, or any other conuincing reaſon, they would forbeare to ſignifie the
ſame, eſpecially being ſo greatly vrged thereunto?*

11. *Beſides the manner alſo of my* Aduerſaries
*handling this cōtrouerſie, in corrupting my words,
peruerting my meaning, concealing my anſwers, altering the true ſtate of the queſtion, confounding the
Readers vnderſtanding with ambiguous words and
ſentences, and being requeſted to inſiſt vpon any one
place of holy Scripture, authoritie of ſacred Councell, or any other Theologicall reaſon, which they
ſhall thinke to be moſt conuincing, that thereby the
controuerſie may quickly bee at an end, their flying
from one place of holy Scripture to another, from one
Councell to another, from one Theologicall reaſon to
another, their fallacious arguing from the facts of
the* Apoſtles, *yea alſo and of thoſe* Prophets, *who
were no Prieſts, which were done miraculouſlie, and
by an extraordinarie power, or by the ſpeciall command of Almightie God, to prooue the like ordinarie power to be in ſpirituall Paſtours, from the practiſes*

ctiſes of certaine Popes, who were reſiſted therein
both by Chriſtian Princes and people to inferre the
practiſe of the Church, which is a congregation of
all the faithfull &c. from the opinion of very many
Doctours, or alſo of the Church onelie probably
iudging or thinking, to conclude the faith of the
Church firmely beleeuing or defining, from the
Popes power to command temporals, to gather the
Popes power to diſpoſe of temporals, from the Popes
power to impoſe temporall puniſhments to deduce a
power in the Pope to inflict or vſe temporall puniſhments, or which is all one, to conſtraine with tem
porall puniſhments, & from a power which is granted to the Church, as the Church is taken for the
Chriſtian world conſiſting both of temporall and
ſpirituall power, to conclude the ſaid power to be in
the Church, as the Church is taken for the ſpiritual
Kingdeme of Chriſt, which conſiſteth only of ſpirituall power, and ſuch like pittifull ſhifts to confound
therby their Readers vnderſtanding, & at the laſt,
in regard either of their preſence or preheminece in
the Court of Rome, to cauſe by their euill information his Holineſſe to conſent to the forbidding of
their Aduerſaries bookes, that thereby neither their
legerdemaine and fraudulent dealing may bee laid
open to the view of the world, nor the Reader may
ſee what we alledge againſt them, or in defence of
our ſelues, but in that lame and corrupt manner, as
they ſha' pleaſe to deliuer it, doth euidently ſhew, that
they are not deſirous to ſatisfie mens vnderſtan-
dings, and to ſearch and finde out the truth by a ſincere debating of this dangerous and difficult contro-
C 3 verſie,

"erſie, *but rather that they themſelues doe (uſpect their owne cauſe, which becauſe they haue once ta-ken in hand to defend, they will* per fas & nefas, *by fraud and violence ſeeke ſtill to maintaine.* But *truth will neuer be ouerthrowen, it may for a time by fraud and violence be ſuppreſſed, but maugre all the ſleights of the impugners thereof, it will in the end preuaile.*

Whereas my plaine, ſincere, and perſpicuous handling this queſtion, and requeſting my Aduer-ſaries, that they will inſiſt vpon any one text of holy Scripture, which ſhall ſeeme to them to be the moſt pregnant place, whether it be, whatſoeuer thou ſhalt looſe, &c. Feed my ſheepe. If you ſhall haue Secular iudgments &c. *or any other; or vpon any one decree of Popes, or generall Coun-cells, whether it be,* can: Nos Sanctorum, Iura-tos, Abſolutos, *or any other, whether it be the Councell of* Trent, *of* Lyons, *of* Laterane, (*which now of late is ſo greatly vrged by ſome, whereof in former times was made ſo ſmall account for the proofe of this point,) or vpon any one Theologicall reaſon, which ſhall ſeeme to them to be the moſt vn-anſwerable, whether it be taken from the* ſubor-dination *of the temporall power to the ſpirituall, or from the* neceſsitie *of defending the Church, repreſſing hæreſies, puniſhing wicked Princes, de-fending innocent people, or from the promiſe which Chriſtian Princes make to the Church, either in Baptiſme, or at their Coronation, or any other which ſhall like them beſt, proteſting withall,* [k] *that if any man ſhall ſhew by any convincing reaſon that)*

k *In Reſp: A-pologet. num. 1.*

*that the doctrine for the Popes power to depose
Princes is a point of faith, and consequently the
contrary not* probable ; *I will presently yeeld, neither (hall any hope of gaine, or feare of punishment
withdraw me from embracing forthwith and publishing also the truth, doe sufficiently demonstrate,
that my only desire is to finde out, and follow the
truth in this controuersie, which doth so neerely
touch our soules and saluation and our obedience
due by the law of Christ to God, and our temporall
Prince.*

13 *Wherefore my earnest request at this time,
and vehement desire onely is,* Deare Countrymen, *that you will be pleased to examine diligently
your spirituall, and temporall obedience, your dutie
to* GOD & CAESAR, *and that you will be led
and guided by true reason, and not caried away by
blinde affection, hope of preferment and credit, or
feare of disgrace and want, and not to be desirous
so to please the* Pope, *as to neglect your dutie, and
obedience, which by the command of* Christ, *and
vnder paine of eternall damnation you owe to your
temporall Prince.* Be not deceiued, God is not
mocked. Cœca obedientia, blinde obedience
*in this case is dangerous, and damnable, and your
ignorance herein, you hauing now so iust cause to
doubt, and therefore, according to the doctrine of
all Diuines, are bound to examine the truth, will
be affected, grosse, wilfull, and culpable, like to that,
whereof the* Prophet *spake,* ᵒ Noluit intelligere | ᶫ *Pſal:* 35.
vt bene ageret, hee would not vnderstand that
he might doe well. *For although it be lawfull,*
and

and alſo very commendable to obey your Superi-
ours command, without examining what authoritie
he hath to impoſe vpon you ſuch a command, when
by obeying, you incurre no danger of diſobeying
God, of wronging your neighbour, whom by the
law of God you are bound not to wrong, or of diſo-
beying another Superiour, whom by the law of God
you are bound alſo to obey, yet this is alſo certaine,
that when there is a controuerſie, that your obeying *an earthly Superiour is a* diſobedience *to God,*
or a rebellion againſt another ſupreme Superiour,
whom God hath commanded you to obey, vnleſſe
you duely examine the matter, and in what manner
by obeying that earthly Superiour, although it be
the Pope, *you doe not diſobey* God, *nor commit*
rebellion againſt your Prince, *whom* God *com-*
mandeth you to obey, no pretence of aduancing Ca-
tholike Religion, of deuotion to the See Apoſtolike, *or of any other good end whatſoeuer can ex-*
cuſe you from committing a mortall ſinne.

14 *The pretence of furthering the common*
good, of aduancing Catholike Religion, of depreſ-
ſing hæreſies, of puniſhing wicked Princes, of de-
fending innocent people, and ſuch like, may be co-
lourable clokes to excuſe many damnable and deui-
liſh attempts, many wicked backbytings, ſlåderings,
and other wrongs both by words and deeds, as by
late experience may be ſeene in the execrable mur-
thers of the two moſt Chriſtian Kings of France,
in the abhominable Conſpiracie *of the* Powder
Traitours, *in the vncharitable proceedings againſt*
the Appellants, *and thoſe who fauoured them, and*
now

and now againſt thoſe Catholikes, who do any waies fauour the Oath, *(to omit many other exorbitant dealings vnder this pretence of furthering the common good, which if it were needfull I could make manifeſt)but aſſure your ſelues that neither good ends are ſufficient to excuſe bad practiſes, nor the zeale of the perſon is a ſufficient warrant to iuſtifie all his actions, nor iniuſtice is to be done to any man be he neuer ſo wicked.*

I 5 *Call to minde, I beſeech you, the doctrine of the ancient Fathers, and the practiſe of the primitiue Church, obſerue the cauſes of the beginning and increaſe of this practiſe, and doctrine for the Popes power to depoſe Princes, and the continuall contradiction thereof, and you ſhall finde, that no man of any learning can perſwade his conſcience, that this doctrine is certaine, and of faith. For the zeale of* Pope Gregorie *the ſeuenth, the wickedneſſe of* Henry *the fourth Emperour, the diſcord of the* German *Princes, the riches of the Counteſſe* Mathildis, *the warlike forces of the* Nortmans, *and the deſire of all men that the Emperour might be reſtrained from doing ſuch euills, were the firſt occaſions,* ᵐ *that this doctrine began firſt to bee practiſed by the ſaid Pope* Gregorie, *and afterwards, it being in regard of the ſtrangeneſſe thereof, ſo greatly contradicted, iuſtified by him to bee lawfull, for which cauſe it was by* Onuphrius ⁿ *called,* a thing not heard of before that age, *and by* Sigebert *a learned, and vertuous Catholike, and no* Schiſmatike, *as I will proue beneath* ᵒ *, it was taxed of* noueltie, not to ſay of hereſie, *and confuted*

D

m See beneath part: 1. cap: 6. nu: 24.

n See in the place aboue c ted.

o Part: 1. *cap.* 6. *num.* 20. *& ſeq.*

ted by him at large.

16 Secondly, *the aduancing of them, who did maintaine this doctrine, the depreßing of thofe, who did impugne it, the fuppreßing of Bookes, and the threatning of Eccleftafticall Cenfures, which neuertheleffe if they be vniuft, are not of force in the* p *Suarez de Cenfuris Difp. 4. fec. 7. nu. 2. 4. 23. & feq.* P *Court of Confcience, and the indiligence of temporall Princes to maintaine their Soueraigntie (the caufes whereof I dare not prefume to examine) befides the former reafons, and pretence of aduancing Catholike religion &c. were the chiefe caufes, why the defenders of this doctrine, did fo increafe in number from the time of Pope* Gregorie *the* 7. *in comparifon of thofe who did impugne it. But if temporall* Princes *would yet be pleafed, to vfe hereafter thofe meanes to defend their right, and Soueraigntie, which* Popes *haue heretofore, and doe continually vfe to maintaine their pretended temporall authoritie ouer* Kings *and* Princes, *to depofe them, to difpofe of their temporalls &c. in order to fpirituall good, I do not doubt, but that the ftreame of Doctors would quickly turne backward, and my* Aduerfaries *would haue fmall caufe to brag (confidering efpecially the weakneffe of their grounds, and that their doctrine is ouerfwaied by authoritie, and not by reafon) that fo many Authors fauour the* Popes *power to depofe* Princes, *and fo few the right of* Princes *not to bee depofed by the* Pope.

17 *Neuertheleffe it is alfo manifeft, that it hath euer been contradicted by* Chriftian *Princes and people, and notwithftanding the forefaid motiues, and*

and alſo the feare that ſome might haue, leſt wicked Princes might be in ſome ſort incouraged to perſeuere in euill by impugning that doctrine, which ſeemed to be a bridle to reſtraine their bad purpoſes) it hath continually been impugned, diſproued, and confuted by learned Catholikes, as I haue cleerely proued in this Treatiſe. And therefore remember*, into what danger of ſoule, bodie, and temporall fortunes, you (for want of reading and due examining,) doe throw headlong your ſelues, and many innocent men, who doe follow your example and counſell, for the which at the day of iudgement you are to make a moſt ſtrict account, where no fauour of* Man *can helpe you, and willfull ignorance will not excuſe you, but condemne you, and it will be too late to ſay then* Non putaram*, vnleſſe you doe now, abſtracting from all humane affection & reſpects, examine duely what dutie you beare* God *and* Cæſar*, what obedience you owe to the* Pope, *and your temporall* Prince.

18 *But perhaps ſome of you will demand, how can you by reading examine this controuerſie, ſeeing that the* Bookes *, which treate thereof are forbidden by the* Pope? *In anſwer to this I will onely propound at this time to your prudent conſiderations, whether if there ſhould ariſe a controuerſie betwixt the* Pope, *and a temporall* Prince *concerning the title to any kingdome, eſpecially which that temporall* Prince *hath in his poſſeſſion (as there is betwixt the* Pope, *and the* King *of* Spaine *touching the Kingdomes of* Naples, *and* Sicilie) *the* Pope *hath authoritie to command that temporall* Prince *, and his* Subiects *not to read, and peruſe thoſe euidences,*

D 2 *which*

which doe make in fauour of his owne title, but onely thofe euidences, which doe proue the Popes *title?*

19 *Now if the reafon, why my bookes are forbidden by the* Pope, (*or rather by the euill information, importunitie, and iudiciall fentence of* Card. Bellarmine, *againft whom, as my principall* Aduerfarie *in this caufe, I did write both my* Apologie *for the right of* Princes, *and alfo my* Theologicall Difputation *concerning the* oath *of* Allegiance, *which two bookes are onely forbidden, and who therfore was pleafed to bee an* Accufer, Witneffe, *and* Iudge, *in his owne caufe*) *be, for that they doe fauor the* oath *of* Allegiance, *and impugne the* Popes *power to depofe* Princes, (*as all my* Aduerfaries *confeffe, that for this caufe they are forbidden to bee read*) *then you may cleerely perceiue, that therefore my bookes are forbidden, for that they doe fhew, and declare the euidences, which doe make for the right and title of temporall* Princes, *and their right not to be depriued, or thruft out of their kingdomes by the* Popes *pretended authoritie, but efpecially of our* Soueraigne, *whofe cafe concerning this point is more fingular, and concerneth him more neerely, confidering the oppofition betwixt him, and the* Popes Holineffe, *with whom he is not linked in vnitie of religion and friendfhip, then it doth concerne other Chriftian* Princes, *who haue not the like reafon to feare tumults, rebellions, and* Powder-treafons, *vnder pretence of reftoring* Catholike *religion in their Countrey, and of hauing the* Popes *expreffe or virtuall licence for the fame; which prohibition of the* Pope

to

to forbid fuch kinde of bookes, *how far it can binde either thofe* Princes, *to whom it belongeth by the law of* God *and nature to defend their Soueraigntie, or elfe their Subiects, who alfo by the fame Lawe of* God *and nature are bound to examine the reafons and euidences of their Princes title, authoritie, and Soueraigntie, leaft that for want of due examination they fhould deny to* God, *or* Cæfar, *that which is their due, I remit to the prudent confideration of any iudicious Catholike man.*

20 Laftly, *confider, I pray you, the manifold wrongs, which for the loue and paines I haue taken for your fakes, I haue receiued from diuerfe of you, whom I could name, if it were needfull, both in reprochfull words, and vncharitable deeds, not befeeming, I will not fay,* Religious Priefts, *but morall honeft men. For long before I did put pen to paper, I had throughly examined this controuerfie, and all which in my iudgement could bee obiected on either fide, and for my owne part I was fully fetled in my opinion ; but perceiuing all men to bee filent in a matter of fuch importance, and necefsitie as this is, and which alfo concerneth vs all, the zeale, affection, and dutie, which I bare to* Catholike Religion, *to the* See Apoftolike, *and to my* Prince *and* Countrey, *with a vehement defire, that the truth in this important controuerfie, which concerneth our obedience, which by the command of* Chrift, *wee owe to* God *and* Cæfar, *to the* Popes *Holineffe, and to our temporall* Soueraigne, *compelled mee firft to write, and now alfo to continue, for which*

although

*although I fhall hereafter fuffer, as hitherto I haue
done, reproch, infamie, difgrace, loffe of friends,
and other euils, yet I will ftill pray for my perfecu-
tors, and remit my caufe to* GOD *aboue, affuring my felfe, that in time conuenient he
will in this world, or the next, or
both, be a iuft Iudge, reuenger, Protector, and re-
warder of the
Innocent.*

THE

THE
PREFACE TO
the Reader.

Wherein
Mr. FITZHERBERTS PREFACE
is confuted, the matter which WIDDRING-
TON handleth, and the manner how he proceedeth therein, is declared, and his doctrine proued to be truely *probable,*
and neither *preiudiciall* to his
MAIESTIES *seruice,*
nor to the *Consciences* of
Catholikes.

I. T is not vnknowne to
thee, *Courteous Reader,* the
great controuersie hath
been of late yeares, especially among vs Englilh
Catholikes, concerning
the new oath of Allegi-
ance, which his *Maiestie*
by Act of Parliament
hath ordained *to make triall how his Catholike Subiects
stand affected towards him in point of there loyaltie, and
due obedience.* For although his *Holinesse,* by the insti-
gation and importunitie no doubt of others, hath by
three feuerall Breues declared the faid oath to be vnlawfull,

lawfull, and to containe in it many things cleerely
repugnant to faith and faluation, and many learned
men, efpecially *Iefuites* , as Card. *Bellarmine* Fa:
Gretzer,*Leffius*, *Becanus*,and now laftly *Suarez*,haue
by publike writings endeauoured to conuince the
fame, neuerthelelfe fince that Mr. *George Blackwell*
then Archpræsbiter, and many other learned Priefts
did from the very fiift publifhing of this oath defend
it to bee lawfull, and not to containe in it any thing,
which either exprelfely, or couertly is contrarie to
Catholike faith or faluation, the faid oath hath been
maintained as lawfull by many learned Catholike
Priefts, and hath been taken by the moft part of thofe
Lay-Catholikes, to whom it hath been tendered ; affuring themfelues that his *Holineffe* command for the
refufing thereof, being onely a declaratiue precept,
and not grounded vpon any infallible definition,but
at the moft vpon a probable opinion, that the *Pope*
hath power to depofe Princes (which is the maine
subftance of the oath, as my *Aduerfarie* here [a] con-
felfeth, and Fa : *Suarez*, [b] alfo before him exprelfely
acknowledgeth, is not, according to *Suarez* doⱷrine,
of force to binde them, efpecia.ly with fo great preiudice to his *Maieftie* and themfelues, to embrace an
vncertaine and doubtfull opinion, or to obey the
Popes declaratiue precept grounded therevpon.

    2 I therefore with other Catholikes confidering
how greatly this oath doth concerne our allegiance,
and obedience due to *God* and *Cæfar*, and the great
harme both fpirituall and temporall, which may en-
fue by breach thereof, thought it our beft courfe, to
fet downe fincerely all the chiefeft arguments,which
haue been hitherto by any Author,or which might in
our iudgements be obieⱷed by any againft the faid
oath, together with the anfwers, which haue been,or
might be brought to the fame Obieⱷions, and withall dutifull fubmiffion to propound them to his *Ho-*
lineffe,

a *In the end of*
his ℙ*reface.*
b *Lib.6.defenf.*
4 cap.2.

lineſſe,humbly requeſting him,that he would be pleaſed diligently to peruſe them, and in regard of his
Paſtorall Office would vouchſafe to inſtruct vs in the
Catholike faith, ſatisfie the difficulties, which doe
perplex our conſciences,& to make knowne vnto vs,
what clauſes of the oath are, I doe not ſay, according
to the opinion of Card. *Bellarmine*, or ſome other
Catholike Doctors, who are no neceſſarie rule of the
Catholike faith,but according to Catholike doctrine
neceſſarily to be beleeued by all men, repugnant to
faith and ſaluation, as his *Holineſſe* affirmeth in his
Breues. And this I performed in my *Theologicall Diſputation*, partly at the requeſt of many Catholikes,
whoſe caſe I greatly pittied, but chiefly for the duty
I owed to God, Religion, my Prince and Countrey:
Neither did I intend in that *Diſputation* to affirme any
thing of my ſelfe, but as repreſenting the perſons of
thoſe, who were perſwaded, that the oath may, or
may not be lawfully taken. And becauſe when the ſaid
Diſputation was in the preſſe,& almoſt finiſhed, there
came to my hands an Engliſh booke compoſed by
F.T. and entituled a *Supplement to the Diſcuſsion &c.*
wherein this Authour endeauoured to proue the ſaid
oath to bee repugnant to all lawes both humane and
diuine, and therefore iuſtly condemned by his *Holineſſe*,in that it doth exempt temporall Princes from
Excommunication and depoſition by the Pope, I
thought good to touch briefely in an *Admonition* to
the Reader, both the ſubſtance of this Authors diſcourſe, and of the chiefeſt arguments which hee
brought againſt the oath, and alſo the anſwers, which
might bee made to them; to the end his *Holineſſe*,
might be fully informed of all the reaſons, which are
alledged as well againſt as for the taking of the oath.
And this was the cauſe, that I writing in Latin,did to
informe his *Holineſſe* briefely ſet downe what hee had
written in Engliſh againſt the aforeſaid oath.

E　　　　　　3　But

c *In the Pre-*
face nu. 2.

3 But the said Authour *F. T.* who now hath tur-
ned backward the first letters of his name into *T. F.*
and is knowne, acknowledged, yea and boasted of by
his fauourers to be M^r. *Thomas Fitzherbert* now an
Englilh Iesuite (for which cause I was the more bold
to expreſſe his name) hath of late set forth a *Reply* in
English in defence of his arguments, which I briefely answered in Latine, to the end, saith he, *that our
Countreymen, whom it most importeth to vnderstand well
the qualitie, and state of this controuersie, may discouer
my weakeneſſe, and auoide the danger of their soules,
whereto they may be drawne by the false fame, and opinion, that many haue conceiued of my sufficiency.* But
howsoeuer my *Aduersarie,* or any other bee concei-
ted of my weakeneſſe or sufficiencie (for time will
make knowne the weakeneſſe or sufficiencie of vs
both) I doe not doubt (God willing,) but notwithstanding all his vaunting bragges, to discouer cleerely the weakeneſſe and insufficiencie of his Reply, albeit hee hath beene furthered with the former writings of many learned men, especially Card. *Bellarmine,* Fa : *Lessius,* & now lastly of *Suarez* (from whom
he borroweth the chiefest Replyes he bringeth to my
answeres, yet concealing their names) to omit the
many other helpes I want, which he may haue in the
place where hee liueth, both by the conference of
learned men, & the commoditie of all sorts of books,
wherewith that place is furnished. And although hee
vseth very spiteful, and slanderous speeches against
me (for the which I pray God to forgiue him) thinking thereby to magnifie himselfe, disgrace me, and
promote his owne cause; but in the end hee will finde
that such exorbitant and irreligious courses will tend
to his owne disgrace and not mine, and bee greatly
preiudiciall both to his cause and conscience, yet I wil
abstaine from such vncharitable and vniust proceedings, and with all modestie I will defend my owne
                                                    innocencie,

innocencie, by anfwering all his obiections, and by
clearing my felfe of all thofe imputations, which hee
hath falfly laid to my charge: and if in defending my
felfe I lay open his fraude, and ignorance, and returne
his flanders backe vpon himfelfe, I ought not therefore to be taxed of calumniation, feeing that, *to detect
the flanders of the Aduerfarie is not*, to vfe Card. *Bellar-*
mines owne words, *to be accounted a defaming.* Now
to draw neere vnto the matter.

d *Cap.* 5. *Apo-*
logiæ.

4. Before my *Aduerfarie* come to examine my
Anfwere to his arguments, he thinketh it not amiffe
to fay fomewhat concerning me, the matter which I
handle, and the manner how I proceede therein. Firft
then touching me he affirmeth, ᵉ *that whereas I call*
my felfe by the name of Widdrington, *it is well knowne to*
many, that M. Roger Widdrington, *vnder whofe fhad-*
dow I fhroude my felfe, is farre different from me in quali-
tie, habit, and profeffion. And albeit ᶠ *he is not ignorant*
what my true name, and qualitie is, yet he forbeareth to de-
clare it for iuft refpects, and will only fay of me for the pre-
fent, that whereas our Aduerfaries haue heretofore leuied,
and Preft many fouldiers of their owne profeffion to main-
taine their quarrells againft vs, they haue now in this late
quarrell of the oath Preft one of ours (*I meane* faith he,
this Authour) *who fo much prefumeth of his owne skill and*
ftrength, that albeit the prouerbe faith, Ne Hercules contra duos, *yet he feareth not to encounter tenne at once, yea*
hopeth, as it feemeth, to wreft the club out of Hercules *his*
hand, and to beate him with his owne weapon. For he taketh
vpon him to ouerthrow Card. Bellarmine *with his owne*
arguments, to batter the fortreffe of the Catholike Church
with her owne Canons, and conftitutions &c.

e *In his Pre-*
face num. 3.

f *Num.* 3.

5. But firft, whether *Roger Widdrington* be the true
or fuppofed, the fole, or ioint Authour of that Difputation, it little auaileth to the matter, which is now in
controuerfie : and when my *Aduerfarie* fhall name
more plainely that perfon, whom he forbearing, as he
　　　　faith

faith, to name, yet cunningly nameth, I doubt not, but that hee will not be afraid to anſwere him more fully ; neither will all my *Aduerſaries* clamours, and threatnings diſcourage him from defending the truth, his Prince, and Countrey, for the loue wherof, & not for any hope of temporall luce or preferment, or for to ſhew his wit as my *Aduerſary* falſly affirmeth, he will not be aſhamed to be Preſt on to write againſt M^r. *Fitzherbert*, or any other ſuch like Authour, who liuing in other Countries, and out of danger to looſe any thing, but rather in hope to obtaine preferment by their writings, would preſſe Engliſh Catholikes to defend with danger of looſing all they haue, and of incurring his *Maieſties* high diſpleaſuer that doctrine for the Popes power to depoſe Princes to be of faith, which the *State of France* hath accounted *ſcandalous*, *ſeditious, damnable*, and *pernicious*. In the meane time let this ſuffice, that he is a childe of the *Catholike* Romane Church, and as good a Catholike, if not better then M^r. *Fitzherbert* is, if we will dulie conſider the true nature and definition of a *Catholike*, and that he is no true *Catholike*, who with true *Catholike* and ſupernaturall faith beleeueth doubtfull, diſputable, and vncertaine opinions, and which conſequently are ſubiect to errour, to which true *Catholike* faith cannot in any wiſe be expoſed.

6. Secondly, it is vntrue, that I doe preſume ſo much of my owne skill and ſtrength, that I dare aduenture to wreſt out the club of *Hercules* his hand, as my *Aduerſarie* affirmeth, or to encounter vpon equall tearmes with *Card. Bellarmine*, or any one of thoſe learned writers, whom I named in my *Diſputation*, accounting my ſelfe to be farre inferior to euery one of them in skill and ſtrength (only excepting this my *Aduerſarie*, whoſe skill and ſtrength I doe not greatly feare, it being well knowne of what ſufficiencie he is, and that his skill in Philoſophie, or Schoole Diuinitie

tie is not great, although he hath prettie skill in making vſe of other mens labours, and anſwering in Engliſh, what other men haue before replied in Latine) but if *Hercules* will leaue his club, and fight with a bulruſh, it is no great maiſtrie for a weaker man to withſtand him; if *Card. Bellarmine* inſteed of the expreſſe words of holy Scripture, and the true meaning thereof ſo declared to be by the ancient Fathers, or the vniuerſall Church, or vndoubted definitions of Generall Councels, or neceſſarie inferences dedu&ed from them (which are the only weapons wherewith Catholike do&rine can be conuinced) will flie to ouerwreſted ſimilitudes, falſe, or at the moſt probable ſuppoſitions, doubtfull and vncertaine colle&ions, to proue an infallible do&rine of the Catholike faith, as he, and the reſt, who follow him in this controuerſie for the *Popes* power to depoſe Princes haue done, it is an eaſie matter for one, who hath leſſe skill and ſtrength then they haue, to withſtand them, yea and to vanquiſh them, and a hundred ſuch others being ſo weakely armed.

7. And therefore very falſe, and friuolous is that, which my *Aduerſarie* affirmeth that Widdrington (for ſo ſtill I will call my ſelfe) *taketh vpon him to batter the fortreſſe of the Catholike Church with her owne Canons, and conſtitutions, and to vndermine the immoueable rocke of* S. Peter *with his owne inſtruments, and all this he doth with ſuch art and ſleight, that whiles he fighteth againſt the Church, he pretendeth to be a friend and childe of the Church, and albeit he impugne the Popes authority, yet he dedicateth his booke to the* Pope, *laughing vpon him, whiles he woundeth him, and betraying* Chriſt *with a kiſſe, as* Iudas *did. But how vainely he laboureth in all this, he may eaſily ſee, if he call to minde, what he hath learned in the Catholike Church, to wit, how inexpugnable is the rocke, and ſeate of* Peter, which the proud gates of hell *cannot ouercome.* For I doe not batter the fortreſſe of

g *Num.* 4. and 5.

the Catholike Church whom I reuerence and loue as
my deare mother (and to whofe Cenfure I euer haue
and do alfo now moft humbly fubmit my felfe and all
my writings) but the priuate opinions of fome few
Catholikes, efpecially *Iefuites*, who will needes enforce vpon the Chriftian world, doubtfull, difputable
and vncertaine opinions, for infallible grounds of fupernaturall faith, which onely is the fortreffe of the
Catholike Church.   Neither doe I vndermine that
immoueable rocke of S. *Peter*, whereon *Chrift* hath
built his Church, but thofe *fcandalous*, *feditious*, *damnable* and *pernitious* pofitions (for fo the *State of
France* doth call them) of murthering Princes, and
thrufting them out, contrarie to the rules of law and
reafon, of the lawfull poffeffion of their kingdomes,
by an authority which is only doubfull and queftionable : Neither do I impugne that authoritie of the
Pope, which is certainely knowne to be granted him
by *Chrift*, but that new doctrine of fome few writers,
which doth attribute to the *Pope* that authoritie, as
certainly giuen him by *Chrift*, which at the moft is
difputable, whether *Chrift* hath giuen it him or no.

8. I do honour and reuerence in good truth *Card.
Bellarmine*, as alfo many other learned men of his Society, and their fingular learning I doe greatly admire, but that their learning or authoritie ought to be
fo greatly efteemed of by Catholikes, that whatfoeuer they thinke to be a point of faith, it is prefently
to bee taken for a diuine Oracle, and the contrarie
opinion of other learned Catholikes, who haue feene
and examined all their grounds, reafons, and authorities, is not to be accounted an opinion, but an *herefie*, and that in a matter of fuch importance, which
concerneth the dutifull obedience of euery Chriftian
to *God* and *Cæfar*, this is that which I cannot take in
good part. And might not, I pray you, the *Canonifts*,
who do vehemently defend the *Popes* direct power

to

to difpofe of all temporalls againſt Card. *Bellarmine*
and others, whom they are not afraide to call *impios
politicos wicked politicians*, ᵸ pretending thereby to
ſtrengthen the fortreſſe of the Catholike Church, to
confirme the immoueable rocke of *S. Peter*, and to
maintaine the Popes authoritie, retort the very ſame
inueƈtiue, which my *Aduerſarie* hath borrowed of
Card. Bellarmine, ⁱ vpon *Card. Bellarmine* himſelfe,
who doth vehemently impugne the aforeſaid direƈt
authoritie, which the Canoniſts do yeelde vnto the
Pope, and with the ſame facilitie crie out with my *Aduerſary, that he taketh vpon him to batter the fortreſſe of
the Catholike Church with her owne Canons, and conſtitutions, and to vndermine the immoueable rocke of* S. Peter
*with his owne inſtruments, and all this he doth with ſuch
Art and ſleigth, that whiles he fighteth againſt the
Church, hee pretendeth to be a friend and childe of the
Church; and albeit he impugne the* Popes *authoritie, yet
he dedicateth his booke to* Pope Sixtus *the fift, laughing
vpon him whiles he woundeth him, and betraying Chriſt
with a kiſſe, as* Iudas *did &c.* And thus much concerning me.

9. Now as touching the matter which I handle,
and the manner of my proceeding therein, *Widdringtons ſpeciall purpoſe* (ſaith my *Aduerſarie*) *in this his
late worke is to defend the new* oath of allegiance, *and to
confute all the chiefe arguments, that haue beene made by
any againſt the ſeuerall clauſes thereof; which neuertheleſſe
he meaneth no other waies to performe* (as he himſelfe often
proteſteth) *but only by ſhewing probably, that the ſaid Oath
may be taken by Catholikes, and that nothing hath beene
hitherto, or can be obiected againſt it, which hath not been
or cannot be probably anſwered.* And from hence my
Aduerſary gathereth certaine admonitions to the Reader, *which*, as he ſaith, *are worthy to be noted.*

10. But before I come to ſet downe his worthy
admonitions, I thinke it fit, to put thee in remem-
brance

ᵸ *Alexander Carerius.*

ⁱ *Againſt* Bar-clay *cap. 1. and in the Epiſtle Dedicatory of his* Schulcke-nius *againſt me.*

ᵏ *Num.* 6.

brance (Curteous Reader) what is the true state of the queſtion betwixt vs concerning the Popes power to depoſe Princes, and what was my chiefe intent in making that diſputation of the Oath. *The maine queſtion therefore betwixt me*, and theſe my *Aduerſaries*, as my *Aduerſarie* T. F. alſo confeſſeth, [1] *is touching the Popes power to depoſe Princes, which ſpecially is denied in this new oath :* to wit, whether it be a point of faith, and not to be denied by any Catholike without note of hereſie, or errour, that the *Pope* hath by *Chriſt* his inſtitution power to depriue temporall Princes of their Kingdomes for any crime whatſoeuer. For whereas ſome very few late writers eſpecially *Card. Bellarmine* and other *Ieſuites*, could not bee content to defend this doctrine for the Popes power (call it temporall, or ſpirituall as you will) to depoſe Princes in a moderate manner, but would needes take vpon them to make it a point of the Catholike faith, and cleerely to demonſtrate by the teſtimonie of holy Scriptures, of ſacred Councells, and by inuincible reaſons, that *Chriſt* hath giuen to *S. Peter*, and his Succeſſors ſuch a temporall power ouer Soueraigne *Kings* and *Princes* (a doctrine neither practiſed, nor knowne by the Fathers of the Primitiue Church, and which hath beene a chiefe occaſion, why this Kingdome is departed from the obedience to the See Apoſtolike) and to condemne all thoſe Catholikes of *hereſie*, who do not runne with them in this their violent courſe, when I ſeriouſly conſidered with my ſelfe, what ſcandall this new doctrine maintained with ſuch violence brought to Catholike Religion, what danger to our Prince and Countrey, and what great calamities and diſgrace Engliſh Catholikes do daily ſuffer thereby, as not being accounted true, and loyall Subiects to their Prince, euen according to the doctrine of thoſe, who are eſteemed to bee the chiefe pillars of the Catholike Church, but ſo long only as it ſhall pleaſe the Pope, I thought

1 *In the end of his Preface.*

thought my felfe bound by the duty which I do owe
to the Catholike Religion, & to my Prince & Country, to take away as much as lieth in mee (notwithftanding the manifold flaunders, which I fore-faw
fome perfons would therefore raife againft mee) the
aforefaid fcandals, dangers and difgraces, and to anfwer *probably* all the arguments which Card. *Bellarmine* hath from the chiefeft Authors, who haue handled this queftion collected, to demonftrate that it is
a certaine and infallible doctrine, and the contrary,
not fo much an *opinion*, as an *herefie*, that the Pope
hath by *Chrift* his inftitution authority to depriue
Soueraigne Princes of their temporall Kingdomes
and dominions.

11 Wherefore the prefent controuerfie betwixt
me and my Aduerfaries is not at this time concerning
the *abfolute* propofition, to wit, whether the Pope
hath or hath not power to depofe, (the reafon why I
doe not difpute of this *abfolute* propofition I will declare beneath ᵐ) but concerning the *modall*, whether ┃ m *Num.*78.79
it be certaine, without coutrouerfie, and a poynt of
faith, that the Pope hath power to depofe, as this
Author T.F. following Card. *Bellarmine* and fome
few *Iefuites*, will needes haue it to be, and I with other
Catholikes, and the Kingdome of France, as *Petrus
Pithæus* witneffeth ⁿ, doe vtterly deny the fame, And
from hence it euidently followeth, that although ┃ n *In Cod.libert.
Card. *Bellarmine* fhould alledge an hundred Catho- ┃ Ecclef.Galli.*
like Authors, who doe affirme, that the Pope hath
power to depofe Princes, yet if they doe not alfo affirme that it is *certaine*, and to be beleeued as a *point
of faith*, that the Pope hath fuch a power, they neither
confirme his opinion, nor gainefay mine concerning
the prefent controuerfie, which is now in hand. And
thus much concerning the matter and manner of my
Apologie for the right of Princes. Now touching my
Theologicall Difputation concerning the oath of Alle-
　　　　　F　　　　　　　　　　　geance,

geance, although in very deede hitherto I haue not
feene any fufficient reafon to condemne the fayd
oath as vnlawfull, and from the doctrine which I
taught in my *Apologie* it doth neceffarily follow, that
with a probable and fafe confcience it may bee taken
by any Catholike, confidering that the Popes power
to depofe Princes,as my *Aduerfarie* heere confeffeth,
is the maine queftion betwixt him and me,and which
is fpecially denied in this oath, neuertheleffe I did
not intend in that *Difputation* pofitiuely to defend
the fayd oath, but fincerely to propound vnto his
Holineffe, who as I am fully perfwaded, was neither
truely, nor throughly informed of the reafons, why
Englifh Catholikes thought the fayd oath to bee
lawfull, all the arguments on both fides,which might
be vrged againft or for the oath, affirming nothing of
my felfe,but as reprefenting the perfons of thofe,who
either impugned or approoued the fayd oath; humbly requefting his *Holineffe*,that after he had diligently examined the reafons on both fides, he would bee
pleafed to fatisfie thofe difficulties, which wee propounded, and to make knowne to vs Englifh Catholickes, thofe many things, which he in his *Breues* had
affirmed to be in this oath cleerely repugnant to faith
and faluation.

12 Now let vs fee thofe worthy admonitions,and
thofe things, which my *Aduerfary* fayth,*are worthy to be*
noted. Firft therefore, fayth he, o *Widdrington doth*
not account his owne opinion and doctrine in this point to be
certaine and affured, but only probable, *neither yet con-*
demneth our doctrine as manifeftly falfe, or repugnant to
faith,or to the faluation of foules : befides that he confeffeth
alfo elfewhere, p *that his* Holineffe *in three feuerall* Breues *declared the contrary doctrine contained in the oath*
to be repugnant to the Catholike faith q: *whereupon I in-*
ferre, that it were no leffe then moft dangerous temeritie,
and extreme folly to reiect our doctrine, and to adhere to
his

o *num.* 10.

p *In Epift.*
Dedicat. & in
Difp. Theolog.
cap. 3. *num.* 1.
q *Num.* 11.

his ; for if it be wisdome in doubtfull matters to take the
surest way, it cannot with reason be denied, but that albeit
his opinion seeme probable *to him,yet the contrary is much*
more to be imbraced, seeing that by his owne confession it is
at least probable, *and therefore may be imbraced without*
danger, whereas his is not onelie doubted of, but also decla-
red to be contrarie to the Catholike faith, both by his Holi-
nes, *& also by very many learned Catholikes (as he him-*
selfe also confesseth: r *) besides that he acknowledgeth also*
afterwards,that there are very few Authors extant,which
doe deny our doctrine in comparison of those that teach and
defend it ; whereto I also adde, that it is altogether con-
forme to the practise of the Church, confirmed by diuerse
generall Councels,as I haue shewed particularly in my Sup-
plement ; so as no man, that hath care of his soule,can haue
any reason to venter it vpon his opinion, impugned and con-
demned by so great authority, when our doctrine may by his
owne confession be securely followed without doubt or dan-
ger.

13. But marke (Courteous Reader) how many
frauds, and falshoods my *Aduersarie* hath here committed. And *first* how cunningly hee would deceiue
thee by not distinguishing the *absolute* proposition
concerning the Popes power to depose Princes,
which is not now in question, from the *modall,* which
onely is now in controuersie. For although I do not
take vpon me at this present to condemne that opi-
on for the *Popes* power to depose Princes as manifestly false, or to defend the contrary as certaine and
without controuersie, yet it is vntrue, that I doe not
assuredly account that opinion and doctrine, which
affirmeth it to bee a *point of faith,* that the *Pope* hath
power to depose Princes, and the contrary to be *here-*
ticall, to be absolutely false, and to vse the words of
the *Parliament* of Paris against *Suarez* doctrine, to be
scandalous, seditious, damnable and *pernicious.*

14. *Secondly,* it is also vntrue, that I doe acknow-

r *Vbi supra.*
f *Cap.* 3 *sec.*3.
num. 15.

t *Supplem. cap.*
2. *nu.* 76.77.

ledge that there are very few Authors extant, which doe deny their doctrine concerning the *modall* propofition, in comparifon of thofe, that doe teach and defend it : for although I affirmed, that very few Authors, whofe writings are now extant, in comparifon of others, who defend this temporall power of the Pope, are to be found that deny his authority to depofe Princes, (the reafons whereof which I alledged in that place and before in my *Apologie*, becaufe they clean ouerthrow the common argument taken from the multitude of Authors, who doe cleaue to their opinion touching the *abfolute* propofition, both my *Aduerfarie*, and D. *Schulckenius* alfo do altogether conceale,) yet touching the *modall* propofition I confidently auerred, that there were very few writers, and thofe for the moft part *Iefuites*, who doe hold this doctrine for the Popes power to depofe Princes to be a *poynt of faith*. For behold my expreffe words.^u *And frō hence any man may plainly perceiue, that* Widdrington *doth not oppofe himfelfe either againft all Diuines, or againft the common opinion of the Church, or Doctours, but onely againft very few writers, confidering that among thofe feuentie Authors related by* Card. Bellarmine *very few are to be found, who (although they are perchance of opinion, that the* Pope *by* Chrift *his inftitution hath authoritie to depofe* Princes *for enormious crimes) doe fo peremptorily adhere to that opinion, as to taxe them with* herefie, *who doe maintaine the contrary. And if* Card. Bellarmine *in the later Editions of his bookes, yet bringing no new reafon to confirme his former opinion, had not condemned the contrarie opinion of Catholikes as* hereticall, *but had fuffred euery man to perfeuere without note of* herefy, *in his owne opinion, which he fhould thinke to be the truer, he fhould not doubtleffe haue had* Widdrington *to be his Aduerfarie, or to haue attempted to ouerthrow his reafons as infufficient to* demoftrate *an vndoubted point of faith.*

15   *Thirdly*, it is alfo vntrue, that confeffe the

Popes Holineffe to haue declared in his *Breues*, that the doctrine, which denyeth his power to depofe Princes, is contrary to the Catholike faith: I onely confeffe, that in his *Breues* he hath declared the Oath to be vnlawfull, for that it containeth in it many things flat contrary to faith and faluation; but what thefe many things be, his *Holineffe* doth not expreffe in his *Breues*, neither as yet hath he been pleafed to fignifie it vnto vs, although we haue both by priuate letters, and alfo publike writings moft humbly and inftantly requefted it at his hands. I did indeede confeffe, that his *Holineffe* was by all likelyhood mif-informed of thofe many things, which he thought in this oath to be flat contrary to faith and faluation, by *Card: Bellarmine*, who hath publikely in his bookes declared, that the Popes fpirituall Primacie, his power to excommunicate, and to binde and loofe are plainely denied in this Oath, and the Kings fpirituall Supremacie is therein acknowledged, but how vntrue this is, I haue fufficiently fhewed in my *Theologicall Difputation*, and beneath I fhall haue occafion to repeat againe. And albeit his *Holineffe* had in his *Breues* particularly declared the doctrine for his power to depofe Princes to be *of faith*, and the contrary to be *hereticall*, (as likewife *Pope Celeftine* the 3. did in a *Breue*, or *Decretall* letter of his, which was in times paft for almoft two hundred yeeres together extant in the Canon Law, declare, that *Marriage was fo diffolued by herefie, that the partie, whofe confort was fallen into herefie, might lawfully marry another*, which doctrine is now flatly condemned in the *Councell of Trent*) yet this declaration of the *Pope* being no infallible definition, but onely a fignification of his opinion as I proued abundantly in the forefaid booke, no Catholike is bound in confcience to follow it, neither to obey his declaratiue precept grounded thereon as out of *Suarez* doctrine I fhewed in that place.[x]

x *Diſp: Theo-
log. cap: 10.
ſec. 2.*

y In the Ad-
ioinder num:
106. & ſeq.

16   *Fourthly*, it is alſo vntrue, that I confeſſe the contrary doctrine of theirs touching the abſolute propoſition to be at leaſt *probable*, and that it may be ſecurely followed *without doubt or danger*; for touching practiſe I doe vtterly condemne that doctrine as abſolutely *falſe, impious, dānable, ſeditious*, yea & in ſome ſort *hereticall*, as ſhall appeare beneath y, and for ſpeculation, I doe neither approue it as *probable*, nor condemne it as *improbable*, becauſe with the probabilitie or improbabilitie of the *affirmatiue part* of this queſtion, I do not at this time intermeddle. That only, which I affirme, is touching the negatiue part of the queſtion, to wit, that it is *probable*, that the Pope hath not power to depoſe Princes, but whether it be probable, that he hath power to depoſe Princes I neither confeſ nor deny, but only for Diſputation ſake I doe grant, that although it be *probable*, that the Pope hath ſuch a power, yet it doth not therefore follow, that it is *certaine* and of *faith*, and the contrarie *heres ticall, improbable*, and not to be imbraced by any Catholike without note of *hereſie, errour*, or *temeritie*.

And by this you may alſo eaſily perceiue, another fraude, and cunning of my *Aduerſarie*. For whereas he affirmeth, *that my ſpeciall purpoſe is to ſhew* probably, *that the ſaid oath may lawfuly be taken by Catholikes*, he doth heere turne cunningly the queſtion an other way, affirming, that it is alſo *probable*, yea & the more *probable* opinion, that the oath may lawfully be refuſed by Catholikes, with which queſtion I doe not intend at this preſent to intermeddle, but only to proue by true *probable* arguments, that the oath may lawfully be taken by Catholikes. For be it ſo for Diſputation ſake, that it is *probable*, yea and the more probable opinion, that Catholikes may lawfully refuſe the oath, (by reaſon that ſo many learned men, yea and the Pope himſelfe, doe thinke it to be vnlawfull) which neuertheleſſe I will not at this time either affirme,

firme,or denie,for the reason I will alledge beneath[z],
yet can it not from thence be rightly concluded, that
therefore it is not *probable*,that the oath may lawfully
be taken,or that it is a *most dangerous temeritie and extreme folly*, as my *Aduersarie* seemeth to insinuate, to
follow an opinion which is *truly probable* against the
more probable opinion of the *Pope*,and other Diuines,
as out of the doctrine of *Uasquez* affirming it also to
be the more opinion of Diuines, I did in my *Theologicall Disputation* [a] cleerely convince. It is sufficient
for my purpose at this present, that Catholikes may
lawfully take the oath, but whether they may also refuse it, I at this time will neither affirme nor denie.
This onely I will say,that if Catholikes may lawfully
take the oath,and so auoide his *Maiesties* indignation
against them, and also their owne temporall ouerthrow, and will not,they may thanke themselues, &
such like violent spirits, as my *Aduersarie* is,who by
sleight and cunning endeauoureth to perplexe their
consciences, & guilefully to perswade them, that it is
the more safe and the more probable way to suffer all
temporall miseries and disgraces, which he himselfe
in my opinion,if hee were in their case would not
suffer,then to do that which with a safe and probable
conscience they may doe.

18   *Fiftly*, it is also vntrue, *that the doctrine for the
Popes power to depose Princes is conforme to the practise
of the Church*, although it be indeed conforme to the
practise of diuers *Popes* since the time of *Gregorie* the
seuenth, who was the first Pope, that *trusting to the
power and riches of other men*, *contrary to the custome of
his Ancestours*,*contemning the Emperours authoritie*,*depriued him of his Empire*, *a thing before those times not
heard of*, saith *Onuphrius* [b],which practise neuertheles
was then, and hath been euer since contradicted by
Catholike Princes and subiects. As also it is vntrue,
*that this doctrine is confirmed by any one Generall Coun-
cell,*

z *Num:*78.79.

a *Cap.*10 *sec.*2.

b *De varia
creat. Rom:
Pont: lib.* 4.

cell, that it is a point of faith, or the contrary doctrine *hereticall*, or *improbable*, as I haue partly shewed in the *Preface* of my *Apologeticall Anfwer*, where I anſwered all thoſe nine Councells, which *Card: Bellarmine* in his Anſwer to *D. Barclay* brought to proue his doctrine in this point to be of *faith*, and the contrary not *Catholike*, and partly I will ſhew beneath, when I ſhall anſwer to the Replies, which haue been made by *Fa: Leſſius*, maſked vnder *D. Singletons* name, (from whom my *Aduerſarie* borroweth the third part of his booke, to wit, eight whole Chapters which he conſumeth in defence of the *Councell of Lateran*) to the anſwers I made to that Decree of the ſaid *Lateran Councell*, whereon this new doctrine of *faith* according to theſe men is chiefely grounded.

19   Wherefore vnleſſe my *Aduerſarie* be able to convince, as without doubt he is not, that the opinion, which denieth the Popes power to depoſe Princes, is altogether improbable, and the *State* of *France*, beſides many other Doctors, as thou ſhalt ſee beneath, to be extreame fooles, he will neuer be able to *demonſtrate*, that *it is moſt dangerous temeritie*, *and extreme folly* to adhere to that opinion, (which my *Aduerſarie* to perſwade his Reader, that it is a ſingular opinion of one onely Authour, and as he vntruly ſaith, of no one *Catholike*, euer calleth it my opinion) conſidering that according to *Uaſquez* doctrine, which is, as he ſaith c, *the common doctrine of the Schoole men*, it is neither follie nor temeritie, to follow a probable opinion againſt the more probable, the more common, and the more ſure opinion of the Pope and other learned men, although they ſhould pretend to convince their opinion by the authoritie of holy Scriptures, declarations of Generall Councells, the practiſe of the Church, and other Theologicall reaſons, which ſeeme to them invincible. For it is vſuall in a controuerſie among Catholike Doctors, to alledge

c *1ª.2ᵉ. diſp. 62. cap: 4,*

ledge for confirmation of both opinions the aforesaid authorities and proofes, which neuerthelesse
doth not discourage either part from maintayning
their opinions, as it is manifest in the question concerning the superioritie of the *Pope* and *Generall
Councells*, the conception of our *B. Lady* in originall
sinne, and many questions concerning the Popes
authoritie to dispence, and now of late in the question touching grace, and freewill, betwixt the *Domi-
nicans*, and the *Iesuites*.

20 Therefore it is rather *great temeritie*, *and extreme folly*, that you, my Catholike Countrymen,
should venter your soules and whole estates vpon
this my *Aduersaries* writings, whose knowledge in
Diuinitie, is knowne to be but small, and his desire
to ease your griefes, as you shall perceiue beneath [d],   d *Num:* 81.82.
is also no whit lesse: besides he handleth this controuersie, which doth so greatly concerne your spirituall, and temporall good or harme, and your obedience due to G o d and C ae s a r, so vnsincerely,
and corruptly, that either he concealeth my answers,
or peruerteth the true meaning of my words, rather
thereby to disgrace me with the Reader, and to make
him to haue a preiudicate conceipt of what I wrote,
then really and sincerely to finde out the truth, and
by a cleere and moderate debating of the controuersie to satisfie his Readers vnderstanding. And this
very argument taken chiefly from the *Popes Breues*,
which this man to terrifie, and perplexe the timorous conscience of the deuout Catholike Reader vrgeth here, I haue so largely answered in my *Theolo-
gicall Disputation* [e], wherein I fully satisfied this ob-   e *Cap.* 10 *sec.* 2.
iection taken from the authoritie of the *Popes Breues*,
and of so many learned men, who condemne the
oath as contayning in it many things cleerely repugnant to faith and saluation, that I thought he would
haue blushed to repeat the same argument here a-
　　　　　G　　　　　　　gaine

gaine so nakedly, which I my selfe vrged there more plainly and strongly, without making any *Reply* , or taking any notice of the answers I made in that place thervnto. For there I shewed the difference according to *Vasquez* doctrine between a *doubtfull* and disputable question , and that there is neither *doubt* nor *danger* of any imprudence, temeritie, disobedience, or of any other sinne not to obey the *Popes* declaratiue command, when it is grounded vpon an opinion, or doctrine which is not certaine, but disputable , for that diuers *Popes* haue in their *Breues*, or *Decretall letters* declared and taught falfe and also hereticall doctrine, and that the *Popes* declaratiue command hath no greater force to binde, then hath the doctrine or opinion whereon it is grounded, as *Suarez* , whom I related in that place, doth expresly affirme. And thus much concerning my *Aduersaries* first *Admonition*.

f *Num.*12.

21 *Secondly, whereas* Widdrington, saith my *Aduersarie* f *professeth not to giue for his opinion any assured, and certaine proofes, which may breed in the hearers , or Readers a firme and doubtlesse assent, but onely probable reason drawne from credible principles, which may induce a probable perswasion, hee sheweth euidently, that his meaning is not to seeke out the truth, but rather to obscure it by wrangling and cauilling, to shew his wit, labouring to maintaine paradoxes with some shew of probabilitie , knowing right well, that as* Cicero *saith,* there is nothing so incredible, but it may bee made probable by discourse &c. *And what else may this man be thought to intend, but to shew his wit, seeing that hee pretendeth to produce no other proofe of his opinion, but onely probabilitie, and withall acknowledgeth, that the contrarie doctrine is , and hath been professed, and held by almost all the learned Catholikes that euer haue written, at least whose workes are now extant. Is it likely then, that hee meaneth to establish the truth, or to quiet mens consciences by the discussion thereof?*

No,

No truely. But rather that he seeketh, as I haue said, to ob-
scure it, and make it doubtfull, when he can not ouerthrow
it, which is the most diuellish deuise, that any man could
inuent to impugne any point of the Catholike faith ; to wit,
not to doe it all at once, but by degrees, seeking to shake the
foundation of it, first calling it in question, and then teach-
ing it to bee but probable, *and consequently* doubtfull, *to*
the end that the mindes of men hanging in suspence, may
be disposed to admit, as well the errour, as the truth.

22 But whether I or my Aduersarie doth intend
to establish the truth, or rather to obscure it by wrangling and cauilling, seeing that hee still persisteth in
misinterpreting the meaning of my words, and in dif-
sembling the true state of the question concerning the
modall proposition, which is the maine controuersie
betwixt him, and me, (wherein although hee sheweth
in deede in some part his wit, yet verily he sheweth no
sincere and vpright dealing) I leaue to the iudgement
of the indifferent Reader. For first it is vntrue, that
I professe, (as my *Aduersarie* affirmeth) to giue for my
opinion no assured and certaine proofes which may
breed a firme and vndoubted assent, which the Reader would quickly haue perceiued, if my *Aduersarie*
had been pleased to haue entirely related my words,
which are these : *wherefore the present controuersie be-*
tweene me, and Card. Bellarmine *is not concerning this*
absolute *question, or proposition, whether the Pope hath,*
or hath not power to depose Princes for heresie or no, but
concerning the modall *proposition, whether it bee so cer-*
taine, that the Pope by Christ his institution hath such a
power to depose Princes, as that those, who defend the
contrarie opinion, doe expose themselues to manifest dan-
ger of heresie, errour, or of any other mortall sinne.
Wherefore although in my Apologie *I brought certaine*
arguments drawne from inconueniences, which the Logi-
cians call, ad impossibile, *to proue that* Christ *our Lord*
did not grant such an authoritie to the Pope, which is the

abſolute propoſition, *yet whoſoeuer will diligently pe-*
ruſe my Apologie, *will preſently perceiue, that my intent*
was not to bring conuincing reaſons, and which doe cauſe
a firme and vndoubted aſſent, to wit, of the aforeſaid abſolute propoſition, *but onely,* probable, *and ſuch as are*
grounded vpon credible principles, and are able to cauſe a
probable *perſwaſion,* of that abſolute propoſition, of
which propoſition I did there onely ſpeake.

    23   Marke now the fraudulent proceeding of my
Aduerſarie, I affirmed, that my intent was not to bring
conuincing reaſons to proue, that Chriſt our Lord did
not grant authoritie to the Pope to depoſe Princes,
which is the *abſolute* propoſition. Now my *Aduerſa-*
rie affirmeth, that I did not intend to giue any aſſured or certaine proofes for my opinion, and concealeth the difference of my opinion touching the *mo-*
dall and the *abſolute* propoſition, and the difference
of proofes, which in all learned mens opinions are
required to them both. For the very ſame proofes,
which in reſpect of the *abſolute* propoſition are onely
probable, in reſpect of the *modall* propoſition, ſuppoſing that they be *probable,* are *conuincing* proofes; and
although they are of force to cauſe onely a *probable*
perſwaſion of the *abſolute* propoſition, yet they are
of force to cauſe a firme, aſſured, (ſpeaking of moral
aſſurance) and vndoubted aſſent of the *modall.* For
conſidering that according to the knowne, and approued rule of the Logicians, which is taken from the
g *Lib.* 1. *Prior.*
cap. 1.
definition of a *Syllogiſme* aſſigned by Ariſtotle, g *in a*
good Syllogiſme the concluſion is neceſſarily inferred from
the premiſes, if wee once ſuppoſe the premiſes to bee
probable, of necesſitie the concluſion muſt bee pro-
pable, and conſequently the contradictorie propoſition can not bee certaine, and a point of faith.

    24   As for example, concerning the *Conception* of
of our *B. Lady* in originall ſinne, although wee haue
onely a *probable* aſſent of the *abſolute* propoſition, to
wit,

wit, that shee was, or was not conceiued in originall sinne, yet we haue an vndoubted assent of the *modall:* to wit, that it is a disputable question, whether shee was conceiued in originall sin, or no. And although in this question touching our *B. Lady* hir Conception the case be more cleere, it being in some sort declared by the *Councell* of *Trent*, that the question is as yet disputable, yet wee may proportionally perceiue the like in all disputable questions, wherein wee haue onely a *probable* assent of the *absolute* proposition, and yet of the *modall*, to wit, that the question is disputable, wee haue a firme, assured, and vndoubted assent.

25 So in this question of the *Popes* power to depose Princes, although I thinke it *probable*, that the *Pope* hath no power to depose, yet I thinke it *certaine* and assured (speaking of morall assurance to exclude metaphysicall and diuine certainty, to which euident demonstrations, or supernaturall reuelations are required) or, which is all one, my firme, constant, and resolute opinion is, that it is not a point of faith, or a doctrine defined by the Church, that the *Pope* hath power to depose Princes, and I am fully and assuredly perswaded, that the contrarie is questionable, disputable, and is and may lawfully bee maintained by Catholikes. And I would gladly, that M^r. *Fitzherbert*, who is now become so publike a writer, teacher, and Professour in these most high, and difficult points of Diuinitie, before hee hath had for ought I can learne any Maister therein, would teach and instruct vs, what manner of arguments, or proofes, he would bring to proue any doctrine, which is in question, to be *probable*, or disputable ; Doubtlesse hee can bring no other arguments then *probable*, for euident demonstrations, or diuine reuelations do proue the doctrine to be certaine, and without all controuersie, and the contrarie not to be *probable*, what rea-

son

son then can my *Aduersarie* haue to taxe me, for not bringing any *assured* or certaine proofes, but onely *probable*, to proue that it is *probable*, that the *Pope* hath not power to depose Princes.

26 Wherefore to establish and confirme this do-ctrine, that it is not a point of faith, that the *Pope* hath power to depose Princes, or that it is not *impro-bable*, that he hath no such power, it is sufficient to an-swere *probably* all the reasons and authorities to the contrarie, and to bring *probable* proofes; which may cause a *probable* perswasion, that he hath no such au-thoritie: considering that according to the approued ground of all Philosophers, and Diuines, *certaintie* of one part of the contradiction cannot stand with *probabilitie* of the other, taking *probable* in that sense, as the Diuines doe take it, and not for that, which hath onely a shew of *probabilitie*, and is not truely *probable*; for if it bee certainely true, that the *Pope* hath power to depose, it is certainely false, and there-fore not *probable*, that hee hath not power to depose. And therefore my *Aduersarie* rather, seeketh to ob-scure the truth, and to intangle mens consciences by wrangling and cauilling, whiles first he requireth *eui-dent* demonstrations, to proue a *probable* doctrine, and secondly dissembleth the true state of the question, confounding the *absolute* proposition and the proofes thereof with the *modall*, which distinction doth ex-presse the true state of the question, and discouereth both his fraude and weakenesse, not onely in this, but almost in all the rest of his Replyes, and *thirdly* he concealeth the answere, which I gaue to this argu-ment taken from the authoritie of the *Popes* Breues and of other learned men, and also the reasons, why so many learned Catholikes whose bookes are now extant, haue from the time of Pope *Gregorie* the se-uenth defended this opinion for the Popes power to depose Princes. And thus much concerning my

Aduersaries

Aduersaries second admonition, the weakeneſſe whereof will alſo preſently more cleerely appeare by my anſwere to his third and fourth admonition.

27 *Therefore it is to be conſidered for the third point,* ſaith my *Aduerſarie,* ʰ *what* Widdrington *meaneth by a* probable *opinion, or a* probable *anſwere, which no doubt, he vnderſtandeth ſo, that whatſoeuer he ſaith, muſt be held for* probable, *how abſurd ſo euer it be ; for otherwiſe he could not challenge to himſelfe ſuch a priuiledge of* probabilitie *as he doth, his arguments and anſwers being ſo weake and impertinent, as you ſhall finde them to be ; in which reſpect he is faine to diſſemble the anſweres already made by ſome to his former arguments, and authorities in his* Apologie, *whereto he now remitteth his Reader very often, without taking ſo much as any knowledge of the confutation thereof, as though the ſame had neuer been anſwered, or that euery aſſertion or poſition of his, being once laid downe, muſt needs ſtand for an eternall law, or were a decree of the* Medes *and* Perſians*, quod non licet immutari.*

ʰ *Nu.*15.

i *Dan* 6.

28 But not to returne theſe bitter ſpeeches of my *Aduerſarie* backe vpon himſelfe, which with the ſame facilitie, and with farre better reaſon I might doe, *firſt,* It is very vntrue, that I take *probable* for *whatſoeuer I doe ſay how abſurd ſo euer it be,* as this man, if it were lawfull for mee to vſe his *abſurd* word, very abſurdly affirmeth, *that without doubt I doe*; Neither doe I take *probable* for that, which hath onely *a ſhew of probabilitie,* as *Cicero* tooke *probable* in his Paradoxes, but I take *probable,* as Philoſophers and Diuines doe take it, as it is diſtinguiſhed from *demonſtratiue and fallacious,* to wit, for that, *which is approued by wiſe and learned men in the art, which they profeſſe,* which therefore as in ſpeculation may be embraced without any imputation of errour or folly, ſo in practiſe it may bee followed without any note of imprudence, or ſinne:

finne: As in a matter of Phyficke, that is accounted *probable*, which is approued by learned Phyfitions, of Law by learned Lawiers, and of Diuinitie
by learned Catholike Diuines. *Secondly*, it is alfo vntrue, *that I haue* in my *Theologicall Difputation diffem-
bled the anfweres made by fome to my former arguments
and authorities in my Apologie, whereto I remit my
Reader oftentimes*, confidering that my *Theologicall
Difputation* was wholly finifhed, and in the preffe,
before the Replyes of D. *Schulkenius*, and of D. *We-
fton*, and alfo my *Aduerfaries Supplement* were publifhed, fo that I could take no notice of them in my
Difputation; for which caufe I was conftrained to
touch them briefely onely in an *Admonition* to the
Reader. But my *Aduerfarie* himfelfe to make his
owne *Replyes* to feeme the more *probable*, and my
anfweres abfurd, foolifh, impertinent, ridiculous (for fo
hee is pleafed to call them) is not afhamed to diffem-
ble in many points the true ftate of the queftion, and
alfo the anfweres, which in my *Theologicall Difputation* I made to his chiefeft Replyes, efpecially thofe
whereby hee laboureth to terrifie the timerous confciences of vnlearned Catholikes, with the pretence
of his new *Catholike faith*, with the authoritie of the
Popes Breues, and the teftimonies of fo many learned men, who haue condemned the oath, as containing in it many things flat contrarie to faith and
faluation.

29. Now let vs fee his fourth confideration, by
which the Reader may perceiue, how infufficiently he
declareth what is a *probable* argument, or opinion, and
how little he fatisfieth the vnderftanding of vnlearned
Catholikes, who by his obfcure, and confufe defcription of a probable argument, cannot perceiue, what

k *Num.* 17.

argument or opinion is *probable*. *Fourthly*, faith he, *it
is to be confidered, that to make an argument, or proofe*
probable, *it fufficeth not that it feeme good and true in it
felfe,*

felfe, but it muſt alſo be able in ſome ſort to counterpoyſe the arguments and proofes of the contrary opinion : for often it falleth out that the reaſons of one part are ſo pregnant, that they ſeeme to conuince, and yet when they are weighed with the reaſons of the other part, they are neither pregnant, nor ſo much as probable : *for according to the old prouerbe,* one tale is good vntill an other be heard.

30. *To which purpoſe it is to be conſidered , that many heretikes, and namely the* Arians (*of whom there are many euen at this day*) *both doe, and may well pretend a farre greater probabilitie for their opinion, than* Widdrington *doth or can for his, conſidering their aboundant allegation of Scriptures, their ſubtill ſhifts in anſwering the arguments and obiections of the* Catholikes *, the great multitude of learned men of their Sect in times paſt, and their dignitie in the Church, the Conuenticles aſſembled, and held in their fauour, and finally the ample propagation of their opinion and Sect, eſpecially in the time of* Conſtantius *the Emperour. For which reſpects their followers , at this day , doe hold their doctrine not only for* probable, *but alſo for infallibly true, and condemne the contrary for pernicious* hereſie : *whereas* Widdringtons *grounds and proofes of his opinion ſeeme to himſelfe ſo weake, that he dare not affirme them to be more then* probable.

31. *Therefore as there is no good Chriſtian that doth now hold the arguments of the* Arians *to be ſo much as* probable, *conſidering the potent reaſons, and proofes of the Catholike doctrine in that point, ſo albeit the arguments and authorities , which* Widdrington *produceth , were they farre more plauſible and pregnant then they are , yet no Catholike could eſteeme them to be any way* probable, *being compared and ballanced with the irrefregable proofes of the other part ; I meane the arguments, and neceſſarie conſequences drawne from the holy Scriptures , the authoritie of almoſt all the learned Doctors and Diuines that haue written of that point, and the practiſe of the Church for ſome hundreths of yeares confirmed by nine or ten Coun-*

l *See Supplem.*
chap. 2. *num.*
76. 77.

cells [1]*, whereof some haue been the greatest that euer were in Gods Church; and therefore I say that all this being well weighed, no Catholike man of sound wit , or iudgment can imagine this mans arguments (which he himselfe houldeth but for* probable) *to haue any* probabilitie *in the world, or to proue any thing else but his weakenesse, wilfulnesse, and folly in propounding and mainteining them.*

m *Disput. The-*
olog. cap. 10.
sec. 2. *num.* 7.
vsque ad num.
21.

32. *For albeit he teacheth out of* Vasquez [m] *, and o-thers, that of two opinions the lesse* probable *and lesse safe may securely be followed, and that the opinion of a few, yea of one approued Doctor, sufficeth sometimes to make an opi-nion* probable, *though many hold the contrary to that one Doctor (to which purpose he filleth aboue a dozen pages of his booke with* Vasquez *his doctrine and text) yet he is* absurd *in applying the same to this our case ; for although* Vasquez *dse teach* [n] *that a man may in doubtfull cases or questions securely follow the opinion of a few learned Doc-tours, though the same be lesse safe , and* probable *, then the contrarie opinion held by many , yet he is to be vn-derstood to speake only of such disputable questions , as my* Aduersary Widdrington *himselfe alleageth* [o] *for exam-ple sake out of* Vasquez *, to wit,* whether there are any habits infused by God alone, *concerning which question* Vasquez *saith,* [p] *that albeit* Pope Clement *the fift did determine expressely in a Councell held at* Vienna, *that there opinion who held that there are such habits , is more* probable, *then the negatiue, yet it was neuer either by that decree, or any other of* Pope, *or Councell determined to be more then* probable, *in which respect he doth not condemne the contrarie doctrine for* heresie, *notwithstanding that he, and the farre greater part of learned men do hold the other to be certainely true.*

n Id. 2a. *disp.*
62. *cap.* 1. *nu.* 1.

o *Ibidem num.*
26.

p *Vbi supra*
disp. 79 *cap.* 1.
& disp. 86.

33. *So as* Vasquez *is to be vnderstood to speake of questi-ons and opinions altogether vndecided , and not of such a doctrine as ours , touching the* Popes *power to depose* Princes, *which, as I haue said, hath not onely beene taught by the learnedst men of many ages, but also is grounded vp-on*

*on the holy Scriptures, and confirmed by the practise and
decrees of diuers Popes and Councells, as well* Generall *as*
Prouinciall, *as* (*to omit the other mentioned in my Supplement* q) *it is euident by the decree of the famous Councell of* Lateran, *which expressely ordained the practise of it
in some cases, and did therefore neeessarily suppose, and
firmely beleeue the verity of the doctrine, as I will clearely
prooue* r *hereafter in this Reply, and withall shew the ridiculous absurditie of* Widdringtons *arguments and instances against the same, yea and conuince him* s *euen by his
owne testimonie to be falne* (*to vse his owne words*) *into
errour or heresie, for not beleiuing this doctrine, which
that famous General* Councell *beleiued, and ordained to
be practised.*

q *Cap. 2. num.*
76. 77.

r *Cap. 15. nu.*
6. 7. 8.
s *Ibidem num.*
9. 11. 12.

34. *In the meane time he is to vnderstand, that whereas to shew the probabilitie of his doctrine, he bringeth many Authors, partly in his* Theologicall Disputation, *and
partly in his* Apologie, *I remit him to* D. Schulckenius ;
*who hath answered particularly to euery one of them, and
proued clearely, that diuerse of them doe make flatly against
him, and many nothing at all for him* (*being truely vnderstood*) *and that some others are worthily reiected, being either so* absurd, *that they are easily confuted by the circumstances of the places alledged, or else* Heretikes (*as it appeareth by their doctrine in other things*) *or knowne* Schismatikes, *who liuing in the time of the* Emperors *or* Kings
*that were deposed, wrote partially in their fauour, of which
sort neuerthelesse there are very few ; so as of all the Authours, that he hath scraped together to make some skew of
probability in his doctrine, he hath no one cleare and sufficient witnesse to iustifie the same.*

35. *And therefore seeing that all his pretended, probabilitie consisteth partly in the authoritie of the* Authors,
and partly in the sufficiencie (*as he supposeth*) *of his answeres to our grounds, arguments, and authorities, which
answeres I shall haue occasion to confute in this* Treatise,
*and to shew them to be so farre from probabilitie, that
they*

H 2

they are wholly impertinent, *and sometimes* ridiculous *for their* absurdity ; *therefore I conclude, that he cannot any way cleere or excuse himselfe from the note of great te-*merity *and grosse* errour *(yea flat* heresie *if he bee obstinate) in impugning our doctrine grounded upon such assured and solid foundations as I haue here signified, and will more particularly and manifestly declare heereafter : as also I will put thee in minde* (good Reader) *oftentimes by the way to note how* probably *or rather (to say truely) how* absurdly *he argueth and answereth, to the end thou maiest the better iudge, how dangerous it will be for thee to venter thy soule vpon his pretence of* probability, *which is no o-ther but such as any* heretike *may haue for his doctrine.*

36. *For all* Heretikes *doe thinke themselues and their fellowes as good and sufficient* Doctors *to make an opinion* probable, *as he either is, or esteemeth his Authors to be ; and they neuer want Scriptures and Fathers that seeme to them to confirme their opinions, and doe make as* probable *answers to our obiections out of Scriptures and Fathers as hee doth, and many times much more* probable, *then he, yea and they may either with his arguments and instances, or other as* probable *as they, impugne the authoritie of any decree of a* General Councel, *be it neuer so expresse against them, saying that the fathers who made it followed, but a probable opinion, and so might erre, as you shal heare* t *he answereth to the decree of the* Councell of Lateran.

t *Infra chap.* 13. *num.* 1.

37. *And so you see, that if his pretended* probability *be admitted against the common doctrine, practise and decrees of the* Church, *any heretike will not onely easily defend, but also establish his heresie : and any point of Catholike faith may easily be called in question & made only* probable, *and consequently doubtfull, obnoxious to error, and to be reiected by any man that list to embrace the contrary : which truely I leaue* (good Reader) *to thy consideration, whether it bee not the right way to ouerthrow* Catholike Religion, *and to introduce all* Heresie *and* Atheisme.

38. This is my *Aduersaries* fourth admonition, the
subftance

substance whereof although I could haue comprised in few lines, yet I thought good to set it downe entirely word by word as it lieth, to the end the Reader may more plainely perceiue his fraudulent, vncharitable, and insufficient proceeding therein. And *first* he declareth, what is requisite to a *probable* argument. *Secondly*, he affirmeth, that *Vasquez* doctrine, which I related in my *Theologicall Disputation*, for following of *probable* opinions is to be vnderstood to speak only of questions & opinions altogether vndecided, & not of such a doctrine as theirs is touching the *Popes* power to depose Princes, *which hath beene taught by the learnedst men of many ages, is grounded vpon the holy Scriptures* & c. *Thirdly*, he inferreth, that any *heretike*, and namely the *Arrians* may pretend as great, yea and farre greater *probability* to prooue their *heresie*, then I doe, or can doe to prooue my doctrine. *Fourthly*, he auerreth, that all my pretended *probability* consisteth partly in the authoritie of those Authors, which I bring in my *Theologicall Disputation* and also in my *Apologie*, and partly in the sufficiencie, as I suppose, of my answers to their grounds, arguments and authorities; for confutation of the first my *Aduersarie* remitteth his Reader to D. *Schulckenius*, and for the second he himself promiseth to shew them to be so far from *probabilitie*, that they are wholly *impertinent*, and sometimes *ridiculous* for their *absurditie*, and that therefore I cannot any way cleere or excuse my selfe from the note of great *temerity* and grosse *errour*, yea, flat *heresie, into which he will*, forsooth, *conuince me euen by mine owne testimonie to be falne, for not beleeuing this doctrine touching the Popes power to depose Princes, which that famous Generall* Councell *of* Lateran *beleeue d, and ordained to be practised*. But how vaine are the brags of this glorious boasting man, and who in very deede is the *impertinent, ridiculous* and *absurd*, thou shalt haue (good Reader) a taste by my answer to this his admo-

H 3 nition

nition, and by my anſwers to the reſt of his Replies
thou ſhalt more fully perceiue, as alſo that I am free
from all note of *temerity*, *errour* or *hereſie*, and how
dangerous it is for thee to venter thy ſoule and whole
eſtate vpon the credit of this vnlearned and vncharitable man, who as hee is knowen to bee a man of
no great learning, ſo alſo both heere and in the greateſt part of his Replies ſheweth great want not
onely of *learning*, but alſo of *charity*, *finceritie*, and alſo of *Chriſtian modeſtie*, as partly thou haſt ſeene already and heereafter ſhalt moſt cleerely vnderſtand.

39. *Firſt* therefore conſider (*Courteous Reader*)
whether M^r. *Fitzherbert* by his deſcription of a *proba-*
ble argument intendeth to quiet and ſatisfie, or rather
to diſturbe and perplexe the timorous conſciences of
vnlearned Catholikes, who cannot vnderſtand what
he meaneth by thoſe words, *in ſome ſort*, and how an
argument, which is far the leſſe *probable*, can by thoſe
words be diſtinguiſhed from an argument, of the contrarie opinion, which is by much, the more *probable*.
For although it be true, that *probable* arguments for
one opinion muſt be able *in ſome ſort* to counterpoiſe
the arguments of the contrary opinion in the iudgement of thoſe, who thinke that opinion to bee *proba-*
ble, and are able to weigh and ballance the intrinſecall
grounds, or arguments on both ſides, yet vnlearned
men, who are not able to iudge & examin the intrinſecall grounds of any opinion, but are onely led by
authority, can not eaſily diſcerne, how farre this, *in*
ſome part, which hath ſo great a latitude, is to bee extended. Neither is my *Aduerſarie*, as I ſuppoſe, ſo
ignorant in philoſophy, although perchance he hath
ſpent ſmal time in the ſtudie therof, as to imagin, that
probability, is in the thing it ſelfe, as truth and falſhood
are, according to that ſaying of the philoſophers, *ex*
eo quod res eſt vel non eſt, propoſitio dicitur vera vel falſa :
a propoſition is ſayd to bee true or falſe, for that the
thing

thing it felfe, which is affirmed or denyed is, or is not.

40   For *probabilitie* is not in the thing it felfe, but in the vnderftanding of him, who approueth the opinion or doctrine, in fo much that although an opinion, which once is true, can afterwards neuer be falfe, nor which once is falfe, be afterwards euer true, yet an opinion, which once was *probable*, may afterwards be *improbable*, and contrariwife, which was once *improbable*, may afterwards proue *probable*, according as it fhall be approued or difproued by men skilfull in the arte which they profeffe : yea an opinion, which to fome Doctors is *improbable*, and alfo *hereticall*, to others may be *probable*, yea and approued as the more true opinion : And this proceedeth from the diuerfitie of mens iudgements and opinions, where oftentimes are feene, according to the vulgar faying, *quot capita tot fententiæ*, *as many heads fo many opinions*. That is *probable*, fay the *Philofophers*, taking it from *Ariftotle* [u], *which is approued by wife and skilfull men in the arte, which they profeffe :* fo that what argument or opinion learned men doe approue, is a *probable* argument or opinion. And this defcription of *probable* is not obfcure and intricate, but cleare and perfpicuous euen to ignorant men, who can eafily difcerne, what opinion or argument learned men do approue. And therefore well faid *Armilla* [x], whom I cited in my *Theologicall Difputation* [y], *that a man is not bound alwaies to follow the better opinion, but it fufficeth that he follow that, which fome skilfull Doctors iudge to be true :* and learned *Nauarra*, whom I alfo related in that booke [z], for the quieting of fcrupulous confciences affirmeth, [a] *that in the Court of Confcience, to the effect of not finning, it fufficeth to choofe for true his opinion, whom for iuft caufe we thinke to be a man of a good confcience, and of fufficient learning.*

41   Wherefore when my *Aduerfarie* affirmeth, that

u 1. *Top: cap.* 1.

x *Verbo opinio nu:* 2.
y *cap:* 10. *fec.* 2. *nu:* 21.

z *cap:* 3. *fec:* 3. *nu:* 14.
a *in Manuali cap:* 27. *num.* 288.

that *to make an argument probable, it sufficeth not, that it seeme good and true in it selfe, but it must also be able in some sort to counterpoyse the arguments of the contrary opinion,* if he meane, that *it must alwaies be able in some sort to counterpoyse the arguments of the contrarie opinion,* in the iudgements of thosewho are not of the contrary opinion, and doe not approue the argument for good, this, if it were lawfull for me to vse my *Aduersaries* vndecent words, is abfurd and ridiculous, for that oftentimes it falleth out, that some Doctours doe thinke an opinion to be *improbable and hereticall,* which other Doctours of the contrary opinion doe thinke not onely to bee *probable,* but also to bee the more true opinion, as it is euident in the question touching the superioritie of the *Pope* and *Councells.* For the ancient Doctors of *Paris,* as *Ioannes Maior,* & *Iacobus Almainus,* who wrote againlt *Cardinall Caietane* concerning this queltion, thought the opinion, which held the *Pope* to be aboue a *Generall Councell,* to be *improbable,* yea and other Doctors, as *Cardinalis Cameracenfis,* and *Iohn Gerfon,* thought it to be *erroneous* and *hereticall,* which neuerthelelfe *Cardinall Caietan* defended to be the more true opinion.

Maior de au-
ctoriti: Ecclesiæ
circa finem.
Almainus de
authorit: Ecclesia cap. 7.
Card: Camerac. de authorit. Ecclef part.
3. cap: 4.
Gerfon in li-
bello contra
Petrum de Lu-
na. artic: 22.
& alibi.

42 But if my *Aduersarie* meane, as needs he must, if he will fpeake with reafon, that *to make an argument probable, it must alwaies be able in some fort to counterpoyse the arguments of the contrary opinion,* in the iudgements of thofe, who either are not of that contrary opinion, or elfe doe not reiect the argument as *improbable;* this is molt true: for in the iudgments of thofe, who do not onely reiect the argument as *improbable,* but doe abfolutely approue it for good, and for the more *probable,* it doth not only *in fome fort counterpoyfe,* but it doth alfo *in fome fort overpoyfe* the arguments of the contrarie opinion, as any man may plainely perceiue by *Vafquez* doctrine, which becaufe itfully cleareth this prefent difficultie, and is able to

quiet

quiet the conscience of any man, be he neuer so ignorant, I related word by word in my *Theologicall Dispu-*
tation, b which doctrine because my *Aduersarie* knew
right well, that it did amply declare what is a *probable*
opinion, and how farre forth both vnlearned , and
learned men may follow a *probable* opinion against
the more common, the more *probable*, and the more
secure opinion of Catholike Diuines , he cunningly
concealeth, as you shall see, the chiefe and principall
point thereof, and yet he carpeth at me for filling
aboue a dozen pages of my booke with *Vasquez* doctrine and text, affirming withall, that I am *absurd* in
applying *Vasquez* doctrine to this our case , but who
is the *absurd*, you shall forthwith perceiue.

43   For whereas *Vasquez* doth teach , *that if a*
learned and skilfull man, who hath taken no small paines
in studies, and hath also throughly seene and examined all
the reasons of the contrarie opinion , shall iudge against all
other writers, who haue gone before him , that his opinion
is the more probable, he may although it be the lesse secure
opinion, lawfully embrace it, and in practise follow it, whose
opinion also an vnlearned man, who ought according to rea-
son, saith Vasquez, *giue credit to the learning and hone-*
stie of a learned and vertuous man, may lawfully follow,
my *Aduersarie* affirmeth, that *Vasquez* is to be vnderstood to *speake of questions and opinions altogether vnde-*
cided, as is that , which I cited there out of Vasquez,
concerning the infusing of habits by God alone , and not of
such a doctrine, as is this concerning the Popes power to
depose Princes , which hath not onely been taught by the
learnedst men of many ages , but also is grounded vpon
holy Scriptures, and confirmed by the practise, and decrees
of diuers Popes and Counsells &c. But whether I be
absurd in accounting that doctrine to be *probable*, vndecided, and questionable among Catholikes , *about*
which the Schoolemen are at strife, and as yet the contro-
uersie is not decided by the Iudge, saith *Trithemius* c, and
    I   which

b *Cap:* 10. *sec:*
2.

c *In Chron:*
monast: Hir-
saug: ad annum
1106.

d *De dominio nat: ciu: & Eccles. in probat: 2. concl.*
e *in Cod.libert. Eccles. Gallic.*

which very many *Doctors doe defend*, saith *Almainus* d, and *which the Kingdome of France hath alwaies approued for certaine* saith *Pithæus* e , and which the late proceeding of the *Parliament* of *Paris* against the contrarie doctrine taught by *Suarez, Card: Bellarmine,* and others hath cleerely confirmed (to omit the forme of oath lately propounded by the tiers Estates,) and that *Card: Peron* himselfe doth not reiect it as *improbable*, I remit to the iudgement of the indifferent Reader.

44 Yea my *Aduersarie* himselfe, although hee vntruly and vnlearnedly, as you shall perceiue beneath, chargeth me with *heresie*, for defending the aforesaid doctrine as *probable*, or to vse *Cardinall Perons* word, as *problematique*, dare not auouch, that the doctrine is defined by any *Generall Councell,* which neuerthelesse, as I shewed in my *Theologicall*

f *Cap: 10. sec. 2. num. 32.*

Disputation f out of Card: *Bellarmine*, and *Canus*, is necessarie that a decree of a *Generall Councell* can make a point of faith, and the contrarie doctrine to be hereticall, but with mincing tearmes onely affirmeth, *that it hath been taught by the learnedst men of many ages, is grounded vpon holy Scriptures, and confirmed by the practise and decrees of diuers Popes and Councells, especially of the great Councell of Lateran, which expresly ordained the practise of it in some Cases, and did therefore necessarily suppose, and firmely beleeue the veritie of the said doctrine.* But besides that here is no speech of any *definition*, which onely can make any doctrine to be of faith, and the contrarie to be hereticall, and also it is vsuall among Diuines to affirme, that their doctrine hath been taught by the learnedst men of many ages, is grounded vpon holy Scriptures, is not onely *confirmed* by the practise, but is also expresfely *defined* by the decrees of *Generall Councells*, which neuerthelesse doth not terrifie other learned men from impugning their doctrine and opinions, I will

shew

shew beneath g, that the *Councell of Lateran* did neither ordaine the practise of that doctrine, nor necef-
farilie suppofe or firmly beleeue, efpecially with diuine and fupernaturall beleefe, the veritie thereof; and
I will anfwer all the Replyes, which my *Aduerfarie*
hath taken out of *Fa: Leffius* (masked vnder *D. Sin-*
gletons name) againft my anfwers, and hath filled not
only a dozen pages, but well neere foure dozen pages
of his booke with *Fa: Leffius* his doctrine & text, yet
concealing his name, belike to make his Reader beleeue what a learned Diuine he is now become, and
that thofe Replyes were not the fruits of other mens
witts, but the fubtle inventions of his owne fertile
braine, whereas it is well knowne, what fmall skill
M^r. *Thomas Fitzherbert* hath in Theologicall learning.

45   But if my *Aduerfarie* had been refolued fincerely to handle this queftion, and really to finde out
the truth, he might eafily haue gathered out of *Vaf-*
quez doctrine, the anfwer to this his *Reply*. For when
Vafquez affirmeth, that *if a learned man, who hath*
throughly feene, and examined all the reafons of the con-
trary part, fhall iudge againft all other writers, who haue
gone before him, that his opinion is the more probable, *he*
may although it be the leffe fecure opinion, embrace it, and
in practife follow it, his affertion is generall, whether it
be concerning any doctrinal point, which is thought
to belong to faith, or any text of holy *Scripture*, or
any decree or definition of *Pope* or *Generall Councell,*
which are in controuerfie among Catholikes. Yea
according to *Vafquez* doctrine, it is lawfull for other
men, who hold the contrarie opinion to be the more
probable, without any note of *temeritie,* to embrace it,
and in practife follow it, vnleffe it be a fingular opinion and of one onely Doctour (as this doctrine
which denieth the Popes power to depofe Princes is
not fingular and of one only, but of many, as I will

I 2   shew

g In the third
part, chap. 9.
and the reft.

shew beneath:) for then, saith Vasquez, *if it be a sin-*
gular opinion, and of one onely Doctor, although it may be
probable *to that Doctour* (who is not therefore so easily to be condemned of *temeritie*) *yet to him, who li-*
keth not the proper and intrinsecall grounds of that singu-
lar opinion, and of one onely Doctor, and seeth it to bee
grounded vpon the authoritie of one onely Doctor, hee
ought not to account it probable *to this effect, that he may*
prudently follow it in practise against his owne, and the
common opinion of a'l others.

46   But if it be not a singular opinion and of one
onely Doctour, although the learned men of the
contrarie opinion doe vrge for their doctrine some
law, decree, or definition, which the contrarie part
hath seene and examined, and hath in some sort answered therevnto, it is lawfull for any learned man
according to *Vasquez*, to follow in practise that other
lesse secure and lesse common opinion, against his
owne opinion, albeit it be the more secure and common opinion. *For when we perceiue,* saith Vasquez,
that the Authors of the contrarie opinion haue seene, and
considered all the grounds and reasons for our opinion, and
haue obserued that obiection taken from that law or de-
cree, and haue endeauoured to answer them, and that they
were not conuinced by them, we may iustly thinke, that we
may prudently and lawfully follow in practise the opinion
of those other men against our owne, neither ought wee to
suppose that our reasons are euident demonstrations, and
which doe make the contrarie opinion to be voide of all
probabilitie.

47   And this doctrine of *Vasquez* is euident in the
question concerning the superioritie of the *Pope* a-
boue a *Generall Councell,* which hath been so long debated betwixt the Doctors of *Rome* and *Paris.* For
both of them affirme, *that their opinion is grounded vpon*
holy Scriptures, is confirmed by the practise and decrees, yea
and definitions of Generall Councels, and yet both of
                                                   them,

thē,becauſe they are approued by learned Catholike Diuines, are *probable*, although, as *Nauarra*, h out of *Ioannes Maior* a learned Diuine of *Paris* relateth, *that the opinion of the Pariſhioners is not permitted to bee defended at Rome, nor the opinion of the Romanes to bee defended at Paris.* And therefore into what ſowle tearmes, trow you, would my *Aduerſarie* breake, if the *Doctors* of *Paris*, who doe reſolutely hold, that the *Pope* is inferiour to a *Generall Councell*, ſhould argue againſt Card. *Bellarmine* and others of his opinion, in the ſame manner, as this fowle mouthed man, who hath ſtill in his mouth *abſurd, ridiculous, impertinent, fool, impudent, temerarious, impious, hereticall,* or erroneous, that their doctrine *hath not onely beene taught by the learnedſt men of many ages, but alſo it is grounded vpon holy Scriptures, confirmed by the practiſe and decrees of diuers* Counſels, *but eſpecially of the famous Councell of* Conſtance, *which did not onely ordaine the practiſe of it in ſome caſes, and therefore neceſſarily ſuppoſe and firmely beleeue, but did alſo expreſſely define, and conſequently command all Chriſtians to beleeue the verity of that doctrine, and that therefore* Card. *Bellarmine is falne into* hereſie, *for not beleeuing that doctrine, which that famous Generall Councell, beleeued, defined,* and *ordained to be practiſed* and alſo to be beleeued.

48 By this it is apparant, that *Vaſquez* doctrine is to be vnderſtood generally of all caſes, queſtions, and opinions, which are in controuerſie among learned Catholikes, although one or both parts doe pretend their doctrine to be *of faith*, and to be grounded vpon the authoritie of *holy Scripture*, or ſome decree of *Pope*, or *Generall Councell*, and that learned Catholikes ought not, according to *Vaſquez*, to bee eaſily condemned of *temeritie*, and much leſſe of *errour* or *hereſie*, who doe not follow the more common, the more probable, and the more ſecure opinion of other Catholike Doctors, although this common opinion

h *In cap. Nouit de Iudicijs notab.3.nu.84.*

feeme to fome followers thereof to be an vndoubted
doctrine, and to be confirmed by fome *Decree,Law*,
or *Canon* of *Pope*, or *Generall Counfell*, which *Decree*,
Law, or *Canon* thofe learned Catholikes haue feene,
examined, and anfwered, although their anfweres
doe not fatisfie the contrarie fide. And conformably
to this doctrine did *Vafquez*, as I obferued in my
Theologicall Difputation, difpute that queftion, *whe-*
ther there be any habits, which are infufed by God alone.
For although he expreffely affirmeth, *that it is the con-*
ftant, without controuerfie, and vndoubted opinion of the
Schoole-Diuines, that there bee certaine vertues called
Theologicall, Faith, Hope, and Charitie, which of their
owne nature are infufed by God alone, and that fome Do-
ctors, as Andreas Vega, doe hold this doctrine to bee of
faith, and the contrarie to be hereticall, or erroneous, en-
deauouring to proue the fame, not out of the Councell of
Vienna, which did onely declare it to be the more probable
opinion, but out of the Councell of Trent, yet *Vafquez*
would not condemne the contrarie opinion not onely of *herefie*, as my *Aduerfarie* would cunningly perfwade the Reader, but not fo much as of *temeritie*.
From whence I inferred, that, according to *Vaf-*
quez doctrine, which my *Aduerfarie* fraudulently
concealeth, *the conftant, without controuerfie, and vn-*
doubted opinion of Schoole-Diuines, and which fome of
them thinke to be a point of faith, may fometimes bee re-
iected without any note, not onely of herefie or errour, but
alfo of temeritie, which doctrine doth cleerely fatisfie
the common argument drawne from the authoritie
of learned men, who hold the doctrine for the *Popes*
power to depofe Princes to bee a point of faith, and
confequently the oath to bee repugnant to faith and
faluation. And thus much concerning the firft
and fecond point of my *Aduerfaries* fourth Admonition.

49   As touching the third point it is apparantly
vntrue,

vntrue, and very iniurious to Catholikes, and to Catholike Religion to affirme, *that the* Arrians , *or any
other heretikes may well pretend a farre greater probabi
litie for the establishing of their herefies , then may I and
those other Catholikes, who hold it* probable,*that the Pope
hath not power to depose Princes.* For (besides that the
Arrian herefie was expreffely condemned in the firft
eight *Generall Counfels*, and afterwards in many o-
thers, and the *Arrians* haue euer been accounted heretikes by ancient Fathers and all other Catholikes ,
wheras there cannot be alledged fo much as any fhew
or colour of any one definition of a *Generall Councell,*
wherein the doctrine which denyeth the Popes power to depose Princes is condemned for *hereticall,*
but all the proofes that my *Aduerfaries* alledge, that
the *Pope* hath fuch a power, are onely ouer-wrefted
fimilitudes, facts, examples, inferences, and fuppofi-
fitions of their owne, drawne from the authoritie of
holy Scriptures, Popes, or Councels) when the Philofophers and Diuines doe affirme, that the authoritie of learned and skilfull men fufficeth to make the
doctrine or opinion *probable* , which they approue,
they vnderftand of learned and skilfull men appro-
uing a doctrine belonging to the art, which they profeffe, according to that vulgar maxime, *vnicuique in
fua arte perito credendum eft, we muft giue credit to euery
man skilfull in his art.*
　50 So that in a point of Law, the authoritie of skilfull Lawiers, and not of skilfull Phyfitions, in a point
of Phyfike the authoritie of skilfull Phyfitions and
not of Lawiers, and in a point of Catholike Religion,
the authoritie of learned Catholikes , and who are
skilfull in points of Catholike Religion which they
profeffe, and not of heretikes, and who doe not profeffe Catholike Religion, doth make the opinion, or
doctrine which they approue to bee *probable.* And
therefore my *Aduerfarie* very infufficiently (not to
　　　　　　　　　　　　　　　　　　　vfe

vſe thoſe fowle words abſurdly & ridiculouſly, which
hee ſo often vſeth againſt mee) argueth from the
authoritie of learned Catholikes to the authoritie of
heretikes, whoſe doctrine according to the definition
of *probable*, can neuer make the opinions, which they
approue in points of Catholike Religion, which they
doe not profeſſe, to be *probable*. Neither by this can
any point of Catholike faith, which is knowne to all
learned Catholikes to bee a point of Catholike faith,
be eaſily called in queſtion, and made onely *probable*,
for that no learned Catholike will cal in queſtion any
doctrine, which is cleerely knowne to be the Catholike faith, and as for heretikes their authoritie can
neuer make any doctrine belonging any way to Catholike Religion, which they doe not profeſſe, to be
probable.

 51 But if there ſhould ariſe any controuerſie a-
mong learned Catholikes, whether this or that doctrine be of faith, and in what ſenſe the words of ſuch
a text of holy Scripture, or of ſuch a Canon, or Decree of Pope or Councell are to be vnderſtood, there
is no doubt, but that the authoritie of learned Catholikes may in thoſe caſes make their opinion *probable*
although other Catholikes would be ſo ſtiffe in their
owne opinion, as to condemne the contrarie part of
hereſie, errour, or *temeritie*. A manifeſt example hereof we haue in the *Councell* of *Conſtance*, wherein according to *Iohn Gerſon* and other learned men, who
were preſent at that Councell, it was expreſſely defined, that the Pope is inferiour and ſubiect to a Generall Councell lawfully aſſembled, and therefore the
contrarie to be flat *hereticall*, but ſince that other Catholikes, eſpecially Romane Diuines haue called that
Decree in queſtion, and haue endeauoured to anſwer
therevnto, affirming that it was only meant of Popes
in time of Schiſme, or that the aforeſaid Decree was
not confirmed by *Pope Martin* in the end of the
              Counſell

Councell, which answeres neuerthelesse doe not satisfie the Doctors of the contrarie opinion, I doe not
thinke, but that my *Aduersarie* will confesse, that the
opinion of the Romans may bee accounted *probable*,
and that the calling of that Decree in question was
not the right way to ouerthrow Catholike Religion, and to introduce all *heresie* and *Atheisme*.

52. But if it should perchance fall out, that some
Catholikes would be so selfe opinatiue, as to affirme
without any definition at all of the Church, although
vnder pretext of zeale and deuotion to the See Apostolike, any doctrine to be of *faith* and the contrarie
to be *hereticall*, and other Catholikes although the
farre fewer in number should deny the same, especially in a matter which concerneth our obedience due
to God and Cæsar, if the first part only should be permitted to write freely what they please, and to taxe the
other part of *heresie*, to omit *errour, temeritie, folly*, *ridiculous absurditie* and such like, and this other part
should be forbidden to defend their good names, and
to answere for themselues, I leaue (good Reader) to
thy consideration, whether this be not the right way
to ouerthrow Catholike Religion and the vndoubted
grounds thereof, and to introduce vncertaine opinions for an infallible doctrine of the Catholike faith,
which is to open a wide gap to heresie, Atheisme, and
euident iniustice, and to make among Christians a
perpetuall dissention betwixt the Cleargie, and Laity,
the temporall and spirituall power. Now that this
doctrine for the Popes power to depose Princes is not
by any *definition* at all of the Church declared to bee
true, my *Aduersary* cannot denie, and that it euer
hath been and is impugned by learned Catholikes,
and the contrarie hath euer beene, and is by them approued, and therefore it is truly *probable*, and not only
hath a pretence of *probabilitie* I will shew beneath,
where I will both relate the Catholike Authours, who

K   deny

deny this authoritie of the Pope to depofe Princes, which only is fufficient to make their doctrine *probable*, and alfo I will difcouer the infufficiencie of thofe *Replies*, which my *Aduerfary* hath made againft my anfweres. And thus much concerning the third point.

53. For the *fourth* and laft point, confider, *Catholike Countreimen*, whether Mr. *Fizherbert* intendeth to declare vnto you plainly and fincerely this prefent controuerfie, and by a cleare explayning of the queftion to quiet your confciences, or rather by wrangling and cauilling to obfcure the difficultie, and blind your vnderftandings. The queftion betwixt him and mee at this prefent is, whether it be a *probable* doctrine, that the *Pope* hath not any power by the inftitution of *Chrift* to depriue Soueraigne Princes of their tempo rall power, and Regall authoritie : And there are two only grounds to perfwade any man , that this or that doctrine or opinion is truely *probable*. The one are called *intrinfecall groundes* , to wit , the arguments and reafons, which are drawne from holy Scriptures, facred Canons, Theologicall reafons and fuch like, to proue that doctrine or opinion : and thefe groundes are proper only to learned men, who are able to weigh and examine the arguments on both fides ; The other are called *extrinfecall grounds*, which doe onely confift in the authority of thofe learned men , who doe hold that doctrine or opinion , becaufe according to that which hath been faid before , that doctrine is trulie *probable*, which is approued by wife and skilfull men in the art which they profeffe ; and by thefe onely grounds vnlearned men can be perfwaded , that any doctrine or opinion is truly *probable*.

54. Now my *Aduerfarie feeing*, as he faith, *that all my pretended probabilitie confifteth partly in the authority of thofe Authours, which I haue brought in my* Theologicall Difputation, *and in my* Apologie, *and partly in the fufficiencie,*

sufficiencie, as I suppose, of my answeres to their groundes, arguments and authorities, yet he taketh vpon him in this *Reply* only to confute some of my answers to their *intrinsecall grounds,* and for the confutation of the *authorities* which I bring, hee remitteth his Reader, to *D. Schulckenius, who,* as he saith, *hath answered particularly to euery one of them.* Seeing therefore that there is no sufficient way to satisfie the vnderstandings of vnlearned men, that the doctrine, which holdeth the Pope to haue no authoritie to depose Princes, is not truely *probable,* but by shewing that no learned Catholikes do approue the same, for that vnlearned men are not able to examine the *intrinsecall grounds* of any Theologicall question, but are only led by *authoritie,* and *extrinsecall grounds,* and if they once perceiue, that learned Catholikes doe approue any doctrine, they will presently also perceiue that doctrine to bee truly *probable,* is there any likelihood, that M.r *Fitzherbert* intended to giue satisfaction to his vnlearned Countreimen, by replying to some of the answeres, which I made to their arguments, and *intrinsecall grounds* of their doctrine, which *intrinsecall grounds* vnlearned men cannot examine, and for an answere to the *authorities and extrinsecall grounds* which I brought, which only grounds vnlearned men can vnderstand, to remit his English Readers, and who for the most part vnderstand not Latine to D. *Schulckenius* a Latine writer.

55. Besides, from my *Aduersaries* own wordes the Reader may easily perceiue a great fraude of his. For my *Aduersarie* confesseth, that I haue brought *many Authours partly in my Theologicall Disputation,* and *partly in my Apologie,* which is very true; for in my *Theologicall Disputation* of set purpose I chose out certaine *Authours* named in my *Apologie,* which I thought did speake more plainly, and against which no iust exception could be taken; whereunto also I added certaine

other *Authours* which in my *Apologie* were not named at all: And yet my *Aduersarie* remitteth his Reader for an anſwere to them all, to D. *Schulckenius*, who hath only anſwered (but how inſufficiently you ſhall ſee beneath) thoſe authorities which I brought in my *Apologie* : for my *Theologicall Diſputation* he could not at that time ſee, it being then but in the P R I N T E R S hands. But the plaine truth is, that vnleſſe my *Aduerſarie* would haue ſhewed apparantly to wrangle and cauill, hee could take no iuſt exception whereby his Reader might be fully ſatisfied, againſt thoſe *Authours*, which I brought in my *Theologicall Diſputation*, and therfore he thought it his beſt courſe cunningly to ſhift them of, and not to meddle with the anſwering of them at all, leaſt the *Reader* perceiuing ſo many learned Catholikes to ioyne with *Widdrington* in denying this doctrine for the Popes power to depoſe Princes eſpecially to be a point of faith, ſhould preſently obſerue both the fraudulent proceeding of my *Aduerſarie*, who laboureth to perſwade his Reader, that only *Widdrington* doth impugne this authoritie of the Pope to depoſe Princes, and alſo that the contrarie doctrine being approued not only by *Widdrington*, but alſo by ſo many learned Catholikes is, and ought to be accounted truly *probable*, and therefore may according to *Vaſquez* doctrine without any note of *temeritie* be embraced by any Catholike. But of theſe authorities I will treat more at large beneath. And thus much concerning my *Aduerſaries* fourth Admonition, and all the foure points thereof.

 56. Now to come to my *Aduerſaries* fift and laſt admonition, which indeede, as he truely ſaith, *is worthie to be noted,* but not for any truth therein to be obſerued, but for the manifeſt fraud and falſhood therin contained: *The firſt and laſt conſideration ſhall be,* ſaith my *Aduerſarie,* *that Widdringtons *doctrine is dangerous and pernicious not onely to the conſciences of Catholikes,*

likes, (as I haue shewed) but also to his Maiesties *seruice,
which he pretendeth to further and aduance thereby* ; *for
he cannot denie, but that the contrary opinion being* probable (*as he confesseth it to be*) *may bee lawfully imbraced
by all men* ; *whereupon it followeth, that any man may not
only refuse the oath lawfully, but also hold, that his* Maiestie *may be deposed by his owne subiects vpon a sentence of
Excommunication and Deposition, and that consequently
they may lawfully take armes against his* Maiesty *in that
case* ; *and this being so, what security hath his* Maiesty, *or
aduancement of his seruice by this mans doctrine* ? *For albeit many doe now take the Oath, and sweare that they
thinke in their conscience, that the Pope cannot depose the
King* ; *yet for as much as it is, and alwaies will be probable,
in the opinion of some learned men, that they haue sworne a
thing, which is false, and consequently that their Oath is
inualide, it followeth (according to the grounds of his doctrine) that they may breake their Oath, seeing that they
may alwaies probably perswade themselues, that they pro-
mised and swore a thing false and vnlawfull, and that therfore they are not bound to obserue it.*

57. *Furthermore, if his* Holinesse *should at any time
dispence with them particularly for their Oath, or excommunicate and depose his* Maiestie, *discharging his Subiects of their bond of fidelitie, and all others of Allegeance,
this man cannot deny, but that it is* probable *at least, that
then they are free from the Oath, and consequently that
they may (euen according to his doctrine of* probabilitie)
concurre to the deposition of his Maiestie: *and therfore seeing that his doctrine doth not giue any security to his* Maiestie, *and that according to his opinion any man may as
lawfully condemne and refuse the Oath, as approoue and
take it, it is euident, that his sayd doctrine is not onely vaine
and fruitlesse to his* Maiestie, *but also dangerous and pernicious, no lesse impugning the authoritie of his* Maiestie
commanding it to be taken, then of his Holinesse *forbidding it.*

58: *Where-*

58. *Whereupon I inferre three things ; the first, that he is neither so good a subiect to his* Maiesty, *as he pretendeth, nor such an obedient childe to the Church as he professeth to be. The second is, that his bookes deserue to be prohibited no lesse in England then* Rome ; *and therefore truely wise men in these parts doe greatly maruel how it can stand with the wisdome of his* Maiesties Councell *to permit them to be printed and published in England as we see they are. The third is, that he is one of those, whom* God *threatneth in the* Apocalyps, *to spit out of his mouth, saying of such indifferent men as he,* Vtinam esses aut calidus, aut frigidus &c. *I would thou wert either hot or cold, but because thou art luke-warme, I will beginne to vomit thee out of my mouth.*

Apoc. 3.

59. *And this shall suffice,* good Reader, *for the present, touching those aduertisements and considerations, which I meant to giue thee concerning* Widdringtons *doctrine in generall: and therfore I will now passe to the examination of his answers to me in particular, and lay downe in order as much of the text of his* Admonition, *as concerneth me, to the end that he shall not haue occasion to say, that I haue concealed or dissembled any thing that he hath said against me ; as also that thou maiest see, how probably he hath answered me, and thereby the better iudge of the probability, as well of his answers to other men, as of his whole doctrine in his* Theologicall Disputation, *which as I understand, thou shalt shortly see fully confuted in Latine to his confusion, Besides that, I doubt not, but thou shalt also, euen in this my* Reply, *see a cleere confutation of the chiefe grounds of his doctrine, and of his principall arguments and answers touching the* Popes *power to depose* Princes, *which is the maine question betwixt him and vs, and specially impugned, and abiured in the new oath.*

60. But what strange paradoxes and positions void of all *probabilitie* Mr. *Fitzherbert* dare aduenture to maintaine, yea and to perswade his *Maiestie,* and the wisdomes of his most *honourable priuie Councell,*

that

that it is dangerous to his *Maiesties* safetie, to haue
this doctrine for the Popes power to depose his *Maiesty*, to be so much as called in question in his Dominions, thou maiest, *good Reader*, cleerely perceiue by
this his last *Admonition*, wherein thou shalt obserue
the manifest fraud and falshood of this man. For if
M^r. *Fitzherbert* had either sincerely, or entirely related my opinion and doctrine, or else had put in mind
his Reader against what kind of *Aduersaries* I do op-
pose, any man of meane vnderstanding would presently haue perceiued (as I obserued elsewhere, which
my words I thinke it not amisse to set downe heere
againe) that it is too too apparantly and shamefully
vntrue, that my manner of handling this question
probably can be dangerous or pernicious to his *Maiestie*, as my *Aduersarie* endeauoureth to perswade his
Maiestie, not for any loue that he is knowen to beare
vnto the State, but to the end by all likely-hood, that
he and such like violent spirits may write more freely
of this subiect, and without being controlled or contradicted by Catholikes, who, as he is perswaded, do
little regard the writings and opinions of Protestants
concerning this or any other doctrine.

    61. For it may bee dangerous to his *Maiesty* to
handle a question *probably* against one *Aduersary*,
which will be nothing dangerous to handle it *probably*
against another. As for example, if it wer agreed vpon by all Catholikes, that the *Pope* hath no power to
depose his *Maiestie*, then it would bee dangerous to
his *Maiestie*, that any Catholike should call this in
question, and dispute it *probably*: but if on the contrary side all Catholikes should agree in this, that it
were *certaine*, *vnquestionable*, and a *poynt of faith*, that
the *Pope hath power to depose his Maiestie, and to absolue
his Subiects of their Allegeance, to command them to take
armes against him &c.* then if a Catholike should call
this in question, or which is all one, dispute it *probably*,
and

i In the Ad-
monition to
the Reader
before my
English Pur-
gation sent to
his Holinesse.

and maintaine, that it is not certaine, that the *Pope* hath such an authoritie, but that it is *queſtionable*, and *probable* that he hath it not, no man of any ſenſe or vnderſtanding can affirme, that ſuch a manner of diſputing this queſtion *probably* againſt thoſe *Aduer-ſaries*, who hold it for *certaine* and *vnqueſtionable*, can bee any way dangerous or pernicious to his *Maieſtie*.

62   Now behold the manner, which I haue taken in handling this controuerſie. *Card: Bellarmine, Fa: Gretzer, Leſſius, Becanus, Suarez*, and ſome other Diuines, eſpecially of the Societie of Ieſus, whom M^r. T. F. in euery ſtep, as though he were their creature, (as now he is become one of their companie,) doth follow, haue laid this for a ſure and vndoubted ground, that it is *a point of faith*, and to be beleeued as certaine, and vnder paine of eternall damnation by Catholikes, that the *Pope* hath power to depoſe Princes, to abſolue Subiects from their allegiance, and therevpon to command them to take armes, and raiſe tumults againſt their Prince ſo depoſed. So that you ſee, that theſe men haue already laid the danger and vndoubted ouerthrow to his *Maieſties* Perſon and Crowne, if the *Pope* ſhould perchance depoſe him, in that they affirme, that all Catholikes are in that caſe bound in conſcience to forſake him, and to fulfill the *Popes* command to the deſtruction of his *Maieſties* Perſon and State. This doctrine, to wit, that it is a *point of faith*, and an vndoubted principle of Catholike Religion, that the *Pope* hath power to depoſe Princes, and to inflict all temporall puniſhments by way of coercion, and that all Catholikes are bound in conſcience to forſake his *Maieſtie*, and to take armes againſt him, I haue taken vpon me for two principall reaſons to impugne, and doe not doubt clearely to maintaine the ſame, againſt the clamours of M^r. T. F. or any other whatſoeuer.

63   My

63   My *first* reason was, for that it is against the truth and puritie of the Catholike Church , *Shee* being a *pillar and ground of truth,* that doubtfull opinions, and which among Catholikes are onely in controuersie, and by the *Parliament* of *Paris* haue been condemned as *scandalous, seditious, damnable,* and *pernicious,* should be enforced vpon English Catholikes, as an vndoubted doctrine of the Catholike faith, to the vtter ouerthrow of themselues , and their whole posteritie, by men who are in no danger to loose, but rather to gaine temporall aduancement by their writings.   My *second* reason was to assure his *Maiestie,* that all English Catholikes may, if they will , according to the grounds of Catholike Religion be true and constant Subiects to his *Maiestie* , and that notwithstanding any sentence of Excommunication or depriuation denounced, or to be denounced against his *Maiestie* by the *Pope,* whereby his Subiects should be absolued from their Allegiance , or commanded not to obey him in temporall causes, they *may* with a safe conscience, & also in practise (marke well what I say) they are *bound* to adhere to his *Maiestie,* to obey him in temporall causes, as still remayning their true and lawfull Soueraigne , and to resist any such sentence of Excommunication or depriuation.

64   The reason wherefore I affirmed, that Catholikes *may* with a safe conscience adhere to his *Maiestie,* and resist the *Popes* sentence of depriuation, was, for that it is a *probable* opinion, and which with a safe conscience, and without danger of *heresie, error,* or *temeritie* may be embraced by Catholikes, that the *Pope* hath no authoritie to depose Princes , nor to inflict any temporall punishments by way of coercion, but that the last punishment , to which the coerciue power of the Church doth extend , are onely Ecclesiasticall and spirituall Censures.   Wherefore that which my *Aduersarie* affirmeth, *that I confesse, it to be*

L   *probable,*

probable, *that the Pope hath power to depose Princes*, *and that the oath cannot lawfully be taken,*is very vntrue, vnles he meane that I confes it for Difputation fake, or, as we vfually fay, *Dato, fed non conceffo, it being admitted, not granted,* for that it makethnothing for, or againft the queftion which is in hand. Therefore pofitiuely I neither confeffe it, nor deny it, approue it, or condemne it, nor with that part of the contradiction, whether it be *probable,* that the *Pope* hath power to depofe Princes, and whether it be *probable,* that the Oath may not be taken, doe I at this time intermeddle, but whereas my *Aduerfaries* doe fo violently maintaine, that it is *certaine,* and an *vndoubted doctrine of faith,* that the *Pope* hath power to depofe Princes, and that the oath is repugnant to faith and faluation, and therefore can not lawfully be taken, I at this prefent doe affirme the contrarie, to wit, that it is *probable,* that the Pope hath not power to depofe Princes,and that the oath may lawfully be taken.

65   But the principall reafon, which I brought for the fecuring of his *Maieftie* (which M^r. *Fitzherbert* fraudulently concealeth)that Englifh Catholikes not onely *may* for the reafon aforefaid, but alfo in practife are *bound* to adhere to his *Maieftie*, and to refift the *Popes* fentence of depriuation, was, for that fuppofing it to be fpeculatiuely vncertaine, whether the *Pope* hath any fuch power to depofe a King or no, it is an vndoubted rule ^k among the Lawyers, and grounded vpon the light of nature and principles of Diuinitie, that *in caufa dubia fiue incerta melior eft conditio poffidentis,* *In a doubtfull or difputable cafe, the ftate of him that hath poffeffion is the better.* And againe, *Cum funt iura partium obfcura, fauendum eft Reo, potiùs quàm Actori,* *when it is vnknowne whether of the parties who are in fuite, hath right, the defendant is to be preferred or fauoured before the plaintiffe.* Seeing therefore that from the very firft beginning of this

k *De regulis Iuris in* 6°.

contro-

controuerſie, concerning the authoritie of *Popes*, and
Soueraigntie of *Kings*, that is, from the time of *Pope*
Gregorie the ſeuenth, who was the firſt *Pope*,that challenged vnto him this temporall power ouer Kings
(call it *temporall* or *ſpirituall* as you pleaſe,for ſure it is
that the effect is *temporall*) hath been vncertaine, diſputable, and euer contradicted by Catholikes both
Kings and *Subiects*, and therefore it can not bee ſaid,
that the *Pope* was euer in poſſeſſion of this authoritie
(although wee ſhould grant, that power, right, or authoritie may be ſaid to bee poſſeſſed) it conſequently
followeth , that what opinion ſoeuer any Catholike
follow *in ſpeculation*, concerning the *Popes* power to
depoſe Princes, yet *in practiſe*, vntill this Controuerſie concerning the *Popes* power to depoſe Kings,and
the right of Kings not to be depoſed,ſhall be decided,
as yet it is not, hee can not with a good conſcience
endeauour to thruſt out a *King* ſo depoſed from the
Kingdome or Dominions which hee lawfully poſſeſſeth.

66 Wherevpon in the end of my *Apologie* I inferred this concluſion, whereof alſo in my *Epiſtle Dedi-*
catorie to his *Holineſſe* I made mention : *And therefore*
if either Pope,Prince, *or any other of a forraine countrey*
ſhould attempt to thruſt an hereticall Prince out of the
kingdome, which he poſſeſſeth, this controuerſie concerning
the depoſition of Princes being vndecided, hee ſhould con-
trarie to the rules of iuſtice doe that Prince moſt manifeſt
wrong. And much more a Subiect can not be excuſed from
manifeſt treaſon, what ſoeuer opinion in ſpeculation he doth
maintaine concerning the Popes temporal power,who ſhould
in practiſe, vnder pretence perchance of deuotion to the
See Apoſtolike, *not duely alſo conſidering the bond of his*
Allegiance towards his Soueraigne, *endeauour to thruſt*
his lawfull Prince *out of his kingdome,which he poſſeſſeth,*
notwithſtanding any Excommunication or ſentence of de-
priuation denounced againſt him by the Pope.

67 But becaufe D. *Schalkenius* hath endeauoured
to confute that reafon, which I out of the aforefaid
rule of the Law, *In caufa dubia melior eft conditio poffi-*
dentis, I brought to proue,that no man in *practife* can
with a fafe confcience obey the *Popes* fentence of depriuation, fo long as this controuerfie concerning the
Popes power to depofe Princes remaineth vndecided,
I will briefely declare,how infufficiently he obiecteth

1 *Cap.*15.*ad nu.*
468 *pag.*629.
*& pag.*633.
*ad nu.*470.

againft that reafon. Firft therefore he affirmeth[1] , *that*
this doctrine to depofe Princes is not doubtfull or in contro-
uerfie among Catholikes, but it is certaine and of faith, and
none but heretikes and fchifmatikes doe defend the contra-
rie , and therefore that rule In caufa dubia &c. In a
doubtfull or difputable caufe the condition of the
poffeffour is the better, *can not bee applyed to the Popes*
power to depofe Princes, But how vntrue this is,and alfo
how flanderous and iniurious it is to many learned
Catholikes efpecially to the moft Chriftian Kingdom
of France , I will cleerely fhew beneath, in fo
much that for this caufe onely if there had been no o-
ther,his book was deferuedly burnt publikly at *Paris*.
68 *Secondly*, D. *Schulkenius* would feeme to affirme, that the aforefaid rule, *In caufa dubia, & c. In a*
doubtfull, or difputable caufe the ftate of him , who hath
pofsefsion is the better, is not a rule of the Law, *for that*
faith he, *I finde not in the rules of the Law, In a doubtfull,*
or difputable caufe,but, In a like or equall cafe the ftate or
condition of him, who hath poffeffion is the better. But
if D. *Schulkenius* will cauill about the words , and
not regard the fenfe, I may likewife fay, that hee
findeth not in the rules of the Law , *In an equall*
or like cafe but *in an equall and like caufe the ftate*
of him , who hath poffeffion is the better. But becaufe
caufe and *cafe,like, equall,doubtfull, vncertaine*,and *dif-*
putable haue all one fenfe, for that if two caufes or cafes be *doubtfull, vncertaine*, or *difputable* , they are *like*
or *equall* in that, therefore I regarding the fenfe, and
not

not the words, did rather vſe the words, *doubtfull, vncertaine* and *diſputable*, then *like*, or *equall*, both for
that the former words doe declare the ſenſe of the
rule more plainely, and alſo becauſe Diuines in alled-
ging that rule of the Law do commonly vſe the word
doubtfull, as it may be ſeene in *Dominicus Sotus*,[m] *Ioannes Azor*,[n] *Ioannes Salas*,[o] and *Gabriel Vaſquez*,[p] and
therefore *Vaſquez* citing the aforeſaid rule taketh *like*
and *doubtfull* for all one, *The aforeſaid rule*, ſaith hee,[q]
*In dubijs, ſeu in pari cauſa &c. In doubts, or in a like cauſe
the ſtate of the poſſeſſor is the better &c.*

69 Wherefore D. *Sculckenius* perceiuing, that thi
exception of his againſt the aforeſaid rule is only ver-
ball, will not abſolutely deny the rule, but anſwereth
thirdly, that if there be ſuch a rule of the Law (as without
doubt in ſenſe there is both in the *Canon*, [r] and *Ciuill
Law*, and in expreſſe words the Diuines and Lawiers
doe cite it ſo) *it doth make for the Pope, who hath beene
for many hundred yeares in poſſeſsion to iudge and depoſe
Seclar Princes, eſpecially in a cauſe belonging to faith.* But
this anſwere of D. *Sculckenius* is very inſufficient. For
firſt, although we ſhould grant, that right, power, or
authoritie may bee ſaid to be poſſeſſed, in that ſenſe,
as *Poſſeſſion* is taken in Law, (whereas according to
the Lawiers, as *Molina* the Ieſuite obſerueth,[t] *poſſeſſion* properly is onely of corporall things, and right, power, and ſuch like ſpirituall things are onely ſaid to
bee as it were poſſeſſed , yet ſuppoſing that it is a
doubtfull, vncertaine, and diſputable queſtion, whether the Pope hath power to depoſe Princes or no, as
the *Pope* is ſaid to be in poſſeſſion of his right to depoſe *Princes*, ſo *Princes* may be ſaid to bee in poſſeſſion of their right not to be depoſed by the *Pope* ; and
therefore in this cauſe is like, or equall, doubtfull or
diſputable, as well for *Princes* right not to be depoſed,
as for the *Popes* right to depoſe them ; and on the o-
ther ſide *Princes* are not onely in poſſeſſion of their

L 3 right

right not to bee depoſed by the *Pope*, but alſo in quiet, peaceable, and lawfull poſſeſſion of their Kingdomes and temporall Dominions, which onely are properly ſaid to be poſſeſſed, in reſpect whereof this rule fauoureth onely *Princes*, and not the *Pope*, and therefore in this doubtfull and diſputable caſe of the *Popes* power to depoſe *Princes*, the ſtate and condition of *Princes*, who are in lawfull poſſeſſion, not onely of their right not to be depoſed by the *Pope*, but alſo of their Kingdomes and Dominions which they poſſeſſe, is, according to the aforeſaid rule, to be preferred.

70. Moreouer, that the *Popes* right, power, or authoritie to depoſe *Princes* may be ſaid to be poſſeſſed, (if poſſeſſion properly be of rights) it is neceſſarie, that hee exerciſe that power to depoſe Kings, they knowing thereof, and bearing it patiently and without contradiction , as may clearely be gathered out of ^u *Molina*, and ^x *Leſſius* : And the reaſon is euident, for otherwiſe if any man ſhould challenge a right , bee it good or bad, and ſhould exerciſe that pretended right, the contrarie part contradicting, he may neuertheleſſe be ſaid to be in lawfull poſſeſſion of that right. And ſo if temporall Lords ſhould pretend to haue a ſpirituall Iuriſdiction ouer temporall and ſpirituall perſons, and ſhould exerciſe that pretended ſpirituall Iuriſdiction ouer them , they contradicting and excepting againſt the ſame, they might neuertheleſſe be ſaid to be in poſſeſſion of that ſpirituall Iuriſdiction. But Chriſtian Kings from the time of *Henry* the fourth Emperour, who was the *firſt Emperour*, that euer was depoſed by the **Pope**, vntill the time of *Henry* the fourth moſt Chriſtian King of France, who was the *laſt King*, whom the Pope depoſed, haue euer reſiſted and contradicted this authoritie of the Pope to depoſe them. And therefore although Popes haue for as many hundreds of yeares, as haue beene ſince the

time

time of Pope Gregorie the feuenth, challenged this authoritie to depofe Kings, yet they cannot be faid to haue been for one yeare, or one day in polfeffion of that authoritie ouer Kings, feeing that Kings haue euer gainfaid and contradicted it. And although there fhould perchance haue beene fome one, or other Chriftian King, who for fome priuate, or publicke refpect hath not refifted the Popes fentence of depriuation denounced againft him, but rather yeelded thereunto, yet this cannot be a fufficient warrant to preiudice his Succeffours, or that the Pope may bee faid to be in polfeffion of his pretended authoritie to depofe Kings in generall, but at the moft to depofe that King in particular, who did not refift or gainfay, but rather acknowledged the authoritie, which the *Pope* claimed to depofe him.

71. *Fourthly*, and laftly D. *Schulckenius* anfwereth, *that the aforefaid rule is to be vnderftood, when the controuerfie is betwixt two inferiour parties who are in fuite, and not betwixt the Iudge, and the partie accufed, or if wee will apply it to the Iudge, and the partie accufed, the Iudge is to be preferred before the partie accufed, but the Pope is Iudge ouer all Chriftian Kings and Princes, and therefore this rule,* faith he, *is in fauour of the Pope.* But how vnfound and infufficient is alfo this *Reply* of D. *Schulckenius,* it is very apparant. For *Firft*, although the *Pope* be *Iudge* ouer all Chriftian Kings and Princes in fpirituall caufes and punifhments, yet in temporall caufes and punifhments they haue no *Iudge,* or *Superiour* befides *God,* the fupreme Iudge of all both Kings and Popes; and therefore well faid our learned Countreiman *Alexander* of *Hales*, ᵞ *expound thofe words, A King is to be punifhed by God alone*, with *materiall punifhment :* And againe, *A King hath no man, who may iudge his facts to wit, to inflict corporall punifhment :* And againe, *A king doth excell, as it is written* 1. Pet. 2. *it is true , in his degree, to wit, to exercife corporall punifhment , with which punifhment,*

y 3. part. q. 40. mem. 5. q. 4.

punifhment, if he offend, he hath none to punifh him but God alone.

72. Yea rather contrariwife the Roman Emperors were in times paft Iudges in temporall caufes of all the Romane Empire, and of euery member thereof both Cleargie and Laitie: but the depofition of Kings is a temporall caufe and punifhment, for what crime foeuer whether temporall or fpirituall a King be depofed: and therefore the controuerfie about depofing Kings betwixt the *Pope* challenging to himfelfe that authoritie, and *Kings*, who are fupreme Iudges in temporalls denying it, is not betwixt the *Iudge* and the party accufed, but at the leaft betwixt two equalls in temporall caufes, whereof the *Pope*, who firft challenged this power to make Kings no Kings is the plaintiffe, and Kings who defend their ancient right, and prerogatiue not to be depofed by the Pope, are the defendant: and fo alfo that fecond rule of the Law, *Cum funt iura partium obfcura &c.* When it is not cleare whether of the parties, who are in fuite, haue right, the defendant is to be preferred before the plaintiffe, fauoureth, *Kings*, and not the *Pope*, who only from the time of *Gregorie* the feuenth claimed this authoritie to make Kings no Kings.

73. *Secondly*, I doe not thinke, that any Lawyer will affirme, that if a Iudge, who is onely knowne to haue authoritie in ciuill matters, as ciuill is oppofed to criminall, fhould challenge a Iurifdiction in criminall caufes, and condemne a man to death, before he fhewed that hee had fufficient warrant from the Prince fo to doe, the partie condemned is bound to obey that Iudge, or that the aforefaid rule, *In a like or doubtfull caufe hee that hath poffeffion is to be preferred*, fhould fauour the aforefaid Iudge, and not the party condemned, who is not onely in poffeffion of his life, but alfo hath right to defend his life, vntill the Iudge fhew fufficient warrant, or it is otherwife publikely knowne,

knowne, that he hath authoritie to take it away. Neither is it a sufficient warrant for the Iudge, that it is knowne, that he is a Iudge in ciuill matters, vnleſſe it be alſo knowne that he is a Iudge alſo in criminall cauſes, as likewiſe it is not a ſufficient warrant for the Pope to depriue Kings of their temporall kingdomes, that it is cleare that he is a Iudge in all ſpirituall matters, vnleſſe alſo it be cleare, as yet it is not, that he is alſo a Iudge in temporall cauſes, and to inflict temporall puniſhments by way of coercion, as without doubt are the taking away of temporall kingdomes, for what crime ſoeuer they be taken away.

74. Wherefore that Dialogue, which D. *Schulckenius* maketh betwixt the Pope, and a conuicted heretike, whoſe goods are without any controuerſie confiſcated both by the Ciuill and Canon Law, is vnaptly applyed to the depoſing of Kings, which hath beene, and is at this preſent in controuerſie among Catholikes. Beſides, that this Dialogue alſo ſuppoſeth, that the Pope is in poſſeſſion of his authoritie to depoſe Kings, and that Kings are not in poſſeſſion of their right not to bee depoſed by the Pope ; and that the Pope is a Iudge of temporall Kings in temporall cauſes, and to puniſh them with temporall puniſhments by way of coercion : and alſo, that the aforeſay'd rule fauoureth the Iudge, and not the perſon conuented before the Iudge, when the authority of the Iudge ouer the perſon conuented is not ſufficiently knowen, all which, as I haue ſhewed before, are very vntrue. And by this thou maieſt perceiue, *good Reader*, how inſufficient are the exceptions, which D. *Schuclkenius* bringeth againſt my argument grounded in the aforſaid rule of the Law, as in very deed are al the reſt of his Replies againſt my *Apology*, as God willing ere long, (for I cannot anſwer fully and exactly as I intend all my *Aduerſaries* at once) I will moſt cleerely ſhew.

M　　　75. Conſider

75. Conlider now *(deare Couxtry men)* firft, the vnlincere dealing of this my *Aduerfarie* T. F. who concealeth the chiefeft part of my opinion and doctrine for the fecuring of his *Maiefty* of the conftant loyaltie and allegeance, wherein all his Catholike Subiects are in confcience bound vnto him, that thereby he may caufe his *Maieftie* to bee iealous of my fidelity, and to account me no good Subiect, as this man flanderoufly affirmeth, *that I am neither a good Subiect, nor a good Catholike, or child of the Church, as I profeffe my felfe to be, but that I am falne into flat herefie, from which I cannot any way cleere or excufe my felfe, for impugning that doctrine for the Popes power to depofe Princes, which is grounded vpon fuch affured and folid foundation, as this man* (forfooth) *heere hath fignified but how guilfully and vnfoundly you haue partly feene) and he will more particularly and manifeftly declare heereafter,* where alfo his particular frauds and falfehoods I will more particularly and manifeftly lay open to his owne fhame and confufion. But for all his flanderous words, I truft in God, that it wil appear to all men, that *infurrexerunt in me teftes iniqui,* ^z *& mentita eft iniquitas fibi ; that falfe witneffes haue rifen vp againft me, and that wickedneffe hath belied her felfe :* and that I will euer prooue my felfe to bee both a good Subiect to his *Maieftie,* and alfo a good *Catholike,* and a dutifull childe of the Catholike Church, as partly I haue prooued heere already, and will more particularly and manifeftly declare heereafter. In the meane time let M^r. *Fitzherbert* examine well his *Catholike faith,* and confider what a kinde of *Catholike* hee is, who fo ftiffely maintaineth vncertaine opinions for the *Catholike* faith, which, if it bee truely *Catholike,* cannot be expofed to any falfhood or vncertainty, as this doctrine for the Popes power to depofe Princes, which with *Catholike* faith hee pretendeth truely to beleeue, may in very deede bee falfe, and without all doubt

z Pfal. 26.

doubt is vncertaine and queftionable among Catholikes.

76. *Secondly* confider, how vntruely M^r. *Fitzherbert* affirmeth, that my manner of difputing this queftion *probably* concerning the Popes power not to depofe Princes, and the lawfull taking of the Oath, doth not onely giue no fecurity to his *Maieftie*, but is alfo dangerous and pernicious to his Maiefties *fafety*, and how vnlearnedly hee argueth from fpeculation to practife. For although I fhould admit not onely for Difputation fake, as onely I doe, but alfo pofitiuely confeffe, that in fpeculation it is *probable*, that the Pope hath power to depofe Princes (whereas with that affirmatiue part of the queftion, to wit, whether it bee *probable* that the Pope hath power to depofe Princes I do not intermeddle, but I do only handle the negatiue part, and doe affirme, that it is *probable* he hath no fuch power, which manner of difputing againft fuch *Aduerfaries*, who hold it not onely *probable*, but *certaine*, that he hath fuch a power, can in no fort be dangerous or pernicious to his Maiefties fafetie, as I cleerely fhewed before) neuertheleffe this my *Aduerfarie* very vnfoundly from hence inferreth, that becaufe in fpeculation it is *probable*, that the Pope hath power to depofe Princes, therefore in practife it is lawfull to concurre to the actuall depofing or thrufting them out of the poffeffion of their Kingdomes, or for Subiects notwithftanding any fentence of depofition to beare armes againft them, fo long as this queftion concerning the Popes power to depofe Princes remaineth difputable and vndecided. Wherfore my firme, refolute and conftant opinion is, that the Pope hath not power to difpéce or abfolue any of his Maiefties Subiects what opinion foeuer in fpeculation they follow concerning the Popes power to depofe Princes, from anie promifforie parts of the Oath, which onely doe belong to practife, and as for the affertory

fertory parts of the Oath, which belong to fpeculation, they are not fubiect to the Popes power of di-
fpencing, as I fhewed at large in my *Theologicall Di-*
fputation ᵃ.

a *Cap. 6. fec. 3.*

77. Now whether this my doctrine doth not
onely giue no fecuritie to his *Maieftie*, but is alfo dangerous and pernicious to his *Maiefties* fafetie (as this
my *Aduerfarie* to procure his *Maiefties* difpleafure
againft me falfely and vnlearnedly affirmeth) if the
Pope fhould denounce any fentence of depriuation
againft him, I leaue to the iudgement of any fenfible
man. Neither is it vnfuall that an opinion or doctrine may in fpeculation bee *probable*, which yet in
practife it is not lawfull to follow, as may bee feene in
the miniftring of corporall phyficke, and of thofe Sacraments which are neceffarie to faluation. For although it bee *probable*, that fuch a medicine will cure
fuch a dangerous difeafe, for that learned Phyficians
are of that opinion, although other learned Phyficians thinke the contrarie to be true, or that fuch a matter or forme be fufficient to the validitie of the Sacrament, for example fake of *Baptifme*, becaufe learned
Diuines hold it to bee fufficient, although other learned Diuines bee of the contrarie opinion, and fo in
fpeculation both opinions be *probable*, yet in practife
wee are bound by the law of charitie to apply to our
neighbour thofe remedies either fpirituall or corporall, which are out of queftion and controuerfie, and
to leaue thofe that are queftionable, if certaine and
vndoubted remedies can be had : So likewife althogh
it be *probable*, that fuch a houfe or land doth not by a
lawfull title belong to him who is in lawfull poffeffion thereof, for that learned Lawyers are of that opinion, although other learned Lawyers thinke the
contrarie to bee true, and fo in fpeculation both opinions bee *probable*, yet in practife wee are bound by
the rules of Iuftice not to difpoffeffe him by violence
of

of that howfe or land, before the Iudge hath decided the controuerfie.

78　*Thirdly*, confider the reafon, why this my *Aduerfarie* T. F. is fo greatly offended, that I for this prefent doe onely take in hand (by anfwering *probably* all the arguments which are obiected on the contrarie fide) to fhew, that it is *probable*, that the Pope hath no authoritie to depofe Princes; and confequently that any man may with a fafe and probable confcience take the Oath; for that the doctrine concerning the Popes power to depofe Princes, is by this my *Aduerfaries* owne confeffion, the maine queftion betwixt him & me, and the chiefe ground wherefore the Oath is iudged to be vnlawfull. His reafon therfore is, for that he faw right well, what great aduantage I had againft him, and what little aduantage hee had againft me in arguing or rather anfwering in this manner; and therefore he calleth it in heate of his zeale, as you haue heard, *The moft deuilifh deuice that any man could inuent.* And truly if I fhould at this firft beginning haue treated of this controuerfie in any other manner, then by handling it *probably* in that fenfe as I haue declared, I might worthily haue been taxed of great imprudencie in giuing my *Aduerfarie* more aduantage againft me then was needfull. For this is the ftate of the queftion, *whether it can bee clearely convinced by the authoritie of holy Scriptures, ancient Fathers, Generall Councells, or by neceffarie inferences from any of them*, as my *Aduerfaries* pretend to convince, *that it is an vndoubted doctrine of faith, and the contrarie not to be maintained by any Catholike, that the Pope hath power to depofe Princes, and confequently that the Oath can not lawfully be taken.* This is the queftion.

79　Marke now the aduantage I haue. For *firft* I am not to proue, but only to anfwer, to defend, not to oppofe. *Secondly*, it is fufficient for me, that my

M 3　　　　　　　　Anfwers

Anſwers be onely probable, but their Replyes muſt not be onely probable, but alſo convincing, and which can not with any probabilitie be anſwered. So that if I ſhould goe about at the firſt to proue my opinion to be moſt true, which my *Aduerſaries* contend not to be queſtionable, I ſhould, as it is euident, greatly diſaduantage my ſelfe. For in ſuch controuerſies as are ſo violently maintained by the Aduerſarie, that hee will not grant the contrarie part to be queſtionable, it is neceſſarie to proceed by degrees; firſt, to make the thing queſtionable and diſputable, which the aduerſe part will not haue to be called in queſtion; and after this is once agreed vpon, then to examine whether opinion be the trueſt. For perchance it may fall out, that as the opinion for the immaculate conception of the *Bleſſed Virgin*, before *Scotus* did oppoſe himſelfe herein againſt *S. Thomas* and his followers, was ſcarſe accounted probable, yet afterwards it was daily more and more embraced, ſo that it is now eſteemed to be by farre the more true opinion, and as *Alphonſus, Salmeron* [b], and *Franciſcus* [c] *Suarez* doe affirme, *agreed vpon by the conſent almoſt of the vniuerſall Church, and of all Eccleſiaſticall writers, Biſhops, Religious Orders, and Vniuerſities*: And as that opinion, which holdeth, that the Pope can not diſpence in the ſolemne vow of Religious chaſtitie, neither in any lawfull marriage before it bee conſummate, is accounted by very many learned men to be the truer opinion, notwithſtanding the practiſe of many Popes to the contrarie; So it may fall out, that in proceſſe of time, this opinion, which denyeth the Popes power to depoſe Princes, may be accounted by the greateſt number of learned men to be by farre the more true opinion, and may be agreed vpon by the conſent almoſt of the Vniuerſall Church, and of all Eccleſiaſticall writers, Biſhops, Religious Orders, and Vniuerſities, notwithſtanding the practiſe of many

ny

b *in Rom: 5. Diſp: 51.§ deinde.*
c *Tom. 2.Diſp: 3. ſec. 5.*

ny Popes, and the vehement oppofition of the Iefuits at this prefent time to the contrarie.

80 *Fourthly* confider, how little beholding are Englifh Catholikes to this my *Aduerfarie* T.F., who will needs inforce them euen with the temporall o-uerthrow of themfelues, and of their whole pofteri tie, to defend that doctrine to be of faith, which the *State of France* accounteth *fcandalous, feditious, damnable* and *pernicious*, and alfo endeauoureth to perfwade his *Maieftie*, that no Catholike can, according to the grounds of Catholike Religion, be a true and loyall Subiect to his *Maieftie*, but at the Popes pleafure, or which is all one, fo long onely as the *Pope* fhall not depofe him, which he may doe at his pleafure. But we haue great affiance in his *Maiefties* fingular wifdome, and clement difpofition, whereof we haue had both by his *Maiefties* gracious Proclamation, publike bookes, and effectuall deeds, fufficient try all, that he will not be drawne by the falfe fuggeftion of this my *Aduerfarie* (who would haue all his Catholike Subiects to be of the fame violent fpirit as he is) to haue all his Catholike Subiects in the fame degree of iealoufie, but that he will euer make a diftinction betwixt them, who are his true hearted Subiects, and moft loyall in all temporall affaires, and will aduenture all that they haue, and are, in defence of his *Maiefties* Royall Perfon and dignitie, againft any fentence of depriuation whatfoeuer, which fhall be denounced againft him by the Pope (affuring themfelues that it is conformable to the grounds of Catholike Religion which they profeffe, and not repugnant to that fpirituall obedience wherein they ftand bound to the fupreme Paftour of the Catholike Church) and thofe other Catholikes, who thinking it to be a point of faith, that the Pope hath authoritie to dethrone Soueraigne Princes, and to make temporall Kings priuate men, will only defend his *Ma-*

teftie

iestie, and yeeld him temporall obedience, vntill the Pope after his sentence of depriuation shall command them the contrarie.

81   But what small reliefe are English Catholikes to expect from Mᵣ. *Fitzherberts* hands, if it were in his power to relieue them, you may (*Catholike Countrymen*) coniecture by this, that towards the end of *Queene Elizabeth* hir raigne (when those foure *Reuerend Priests* were at *Rome* to seeke redresse of *Pope Clement* the eight, to whom they and other of their brethren had appealed, for the manifold wrongs and slaunders wherewith they were charged both at home and abroad, at which time this my *Aduersarie* running from *Cardinall* to *Cardinall* to informe against them, made no scruple of conscience to disgrace and slaunder them, as *Schismatikes, Spies, Rebells*, and *disobedient persons* to the *See Apostolike* &c. as now in his publike writings he handleth me) hee and some others vpon whom he depended, fearing lest that hir *Maiestie* should shew some fauour, and giue some sort of toleration to such hir Catholike Subiects; whom for their constant loyaltie she might securely trust (for out of hir Princely and mercifull disposition Shee had already shewed ouer great fauour to those oppressed Priests, considering the present lawes of the Realme made against them) had so little commiseration of the continuall calamities of distressed Catholikes, that he was not ashamed to aduise then his *Holinesse* in a little *Treatise*, or Pamphlet written in Italian, that it was not good, or profitable to the Catholike cause, that any libertie or toleration of Religion should be granted by the State to the Catholikes of England.

82   And that this is most true hee can not for shame deny, and I haue also heard diuerse vertuous Priests, and Laymen, who were then at Rome, protest vpon their saluation, that they did

did both see and reade the aforesaid Italian Pamphlet, affirming withall, that it was thought then by diuerse at Rome, that this my *Aduersarie* T. F. was in that businesse onely an agent and instrument for others, vpon whose command and becke hee wholly depended, who feared, least that if her *Maiestie* should haue granted vvhich they then greatly suspected, any toleration or mitigation of the Law to those hir Catholike Subiects, who would giue sufficient securitie of their true, vnfaigned, and constant loyaltie, it would haue beene the ready way to haue thrust all the *Iesuites* quite out of England. Now vvhat designements this my *Aduersarie* can haue, and what construction you may make of such his proceedings, and whether hee sincerely intendeth so much your good, as his priuate ends, and of those vpon whom hee now dependeth, and how diligently you are to examine his words, deeds, and writings, who dare aduenture with such palpable fraude to delude his *Holinesse*, his *Maiestie*, and your selues, as partly you haue seene in this his Preface, and more fully you shall see beneath, I leaue, Catholike Countreymen, to your prudent considerations.

83 Lastly, the applying of those words of the *Apocalyps*, *I would thou wert either hot or cold*, *&c.* to mee being but a slanderous calumnie affirmed without proofe, needeth no confutation. And with the same facilitie might *Carerius*, and the Canonists apply them to *Cardinall Bellarmine* and others of his Societie, for which cause hee calleth them *wicked polititians*, who are so *luke warme*, that they will not grant with the *Canonists*, that the *Pope* is not onely a spirituall, but also a temporall Lord of the whole Christian world. True it is that I am not of so fierie a spirit, as vnder pretence of zeale

N   to

to approue Gunpowder plots, or that defperate doctrine, from whence fuch furious attempts doe proceede, neither vnder colour of feruent deuotion to
attribute to the *Pope* an authoritie ouer the Kingdomes, bodies, and liues of temporall Princes, which
is not knowne to bee granted him by *Chrift*, and
which is more fcalding, to brand thofe Catholikes
with *herefie* that haue not the like feruour : Neither
am I fo cold as to deny either to Pope or Prince, that
authoritie which is knowne to be due to them, all extremities I hate, virtue confifteth in a meane, neither to take from *Cæfar*, and giue it to *God*, nor to
take from God, and giue it to Cæfar, but to render
to *God* and *Cæfar*, that which is their due.

84 And this fhall fuffice (*Deare Countrimen*) touching thofe aduertifements & confiderations, which
M^r. *Fitzherbert* hath giuen you concerning my doctrine in generall, and therefore I will now paffe by
degrees to the examination of his *Replyes* to mee in
particular, and I doubt not to difcouer alfo herein fo
plainly his manifold frauds & falfhods, that you haue
iuft caufe not to hazard your confciences and whole
eftates vpon fuch his fraudulent words and writings,
as partly you haue already feene in this his *Preface*,
how vnfincerely and guilefully in euery one of his
aduertifements and confiderations hee hath procee-
ded, and more cleerely you fhall fee beneath in this
Treatife, which Treatife to the end you may more
plainely vnderftand the chiefe grounds of this controuerfie touching the Popes power to depofe Princes, which is the maine queftion, as my *Aduerfarie*
confeffeth, betwixt him and me, and fpecially impugned in the new oath of allegiance, I will deuide into
three principall parts.

In the *firft* I will fet downe thofe Authors, which
I brought in my *Theologicall Difputation* to proue, that
any Catholike might by reafon of *extrinfecall grounds*,
and

and the *authoritie* of learned Catholikes *probably* perfwade themfelues , that the *Pope* hath not by *Chrift*
his inftitution any power to depofe *Princes*, together
with a confutation of the *Replyes*, which Card. *Bellarmine* masked vnder D. *Schulkenius* his name, to whom
my *Aduerfarie* here remitteth his *Englifh* Reader, hath
made againft them.

In the *fecond* I will examine all the principall arguments which Card. *Bellarmine* hath brought to proue
the vnion and fubordination of the temporall power
to the fpirituall, which fubordination my *Aduerfarie*
here fuppofeth to be a chiefe foundation, whereon the
doctrine for the Popes Power to depofe Princes doth
depend, and alfo the Replyes which D. *Sculckenius*
hath made to confirme the faid pretended vnion and
fubordination.

In the *third* and laft part I will difcouer in particular the infufficiencie of Mr. *Fitzherberts* whole *Reply*,
in the fame manner, order, and number of Chapters, which hee hath obferued in replying to my Anfweres.

The firſt part,

Wherein
THOSE AVTHORITIES AND
teſtimonies of learned CATHOLIKES,
which Mr. FITZHERBERT *cunningly paſſeth*
ouer, and for anſwere to them remitteth his
Engliſh Reader to D. SCHVLCKENIVS
a Latine writer, are briefely, and
perſpicuouſly examined.

Efore I come to examine the
particular points of my *Ad-*
uerſaries Reply, and to make
manifeſt his immodeſt, inſufficient, and alſo vnſincere
proceeding therein, I thinke
it not amiſſe, firſt to ſet
downe the teſtimonies of
thoſe Catholike Authours,
which I brought in my *Theologicall Diſputation* to
proue, that the doctrine for the Popes power to depoſe Princes is not a *point of faith,* and the contrarie
hereticall (as Mr. *Fitzherbert* following the ſteps of
Card. *Bellarmine,* and ſome few others of his Society
would gladly enforce Engliſh Catholikes euen with
incurring their Soueraignes high diſpleaſure, and with

N 3   the

the vtter ouerthrow of their temporall eſtates to beleeue.) to the end the Reader may thereby clearely
perceiue both the ſilly and ſhuffling anſweres of D.
Schulckenius, and alſo the inſufficient and craftie dealing of Mᵣ. *Fitzherbert,* who taking vpon him in this
his *Reply* to ſatisfie Engliſh Catholiks, thoſe eſpecially
that vnderſtand not the Latine tongue (for otherwiſe
he would doubtleſſe haue replyed in Latine, as he by
me was anſwered in Latine) *and to make them ſee,* as
a *In the Pre-
face, num.* 28.
he ſaith,ᵃ *a cleare confutation of the grounds of my doctrin,
and of my principall arguments and anſweres touching the
Popes power to depoſe Princes, which is the maine queſtion
betwixt him and me, and ſpecially impugned and abiured
in the new oath,* neuertheleſſe he cleane omitteth to anſwere my chiefe, principall, yea and only grounds,
which I brought to perſwade vnlearned men, that the
doctrine for the Popes power to depoſe Princes is not
a point of faith, to wit, *extrinſecall grounds,* drawne
from the teſtimonie of learned Catholikes, who maintaine the contrarie doctrine, by which vnlearned men
are chiefely, if not only, lead, and for confutation of
theſe *grounds* he remitteth his Engliſh Reader to D.
Schulckenius a Latine writer, and wrangleth onely a-
bout *intrinſecall grounds,* the ſtrength, or weakeneſſe
whereof vnlearned men cannot comprehend, as
though, *forſooth,* M. *Fitzherbert,* who hath taken out
of Fa. *Leſſius* masked vnder the name of D. *Singleton,*
a whole Treatiſe touching the decree of the *Councell
of Lateran,* and put it here in his *engliſh Reply,* as though
it were the inuention of his owne wit, would haue
ſpared to haue borrowed alſo of D. *Schulckenius* the
anſweres, which he made to thoſe Catholike Authors
by me alledged, if he had thought that thoſe anſweres
would by Engliſh Catholikes haue beene ſo greatly
applauded.

THE

The first CHAPTER,

Wherein the authoritie of Iohn Trithemius *a famous man of the Order of* S. Benedict, *is examined.*

1. He first authoritie, which I brought in my *Theologicall Disputation*, and also in my *Apologie*, was of *Iohn Trithemius* a famous Abbot of the Order of S. *Bennet*, and a man of singular learning and piety, who writeth, that in his time, to wit in this present age, wherein nothing hath been newly defined either by *Popes*, or *Councells* concerning the *Popes* power to depose Princes (for all the *Decrees* of *Popes* or *Councells*, which by Card. *Bellarmine* and others are vsually alledged to confirme the aforesaid authoritie, were long before *Trithemius* his time) this question touching the *Popes* power to depose the *Emperour* was in controuersie among the *Schoolemen*, and as yet not decided by the Iudge. His words are these : [b] *He indeed* (Henry the fourth) *was the first of all the Emperours, who was deposed by the Pope. The Schoolemen, or Scholastikes* [c] *are at strife concerning this point, and as yet the controuersie is not decided by the Iudge, whether the Pope hath power to*

depose

b *In* Chronico monast. Hirsaug. *ad annum* 1106.
c *Scholastici.*

*depose the Emperour, or no, which question for that it be-
longeth not to vs let vs leaue vndiscussed.*

   2. To this authoritie D.*,Schulckenius* anſwereth in
this manner. *If* Trithemius *by* Schoolemen,*or* Scho-
laſtikes *vnderstand those, who treate of Diuinitie scholastically, as* S. Thomas, S. Bonauenture, Ægidius, Durandus, *and others, he is manifestly deceiued, neither is
it any maruell if he be deceiued, seeing that he was not skilfull in that learning. But if he call* Scholemen, *Grammarians,* Historiographers, Poets, *he saith something. For
truely this point is in controuersie among Grammarians, as*
Valla, Historiographers, *as* Sigebert, Poets, *as* Dantes.
*But although it be in controuersie among them, and in their
opinions the* Iudge *hath not as yet decided the question, yet
it is not in controuersie among learned Diuines, and Lawyers, who are not ignorant in holy Scriptures, and in the ve-
nerable Councells of the holy Church. For although a-
mong these there be a controuersie about the manner, how
the* Pope *can do it, yet there is no question whether he hath
power to doe it. And what need is there to aske aduise of*
Trithemius, *who oftentimes hath erred in the historie,
which he professeth, as* Antonius Poſſeuine *hath noted
in his* Apparatus, *seeing that we haue the common opinion
of Doctours, and decrees of* Councells, *which doe make
the matter cleare. Thus anſwereth* D. Schulckenius.

   3. Marke now how many ſhifts, and ſhufflings be
in this anſwere. *If* Trithemius, *saith he, by Schola-
stickes, or* Scholemen *vnderstand those, who treate of
Diuinitie scholastically, as* S. Thomas &c. *he is manifestly deceiued:* As though *forsooth* only *scholasticall Diuines
and scholasticall Diuinitie* were to be had in eſtimati-
on, and *positiue Diuines,* who do not handle thoſe ſub-
tile *Schoole-quirks,* but do treat of holy Scriptures and
other queſtions of Diuinitie after a plaine and poſitiue
manner, as they were wont to be handled by the ancient Fathers, before *Peter Lombard,* the Maſter of
the ſentences his time, were not to be regarded. True
it

it is, that *Trithemius* by the word, *Scholasticke*, doth
commonly vnderſtand, not onely thoſe, who pro-
feſſe *Scholaſticall*, or *School-Diuinity*, as it is now adaies
diſtinguiſhed from *poſitiue Diuinity*, but by *Scola-
ſtikes* he vnderſtood *Schoolemen* and *Students* in generall, whether they profeſſed *Poſitiue* or *Scholaſticall*
Diuinity, as it may euidently appeare by his *Treatiſes*
de *Scriptoribus Eccleſiaſticis*, and de *viris Illuſtribus*,
where he hath this word, *Scholaſtike*, aboue an hundred times, and vſeth it for a *Schooleman*, ſtudent,
ſcholler, or ſchollerlike in generall.

4. And although *Trithemius* by the word, *Schola-
ſtikes* or *Schoolemen*, had vnderſtood not onely *Students* in Diuinity in generall, but particularly thoſe,
that profeſſe *Scholaſticall* Diuinity, as it is diſtinguiſhed from *poſitiue*, yet that he had beene therein manifeſtly deceiued, as D. *Schulckenius* ſo boldly affirmeth, is manifeſtly vntrue. For *Iacobus Almainus*, a
famous Doctour, and *Schoole-Diuine* of *Paris*, and
according to Fa. *Azor* the Ieſuite [e], a *Claſſicall Doctour*, who flouriſhed in *Trithemius* his time, doth alſo
affirme [f], as I obſerued in my *Apologie*, [g] *that very
many, or moſt Doctours*, among which ſome no doubt
were *Schoole-Diuines, are of opinion, that the Pope by the
inſtitution of Chriſt hath not power to inflict any temporall
puniſhment, as death, baniſhment, priuation of goods,
much leſſe of Kingdomes, nay nor ſo much as to impri-
ſon, but that the power, which hee hath by the inſtitution of
Chriſt, is onely extended to Excommunication, or ſome
ſuch ſpirituall puniſhment, and that his vſing of other puniſhments doth proceede meerely from the poſitiue Law,
and priuiledges of Princes. It belongeth*, ſaith hee, *to
the nature of the Laike power, to haue authority to inflict*
(he meaneth by way of coercion and conſtraint) *temporall puniſhment, as are death, exile, priuation of goods
&c. but the Eccleſiaſticall power by the inſtitution of God
can inflict no ſuch puniſhment, yea cannot ſo much as impri-*

ſon,

e *Lib. 2. Inſtit.
cap. 14.*
f *In Lib. de
Dom. nat. ciu.
& Eccl. in pro.
2a. concl.*
g *Num. 122.*

son, vt plerifque Doctoribus placet, *as very many or most Doctours* (for fo much the word, *plerique*, doth fignifie) *are of opinion, but it is extended onely to spirituall punishment, as Excommunication, and the other punishments which it vseth, are from the pure positiue Law.* And a little before he affirmed, *that the Ecclesiasticall and Lay power of Iurisdiction in the externall Court are fo distinguished in respect of the punishments, which can bee inflicted by either of them, that by one onely a corporall punishment, and by the other precisely a spirituall can bee inflicted.* Now what words can bee more cleere then thefe, to which neuertheleffe D. *Schulckenius* giueth no anfwer, and yet my *Aduerfary* after his vfuall manner very boldly affirmeth, that D. *Schulckenius hath anfwered particularly to euery one of the authorities, which I brought either in my* Apologie,*or* Theologicall Difputation.

5. The like words hath *Iohn Gerfon,* another famous Clafficall Doctour, and Schoole-Diuine of Paris,who liued before *Trithemius,* & *Almaines* time. *There are, faith* Gerfon, ^h *who dee affirme, that this punishment of Excommunication is the laft which the Ecclefiafticall power of Iurifdiction by the onely firft inftitution of Chrift can inflict; fo that it is not extended to imprifonment, or that any man bee adiudged to death or corporall whipping, but when the Ecclefiaficall Iudge doth this, he doth it by the grant of Princes, as the Cleargie by the deuotion of Princes hath receiued much authoritie of temporall Iurifdiction,which Iurifdiction or Cenfure is neuertheleffe called fpirituall, as alfo the temporall goods of Ecclefiafticall perfons are called fpirituall,becaufe they are dedicated & applyed to the, who ferue the Church, as alfo the breads of propofitio,the firft fruits,the tithes, alfe the veffels of the Temple, and fuch like were in the olde Law called facred or holy, fo alfo the new Law doth obferue the fame.*

6. Secondly, *it is no maruell,* faith D. *Schulckenius, that Trithemius be deceiued, if by* Schoole-men *he vnderftand*

h *De poteft. Ecclef. confider.* 4.

derſtand Scholaſticall Diuines, *ſeeing that he himſelfe was not skilfull in that ſcience:* As though, *forſooth*, none can know, when men of any profeſſion be at variance touching any difficult queſtion belonging to that Science, but thoſe onely, that be skilfull in the ſame profeſſion. Phyſicians may eaſily know, when learned Lawyers are at ſtrife concerning a point of Law, and ſo both of them may eaſily know, when learned Diuines are at contention about a Theologicall queſtion; and writers of hiſtories may alſo know, when Diuines or Lawyers are at debate about any point of Diuinity or Law, and may alſo, without paſſing the bounds of their profeſſion relate the ſame to others. And therefore it is no maruell, that *Trithemius* being not onely a meere Hiſtoriographer, but alſo a learned poſitiue Diuine, as by his manifold workes it doth cleerely appeare, might eaſily perceiue, that it was at that time a controuerſie among *Scholaſticall Diuines,* whether the *Pope* had authoritie to depoſe the Emperour or no. Neither is it neceſſarie, that the controuerſie ſhould be made knowen by printed books, but it ſufficeth that it bee made manifeſt by word of mouth, and publike oppoſition and contradiction in Schooles, as all men, who frequent the Schools, may by daily experience moſt cleerely perceiue.

7. Thirdly, *but if* Trithemius, ſaith D. *Schulckenius* call *Schoolemen,* Gramarians, Poets, Hiſtoriographers, *he ſaith ſomething. For truely this point is in controuerſie among* Grammarians *as* Valla, Hiſtoriographers *as* Sigebert, Poets *as* Dantes, *and in their opinions the Iudge hath not as yet decided the queſtion.* Marke now the fraud and cunning of this man. For who would not by this his anſwer imagine, but that thoſe three Authours were meere *Grammarians, Hiſtoriographers, Poets,* and not *Diuines?* where as it is manifeſt, that although for *Grammar, Hiſtories,* and *Poetry* they were ſingular, and inferiour to none of their times, yet

they

i *In verbo*
Laurentius
Valla.

k *In verbo*
Dantes.

l *In verbo*
Sigebertus.

they were all of them also learned Diuines, as *Trithe-mius* in his book de *Ecclesiasticis Scriptoribus* doth sufficiently witnesse. *Laurentius Valla,* saith hee, i *a noble man of Rome, the Prince by farre of Grammarians of this age, a Philosopher, Rhetorician, and a most excellent Diuine* &c. *Dantes,* saith he, k *by Country a Florentine, a most great student in his time of all men, as well in Diuine Scriptures as Secular learning, and very learned, a Philosopher, and a Poet inferiour to none of that age. Sigebert,* saith he, l *a monke of the order of S. Benedict, a most great student from his youth in Diuine Scriptures, and very learned, and in secular learning inferiour to none of his time.* And yet D. *Schulckenius* would cunningly perswade his Reader, that *Valla* was a meere *Grammarian, Dantes* a meere *Poet,* and *Sigebert* a meere *Historiographer.* Moreouer, *Trithemius* could not by *Schoolemen* only vnderstand *Valla, Dantes* and *Sigebert* ; for that his words are of the present tence and time ; He doth not say, *It hath beene* a controuersie among the Schoolemen, but *it is* a controuersie among the School-men, *& adhuc,* and *as yet, till now, hitherto, to this present time,* the question is not decided by the Iudge. Therefore *Trithemius* his words are not so to bee vnderstood, as D. *Schulckenius* expoundeth them, that in the opinion of *Valla, Dantes* and *Sigebert,* who all liued aboue a hundred m yeeres before *Trithemius* his time, but according to his owne opinion the question is not at this present decided by the Iudge.

m For *Sige-bert* liued in the yere 1111 *Dantes* in the yeere 1321. *Valla* in the yeere 1420. and *Trithemius* in the yeere 1519.

8   Fourthly, *But what neede is there ,* saith D. Schulckenius, *to aske aduise of* Trithemius, *who oftentimes hath erred in the historie, which he professeth, as* Antonie Poiseuine *hath noted in his Apparatus* ; But *first ,* be it so, that *Trithemius* giuing credit to the relation of others, hath erred sometimes in his historie (for all those oftentimes *Posseuine* doth in particular reduce onely to three) must therefore no credit be giuen to other his relations ; especially, when other

ther Doctours of the fame age doe relate the fame? And doth not *Card: Bellarmine* himfelfe confeſſe, as appeareth by his Recognitions, that he hath oftentimes erred in points of Diuinitie, which depend not ſo much vpon relation, as vpon iudgement? muſt therefore no credit be giuen hereafter to his iudgement in other points of Diuinitie? or will he like it well, that his own words, which he vfeth here againſt *Trithemius*, be retorted backe vpon himſelfe, *what neede is there to aske the aduife of* Card: Bellarmine, *who, as he himſelfe confeſſeth, hath oftentimes erred in points of Diuinitie, which he profeſſeth.*

9 *Secondly,* obſerue *good Reader,* how palpably and groſſely, not to fay ſhamefully, both *Poſſeuine,* and *D. Schulckenius* alſo, giuing credit to *Poſſeuine,* haue themſelues erred, in reprehending vnworthily *Trithemius* his errours.   For three particular things *Poſſeuine* relateth[n], wherein he affirmeth *Trithemius* to haue erred in his hiſtorie. The *firſt* is, in that *Trithemius* affirmeth[o] *Laurentius Iuſtinianus* to haue been of the Order of the *Celeſtines.* And neuertheleſſe *Poſſeuine* himſelfe a little after in the word *Laurentius Iuſtinianus* doth in expreſſe words affirme, that he was of that Order. *Laurentius Iuſtinianus,* ſaith *Poſſeuine, a Venetian, of the Order of the Celeſtines, the firſt Patriarch of Venice &c.* The *fecond* is, in that *Trithemius* affirmeth one *Hugo* a *Dominican* and *Cardinall* to be *Barchionenſis,* and *doth not make mention whether he was of* Barcilona *in France or in Spaine.* But although *Trithemius* was not ſo exact in diſtinguiſhing thoſe two places, yet conſidering that euery errour includeth a falſhood, and *Trithemius* in the aforeſaid relation affirmed no falſhood or vntruth, hee can not iuſtly by *Poſſeuine* be therefore taxed of errour.

10 The *third* errour, wherewith *Poſſeuine* chargeth them, is, in that hee affirmeth *Abbot Ioachim* to haue beene condemned in a generall Councell, where

as

n *In verbo*
Ioannes Tri-
themius.
o *In verbo*
Laurentius
Iuſtin.

as the Councell, ſaith Poſſeuine, *did not condemne the man, but the doctrine, which was againſt the Maſter of the Sentences.* But truly I can not but greatly maruell, how *Poſſeuine* could be ſo groſſely miſtaken, vnleſſe he would of ſet purpoſe forge ſomething, whereby he might diſgrace *Trithemius.* For if he had but briefely runne ouer that place of *Trithemius,* which he citeth, he could not but haue ſeene, that *Trithemiu* did only affirme *Ioachims* doctrine, and not his perſon to be condemned in the Councell. *Tractatus autem quem ſcripſit* &c. *But the Treatiſe* (ſaith *Trithemius* P in the place cited by *Poſſeuine*) *which* Abbot Ioachim *wrote againſt* Peter Lombard *Biſhop of* Paris, *is condemned in a Generall Councell, as appeareth in the beginning of the* Decretalls, Damnamus.

11   Wherefore to returne backe *D. Schulcke-nius* his words, what neede had *D. Schulckenius* to aske aduice of *Poſſeuine* touching *Trithemius* his errours, ſeeing that *Poſſeuine* himſelfe hath therein not onely groſſely erred, but alſo in other his relations, as in affirming *Iohn Gerſon Chancelour of Paris* to be of the Order of the *Celeſtines* (wherein alſo *Card: Bellarmine* in his late treatiſe of Eccleſiaſticall writers hath erred with him) yea and ſometimes which is leſſe excuſable, when of ſet purpoſe he pretendeth to recall and amend his former errour ; as in verbo *Durandus à S. Porciano,* whom in his former Edition, as he ſaith (for I neuer ſaw it) he affirmed to be *Biſhop of Melda,* as truly he was, and of the *Order of S. Dominike :* and now, forſooth, in his corrected Edition he will needs haue him to be *Biſhop* of *Liege,* and to haue liued in the yeare 1035. and that *Hermannus Contractus,* who liued in the yeare 1054.maketh mention of him, and yet he will alſo haue him to be of the *Order of Dominike :* And neuertheleſſe *Poſſeuine* himſelfe a little before 9 affirmed, that *S. Dominike* dyed in the yeare 1221. which was two hundred fourteene yeares after

Durandus)

Durandus flourished. Now let *D. Schulckenius*, or
any other, who maketh so great account of *Possevines
Apparatus*, either accord these two, that *Durandus à
S. Porciano* was according to *Possevine* of the *Order* of
S. Dominike, and yet that according to the same *Posseuine* he liued well neere 200. yeares before *S. Dominike*
did inflitute his Order, or else not to giue hereafter so
great credit to all that *Possevine* affirmeth, seeing that
he hath so grossely erred both in falsly taxing *Trithemius* of those errours, and also (which is more grosse)
when purposely he endeauoured to amend his owne
errour.

12 Lastly, *we haue,* faith D Schulckenius, *the common opinion of Doctours, and decrees of Councells, which
doe make the matter cleare. And therefore although a-
mong learned Diuines and Lawyers there be a controuersie
concerning the manner how the Pope may doe it, yet there
is no question whether he hath power to doe it.* But *first*
we haue the authoritie of *Trithemius, that it is a controuersie among the* Schoolemen, *and as yet not decided by
the Iudge* , not onely in what manner the *Pope* may
depose the Emperour , *but whether he hath any power
at all to depose him.* Then we haue the authoritie of
Almaine a learned *Schoole- Diuine,* and a *Classicall Doctour, that it is the opinion of very many Doctours, that the
Ecclesiasticall power by the institution of Christ can onely
inflict spirituall Censures, and not any temporall punishment, as death, exile, priuation of goods,* much lesse of
kingdomes, *nay nor so much as imprisonment.* And
therefore although it be the more common opinion
of Doctours, that the *Pope* hath power to depose
Princes, especially of Lawyers, who as *Pope Pius* the
fift did plainely confesse to that famous Lawyer *Nauarre* [r], *doe attribute more authoritie to the Pope then is
sufficient* (for that the greatest part of those Authours
cited by *Card: Bellarmine,* who in expresse words affirme, that the *Pope* hath such a power, are Lawyers,
                            men

r *in Comment:
super cap:* Non
liceat Papæ.
12. q. 2. §. 3.
num: 6.

men alſo *for the moſt part vnskilfull in Diuine Scrip-tures, and the law of God,* as *Dominicus Sotus* affirmeth²) yet it is not the more common opinion of Doctours, that it is a cleare and certaine doctrine not to be cal led in queſtion by any Catholike, that the Pope hath ſuch a power.

13. Few only Diuines there are, & for the moſt part *Ieſuites* who of late yeares haue by might and maine endeauoured without ſufficient grounds to make the matter cleare, and to be an vndoubted point of faith. But vntill they bring more cleare decrees of Coun-cells, or more pregnant proofes from holy Scriptures, then hitherto they haue brought, they will neuer make the matter cleare, but ſtill it will remaine a con-trouerſie among Catholikes, not only in what maner the Pope may, but whether he hath any power at all to depoſe the Emperour or no, as it was in *Trithemius* and *Almaines* time, ſince which time no cleare decree of any Councell hath been made to that purpoſe, for all the decrees of Councells, which by *Card. Bellar-mine* are vrged to proue that doctrine, and haue been anſwered by me and others, and ſhall beneath be an-ſwered more at large, were long before their time. And thus much concerning the firſt authoritie of *Tri-themius,* and *Almaine.*

Chap. 2.   *Wherein the authoritie of* Albericus Roxiatus *a famous Lawyer is briefly debated.*

1. T*He ſecond teſtimonie,* which I brought in my *Theologicall Diſputation,* and alſo in my *Apolo-gie* to proue this doctrine for the Popes power to de-poſe Princes not to be certaine, without controuerſie, or a point of faith, was of *Albericus Roxiatus, a moſt famous Profeſſour,* as *Trithemius* writeth, ª *of the Canon*

and

and Ciuill Law, and a man excellently learned, and according to Fa. *Azor* [b], a *Classicall Doctour*, who liued in
the yeare 1340. aboue a hundred yeares since the
Councell of Lateran, which is now so greatly vrged.
For this Authour calleth in question foure of the most
principall *Canons* or *Decrees* of *Popes* regiſtred in the
Canon Law, which do seeme most to fauour their authoritie to depoſe Princes, and to diſpose of the temporalls, eſpecially of the *Romane Emperour* (among
which one is that famous, and so often inculcated by
my *Aduerſaries,* ſentence of depoſition denounced
againſt *Fredericke the Emperour* by *Pope Innocent* the
fourth in the preſence of the *Councell of Lyons*) and he
affirmeth that none of them are in his opinion agreeable to law, or right, but that they were made by *Popes,*
againſt the rights, and libertie of the Empire.

   2. *The Paſtours of the Church,* ſaith he, [c] *putting
their ſickle into others harueſt, haue made foure Decrees,*
or *Decretalls. The one concerning the election of the* Emperour, *which beginneth,* Venerabilem, *and of this it is
there noted by all men. An other is about the depoſing of*
Friderike *the Emperour,* extra *de ſententia & re iudicata*
cap. *Ad Apoſtolicæ* in ſexto, *where also of this it is noted
by all men. An other is concerning the diſcord betwixt*
Henry *the Emperour,* and Robert *King of Sicily, and the
ſentence of treaſon publiſhed by the* Emperour *againſt him:
which Decree is in* Clementina *de ſententia & re iudicata* cap. *Paſtoralis. Another is in* Clementina prima *de
Iureiurando, that the Emperour is bound to ſweare allegiance to the Pope, and concerning ſome authoritie of the*
Pope *ouer the* Emperour. *Which Decretalls, whether
they be iuſt or no, God he knoweth. For I without preiudice
to ſounder aduice do beleeue (and if it ſhould be erroneous
I recall it) that none of them be agreeable to right. Yea I
beleeue that they are publiſhed againſt the rights and libertie of the Empire, and I doe thinke that by God they were
inſtituted diſtinct powers, whereof I haue noted ſufficiently*

            P   lege

b *Lib.* 2. *Iiſt. cap.* 14.

c *In Dictiona-rio* verbo *Ele-ctio.*

lege prima *Cod. de Summa Trinitate & Fide Catholica.*
Thus *Albericus.*

3   Obſerue now, *good Reader*, how ſleightly D.
Sculckenius would ſhift of this authoritie, which is ſo
plaine and manifeſt. *Albericus*, ſaith he, *ſpeaketh wa-*
uering and altogether doubtfull, and he addeth, and if it
ſhould be erroneous I recall it : and he is conuinced of errour
by Azor lib. 10. *cap.* 6. *q.* 3. Theſe be all the exceptions that D. *Schulckenius* taketh againſt this authority.
But firſt this word *doubtfull* or *wauering*, as out of *Vaſ-*
quez I obſerued in my *Theologicall Diſputation* d, may
be taken two manner of waies, either when one is ſo
doubtfull, that he hath no determinate aſſent of either
part, but remaineth perplex betwixt both, iudging
neither part to be either true or falſe, in which ſenſe
that word, *altogether doubtfull*, which D. *Schulckenius*
vſeth here, if he will not ſpeake improperly, can only
be taken ; and when we are thus *doubtfull* concerning
any matter, we are alwaies bound to chuſe the ſurer
part ; neither is it lawfull to do any thing with a *doubt-*
full conſcience, taking doubtfull in this ſenſe : Or elſe
the word, *doubtfull*, may be taken, when wee haue a
determinate aſſent or iudgement that one part is true
or falſe, but yet we are not certaine, and therefore haue
ſome *feare* of the contrarie, which *feare* doth not exclude a determinate aſſent and iudgement that one
part is true, for euery aſſent, iudgement or opinion,
which is only *probable*, doth alwaies imply a *feare* ;
but *feare* conſiſteth in this, that he who is *fearefull*, or
iudgeth with *feare*, hath two aſſents or iudgements,
the one *direct*, whereby he iudgeth determinately, that
one part is true, the other *reflexe*, whereby he iudgeth,
that although he thinketh it true, yet in very deede it
may be falſe, for that it is not certaine, but Diſputable
and in controuerſie among Doctours, and therefore
only probable : and when we are thus *doubtfull* or *feare-*
full concerning any matter, we are not bound to chuſe
the

the furer part, but it is fufficient to chufe that which
is *probable*, neither is it vnlawfull to doe any thing
with fuch a *doubtfull*, or *fearefull* confcience, as in that
place I declared out of *Vafquez.*

4. Now if D. *Schulckenius* by thofe wordes, *wauering* and *altogether doubtfull*, vnderftand, as of necefli-
tie he muft, if he will fpeake properly, that *Albericus*
had no determinate affent, iudgement, or opinion
concerning the vniuftice of thofe *Decretalls*, this is
manifeftly falfe, and thofe words, *I doe beleeue that
they are not agreeable to right, and I doe beleeue that
they are publifhed againft the rights and libertie of the Empire &c.* doe clearly conuince D. *Schulkenius* of apparant vntruth. But if D. *Schulckenius* by thofe
words *wauering* and *altogether doubtfull*, doe onely
meane, that *Albericus* was indeed of opinion, that
thofe *Decretalls* were vniuft, yet he did not hold his
opinion for certaine, and without all controuerfie, and
therefore was not obftinate in his owne opinion, but
was readie to recall it, if it fhould proue to be erroneous, and that hee would not condemne other men,
that fhould thinke the contrarie, (as now adaies it is
too frequent to condemne other men) this is very
true ; for fo much only doe import thofe his wordes,
and I do beleeue vnder correction, or *without preiudice to
founder aduife, and if it fhould be erroneous I recall it*; this
neuerthelelfe doth not hinder, but that we haue the o-
pinion of a man *excellently learned*, and of a *Claflicall
Doctour*, that the fentence of depofition denounced
againft *Frederike* the *Emperour* by *Pope Innocent* the
fourth in the *prefence* of the *Councell* of *Lyons*, and three
other famous *Decrees* of *Popes* regiftred in the *Canon
Law* touching the *Popes* power to difpofe of temporalls, were vniuft, and made againft the rights and libertie of the Empire.

5. *Secondly*, but *Albericus is conuinced*, faith D.
Schulckenius, of error by Azor. But befides that this

letteth

letteth not, but that *Albericus* is of opinion, that the
Pope hath no power to depofe Princes, this alfo is euen
as true, as that which D. *Schulckenius* faid before concerning the errours, which he faid *Poʃʃeuine* had obferued in *Trithemius* his hiftorie. For befides that all
the arguments, which *Azor* bringeth to proue in generall, the *Popes* authoritie ouer the *Emperour* in temporalls, are but triuiall, and haue been alreadie anfwered partly by D. *Barclay*, partly by my felfe, and now
of late very exactly by M^r. *Iohn Barclay*, to whom as
yet no anfwere hath beene made, one only argument
in particular *Azor* vrgeth againft *Albericus*, which is
this, *that the Romane Emperour was inʃtituted by the authoritie of the Church, by whoʃe grant alʃo the Romane
Empire was tranʃlated from the Grecians to the Germanes
or Frenchmen, and that he is created as a Patron, defen-
dour, Protector, and Tutour of the Church,* from whence
he inferreth, *that the Pope did not put his ʃickle into another mans harueʃt, but did vʃe his owne right, when hee
made that Canon concerning the election of the Emperour,
and when he exacteth an oath of the Emperour.*

e *Num* 404.
& *ʃeq.*

    6. But that this is no conuincing proofe, I fhewed
clearely in my *Apologie* e. For the Romane Empire
was not inftituted by the authoritie of the Romane
Church, feeing that he was inftituted before there was
any Romane Church at all, and continued for a long
time together the *Soueraigne Lord* in temporalls of the
Romane Church. Neither was the Romane Empire
tranflated from the Grecians to the Germans or
French men by the grant of the Romane Church, if
by the *Romane Church* be meant onely the *Cleargie of
Rome,* but it was tranflated by the grant, fuffrages, and
authoritie alfo of the *Laitie,* who in the weft parts were
fubiect to the Romane Empire. True alfo it is, that
all Catholike Princes ought to be Patrons, defenders,
and protectours of the Romane Church (but the Romane Emperour more fpecially) they being children
and

and members of the Catholike Romane Church, and
euery member is bound to defend eath other, but
especially to defend the head. And therefore I will
easily grant, that the Pope may exact, if need require,
not only of the Romane Emperour, but also of all o-
ther Catholike Princes an oath of spirituall allegiance,
but that Catholike Princes are subiect to the Pope in
temporalls, and that the Pope may exact of them an
oath of temporall allegiance, this is that I vtterly deny, neither will Card. *Bellarmine*, or any other be able
by any sufficient argument to conuince the contrary;
wherefore it cannot with any shew of probabilitie be
denied, but that we haue the testimonie of *Albericus*,
a man excellently learned, and a Classicall Doctour,
that the Pope hath no authoritie to depose Soueraigne Princes, and to dispose of their temporall dominions.

Chap. 3. *Wherein the authoritie of* Ioannes *Parisiensis, a famous Doctour of Paris, is
examined, and the exceptions of D.*
Schulckenius *against it are proued to
be insufficient.*

1.   THe third authoritie, which I brought in my
Theologicall Disputation [a] and also in my *Apologie* [b], was of *Ioannes Parisiensis.* a famous Diuine of the
Order of S. *Dominike*, and as *Trithemius* relateth [c],
*most learned in the holy Scriptures, and who in the Vniuer-
sitie of* Paris *was for a long time together a publike Professour, and left behind him many Disciples.* He flourished
about the yeare 1280. which was 65. yeares after the
great *Councell of Lateran*, which is now adaies so greatly vrged by our *Aduersaries.* This Doctour therefore
although he be of opinion, *that if a King should become
an heretike, and incorrigible, and a contemner of Ecclesiasticall Censures, the Pope may do somewhat with the people,*

a *Cap. 3. sec. 3.
num. 7.*
b *Num. 121.*
c *In verbo
Ioannes Pari-
siensis.*

ple, *whereby the King may be depriued of his Secular dig-*
nitie, and be depoſed by the people, to wit, *he may excom-*
municate all thoſe, to whom it belongeth to depoſe the king,
who ſhould obey him as their Soueraigne : Neuertheleſſe
he is cleerely of this opinion, *that it belongeth not to the*
Pope, to depoſe iuridically Kings or Emperours for any
crime whatſoeuer although it be ſpirituall, or which is all

d Almainus
de poteſt. Eccl.
q. 2. cap. 8.

one to depriue them **d** of their kingdomes by a defini-
tiue ſentence, *in ſuch ſort, that after the ſentence be pub-*
liſhed they ſhall haue no more regall power and authoritie.

e *De* poteſt.
Regia & Pa-
pali *cap.* 14.
ad 20.

For he affirmeth, **e** *that excommunication,* or *ſuch like*
ſpirituall puniſhment is the laſt, which may be inflicted by a
ſpirituall Iudge. For although, ſaith he, *it belong to an*
Eccleſiaſticall Iudge to recall men to God, and to withdraw
them from ſinne, yet he hath not power to doe this, but by
vſing thoſe meanes, which be giuen him by God, which is
by excluding them from the Sacraments, and participation
of the faithfull. Wherefore although *Pariſienſis* be of
opinion, that the temporall common-wealth hath in
ſome cauſes of great moment authoritie to depoſe
their Prince (with which queſtion I doe not intend
at this time to intermeddle) yet concerning the principall controuerſie, which is betwixt me and *Card.*
Bellarmine, to wit, whether it be hereticall erroneous,
or temerarious to affirme, that the Pope hath no
power to depriue Princes of their Royall right and
authoritie, *Ioannes Pariſienſis* doth moſt plainely, as I
haue now ſhewed, contradict the opinion of *Card.*
Bellarmine. Thus I wrote in my Theologicall Diſputation.

    2   Marke now, *good Reader,* with what fraude
and falſhood *D. Schulckenius* endeauoureth to paſſe

f *Pag.* 64. 65.
66. *ad num:* 4.

ouer this authoritie. *Ioannes Pariſienſis,* ſaith he **f**, *is*
not for the contrarie opinion. For although he giueth leſſe
to the Pope, then he ought, yet he giueth as much as ſuffi-
ceth for our purpoſe. For what doth it appertaine to the
queſtion which is in hand, whether the Pope doe depoſe im-
mediately

mediately by his sentence, or that he may by his right with-
draw his subiects from their obedience and cause them to
depose? But who would not admire the wonderfull
boldnes of this man? For the onely queſtion betwixt
me and *Card. Bellarmine* is, and euer hath been, whether the Pope hath authoritie to depriue Princes of
their Kingdomes immediately by his ſentence, in
ſuch ſort, that after his ſentence of depriuation be denounced, they, who before were Kings and had true
Regall authoritie, are then no more Kings, and haue
no true and lawfull right to reigne; and yet now he
being preſſed with the authoritie of *Ioannes Pariſienſis*,
bluſheth not to affirme, *that it doth not appertaine to*
the preſent queſtion, whether the Pope may depoſe imme-
diately by his ſentence, which neuertheleſſe is the onely
queſtion betwixt him and me, *or by commanding and*
cauſing the temporall Common-wealth to depoſe their
Prince, with which queſtion I haue ſundry times in
my *Apologie* affirmed that I would not intermeddle.
For moſt certaine it is, euen according to *Card: Bel-*
larmines owne doctrine g, that the Pope can not withdraw, diſcharge, or abſolue ſubiects from their obedience immediatly by his ſentence, vnles he haue authoritie to depriue immediately & by his ſentence
their Prince of his Princely power and authoritie,
for that authoritie in a Prince, and obedience in ſubiects
are correlatiues, and one dependeth on the other, and the
obligation of obedience doth ſo long endure in the Subiect,
as the dignitie, power, or Iuriſdiction doth endure in the
Superiour, ſaith Suarez h, and *to deny obedience to a*
Prince ſo long as he remaineth Prince, and is not depriued of his Princely power, *is clearely repugnant,* ſaith
Card: Bellarmine i, *to the law of God,* and nature.

3   This therfore is the opinion of *Pariſienſis* touching
the Popes authoritie to diſpoſe of the temporall
goods, or dominions either of Kings, or priuate men.
And *firſt* concerning the goods of priuate men hee

affir-

g *in Tract:*
contra Barcl.
cap. 21. pag. 202

h *in Defenſione*
fidei & c. lib. 6.
cap: 3. nu. 6.
i *in Tract:*
contra Barcl:
cap. 21. p. 202.

k *De potest.*
Regia & Pap.
cap: 6.7.

affirmeth ᵏ, *that the Pope is not a Lord, to whom the pro-*
pertie of Church *liuings doth belong, but onely a dispencer*
of them, but of the goods of Laymen he is not so much as a
dispencer; vnlesse perchance in extreame necessitie of the
Church, *in which necessitie also he is not a dispencer, but*
a declarer of the law. And because in extreame necessitie
of faith and manners, all the goods of the faithfull, yea and
Chalices *of* Churches *are to be communicated, the Pope,*
who is supreme not onely of the Cleargie, but of all the
faithfull, as they are faithfull, hath authoritie, as he is ge-
nerall informer of faith and manners, in case of extreame
necessitie of faith and manners to dispence in this case the
goods of the faithfull, & to ordaine them to be exposed, as
it is expedient for the common necessitie of faith, which other
wise would be ouerthrown by the inuasion of Pagãs, or other
such like accident. And this ordination of the Pope is only
a declaration of the law, to which he may by Ecclesiasticall
Censures *compell the faithfull. But in cases not of necessi-*
tie, but of some speciall vtilitie, or when it is not apparant,
that the goods of Lay-men doe helpe such vtilitie, or ne-
cessitie, the Pope hath not authoritie to compell any man,
but concerning this hee may giue indulgences for giuing
aide to the faithfull, and no other thing is granted him in
my opinion. Thus writeth *Parisiensis.* wherefore in
his opinion the Pope hath no authoritie to depriue a
Lay-man of his goods, or any part thereof, euen in
necessitie of faith and manners, but onely to declare,
that he is bound by the law of God to giue such part
of his goods, as the necessitie of the Church shall require, which if he neglect to doe, the Pope hath no
other authoritie to compell him therevnto, then by
Ecclesiasticall Censures, which are the last punishments,
which the Ecclesiasticall power by the institution of Christ
can inflict.

4 In the very like manner *Parisiensis* discourseth
of the disposing of Kingdomes, and of deposing
temporall Princes, as I before related out of him.
For

For *firſt* he affirmeth, *that the Pope hath no authoritie to depoſe a King iuridically*, or, which is all one, to depriue him by a iuridicall ſentence of his right to reigne; and *ſecondly*, that the people, or temporall common-wealth may, and in ſome exorbitant caſes are bound to depoſe their Prince; and ſo the Pope not by a iuridicall ſentence of depriuation, but by declaring what the people are by the law of God bound to doe, and by Eccleſiaſticall Cenſures compelling them therevnto, may according to *Pariſienſis*, concurre to the depoſing of a Prince by meanes of the people, which if the people, notwithſtanding the *Popes* Cenſures neglect to doe, the *Pope* hath no further power to depoſe him, for that *Eccleſiaſticall Cenſures are*, according to him, *the laſt puniſhment, which the Eccleſiaſticall power can inflict.*

5 Wherefore two things are affirmed by *Pariſienſis*, the one, that the *Pope* hath no authoritie to depriue Princes immediately by his ſentence of their Princely power, and this is that only, which is in controuerſie betwixt mee and *Card: Bellarmine* : the other, that the people, or temporall common-wealth haue that authoritie in ſome exorbitant caſes : and this is only a philoſophicall queſtion, and wherewith I would neuer intermeddle; as being impertinent to the queſtion concerning the *Popes* authoritie to depriue him. And although many Catholike Doctors doe agree with *Pariſienſis* in this point, yet many other learned Catholikes, whom I cited in my *Apologie* [l], doe diſſent from him herein, to which opinion doe incline very many of the ancient Fathers, who expounding thoſe words of the King and Prophet, [m] *I haue ſinned to thee alone*, doe affirme, that *Soueraigne Princes, for that they are inferiour to God alone*, to wit, in temporalls, *can be puniſhed* with temporall puniſhments *by God alone.* And therefore D. *Schulckenius* may be greatly aſhamed to affirme ſo boldly, that

l *Num. 411.*

m *Pſal: 50.*

Parifienfis doth not make for my opinion, and that it doth not appertaine to the queftion which is in hand, whether the *Pope* may depofe Princes immediately by his fentence, or by meanes of the people, feeing that the onely queftion betwixt vs is, whether the *Pope* hath power to depriue Princes of their Royall power immediately by his fentence, and not what authoritie the common-wealth hath to depriue them.

6 But *D. Schulckenius* perceiuing, that this his anfwer to the authoritie of *Parifienfis* was but a meere fhift and euafion, hath referued but not in this place another anfwer, whereby he imagined to cleane ouer-throw the authority of this famous Doctour and Schoole-Diuine. For hee beneath [n] replying to the answer, which I made to thofe words of *S. Bernard* vrged by *Card. Bellarmine* to prooue the Popes pow-er to depofe Princes, *Quid tu denuo vfurpare gladium-tentas* &c. wherof beneath [o] I will treate more at large; in confirmation of which my anfwer I cited the au-thoritie of *Ioannes Parifienfis*, D. *Schulckenius* writeth thus : *There is no great regard to bee had of the authoritie of* Ioannes Parifienfis *whatfoeuer he faith, for that other his errours are condemned by the Church in the common* Extrauagant *Vas electionis : and alfo in the* 14. chapter *of the fame* Treatife hee mingleth *many errours.* The like anfwer, but more biting maketh *Fa: Leffius* in his *Singleton. It is to little purpofe,* faith he, [p] *what* Ioannes Parifienfis *doth fay, becaufe he alledgeth very many other falfe citations and hiftories, as being a Schifmatike.* Ano-ther cenfure but more temperate *Card. Bellarmine* gi-ueth of him in his booke of *Ecclefiafticall writers. Io-annes Parifienfis,* faith he, [q] *of the Order of the Prea-chers, was famous about the yeere* 1296. *Hee wrote vpon the foure bookes of the fentences, and diuerfe Quodlibets : but efpecially of Kingly and Papall power, and becaufe it was his happe to liue in troublefome times by reafon of the*
difcord

n *Pag.* 394.
ad num. 201.

o *Part.* 2. *ca.* 9.

p *Pag.* 29.

q *Pag.* 380.

difcord betweene Pope Boniface *the eight, and* Philip *the faire, King of France, and hee lined and taught at* Paris, *hee feemeth to be more inclined towards the* King, *then the* Pope.

   ſ But truely it is ſtrange, that men of ſuch ſingular learning, and religious profeſſion ſhould ſo raſhly and without ſufficient grounds be ſo tranſported, as, contrarie to the rules of Chriſtian Charitie and Iuſtice, to defame and ſlaunder learned and vertuous men, and thoſe eſpecially, who beeing dead cannot defend themſelues. For *firſt* it is an apparant and too too maniſeſt ſlander, which *Fa:* *Leſſius*, ſpeaking with all dutifull reſpect to his reuerence, doth affirme *that Ioannes Pariſienſis was a Schiſmatike* ; neither can he out of any approoued Authour, or by any probable reaſon prooue any ſuch thing : and therfore what great account hee hath to make at the dreadfull day of iudgement, for vniuſtly taking away, as much as lieth in him, the good name of ſo famous a man, and in ſo fowle and hainous a crime as Schiſme is, I remit to the examination of his owne conſcience. Beſides, that *Pariſienſis mingleth many errours in the* 14. *chapter of his Kingly and Papall power,* as D. Schulckenius affirmeth, and *that he alledgeth many falſe citations and hiſtories,* as *Fa:* *Leſſius* ſaith, is alſo vntrue, and it had beene fitting for them to haue alledged ſome one of them, that thereby ſome credit might haue beene giuen them for the reſt. Vnleſſe whatſoeuer is not agreeable to D. *Schulckenius* his doctrine, which he thinketh to be certaine muſt bee accounted an errour, and whatſoeuer *Fa. Leſſius* hath not ſeeene, or read muſt be eſteemed a *falſe citation* or *hiſtorie.* True it is, that *Pariſienſis in that* 14. *chapter* doth teach, *that the Pope cannot iudge of temporall cauſes, but in regard of the ſinne, and that hee cannot depoſe Princes by his ſentence, and that the laſt puniſhment, which an Eccleſiaſticall Iudge can inflict, are ſpirituall and Eccleſiaſticall Cen-*

ſures which indeede are no errours, whatſoeuer theſe ſeuere *Cenſours* ſay to the contrary. True alſo it is, that *Pariſienſis* citeth a place out of *Hoſtienſis*, at which Fa. *Leſſius* doth indiſcreetly carp, ^r affirming, *that he findeth no ſuch thing in Hoſtienſis, yea & that* Hoſtienſis *hath not written vpon the chapter* Ad Abolendam *tit. de Hæreticis, as Widdrington iudgeth, as neither vpon other texts.* But neuertheleſſe I found in *Oſtienſis* vpon the chapter *Ad abolendam* that which *Ioannes Pariſienſis* cited out of him ; and to ſay that *Hoſtienſis* did not write vpon that chapter *Ad abolendam,* is ſo manifeſt an vntruth as I obſerued in another place ^ſ, that I wonder how F. *Leſſius*, who is reputed to be a man of ſo great reading, could be ignorant thereof.

6 Moreouer, that *Pariſienſis ſeemeth to bee more enclined to the King then to the Pope, he then liuing and teaching at Paris,* is indeede affirmed, but not prooued by Card. *Bellarmine.* And if this manner of cenſuring learned men and excepting againſt their authority, as men partiall, may be approoued, it is the readie way to ouerthrow the teſtimony almoſt of all the Authours on both ſides. For it may in the ſame manner be anſwered, that as ſuch Authours wrote partially in fauour of *Kings,* ſo others wrote partially in fauour of *Popes* ; And therefore *Pariſienſis* himſelfe foreſeeing this obiection replieth thus : *For to ſay,* ſaith he, ^t *that ſo woorthie men, among whom ſome alſo were Popes, did write againſt their conſcience in fauour of Princes, or for feare of them, is to ſtretch foorth his mouth againſt heauen. For contrariwiſe it might be ſayd more probably, that thoſe Doctours, who doe ſo vnmeaſurably aduance the* Popes *authority, doe ſpeake for feare or fauour of him, ſeeing that they are Eccleſiaſticall perſons, who may by him get greater preferment. And eſpecially ſith that they ſay (although not well) that the* Pope *doth graciouſly embrace them, who do amplifie his authority, & depreſſeth them, who doe* ſay the contrarie.

7. Further

r *Pag.* 30.

ſ In my Latin Appendix againſt Fa: *Suarez* part. 1. ſec.7 num. 14.

t *De poteſt. Regia & Papali* c. 21. ad 41.

7 Furthermore, neither can D.*Schulckenius* in my opinion fufficientlie prooue, that *Ioannes de Poliaco*, whofe errours were condemned by *Pope Iohn* the 22. in that Extrauagant *Vas electionis*, was this *Ioannes Parifienfis*, who made the *Treatife of Kingly and Papall power*, but fome other Doctour of *Paris*, who was called by that name, and liued about that time. And my coniectures are thefe. *Firft*, for that the errours, which *Ioannes de Poliaco* maintained concerning confeffions made to the mendicant Friers, were againft the priuiledges which were granted to the mendicant Friers, and therefore it is not like that he who wrote the Treatife *of Kingly and Papall power*, and was himfelfe of the order of the preaching Friers, would preach and teach againft the priuiledges granted to his Order. *Secondly*, if this *Ioannes de Poliaco* had been of the Order of the preaching Friers, as all Authours affirme that *Ioannes Parifienfis*, who wrote the Treatife of *Kingly and Papall power*, was, it is very like, that *Pope Iohn* the 22. who condemned his errors, would haue named him fo to be in his *Extrauagant* as he did, in his other *Extrauagants* name of what Order thofe Authours were, whofe errours he condemned, as *Michael* of *Cefena*, *William Occam*, *Henricus* of *Cena*, and others: who neuerthelelfe are in fome fort excufed from errour by D. *Sanders* u.

8, *Thirdly*, there is no Authour that I haue read, who faith, that *Ioannes de Poliaco*, whofe errours were condemned, was of the Order of the preaching Fryars, neither doth *Prateolus*, who vfually fetteth down, of what Order thofe Authours whom he relateth, are, affirme, that this *Ioannes de Poliaco* was of that Order, whereas moft Authours, who fpeake of *Ioannes Parifienfis*, that wrote the Treatife of *Kingly and Papall power*, doe affirme, that hee was a Dominican Fryar. *Fourthly*, neither is, there any Authour that I haue read, who doth affirme, that *Ioannes Parifienfis*,

Q 3   who

u *De vifib. monarch. lib.7. num 161.*

who made the Treatiſe of *Kingly and Papall power*, was called *Ioannes de Poliaco*. *Laſtly Ioannes Pariſienſis* was famous in the yeare 1280. according to *Trithemius*, and *Kiſengrenius*, and according to Card. *Bellarmine* in the yeare 1296. both which may very well be true, for that it may very well fall out, that the ſame man may be a famous Teacher ,and Preacher for ſixteene yeares together, but it is very vnlike, that one man ſhould for one and fortie yeares together at the leaſt be a famous Reader and Preacher, which wee muſt grant to be true, if *Ioannes de Poliaco*, whoſe errours were condemned, and he in perſon recalled them before the *Pope* and *Cardinalls* in publike Conſiſtorie at *Auinion* in the yeare 1321. and was commanded to teach and preach in the Schooles, and pulpit the contrarie doctrine, was our *Ioannes Pariſienſis*, who wrote the Treatiſe of *Kingly and papall power*, and was famous in the yeare 1280.

9. But to conclude this point, be it ſo, that our *Ioannes Pariſienſis*, and *Ioannes de Poliaco* were one and the ſelfe ſame man, which yet, as I haue ſhewed, hath no great likelihood, neuertheleſſe the maintaining of thoſe errors doth little repaire the authoritie of *Ioānes Pariſienſis* in this point, but rather from hence a forcible argument may bee drawne to proue, that it is no erroneous doctrine, to hould, that the Pope hath no authoritie to depoſe Princes by his ſentence. For beſides that it was no great blemiſh either to the learning or vertue of *Ioannes de Poliaco*, to hold that doctrine concerning confeſſions, which was condemned in that *Extrauagaut*, ſeeing that both many other learned men at that time as *Henricus de Gandauo* x a famous Doctour of Paris, *Durandus* a S. *Portiano* y a great Schoole-Diuine, yea and the whole *Vniuerſitie* of Paris, as witneſſeth *Ioannes Maior* z, a famous Doctour of the ſame Vniuerſitie, did maintaine the ſame; and alſo that he was readie at the firſt condemnation

thereof

x *quodl.* 2.*q.* 26. *& quodl.* 10. *q.* 1.
y *In* 4. *diſt.* 17. *q.* 2.
z *In* 4. *diſt.* 17. *q.* 6.

thereof to recall it, and to preach the contrary ; if at
that time the *Pope* and *Cardinalls* had alſo beene perſwaded, that it was an *erroneous* doctrine to affirme,
that the *Pope hath no power to depoſe Princes by his ſentence, and that it belongeth to the Pope to recall men to
God, and to withdraw them from ſinne by no other coerciue
meanes, then by excluding them from the Sacraments and
participation of the faithfull,* and *that Excommunication,
or ſuch like ſpirituall puniſhment is the laſt, which may bee
inflicted by the ſpirituall Iudge,* all which *Ioannes Pariſienſis* in his treatiſe of *Kingly and papall power* did publikely maintaine, without doubt the Pope, if hee had
thought this doctrine to be *erroneous,* would alſo haue
compelled him to recall it , it being ſo greatly preiudiciall to his owne Pontificall authoritie. And therefore notwithſtanding all the exceptions, which *Card.
Bellarmine* and Fa. *Leſſius* do take againſt *Ioannes Pariſienſis,* we haue the teſtimonie of this learned Catholike, and famous *Schole-Diuine* , that the Pope hath
no authority to depoſe Princes by his ſentence, which
is the only queſtion at this time betweene me, and
Card. Bellarmine.

Chap. 4. *Wherein the authoritie of* M. Doctour Barclay *a famous and learned Catho-like is breifly examined.*

1.   THe *fourth teſtimony,* which I broght both in my
Theologicall Diſputation[a], and alſo in my *Apologie*[b], was of Mr. *Doctour Barclay* a moſt learned man,
and yet no more learned then religious , (howſoeuer
ſome falſly and vnchriſtianly do ſlaunder him) in his
booke *de Regno* printed at *Paris* in the yeare 1600.
with priueledge of the moſt Chriſtian King of France,
where he affirmeth, *that Kings, who doe omit, or are neg-
ligent, to keepe Gods commandements, to worſhip him reli-
giouſly,*

a *Cap.* 3. *ſec.* 3.
num. 28.

giouſly, and to vſe all care and diligence, that their ſubieɛts do not reuolt from true Religion, *and fall into Idolatrie, Iudaiſme, or hereſie, are to be iudged by* God alone, *becauſe only to* God *they are ſubieɛt, ſpeaking of temporall iudgement and ſubieɛtion, although the* Pope, *being the ſupreme Prince, and vniuerſall Paſtour of the Chuch, hath power to condemn with ſpirituall iudgement all kings and Princes, offending againſt Gods law, as they are Chriſtians; and children of the Church, and to deliuer them to inuiſible tormentours to be puniſhed with the rod of the inuiſible ſpirit, and with the two edged ſword of Excommunication.*

2. But *Card.* Bellarmine in his booke againſt D. Barclay [c] little regardeth his authority; and now in his *Sculckenius* he affirmeth, [d] *that Catholikes will make no more account of Barclay, then they do of* Marſilius de Padua, *and of my ſelfe* (an eaſie anſwer to ſhift off the authoritie of any learned Catholike) And againe, *who doth not maruaile,* ſaith D. *Schulckenius, that ſeeing* Card. Bellarmine *hath in this point clearely and ſoundly after his accuſtomed manner confuted* Barclay, Widdrington *durſt not only aduenture to write againſt him without ſufficient ground, but alſo to oppoſe the ſaid* Barclay, *as a teſtimonie of truth againſt* Card. Bellarmine.

3. But notwithſtanding this glorious brag of D. *Schulckenius* ſo highly commending himſelfe, and his cleare and ſound confuting of *Barcl:y after his accuſtomed manner,* it cannot be denied, but that *Doɛtour Barclay* was a very learned man, and liued and died like a vertuous Catholike, and that hee was in times paſt, as *Poſſeuine* alſo relateth, [e] *a Counſeller to the Duke of Lorraine, and Maſter of Requeſts, and in the vniuerſity of Muſſepont a Profeſſour of the Canon and Ciuill Law, and alſo Deane,* and that his booke was printed at *Paris* with a ſpeciall priueledge of the moſt Chriſtian King of France, and is by *Poſſeuine* related among other approued bookes, and no exception taken by him againſt it. And therefore who doth not maruell, that
                         D. *Schulckenius*

c *Per totum.*
d *Pag.* 110. *ad num.* 28.

e *In* verbo *Gulielmus Barclaius.*

D. *Schulckenius* durst aduenture so bouldly to affirme, that Catholikes will make *no more account of* D. *Barclay*, a famous and learned Catholike, *then of Marsilius of Padua*, a known and condemned heretike, although not for this point touching the Popes power to depose Princes, but for other his assertions which I related in my Appendix against Fa. *Suarez* Wherefore although perchance some Catholikes doe with *Card. Bellarmine* make small account of *Doctour Barclaies* authoritie, as also they would make of the authoritie of any other Catholike, were he neuer so vertuous or learned, that should write against them in this point, neuerthelesse other Catholikes doe greatly regard his authoritie for the aforesaid cause, and they are also perswaded, that they haue as probable reasons to thinke, that he did not write partially in fauour of Princes or any other person, as that Card. *Bellarmine* did not write partially in fauour of the Pope, and some other of his followers in fauour of him, and their Order.

4   Neither hath D. *Schulckenius* in very truth any great cause so greatly to vaunt of his cleare and sound confuting of D. *Barclay*, for that both his sonne M[r]. *Iohn Barclay* a learned Catholike hath most clearely shewed the said confutation to be very vnsound, to whom as yet no *Reply* hath been made, and yet his booke was printed at *Paris* by the Kings Printer three yeeres since; and also the *Bishop of Rochester*, a learned Protestant, hath out of Catholike grounds conuinced D. *Schulckenius* his brag, *of the cleare and sound confuting of* D. *Barclay*, to be but vaine. wherefore let Card: *Bellarmine* first make a cleare and sound *Reply* to the aforesaid Answers, and then he may haue some cause to boast, that he hath *clearely and soundly confuted* D. *Barclay*. In the meane time it can not be denyed, but that notwithstanding all the clamours of our *Aduersaries*, this doctrine, which doth now so

R   vehe-

f *Part.*1.*cap.*2. *num:* 2.

vehemently maintaine the *Popes* power to depose Princes is, and hath euer been impugned by vertuous and learned Catholikes.

Chap. 5. *Wherein the authorities of* Mr George Blackwell, *and of many other English Priests are at large debated.*

a Cap. 3. sec. 3. num. 9.

1. THe *first* teſtimonie, which I brought in my *Theologicall Diſputation*[a], (to which *D. Schulckenius* doth not anſwer) was of Mr. *George Blackwell* a vertuous and learned Catholike Prieſt, and once the Archipræsbyter of the Engliſh Seminarie Prieſts, who maintayned euen vntill death (for not halfe a quarter of an howre before hee dyed he confirmed the ſame) the oath to be lawfull, and that the *Pope* hath not power to depose Princes. to which alſo (beſides Mr. *William Warmington in his moderate defence of the Oath,* Mr. *Iohn Barclay* in his booke againſt Card: *Bellarmine* in defence of his Father, printed at Paris by the Kings Printer; and Mr. *William Barret* in his booke *de Iure Regio,* and many other learned Catholikes of this Kingdome both Prieſts and Lay-men, whoſe names for iuſt cauſes I forbare to ſet downe, for that they had not ſhewed themſelues by publike writings) I added the teſtimonie of thoſe *thirteene Reuerend and learned Engliſh Prieſts* (with whom twice thirtie others would haue ioyned, if their proteſtation had not been made ſo ſuddenly) who, *to giue aſſurance of their loyaltie to the late Queene Elizabeth,* did by a publike inſtrument, written in parchment, *profeſſe, and made it knowne to all the Chriſtian world, that Shee,* being at that time excommunicated by name, and depriued by the ſentence of *Pope Pius* the fifth, of hir Regall power and authoritie) *had* neuertheles *as full authoritie, power, and Soueraigntie ouer them,*

and

and ouer all the Subiects of the Realme, as any hir High-
neſſe Predeceſſours euer had, And that notwithſtanding
any authoritie , or any Excommunication whatſoeuer, ei-
ther denounced, or to be denounced by the Pope againſt
hir Maieſtie , or any borne within hir Maieſties Domi-
nions, which would not forſake the defence of Hir, and Hir
Dominions , they thought themſelues not onely bound in
conſcience not to obey this, or any ſuch like Cenſure , but
alſo did promiſe to yeeld vnto hir Maieſtie all obedience in
temporals.

   2   Now it is euident, that this their proteſtation,
which I did at large ſet downe in my *Appendix* to
Suarez [b], can no way be iuſtified, but vpon ſuppoſall,   b *Part.2.ſec.1.*
that the *Pope* had no authoritie to depoſe the *Queene.*
For if hee had authoritie to depoſe Hir, Shee being
then by the *Popes* ſentence depriued of all hir Regall
authoritie, power, and Soueraigntie, could not haue,
as they profeſſed, *as full authoritie, power, and Soue-*
raigntie ouer thē, and all the Subiects of the Realme, as any
of hir Predeceſſours euer had before : Neither alſo could
they (although Shee had not been then depoſed)
lawfully *promiſe,* as out of *Suarez* I will convince be-   c *Num: 7.8.*
neath [c], *that notwithſtanding any authoritie, or any Ex-*
communication whatſoeuer, either denounced, or to be de-
nounced againſt hir Maieſtie, or any borne within hir Ma-
ieſties Dominions , they would neuertheleſſe yeeld vnto
hir Maieſtie all obedience in temporalls, thinking them-
ſelues bound in conſcience not to obey this, or any ſuch like
Cenſure, vnleſſe they did ſuppoſe, that the *Pope* had
no power to depoſe hir *Maieſtie ,* or to abſolue hir
Subiects from their obedience.

   3   And if perchance any of thoſe Prieſts ſhould
now be of opinion , that the *Pope* hath power to depoſe Princes, and to excuſe his former proteſtation,
ſhould anſwer , that hee onely intended to acknowledge hir *Maieſtie* to be at that time *Queene ,* and to
reigne *de facto,* but not *de iure* (beſides that he ſhould

R 2   ſhew

shew himselfe to be an egregious dissembler, equiuo-
catour, and deluder both of hir *Maiestie*, and also of
his *Holmesse*, and should therefore deserue to be greatly punished, both for deluding the State in a matter
of so great weight, and also for bringing Catholike
Religion in obloquie among Protestants by such de-
testable dissimulation, not to call it flat lying and co-
soning, which ought to be abhorred of all men, but
especially Catholike Priests, who both by their words
and deeds ought to be a patterne to others of Christian sinceritie) this Answer can not stand with the
words which he protested.

4   For *first* marke the *Preamble* to their *Protesta-*
tion, which clearely confuteth the aforesaid answere.
Whereas (say they) *it hath pleased our dread Soueraigne*
Lady to take some notice of the faith and loyaltie of vs,
her naturall borne Subiects Secular Priests (as it appea-
reth in the late Proclamation) and of her Prince-like cle-
mencie, hath giuen a sufficient earnest of some mercifull
fauour toward vs (being all subiect by the lawes of the
Realme to death by our returne into the Country after our
taking the Order of Priesthood since the first yeere of hir
Maiesties reigne) and onely demandeth of vs a true pro-
fession of our Allegiance, thereby to be assured of our fide-
litie to hir Maiesties Person, Crowne, Estate, and dignitie,
Wee, whose names are vnderwritten, in most humble wise
prostrate at hir Maiesties feete, doe acknowledge our
selues infinitely bound vnto hir Maiestie therefore, and are
most willing to giue such assurance, and satisfaction in this
point, as any Catholike Priests can, or ought to giue vnto
their Soueraignes.   First therefore we acknowledge the
Queenes Maiestie to haue as full authoritie, power, and
Soueraigntie ouer vs, and ouer all the Subiects of the
Realme, as any hir Highnesse Predecessors euer had; and
further we protest &c.

5   Now were it not an intollerable deluding and
mockerie, for any of those Priests (this *Preamble* considered)

(idered) to affirme, that by the aforesaid words, hee did onely intend to acknowledge her *Maiesty* to bee *Queene,* and to raigne *de facto,* but not *de iure*? was this the notice, that her *Maiesty* tooke of the faith of Secular Priests, rather then of Iesuites? and did her *Maiesty* by those words (*and onely demandeth of vs a true profession of our Allegeance, thereby to bee assured of our fidelitie to her* Maiesties *person, Crowne, Estate and Dignitie*) demand of them, that thay should acknowledge her to be *Queene* onely *de facto,* but not *de iure*? And can Catholike Priests of other Countries giue to their Soueraignes no other assurance of their loyalty, then onely to acknowledge them to bee their *Kings,* and to raigne ouer them *de facto,* but not *de iure,* as these Priests did *acknowledge themselues to bee most willing to giue such assurance and satisfaction in this point vnto her* Maiesty, *as any Catholike Priests can or ought to giue vnto their Soueraignes*? No man could make doubt, but that shee was *Queene,* and did raigne *de facto,* and so much the whole Christian world, and her sworne enemies could not but acknowledge. So that, according to this shamelesse answer, those Priests did giue no other assurance of their loyaltie to *Queene Elizabeth,* then any man might giue to a knowen and manifest vsurper, and by those words *to haue as full authoritie, power and Soueraignty as any her Predecessours euer had*) did acknowledge her to haue no other power and authoritie, then any knowen vsurper hath, and which her knowen enemies, and who accounted her no lawfull *Queene,* would also acknowledge her to haue, that is to be *Queene,* and to raigne *de facto,* but not *de iure.*

6. *Secondly,* although one may truely acknowledge an vsurper to be *King,* and to raigne *de facto,* for that this doth onely imply an act, fact, or possession, which may bee without any right at all, yet no man can truely acknowledge, that an vsurper, or who is

R 3   King

King *de facto* onely, and not *de iure*, hath authority, which doth import a rightfull and lawfull power, to raigne, and much lesse, to haue *as full authoritie and power*, as euer any his Predecessours euer had, who were Kings, and raigned not onely *de facto* but also *de iure*, or, which is all one, did both actually raigne, and also had *full power and authority* to raigne.

5 *Thirdly*, not onely the aforesayd acknowledgement, that her Maieftie, being at that time depriued by the Pope, had neuerthelesse *as full power and authoritie*, as any her Predecessours euer had before, doth necessarily suppose, that the Pope had no authoritie to depriue her, but also, although shee had not beene at that time depriued by the Pope, the other clause of their protestation, which contained a promise to obey her in all temporal causes, and to defend her &c. accounting it their dutie so to doe, *notwithstanding any authoritie, or any Excommunication whatsoeuer denounced or to be denounced against her Maieftie, or euerie one borne within her Maiefties Dominions that would not forsake the aforesayd defence of her Maieftie &c. thinking themselues not bound in conscience to obey this or any such like Censure*, doth necessarily suppose and imply the same, to wit, that the Pope had no authoritie to depose her, which Fa. *Suarez* arguing against the like clause contained in the new Oath of Allegeance doth most cleerely conuince, whose argument therfore I will set downe word by word, only turning his speech to the Priefts, which he applieth to the Kings Maieftie.

d *In Defenf.*
*lib.*6.*cap.*3.

8. " For to take away all manner of euasion, saith
" *Suarez*, I demand, whether those Priefts doe vn-
" derftand, that the sentence of the Pope deposing
" a baptized Queene for crimes may be iuft, or they
" beleeue that it is alwaies vniuft. The firft they will
" not in my opinion affirme, for otherwise they
" should promise a most wicked thing, to wit, not to
                       " obey

" obey a iuſt ſentence, which implieth in it a iuſt
" command. For if the ſentence bee iuſt, the com-
" mand alſo, which enioyneth ſubiects to obſerue it,
" muſt alſo be iuſt, ſeeing that otherwiſe it cannot be
" put in execution. Alſo if the ſentence of depoſition
" denounced againſt a Queene may bee iuſt, it will
" alſo be effectuall, therefore it hath the effect of that
" puniſhment which it impoſeth. Wherefore ſeeing
" that the puniſhment impoſed by the ſentence of
" depoſition from her Kingdome, is to depriue her
" actually, or effectually of her dominion and pro-
" pertie to her Kingdome, a iuſt ſentence doth effe-
" ctually depriue her of her Kingdome, therefore it
" is againſt iuſtice and obedience due vnto the Pope
" to reſiſt that ſentence, and to defend the Queenes
" perſon againſt the execution of that ſentence, there-
" fore hee that beleeueth the firſt, and neuertheleſſe
" promiſeth this ſecond, doth promiſe a thing cleerly
" vniuſt and wicked.

9 " And beſides it implieth a contradiction to be
" willing to yeeld obedience and allegeance, as thin-
" king thy ſelfe bound ſo to doe. to one whom thou
" knoweſt to be by a iuſt declaration and ſentence ef-
" fectually depoſed from her Kingdome. As if the
" Pope himſelfe ſhould exact of Chriſtians a promiſe,
" that notwithſtanding any ſentence or declaration
" of depoſing him for any crime euen for hereſie de-
" nounced by whatſoeuer generall Councell, they
" will defend him in his See, and will yeelde him the
" ſame obedience and allegeance, their promiſe were
" wicked, for that were a wicked thing, and againſt
" the Church & Faith. Such therfore is the promiſe
" of thoſe Prieſts, if the aforeſaid ſentence againſt the
" Queene bee ſuppoſed to bee iuſt. This therefore
" thoſe Prieſts without doubt will not admit, neither
" alſo are they, as I thinke, ſo inconſiderate of their
" affaires, that if they grant the Popes ſentence de-
                                        " nounced

" denounced againſt a *Queene* may be iuſt, neuerthe-
" leſſe they will deny that againſt the *Queene* of En-
" gland it may haue the ſame iuſtice. For what grea-
" ter immunitie or innocencie can they alledge in the
" *Queene* of England, then in other Princes, who
" haue beene rebells to the Romane Church, or for-
" ſakers and impugners of the faith. Or although
" they do not acknowledge, that the *Queene* for that
" time had not committed any thing worthy of de-
" poſition, how doe they know, that for the time to
" come ſhe cannot ? and yet their promiſe is abſolute,
" *notwithſtanding any authoritie , or any ſentence of Ex-*
" *communication denounced or to be denounced againſt the*
" Queene, *or euery* one *borne within her* Maieſties *Do-*
" *minions &c.* Wherefore there is no doubt, but that
" the ground of this promiſe and profeſſion is, that
" ſuch a ſentence cannot bee iuſt. Wherefore from
" hence we euidently conclude, that thoſe Prieſts by
" the aforeſaid words do profeſſe, that the ſentence of
" depoſition againſt the *Queene* can neither be valid
" nor iuſt. For in very deede this they doe profeſſe,
" when they promiſe not to obey, nor to obſerue ſuch
" a ſentence.

10. Whereupon we do moreouer conclude, that
" thoſe Prieſts doe profeſſe , that the Pope hath not
" power to denounce ſuch a ſentence, ſeeing that for
" no other cauſe they doe beleiue the ſentence to be
" vniuſt, but for that it is giuen without power and
" Iuriſdiction in the *Pope* to depoſe a *Queene.* Nei-
" ther can thoſe Prieſts alledge in ſuch a ſentence any
" other cauſe of iniuſtice , which is perpetuall, and
" may be a ground of this part of their profeſſion.
" for their profeſſion doth not ſpeake of a ſentence al-
" readie denounced, but abſolutely of a ſentence *de-*
" *nounced* or to be *denounced* againſt the *Queene* : ther-
" fore it doth comprehend euery ſentence , whether
" it bee giuen the partie being heard, or not heard,
" whether

" whether for difagreement in religion, or for any o-
" ther crime, or caufe whatfoeuer. Wherefore the in-
" iuftice which thofe Priefts do fuppofe to bee in that
" fentence and wherupon they ground their profeffi-
" on is no other, but for that they beleeue, that it can-
" not proceede from a lawfull power and Iurifdicti-
" on. And therefore I conclude that they profeffe;
" that the *Pope* hath not power and Iurifdiction to
" giue a fentence of depofition againft the *Queene* for
any caufe. Thus argueth Father *Suarez.* So that it is
euident, that thofe *thirteene reuerend Priefts* muft of
neceffitie fuppofe, if they will haue their proteftation
and promife to be iuft and lawfull, that the Pope hath
no power to depriue Princes of their Regall right and
authoritie.

   11. And by this fift teftimonie it is alfo apparant,
that not only M. *Doctour Barclay*, and *Widdrington,*
as Card. *Bellarmine* in his booke againft *Barclay*, and
now in his *Sculckenius* againft me, vntruely affirmeth,
but many other Englifh Catholikes (to omit thofe o-
ther learned *Catholikes* of other *Countries*, of whom I
haue fpoken before, and the *Kingdome* and *State* of
France, of which I will fpeake beneath) g are of opinion, that the Pope hath no authoritie to depriue Soueraigne Princes of their temporall Kingdomes and
dominions. Which alfo may moreouer be confirmed by the *petition,* which fome *Englifh Catholikes* did
exhibite to *Queene Elizabeth* deceafed after the difco-
uerie of *Parries* confpiracie, wherein thefe expreffe
wordes are contained : *In confideration of all which neceffarie points, we doe proteft before the true liuing God,
that all and euery Prieft and Priefts, who haue at any time
conuerfed with vs, haue recognized your* Maieftie *their
vndoubted and lawfull Queene tam de iure, quam de facto.*
who neuerthele ffe was at that time and long before
depriued of her Princely power, right and dignitie by
the publike fentence of *Pope Pius* the fift.

g In the next Chapter.

                 S   12. And

12. And to these authorities we may add the testimonies set downe in the end of M^r. *Blackwells* Latine examination, of *Bishop Watson, Abbot Fernam, Doctor, Cole, Iohn Harpesfield,* and *Nicolas Harpesfield*) all of them very famous and learned Catholikes) who vpon the publishing of the Bull of *Pius Quintus* against *Queene Elizabeth,* being examined by the Magistrate in the yeare 1578. and demanded, *whether notwithstanding the aforesaid Bull, or any other sentence of the* Pope *denounced or hereafter to be denounced against the said* Queene, *they did thinke, that shee was their true and lawfull* Queene, *and that they, and all other English and Irish men did as Subiects owe to her* Maiesty *obedience, faith, and loyaltie, as to their lawfull and true Queene, and Soueraigne Prince,* they did all with vniforme consent acknowledge, and confesse, *that notwithstanding the aforesaid Bull, or any other sentence or declaration of the* Pope *already denounced, or hereafter to be denounced against the said* Queene, *she was their true, and lawfull Queene, and that they did owe vnto her obedience and allegiance as to their lawfull Prince.* And *Nicholas Harpesfield* answered more plainly and distinctly, *that notwithstanding the aforesaid Bull, sentence and declaration of the* Pope, *or any other already denounced, or hereafter to be denounced by the* Popes *authority, he did acknowledge her to be his true* Queene, *and was to be obeyed, as a true* Queene, *and had as ample and full Regall authoritie in all ciuill and temporall causes, as either other Princes haue, or her most noble Progenitours euer had.* The like also M. *Edward Rishton,* and M. *Henry Orton* both learned Priests did answere.

13. But M. *Iames Bosgraue* a learned Iesuite in his declaration made in the yeare 1582. did more plainly and fully set downe his opinion concerning the power it selfe to depose, *that he did thinke and that before God, that the* Pope *hath no authoritie, neither* de facto, *nor* de iure, *to discharge the Subiects of the*
Queenes

Queenes Maieſtie, *or of any other Chriſtian Prince of their allegiance for any cauſe whatſoeuer, and that he was inwardly perſwaded, in his conſcience, that the* Queenes Maieſtie *both is his lawfull* Queene, *and is alſo ſo to be accounted, notwithſtanding any Bull or ſentence, which the* Pope *hath giuen, ſhall giue, or may hereafter giue, and that he is readie to teſtifie this by Oath, if neede require.*

Mr. *Iohn Hart* alſo a learned Ieſuite in his conference with M. *Rainolds* in the tower in the yeare 1584. and in his Epiſtle to the indifferent Reader did anſwere as effectually : *As for that, ſaith he, which* M. Rainolds *affirmeth in one place,* h *that I haue tould him, that my opinion is, the* Pope *may not depoſe Princes, indeede I tould him ſo much. And in truth I thinke, that although the ſpirituall power be more excellent and worthy then the temporall, yet they are both of God, neither doth the one depend on the other. Whereupon I gather as a certaine concluſion, that the opinion of them, who hold the* Pope *to be a temporall Lord ouer Kings and Princes, is vnreaſonable, and vnprobable altogether. For he hath not to meddle with them or theirs ciuilly, much.leſſe to depoſe them, or giue away their Kingdomes : that is no part of his commiſſion. Hee hath in my iudgement the Fatherhood of the Church, not a Princehood of the world :* Chriſt *himſelfe taking no ſuch title vpon him, nor giuing it to* Peter, *or any other of his diſciples. And that is it which I meant to defend in him, and no other ſoueraigntie.*

h *Chap.* 7. *diuiſ.* 7.

14 Mr. *Camden* alſo relateth i, that when *Fa: Campian,* and diuers other Prieſts were demanded by the Magiſtrate, *whether by the authoritie of the Bull of Pius Quintus hir Maieſties Subiects were abſolued from their oath of allegiance in ſuch ſort, that they might take armes againſt hir Maieſtie? whether they did thinke hir to be a lawfull Queene? whether they would ſubſcribe to the opinion of* D. Sanders, *and* Briſtow *touching the authoritie of that Bull? whether if the Pope ſhould make warre againſt the Queene, they would take his or hir*

i *In Annalibus rerum Anglic. &c. pag.* 327. *ad ann.* 1581.

k *tergiuerſando*

*part? Some anſwered ſo ambiguouſly, ſome ſo headily,
others by wrangling* k, *or by ſilence did ſhift off the queſtions
ſo that diuers plaine dealing Catholikes began to ſuſpect,
that they harboured ſome treachery :* and one Iames
Biſhop *a man deuoted to the Pope of Rome did write a-
gainſt theſe men, and did ſoundly ſhew, that Conſtitution,
which is obtruded in the name of the Councell of Lateran,*
(whereon all the authoritie to abſolue Subiects from
their Allegiance, and to depoſe Princes is grounded)
was no other then a decree of Pope Innocent *the third,
and neuer receiued in England : yea and that Councell
to be none at all, nor any thing there decreed at all by the
Fathers.* By all which it is euident, that few Engliſh
Catholikes were of opinion, that the Pope hath
power to depoſe Soueraigne Princes, vntill theſe later
Ieſuites, and ſuch as adhered to their opinions, began
to defend ſo eagerly the *Bull of Pius Quintus*, and to
maintaine with ſuch vehemencie his aforeſaid authoritie to depoſe Princes, as a point of faith, which doctrine how preiudiciall it hath been, and is at this preſent to Catholikes, and Catholike Religion, I leaue,
Catholike Reader, to thy prudent conſideration.

Chap. 6. *Wherein the authoritie of the* King- dom, *and* State *of* France *is at large diſcuſſed.*

a *Cap.3. ſec.3.
num: 12.*
b *Num: 30.
& ſeq.*

1. THe ſixt and laſt teſtimonie which I brought
in my *Theologicall Diſputation* a, and alſo in
my *Apologie* b, and which onely, if there were no o-
ther, would ſuffice to proue that the doctrine for the
Popes power to depoſe Princes is not a *point of faith*,
was taken from the authoritie of the moſt noble, and
moſt Chriſtian Kingdom and State of France, which
euer held the contraie to be the more true, ſound,
and aſſured doctrine. And firſt to omit the authoritie

ritie of *Iacobus Almaine*, a famous Schoole-Diuine of Paris, whereof I spake before, who affirmed, that *very many*, or *most Doctors were of opinion, that the Pope hath not by the institution of Christ authoritie to inflict temporall punishments, no, nor so much as to imprison*, much lesse to depriue Princes of their Kingdomes or liues) in a generall Parliament, or assembly of all the States of France held at Paris in the yeare 1593. the *Cardinall de Pelleue*, and other Prelates, who then were present, tooke exceptions against certaine decrees of the Councell of Trent, which *Laurentius Bochellus* relateth, among which that of the 25. session, chap:19. wherein the Councell forbiddeth Kings to permit single combats, was one. *The Councell of Trent*, say they, *doth excommunicate and depriue a King of the Cittie or place, wherein he permitteth to fight a single combate. This article is against the authoritie of the King, who cannot be depriued of his temporall Dominion, in regard whereof he acknowledgeth no Superiour at all.*

2 Secondly, *Petrus Pithæus, a man*, as Posseuine the Iesuite relateth, *truly learned, and a diligent searcher of antiquitie*, in his booke, *of the liberties of the Church of France*, printed at *Paris* by authoritie of the *Parliament* in the yeare 1594, doth out of a generall maxime, *which France*, as he saith, *hath euer approued as certaine*, deduce this particular position: *That the Pope can not giue as a prey the Kingdome of France, nor any thing appertayning thereunto, neither that he can depriue the King thereof, nor in any other manner dispose thereof. And notwithstanding any admonitions, Excommunications, or Interdicts, which by the Pope may be made, yet the subiects are bound to yeeld obedience due to his Maiestie for temporalls, neither therein can they be dispenced, or absolued by the Pope.*

3 Mark now, *good Reader*, what silly shifts *D. Schulckenius* hath found out to repell the aforesaid authorities. To the first hee answereth, [c] *that it is not credible,*

c *Pag.* 121. *ad num:* 31.

S 3

credible, that the Cardinall of Pelleue, and the other Prelates should affirme that, which Bochellus relateth. For the Councell of Trent, saith he, doth not decree, that Princes are absolutely depriued of the Cittie and place, wherein they shall permit single combat, but with a restriction, that they are depriued of the Cittie, fort, or place, which they hold of the Church, or which they hold in fee farme. Therfore the Councell doth not speake of the King of France, or other absolute Kings, vnlesse Bochellus will haue the Kingdome of France to be giuen to the Kings by the Church, or that the King is not a direct Lord, but a feudarie. Therefore it had been great imprudence and malignitie, to depraue so spitefully the words of the sacred Councell, as Bochellus hath depraued, which ought not to be presumed of the Cardinall of Pelleue, and of the other Prelates.

4   But truly it is not credible, that *Bochellus* durst presume to commit so great, and publike a forgerie, as to falsifie the Records of the highest Court of *Parliament*, and assembly of the three States of the Land, especially printing his booke at *Paris*, where without doubt he should not want men both to finde out easily, and also to punish seuerely so great a forgerie, and withall affirming, that those articles were extracted out of the Register of the assembly held at *Paris* in the yeare 1593, and putting downe such particular circumstances, as naming not only the day of the yeare, but also of the moneth, to wit, *the 19. of Aprill, when the Lord* Abbot *of* Orbais *did on the behalfe of the Lord* Cardinall *of* Pelleue *bring a coppie of them &c.* and setting downe all the articles in *French*, whereas the maine corps of his booke was *Latin.*

5   Neither is the reason, which *D. Schulckenius* bringeth, to make this testimonie seeme incredible, of any great moment. For *first* it is vntrue, which he saith, *that the Councell did not speake of the King of France, and other absolute Kings.* The words of the
Councell

Councell are cleare to the contrarie. *The Emperour,* ſaith the Councell, *Kings, Dukes, Princes, Marqueſſes, Earles, and temporall Lords by what other name ſoeuer they be called, who ſhall grant a place for ſingle combat in their Countries among Chriſtians, let them be excommunicated, and vnderſtood depriued of the Iuriſdiction and Dominion of the Cittie, fort, or place, which they hold from the Church, wherein, or whereat they ſhall permit ſingle combat, and if they be held in fee farme, let them forthwith be taken for the direct Lords: but they that ſhall fight the combat, and they that are called their Patrimi, let them incurre* ipſo facto *the puniſhment of Excommunication, and forfeiture of all their goods &c.* So that it is plaine, that the *Councell* ſpeaketh of *Emperours,* and of other abſolute *Kings* and *Princes.*

6. *Secondly,* although it bee cleere, that thoſe words [*let them bee depriued of the Citty, Fort, or place which they hold from the Church*] beſpoken with a reſtriction and limitation onely to thoſe Citties, Forts, or places, which bee held from the Church, yet the words following [*and if they be held in fee farme, let them foorthwith be taken for the direct Lords*] may abſolutely, and without the aforeſaid reſtriction bee vnderſtood of thoſe Citties, Forts or places, which be held in fee farme either from the Church, or from ſome other Soueraigne Prince, as from the direct Lord of them. So likewiſe the puniſhment of the *confiſcation* of goods may be vnderſtood as well without the territories of the Church, as within the *Popes* dominions, and may alſo bee vnderſtood to comprehend abſolute Princes, if perchance they ſhould either bee Patrimi, or fight themſelues in ſingle combat. And ſo by conſequence it might bee inferred, that, if the *Councell* hath authoritie to depriue abſolute Kings of thoſe dominions, which thy hold in fee farme from other abſolute Princes, or to confiſcate their goods, or elſe the goods of their ſubiects without their con-

sent, the Councell also hath authoritie to depriue for the same cause absolute Princes of their Citties, Forts and places, whereof they are absolute Lords. And so the *Cardinall* of *Pelleue,* and other Prelates of *France* might vnderstand the *Councell* in that sense, as also D. *Weston* in his Sanctuarie [d] doth vnderstand them, and thereupon vrgeth those words of the *Councell* of *Trent* as a principall argument to prooue, that the doctrine for the Popes power to depose Princes is a poynt of faith, and decreed by the *Councell* of *Trent,* who little thought, that he should therefore haue beene censured of *imprudencie* and *malignitie,* as D. *Schulckenius* censureth the *Prelates and Parliament* of *France,* if they should vnderstand in that manner the *Councell* of *Trent,* as *Bochellus* relateth, and D. *Weston* expoundeth it.

6. To the second testimony of *Petrus Pithæus,* D. *Schulckenius* answereth in as shuffling a manner. First, *I answer,* saith he, [e] *that* Antonie Posseuine *commendeth* Petrus Pithæus *for a learned man, and a diligent searcher of antiquity, and relateth all his workes, and also his death, and yet he maketh no mention of this booke, and I confesse I neuer saw it.* But although neither *Posseuine,* nor D. *Schulckenius* euer saw that booke, yet I haue seene it, and read it, and it was printed at *Paris* by the authoritie of the *Parliament* in the yeere 1594. and it hath those maximes and positions which I related in my *Apologie.* And therefore we haue the testimony of a *very learned Catholike, and a diligent searcher of antiquitie,* by *Posseuines* confession, that *France hath euer held this position for vndoubted, that the* Pope *hath no authoritie to depriue the* King *of* France *of his Kingdome, and that notwithstanding any admonitions, Excommunications &c. his subiects are bound to obey him in temporals.*

7. His second answer is, *that whosoeuer is the Authour of that booke, it is cleerely false, that France hath al-*

waies

d *q.* 28.

e *Pag.* 124.

waies approoued that doctrine for certaine. Marke now
the reaſons, which D. *Schulckenius* bringeth to conuince this *very learned man, and diligent ſearcher of antiquity of manifeſt falſhood.* For *firſt it is repugnant,* ſaith
he, *to the Councell of Claramont, wherein* Philip *the firſt
was excommunicated and depriued of his Regall Honour
and Crowne by* Pope Vrbanus *the ſecond,whereof ſee* Iuo
Carnotenſis *in his* 2 8. *epiſtle to Vrbanus.* But it is moſt
cleerely falſe, that *Philip* was in that *Councell* depriued
of his Regall Honour and Crowne, as both I[f], and
M[r]. *Iohn Barclay*[g] haue cleerely ſhewed heeretofore,
for that no Hiſtoriographer writeth, that he was depoſed in that Councell, but at the moſt onely excommunicated, for that hee had forſaken his lawfull
wife *Berta,* and had married *Bertrada,* who was alſo
wife to another man. For *Sigebert, Aimonius, Mat-
thew Paris, Nauclerus, Paulus Æmilius, Robertus Ga-
guinus, Papirius Maſſonius,* the *Authour of the frag-
ment of the hiſtorie of France publiſhed by* Petrus Pithæus
with Glaber, *Genebrard,* and *Vignerius* doe relate that
Philip was excommunicated by *Vrbanus,* and as ſome
of them ſay, in the Councell of *Claramont,* but none
of them make mention, that hee was depoſed or depriued of his Royall honour and Crowne.

   8. Neither can it any way be prooued out of *Iuo,*
that *Philip* was depriued by *Pope Vrbanus* of his *Royall
Honour and Crowne,* for that *Iuo* at that very time,
when *Philip* was excommunicated, did in expreſſe
words account him his *Lord* and *King,* and offered
him *his faithfull ſeruice, as to his Lord and King :* This
onely can be gathered out of *Iuo,* that *King Philip* was
deſirous to honour his new *Queene,* or rather Con-
cubine *Bertrada,* by putting the Royall Crowne or
Diademe on both their heads in a publike ſolemnity,
which for that it was a religious ceremony, and vſually done in the Church at the time of Maſſe, by the
Primate of the Land, and *Philip* was at that time ex-
               T   commu-

f *In Prefat. ad
Reſp. Apol. nu,
36. & ſeq.*
g *In Prolegom.
num.* 7 5.

communicated and depriued of all holy rites and ceremonies of the Church, *Pope Vrbanus* forbad all the Bithops of France to crowne in that fort the *King*, and his new fuppofed Queene, for *Philip himfelfe* was long before crowned *King* of France, and this folemnitie, which *Pope Vrbanus* forbade, or the want thereof did not giue or take away from *King Philip* any iot of his *Royall power and authoritie.*

9. Secondly, *it is repugnant,* faith D. *Schulckenius, to the examples of Gregorie the great, of Zachary, and of other Popes.* But to thofe examples both I haue anfwered at large in my Apology,[h] and alfo fince that M[r]. *Iohn Barclay*[1], to whom as yet r o *Reply* hath beene made, and firft, that thofe words of S. *Gregorie,* [k] *honore fuo priuetur,* let him be depriued, or I *would to God he may be depriued of his honour* (for both wayes it may be Englifhed, as that the verbe *priuetur* may be of the Imperatiue, or of the Optatiue moode) doe not contain a iuridicall fentence, command or decree, as likewife neither thofe words, which are fpoken in the like manner by S. *Gregory, & cum Iuda traditore in inferno damnetur, and let him be damned in hell,* or, *I wifh he may be damned in hell with Iudas the traitour,* but onely either a zealous imprecation [l] againft them, who fhould infringe his priuiledge, if they did not repent, or elfe a declaration, that they were worthie for their contempt, to bee depriued of their honour, and to bee condemned to hell fire with *Iudas* the traitour : from whence it cannot be inferred, that the Pope hath authoritie to depriue by a iuridical fentence thofe Kings who infringe his priuiledge of their Regall Honour, or to condemne them by a iuridicall fentence to hell fire.

10. So likewife to that example of *Pope Zacharie* I anfwered, [m] that he did not by any iuridicall fentence of depriuation depriue *Childerike* of his Kingdome, and create *Pipin* King, but onely gaue his aduife, counfell,

Margin notes

h *Num.* 382. *& feq. & num.* 404. *& feq.*
i *Ca.*40. *& 42.*
k *Lib.*2. *epift. poft.epift.* 38.

l *See* Baronius *ad annum* 1097.*num* 51.

m *Num.*404. *& feq.*

counſell, and conſent, or at the moſt command to the *Peeres* of *France*, that they ought, or might lawfully (the circumſtances which they propounded to *Zacharie* being conſidered) depriue *Childerike* of his kingdome, and create *Pipin* king : but this argueth no authoritie in the *Pope* to depoſe Princes by any iuridicall ſentence of depriuation, but at the moſt an authority in the common wealth to depoſe their *King* in ſome caſes of great moment, which is not the queſtion, which we haue now in hand. And therefore the *Gloſſe* [n] with other graue and learned Authours cited by me in my *Apologie* [o] doe expound thoſe wordes of *Pope Gregorie* the ſeuenth: *Zacharie depoſed Childerik*, thus, *Zacharie gaue his aduiſe and conſent to thoſe who depoſed him* : and thoſe words, which ſome *Chronicles* haue, *Childerike was depoſed by the authoritie of Pope Zacharie*, *Lupolbus Bambergenſis*, *Ioannes Pariſienſis*, and *Michael Coccineus* doe expound in the like maner, that *Childerike* was depoſed by the *authoritie* of *Pope Zacharie* not *depoſing Childerike*, *and creating Pipin King*, but only *declaring, that he might be lawfully depoſed by the Peeres of France*, whereof they were in ſome doubt, for that they had ſworne to him allegiance, and therefore they craued the opinion, and aduiſe of Pope *Zacharie* to be reſolued by him of that doubt, for that the *Vniuerſitie* of *Paris* did not flouriſh at that time, ſaith *Ioannes Maior*, [p] and ſo *Pipin* was annointed *King* by the election of the *Barons*, ſaith *Ioannes Pariſienſis*, and by the *authoritie* of the *Pope declaring the doubt of the Barons, which alſo they might haue done without the* Popes *conſent vpon a reaſonable cauſe.*

11. But becauſe *Card. Bellarmine* will neuer ceaſe to inculcate ſtill the ſame authorities, which by mee, and others haue beene ſo often anſwered, I thinke it not amiſſe to add ſomething here concerning that, which I did in generall words inſinuate in my *Apologie*, [q] and is more expreſly touched by *Nicholas Vinge-rius*

---

n *In* cap. *Alius* 15. q. 6.
o *Num.* 404. & ſeq.

p *Jn* 4.diſt.24. q. 3. circa finē. de poteſt. Regia & Papal.c. 15.

q *Num.* 382 ·

rius in his *Hiſtorie* of the *Church of France*, and more particularly vrged by the *Biſhop of Rocheſter* in his anſwere to *Card. Bellarmines Treatiſe* againſt *Barclay*; to wit, that the priueledge which is ſaid to be granted by *S. Gregorie* to the *Monaſterie* of *S. Medard*, and which is ſo greatly vrged by *Card. Bellarmine*, and others, is not ſo *authenticall*, as Card. *Bellarmine*, and others ſuppoſe it to be, which may be proued by many probable coniectures; as by the ſtile, and phraſe, which is not agreeable to S. *Gregories*, and alſo by the date of the yeare of our Lord, which is not agreeable to the manner of dating of thoſe daies, but *principally* by the perſons, who are ſubſcribed for witneſſes to that priueledge. For S. *Auſtin* Biſhop of *Canterbury*, and *Mellitus* Biſhop of *London*, and *Theodorike* King of France, are ſubſcribed for witneſſes to that priueledge, and yet neither S. *Auſtin*, nor *Mellitus*, were *Biſhops*, nor *Theodorike* King at that time, which Card. *Baronius* alſo doth in expreſſe words affirmer. *But I confeſſe,* ſaith he, *that the ſubſcriptions of the* Biſhops, *and of* Theodorike *King of France do not agree to theſe times: for many* Biſhops, *who are found ſubſcribed, are knowne to be created ſome certaine yeares after*, *as to ſpeake nothing of the reſt*, Auguſtin *Biſhop of* Canterbury, *and* Mellitus *of* London, *who, as it is manifeſt*, *were neither at this time* Biſhops, *nor gone for* England; *neither at this time did* Theodorike *reigne in* France, *but* Childebert, *and* Gunthramn. *Wherefore my opinion is*, *that the ſubſcription was afterwards adioyned.* Thus *Baronius.* But conſidering that *Theodorike* not only in the *ſubſcription*, but alſo in the *priueledge* it ſelfe is named King, at whoſe inſtance S. *Gregorie* ſaith he granted that priueledge, *Baronius* might with the ſame reaſon haue affirmed, that not only the *ſubſcription*, but alſo the *priueledge* it ſelfe was afterwards made, and adioyned to S. *Gregories* Epiſtles, which without doubt *Baronius* would quickly haue acknowledged, if it had not beene for thoſe

r *Ad annum* 893. *num.* 85.

thoſe words *honore ſuo priuetur*, which hee thought made greatly for the Popes power to depoſe Princes, ſeeing that vpon far weaker grounds hee ſticketh nor to deny oftentimes priueledges, and antiquities, which neuer before were called in queſtion.

12. And although Pope *Gregorie* the ſeuenth in his Epiſtle to the *Biſhop* of *Metz* doth not cite this priueledge, of S. *Gregorie* granted to the *Monaſterie* of S. *Medard* (which is no ſmall coniecture, that this priueledge was not extant in thoſe daies among the Epiſtles of S. *Gregorie*, for otherwiſe it bearing ſo great a ſhew of being *authenticall* by the *ſubſcription* of 30 Biſhops, and the *King* and *Queene* of *France*, who were witneſſes thereunto, it would by all likelihood haue beene cited by Pope *Gregorie* the ſeuenth) but an other priueledge granted to an other *Monaſterie* by S. *Gregorie* in his Epiſtle to one *Senator Abbot* [f] wherin S. *Gregorie* did not ſay *honore ſuo priuetur, let him be depriued of his honour*, but *poteſtatis, honoriſque ſui dignitate careat, let him want*, or, *I deſire he may want*, not his honour, but *the worthineſſe of his power and honour*, which words are not ſo forcible to prooue the *Popes* authoritie to depriue *Kings* of their *princely honour and power*, but at the moſt to declare them to bee vnworthy of it for ſome crime committed by them, and to be worthy alſo to be damned in hell with *Iudas* the Traitor, for that many a one may be a true *King*, and haue *princely power and honour* who is vnworthy thereof. Neuertheleſſe, (beſides that the aforeſaid words do containe no ſentence of depriuation, but onely a *curſe*, or *imprecation*, which kinde of imprecations euen containing *anathema* was frequent in the priueledges granted by Lay-men yea and vpon ſepulchres, that men ſhould be fearefull to violate them, as *Baronius* [t] relateth) alſo this priueledge mentioned in S. *Gregories* epiſtle to *Senator*, is not ſo *authenticall*, both for that it hath neither date of any yeare, or day when

[f] *Lib.* 11. *epiſt. epiſt.* 10.

[t] *Ad an.* 1097. *Num.* 51.

it was written, nor subscription of any witnesse, which
by likelihood it would haue had, if there had beene
any *authenticall* copie thereof, and also for that the
Authour of the booke intituled *de vnitate Ecclesiæ* who
is thought to be *Venericus* Bishop of *Vercellis*, and liued
in *Pope Gregorie* the seuenth his tim˙, answering that
epistle of *Pope Gregorie* the seuenth to the *Bishop* of
Metz doth bouldly affirme, that those words, *potesta-*
tis honorisque sui dignitate careat, let him want the worthi-
nesse of his power and honour, were not in those daies extant among the workes of S. *Gregorie.* Whereby the
Reader may easily perceiue, what weake demonstrations and authorities Card. *Bellarmine* doth so often
inculcate to conuince this doctrine for the *Popes*
power to depose Painces *to be a point of faith.*

13   Thirdly, *it is also repugnant,* saith D. Schulckenius, *to those most famous French writers, whom I re-*
lated before.   But although it be true, that the most
part of those seuenteene *French writers* related by
Card: Bellarmine in his booke against *Barclay,* and
now in his *Schulckenius* against me, are of opinion,
that the Pope hath power to depose Princes, this neuerthelesse may also be true, which *Petrus Pithæus*
affirmeth, to wit, *that France,* vnderstanding thereby
the *State of France, hath euer held, the the Pope hath no*
authoritie to depriue the King of France of his Kingdem.
May it not truly be said, that the *Kingdome,* and *State*
of *England* hath from the first yeere of *Queene Eli-*
zabeths reigne, euen to this present time, held, that
the Catholike Romane Religion is not the true Religion, notwithstanding that not onely *seuenteene,* but
seuenteene thousands there haue been of English
Catholikes, since the first beginning of hir reigne, till
now, who haue held the contrarie. wherefore when
Petrus Pithæus affirmed, that *France hath euer held,*
that the Pope hath no authoritie to depose their King, by
France hee did not vnderstand euery particular
French

French-man, but the *State* and *temporall Gouernours* of
the *Kingdome* of *France,* which his aſſertion is alſo
confirmed by the State and Parliament of Paris, firſt
in the cenſuring of *Card: Bellarmines* booke againſt
D. Barclay, then in burning his *Schulckenius* written
againſt me, afterwards in condemning *Suarez* booke
againſt his *Maieſties Apologie* for maintayning ſo
ſtiſly this doctrine for the Popes power to depoſe
Princes, and to diſpoſe of all their temporalls, which
they call a *ſcandalous,* and *ſeditious,* a *damnable,* and
pernicious doctrine, and now laſtly, by the decree of the
Parliament of Paris the ſecond of Ianuarie of this
preſent yeere **1615,** wherein it is ordained, that it
ſhall not bee held for *problematique* ; and alſo by the
new oath of allegiance like vnto that of ours, (but
that ours is more *ſweete,* and more *modeſt,* as the *Car-*
dinall du *Peron* ᵘ aſſirmeth) which thoſe of the lower   u *Pag.* 100.
houſe of the generall aſſembly of all the States of
France, (whom the ſame *Cardinall* du *Peron,* in his
ſpeech to them, confeſſeth to be Catholikes ˣ,) endea-   x *Pag.* 96.
uoured to haue made for a *fundamentall Law.*

14   Laſtly, *it is alſo repugnant,* ſaith D. Schulckenius, *to reaſon, it is repugnant to the principles of the Ca-*
tholike faith. For if the Subiects of the King of France
be bound to obey their King being excommunicated, and
that they can not be abſolued from this obedience by the
Pope, *it followeth that either the King of France can not*
be bound by Chriſt his Vicar with the bond of Excomuni-
cation, or that his Subiects can not be looſed from the bond
of their allegiance and obedience. *Both are repugnant to*
the words of Chriſt, who ſaid to his Vicar, whatſoeuer
thou ſhalt binde vpon earth, ſhall be bound alſo in
heauen, and whatſoeuer thou ſhalt looſe vpon earth
ſhall be looſed alſo in heauen. *Neither did* Chriſt *ex-*
cept the King *of* France, *or his Subiects, and who hath*
excepted them I can not tell. This I know, that no man
could by right except them. and whoſoeuer will not be ſub-
                                                           iect
T 4

ieÊt to the keyes of the Church, I know, and with a cleare
voice I doe pronounce, that hee will neither bee a Chri-
ſtian, nor can hee appertai e to the kingdome of Chriſt.
   15   Great words to ſmall purpoſe. For although
it be true, that Card: *Bellarmine*, *Suarez*, and ſome
few others are, or ſeeme to be of opinion, that it is
againſt reaſon, and againſt the principles of the Catholike faith, to hold, that the Pope hath no authoritie to depoſe Princes, yet it is alſo true, that other
learned Catholikes are of opinion, that it is neither a-
gainſt reaſon, nor againſt the principles of the Catholike faith to hold, that the Pope hath no ſuch authoritie. Muſt the opinion of *Card: Bellarmine*, or of
Suarez, or of any other learned Catholike, be a rule
of reaſon to all other learned Catholikes, or to bee
accounted by all Catholikes the principles of the
Catholike faith? All Catholikes doe confeſſe, that
the Pope hath authoritie to excommunicate a Chriſtian King, and that Subiects are not bound to obey
an excommunicated King in thoſe things, which the
Cenſure of Excommunication of it owne nature, and
by the inſtitution of Chriſt doth forbid ; but to abſolue Subiects from their temporall allegiance either
by vertue of Excommunication (which being a ſpirituall Cenſure hath neither of it owne nature, nor by
the inſtitution of Chriſt ſuch a temporall effect) or by
the ſentence of depriuation, this many learned Catholikes, with the State of France doe affirme not to
belong to the Popes ſpirituall authoritie to *binde*, or
looſe.
   16   True alſo it is, that all Chriſtians are ſubiect
to the keyes of the Church, but theſe keyes are ſpirituall, not temporall, of the kingdome of heauen, and
not of earthly kingdomes ; neither is any Chriſtian
excepted from that authoritie, which *Chriſt* gaue to
S. Peter by thoſe words, *whatſoeuer thou ſhalt looſe* &c.
But thoſe words are not to be vnderſtood of temporall,

rall, but onely of fpirituall bindings and loofings, as I haue often fhewed; neither did any of the ancient Fathers euer extend the *keyes* of the Church, to the abfoluing of Subiects from their temporall allegi- ance, or to the depriuing of Kings and Princes of their temporall liues, libertie, kingdomes or goods, as by fome Catholikes of thefe latter ages, contrarie to the true meaning and inftitution of Chrift, and to the vnderftanding and practife of the primitiue Church, they haue been violently wrefted. To that *whatfoeuer thou fhalt loofe* &c. *I anfwer,* faith Ioannes Parifienfis, *according to* S. Chryfoftome & Rabanus, *that by this is not vnderftood any power to be giuen but fpirituall, to wit, to abfolue from the bond of finnes. For it were foolifh to vnderftand, that by this is giuen a power to abfolue from the bond of debts,* and much leffe from that great and high debt of temporall allegiance.

16. Thefe be all the exceptions which D. *Schulc- kenius* taketh againft thofe authorities, which I broght in my *Theologicall Difputation* : Now let any indiffe- rent Reader iudge, whether he hath fufficiently an- fwered thofe authorities, or rather by cauilling and fhuffling laboured cunningly to fhift them off, and whether Mr. *Fitzherbert* might not blufh to affirme fo boldly, *that D. Schulckenius,* to whom he cunning- ly alfo, as you haue feene, remitteth his *Englifh Rea- der,* for his anfwer to thofe authorities, *hath anfwered particularly to euerie one of them, and prooued cleerely, that diuerfe of them make flat againft* Widdrington, *and many nothing at all for him (being truely vnderftood) and that fome others are worthily reiected, being either fo ab- furd, that they are eafily confuted by the circumftances of the places alledged, or elfe heretikes (as appeareth by their doctrine in other things) or knowen Schifmatikes, who li- uing in the times of the Emperours or Kings that were de- pofed, wrote partially in their fauours, of which fort neuer- theleffe there are very few, fo that of all the Authours,*

that

that Widdrington *hath scraped together ta make some shew of probabilitie in his doctrine,* hee hath no one cleere *and sufficient witnesse to iustifie the same,* which how true it is, or rather most cleerely false, I remit to the consideration of the indifferent and iudicious Reader.

.17. For the testimony of *Iohn Trithemius,* a learned and vertuous Catholike, who expressely affirmeth, *that it is a controuersie among Schoolmen, & as yet not decided by the Iudge, whether the* Pope *hath power to depose the Emperour or no,* partly hee reiecteth, partly that word *Schoolemen* hee ridiculously expoundeth to be *Historiographers, Grammarians, Poets,* as *Sigebert, Valla, Dantes,* who neuerthelesse are by *Trithemius* himselfe related to be also excellent *Diuines,* and partly to repell his testimonie he falsely, grossely, and vnaduisedly taxeth him with errours committed in his historie, and for proofe thereof he remitteth his Reader to *Posseuine,* who, as you haue seene, both in that, and also other points of historie hath shamefully erred himselfe: and neuerthelesse, that which *Trithemius* affirmeth, *Iacobus Almaine* a famous *Schoole-Diuine,* and *classicall Doctour* of *Paris,* who liued also in those daies, confirmeth to be true, whose words D. *Schulckenus* doth cunningly passe ouer without any answer at all. *Albericus,* a *Classicall Doctour* of the canon and ciuill Law, for that hee deliuereth his opinion with submission, & is ready to recal it, if it should prooue erroneous, as euery good Catholike ought to doe, he will haue to speake *mauering,* and *altogether doubtfull. Ioannes Parisiensis,* a most learned Schoole-Diuine partly he will haue to make nothing for my opinion, and yet he confesseth that *Parisiensis* is of opinion, that the Pope hath no authoritie to depriue a Prince of his Kingdome by a iuridicall senrence of depriuation, which neuerthelesse is the maine and sole point, which I contend to prooue: and partly to cleane ouerthrow his testimony he taxeth him without

out ſufficient ground of many errours, which errours neuertheleſſe although he ſhould haue maintained, doe cleerely confirme this doctrine againſt the *Popes* power to depoſe Princes. The teſtimony of Mr. D. *Barclay* a famous, learned and vertuous Catholike he no more regardeth then of an heretike. To M.*Black-well* and thoſe other Engliſh Prieſts he anſwereth nothing. The *Records* of the generall aſſembly of the *States* of *France* related by *Bochellus* with ſuch particular circumſtances, that no man can miſdoubt of them, for a friuolous reaſon hee accounteth incredible, The teſtimonie of *Petrus Pithæus,* a *very learned* Catholike, and *a diligent ſearcher of antiquity* by Poſſe-uines confeſſion, affirming that *France* hath euer held for *certaine, that the Pope hath no authoritie to depoſe their King,* alſo for friuolous reaſons hee vtterly reie-iecteth, which neuertheleſſe the late proceeding of the *Court* of *Parliament* againſt his, and ſuch like bookes hath ſufficiently confirmed. And if this manner of anſwering authorities is to bee admitted, who may not eaſily ſhift off any authorities whatſoeuer, eſpecially when they ſhall haue their trumpetters to extoll all their writings and anſwers to the skie, and to depreſſe their aduerſaries, and who ſhall ſeeme to make againſt them, whether they be liuing or dead, euen to the pit of hell, appeaching them of *hereſie, errour, ſchiſme,* and ſuch like hainous crimes?

18. Many other authorities I brought in my *Apologie,* which doe cleerely contradict Card. *Bellarmines* doctrine (which onely I tooke vpon mee to confute) whereof ſome of them doe expreſſely affirme, that the Church of Chriſt hath onely a *ſpirituall,* and not a temporall ſword; Others, that temporall Princes are in temporall affaires next vnder God, and to bee puniſhed with temporall puniſhments by God alone, and that the temporall power is independant of the ſpirituall: Others, that neither *Childerike* was depo-

ſed,

fed, nor the *Romane Empire* tranſlated from the *Græci-
ans* to the *Germans*, or *French*, by the *Popes* ſole authoritie, but by the conſent, ſuffrages, and authoritie
alſo of the people, which neuertheleſſe are principall
authorities, which by *Card. Bellarmine* and others
are brought to prooue the *Popes* power to depoſe
Princes : Finally others, although they be of opinion,
that the *Pope* hath authoritie to depoſe Princes for *hereſie*, or, which is a farre different queſtion, to declare them to be depoſed (for ſo writeth *Antonius* de
Roſellis) yet they deny that for other temporall crimes
or for inſufficiency in gouernment a Chriſtian Prince
can be depoſed by the *Pope*, whereas *Card. Bellarmine*
doth not limit his authoritie to any crime or cauſe,
but doth abſolutely, *in ordine ad bonum ſpirituale, in
order to ſpirituall good* extend this pretended authoritie.

    19. Neither is it true, that I brought the authority
of anie *heretike* for proofe of my opinion, as M. *Fitzherbert* without anie ſhame or cóſcience vntruly affirmeth : I omitted of ſet purpoſe to name *Marſilius* of
Padua, for that not onely his booke, but alſo himſelfe
is placed among *heretikes* in the *Catalogue* of forbidden bookes. And although I had vrged his authority
in that ſort, as I did vrge it in my *Appendix* againſt Fa.
Suarez, yet it had beene in my iudgement a forcible
proofe ; not for that I thinke the authority of an *heretike*, barely conſidered by it ſelfe, to be of anie force to
prooue affirmatiuely any doctrine to belong to faith,
but for that *Marſilius*, writing a booke of purpoſe to
defend the right and Soueraigntie of *Emperours* and
Kings againſt the *Popes* power to depoſe them, wherin
here and there he ſcattereth many hereſies, he ſhould
by Catholike Authours, who write of hereſies, as
Caſtro, Prateolus, D. *Sanders* and others, bee particularly taxed of thoſe hereſies, and yet his doctrine a-
gainſt the *Popes* power to depoſe *Princes*, which was
the

the principall ſubiect of his booke, ſhould not bee cenſured by them as *hereticall* or *erroneous*, for this is a forcible argument, that thoſe Catholike writers did not account his doctrine in that point to be *hereticall* or *erroneus*, although they thought it perchance to be the leſſe probable doctrine.

20. True alſo it is, that in my Apologie I alledged *Sigebert* for my opinion, for that hee vehemently impugned this pretended doctrine for the Popes power to depoſe Princes, both againſt *Pope Gregorie* the ſeuenth, and alſo *Paſchalis* the ſecond, calling it a *noueltie*, not to ſay an *hereſie*, and *anſwering*, as he ſaith, *with ſtrong arguments of the Fathers the Epiſtle, which the ſaid* Gregorie *wrote to* Hermannus *Biſhop of Metz in reproach of Kingly power*. But *Sigebert*, ſaith D. *Schulckenius, was a Schiſmatike, and his bookes againſt* Gregorie *the ſeuenth, and* Paſchalis *the ſecond are condemned by the Catholike Romane Church*. But truly it is ſtrange, and greatly to be lamented, to ſee ſome Catholikes now adaies, eſpecially who profeſſe ſanctitie of life, and pretend to haue a tender and timorous conſcience ſo eaſily to defame, and ſlander other Catholikes, who diſlike their opinions or proceedings, with ſuch enormious crimes, as are *Schiſme*, *hereſie*, and *Apoſtaſie*. What reaſon had Card. *Baronius*, of whom D. *Schulckenius* hath taken the ſame, to call *Sigebert* a *Schiſmatike* (he being by no other Authour, that I haue read, before *Baronius*, charged with that *heinous* crime, but was euer reputed a learned, vertuous, and religious Catholike) truely I cannot in any wiſe perceiue. *Schiſme* is a *rebellious ſeperation from the vnitie of the Church, or a refuſing to obey the* Pope, *as he is the viſible head of the Church, and Chriſt his Vicegerent on earth.*

21: For *obſerue diligently*, ſaith Card. Caietane ʸ *that to refuſe to obey the* Popes *commaund may happen three manner of waies*. Firſt, *in regard of the thing commanded*.

y 2a.24 q.39. ar. 2. in reſp. ad 2m.

manded. Secondly, *in regard of the perſon commanding:* and thirdly *in regard of the office of the Iudge* , or commander. *For if one doth euen with obſtinacie contemne* the Popes *ſentence, to wit , for that he will not fulfill that, which the* Pope *hath commanded, as to abſtaine from ſuch a warre, to reſtore ſuch a State &c. although hee ſhould moſt greiuouſly ſinne, yet he is not for this a* Schiſmatike. *For it falleth out and that often, that one will not fulfill the command of his* Superiour *acknowledging him neuertheleſſe to be his* Superior. *For if one vpon a reaſonable cauſe hath the* Pope *for a perſon ſuſpeſted , and therefore doth not only refuſe the* Popes *preſence, but alſo his immediate iudgement or ſentence , being readie to receiue from him not ſuſpeſted Iudges , hee neither incurreth the crime of* Schiſme, *nor any other crime. For it is naturall to ſhunne hurtfull things, and to be warie of dangers. And the* Popes *perſon may gouern tyrãnically, & ſo much the eaſier, by how much he is more potent , and feareth no reuenger on earth. But when one refuſeth to obey the* Popes *command or ſentence in regard of his office, not acknowledging him to be his* Superiour, *although he do beleiue he is , then properly he is a* Schiſmatike. *And according to this ſenſe are to be vnderſtood the words of* S. Thomas *and ſuch like, for euen obſtinate diſobedience doth not make* Schiſme, *vnleſſe it be a rebellion to the office of the* Pope *, or of the Church, ſo that he refuſe to ſubieſt himſelfe vnto him, to acknowledge him for Superiour &c.* Thus *Card. Caietane.*

22. Now what Authour euer ſaid , that *Sigebert* refuſed to obey in this ſort *Pope Gregories* command, or that he acknowledged *Guibert* the Antipape , and not *Gregorie,* to be the true and lawful Pope. True it is

that *Sigebert* was blamed by ſome , as *Trithemius* [z] re- lateth, *for that he adhering to the Emperour* Henry *being a perſecutour and rebell to the* Romane *Church, wrote letters and treatiſes againſt* Pope Gregorie *the ſeuenth, whih did not become his profeſſion* , but that *Sigebert* did depart from the vnitie of the Church , or that he refu- ſed

fed to obey and fubiect himfelfe to *Pope Gregorie*, as
not acknowledging him to be his Superiour, which is
necellarily required to make one a *Schifmatike*, or that
he adhered to the *Emperour Henry* in his rebellion to
the Romane Church, and in depofing *Gregorie*, and
creating *Guibert Pope*, neither D. *Schulckenius*, nor a-
ny other is able to prooue out of any ancient or moderne writer.

23. True alfo it is, that *Sigebert* was of this opinion,
that the *Pope* had no authoritie to depofe the Emperour, and therein he oppofed himfelfe to *Pope Gregorie*, and *anfwered, as hee* faith, *all his arguments with
ftrong teftimonies of the Fathers*, and vpon this ground
he adhered to the *Emperour*, acknowledging him to
ftill remaine the true and lawfull Emperour, and re-
fufed to obey *Pope Gregories* command, wherein hee
ftrictly ordained, that no man fhould account *Henry*
the fourth to be true and lawfull Emperour : But confidering that the doctrine for the *Popes* power to dethrone temporall Princes, and the practife thereof,
was then new in the Church of God, and neuer heard
of before, for which caufe it was called by *Sigebert* a
noueltie, not to fay an herefie, and fince that time *there
hath euer beene a great controuerfie*, faith *Azor* [a], *concerning this point, betwixt Emperours and Kings on the
one fide, and the Bifhops or Popes of Rome on the other*,
and *the Schoolemen are at variance about the fame, and
as yet the Iudge hath not decided it*, faith Trithemius, *and
very many Doctours are of opinion that the* Pope *hath no
fuch authoritie*, faith Almainus, and *the State of France
hath euer maintained the fame for certaine*, faith *Pithæus*,
and the late practife of the *Parliament of Paris* (to o-
mit all the authorities of our learned Countreymen)
doth moft clearely confirme the fame, it is neither reafon, nor confcience to charge *Sigebert* with *Schifme*,
for impugning that new doctrine and practife, which
was neuer heard of before in the Church of God. And
therefore

a *Tom.* 2. *lib.*
11. *cap.* 5. *q.* 8.

therefore *many complained*, faith *Azor* in the fame place, *that Gregorie the feuenth did depriue* Henry *the fourth of the adminiſtration of the Empire.*

24 *For although the Biſhops of Rome,* (faith Onu-phrius, *a man,* as Poſſeuine confeſſeth, *of exceeding great reading,* and whom Paulus Manutius calleth *a deuourer of Hiſtories*) *were before honoured, as the heads of Chriſtian Religion, and the Uicars of Chriſt, and the Succeſſours of Peter, yet their authoritie was not exten-ded any farther, then either in declaring or maintayning poſitions of faith. But yet they were ſubiect to the Em-perours, all things were done at the Emperours becke, they were created by them, and the Pope of Rome durſt not preſume to iudge, or decree any thing concerning them. Gregorie the feuenth, the firſt of all the Biſhops of Rome, being aided with the forces of the Nortmans, truſting in the riches of Counteſſe Mathildis, a woman moſt po-tent in Italie, and being encouraged with the diſcord of the German Princes, who were at ciuill warre among them ſelues, contrarie to the cuſtome of his anceſtours, contem-ning the authoritie and power of the Emperour, when hee had gotten the Popedome, did preſume, I doe not ſay, to excommunicate, but alſo to depriue the Emperour, by whom, if he was not choſen, he was at the leaſt confirmed, of his Kingdome and Empire. A thing not heard of be-fore that age. For the fables which are carried abroad of* Arcadius, Anaſtaſius, *&* Leo Iconomachus, *I do no-thing regard.* Thus *Onuphrius* [b].

25 *Laſtly,* it is alſo true, that *Sigeberts* bookes in anſwer to the letters of *Pope Gregorie,* and *Pope Paſ-chalis* are put in the Catalogue of forbidden bookes, but that they are forbidden or condemned by the *Catholike Church,* or *the Catholike Romane Church,* as D. *Schulckenius* affirmeth, vnleſſe by the *Catholike Church,* or *Catholike Romane Church* hee vnderſtand thoſe few *Cardinalls,* and *Diuines* of Rome, who are appointed by the Pope for the examining, permitting and

and forbidding of bookes, (which were a very ſtrange
and ouer-ſtrict deſcription of the *Catholike Church*)
is altogether vntrue. Neither is it knowne, for what
cauſe thoſe bookes of *Sigebert* are put in the Catalogue of forbidden bookes ; as likewiſe two bookes
of mine written eſpecially againſt *Card: Bellarmine,*
haue of late by a ſpeciall decree of the aforeſaid
Cardinalls, and eſpecially of *Card: Bellarmine,* who
hath been pleaſed to be a *Iudge, witneſſe,* and *accuſer*
in his owne cauſe, been prohibited, and I vnder paine
of Eccleſiaſticall Cenſures commanded to purge my
ſelfe forthwith, but the cauſe wherefore they are forbidden is not therein expreſſed, neither as yet haue
they giuen me to vnderſtand, of what crime either in
particular, or in generall, I am to purge my ſelfe, although in my purgation written to his *Holineſſe* long
agoe ᶜ, I haue moſt humbly and inſtantly deſired it,
and haue proteſted to bee moſt ready to purge my
ſelfe of any crime whatſoeuer I ſhall know to haue
committed, which their ſtrange proceeding doth
clearely argue, that they haue no ſmall diſtruſt in
their cauſe, and that the doctrine for the Popes
power to depoſe Princes is not ſo cleare a point of
faith, as *Card: Bellarmine,* and his followers would
haue the *Popes Holineſſe* and the Chriſtian world with
out ſufficient grounds to beleeue.

  26   Seeing therefore that there be many cauſes,
wherefore bookes may be forbidden, and which in
generall are reduced to theſe two heads, either
that they are repugnant to faith, or elſe to good manners, which the late inſtructions for the correcting of
bookes publiſhed by the commandement of *Pope
Clement* the eight, do in ſo large, yet doubtfull a manner extend, that ſcarſe any booke can be found which
treateth of the Popes authoritie, but ſome *Correctour*
or other may eaſily except againſt it, (as thoſe bookes
are to be corrected, which are againſt *Eccleſiaſticall*

            X   *libertie,*

c *The* 24. *of Iune* 1614.

libertie, immunitie, and Iurisdiction, so that if a *Canonist*
be the *Corrector*, he will haue that blotted out, which
denyeth the Popes direct power in temporalls, and
that Cleargie are not exempted by the law of God
and nature from the coerciue power of Princes &c.)
vnleſſe it can be proued, that *Sigebertt* bookes were
put in the *Catalogue* of prohibited bookes, for that
they impugned the doctrine for the Popes power to
depoſe Princes, no good argument can be drawne
from that *Catalogue*, to impeach *Sigeberts* credit for
the impugning of that doctrine. Neither can Card:
Baronius, nor Card: *Bellarmine* be excuſed from gree-
uous detraction, in charging *Sigebert*, who both in
his life and after his death was accounted a learned,
vertuous, and religious Catholike, with that execrable
crime of *ſchiſme*, for which at the day of iudgement
they ſhall render an exact account, vnleſſe they can
proue, that he did ſeparate himſelfe from the vnitie
of the Church, or diſobey the Popes command, as
not acknowledging him to be the true viſible head of
the Church, and the Succeſſour of *S. Peter*.

27   I omit now to declare how Catholikes ought
to carry themſelues in times of *Schiſme*, when more
then one pretend to be the true and rightfull *Pope*, and
whether thoſe, who adhere to a falſe *Pope*, perſwading
themſelues for probable reaſons, that hee is the true
and lawfull *Pope*, are to be condemned of *Schiſme*, and
to bee accounted formall *Schiſmatikes*; concerning
which queſtion read *Iohn Gerſon* in his *Treatiſe* therof.
This only at this preſent I will demand, that if to reiect the teſtimonie of *Sigebert*, or any ſuch like Authour, it be ſufficient without any other proofe, to ſay,
as M*r Fitzherbert* anſwereth, that *they liuing in the
time of the Emperours and Kings that were depoſed, wrote
partially in their fauour*, why may it not with the ſame
facilitie bee anſwered to the authorities of many o-
thers of the contrarie ſide, that they liuing in the time
of

of the *Popes*, who tooke vpon them to depole Kings and Emperours (for *this hath euer been a great contro-uerfie,* laith Azor, *betwixt Kings and Emperours on the one. fide , and the Bifhops of Rome on the other*) wrote partially in their fauour? May not Popes haue their flatterers , and who doe attribute vnto them more ample authoritie , then is fitting, as of the *Canonists Pope Pius* the fift affirmed to that learned *Nauarre* [d], as well as Kings and Emperours? See aboue cap: 3. nu. 6. what *Parifienfis* faith of this flattering.

d *in cap.* Non liccat. 12.q.2. §. nu: 6.

20 Wherefore to make an end of thele Autho-rities, I will onely requeft the iudicious *Reader* , that he will be pleafed to confider thele two things : *first,* the reafons which I brought both in my *Apologie* [e], and alfo in my [f] *Theologicall Difputation* , which D. *Schulckenius* paffeth ouer with filence , why there are to be found fo few Authours at this prefent , whofe writings are now extant, who deny the Popes autho-ritie to depofe Princes in comparifon of thofe , who doe maintaine the fame , which being duely confide-red, the *Reader* will eafily perceiue, that it is a great maruaile to finde in any Catholike booke any one fentence or claufe , which feemeth any way to call in queftion this temporall authoritie of the *Pope :* and neuerthelelfe there are at this prefent , and euer haue been, as I haue clearely fhewed before , many vertu-ous and learned Catholikes , who notwithftanding all the clamours, and threatnings of our ouer-violent *Aduerfaries,* are of this opinion, that the Pope hath no fuch authoritie to depriue Kings and Princes of their temporall dominions.

e *Num.* 449. f *Cap* 3. fec. 3. *nu.* 15. & feq.

21 The *fecond* is , that if the doctrine of that learned *Nauarre,* an *excellent Diuine, and moft skilfull in the Law,* (fayth *Poffeuine*) of *Bartholomæus Fumus* in his *Aurea armilla,* of *Gabriel Vafquez* [g] and of other Diuines be true, *that in the Court of confcience it be fuffi-cient to this effect , that we fhall commit no finne , to choofe*

g *See the Pre-face. nu.*40.43.

X 2   *his*

his opinion for true, whom for good cause we thinke to be a
man sufficiently learned, and of a good conscience, and that
no man is bound to follow alwayes the better opinion, but it
sufficeth to follow that opinion, which some skilfull Doctors
thinke to be true : how much the more may our *Ca-*
tholike Countrimen prudently perswade themselues,
that the *Pope* hath no authority to depose Princes,
which doctrine not oneiy one learned, and vertuous
man, but very many with the *State of France* do approue, and who alfo haue diligently read, examined,
and abundantly answered all the reafon arguments,
and authorities, which their learned *Aduersaries* haue
obiected to the contrarie? And this I hope may suffice for the firft part, and for clearing all thofe authorities, which I brought in my *Theologicall Difputation*
from all the exceptions, which *D. Schulckenius* hath
taken againft them. Now wee will examine
the reafons, and intrinfecall grounds of
this doctrine for the *Popes*
power to depofe
Princes.

T H E

THE SECOND PART

Wherein
ALL THE PRINCIPALL ARGV-
ments, which *Card. Bellarmine* bringeth to
proue the *vnion* and *subordination* of the tempo-
rall and spirituall power, together with the Replyes, which are brought, by D. *Schulckenius* to
confirme the same, are exactly examined.

Chap. 1. *The true state of the question concerning
the* vnion *of the temporall and spirituall power is declared.*

1. Ecause my Aduersarie M^r.
Fitzherbert, and all the
rest, who doe so vehe-
mently maintaine the
Popes power to depose
Princes, doe much rely
vpon the *vnion, and sub-
ordination* of the tempo-
rall power to the spiritu-
all, as vpon a principall proofe grounded vpon the
light of reason, before I come to examine the particular points of his *Reply*, I thinke it not amisse for the
better vnderstanding of what shall be said hereafter
by either of vs concerning this *subordination*, or *vnion*,
to declare, in what sort these two powers are among

X 3 Christians

Chriftians united and fubordained;and what a weake
ground this fubordination is to proue, that the *Pope*
hath power to depofe Princes, to difpofe of temporalls, and to punifh temporally by way of coercion or
conftraint. And to proceede orderly herein, and that
the Reader may clearely perceiue, what is the true
ftate of the queftion, betwixt me and Card. *Bellarmine*
and not be caried away with a confufe concept of I
know not what kinde of *vnion* and *fubordination*, I will
firft fet downe that which is certain, and out of queftion, and *then* what is in controuerfie betweene vs concerning this *vnion* and *fubordination*.

    2. *Firft* therefore I agree with Card. *Bellarmine* in
this, that the ciuill or temporall power *of it owne na-*
ture, and being confidered precifely by it felfe, is a diftinct power from the fpirituall, and no way fubiect

a *Num.*132.&*
feq. & nu.150.
153. 154.

or fubordained to it (as in my *Apologie* a) affirmed
out of Card. *Bellarmine*) but they are two feuerall,
diftinct, and difunited powers, and not depending
one of the other, and haue diftinct ends, diftinct fun-
ctions, diftinct lawes, diftinct punifhments, diftinct,
Magiftrates and Princes. And this is very apparant
partly in *infidell Countries, where there is true ciuill or*

b *Lib.*5. de
*Rom. Pont.*c.6.

temporall power (faith Card. *Bellarmine* b) *without any*
order or refereuce to any true Ecclefiafticall or fpirituall
power : and partly in the time of the Apoftles, who
had true and perfect fpirituall power without any true
fupreme temporall or ciuill authoritie. And from
hence it followeth, that as the fupreme fpirituall
Prince, or Paftour is fubiect to none in fpiritualls, fo
alfo the fupreme temporall Prince is fubiect to none
in *temporalls*.

    3. *Secondly*, we do alfo agree in this, that although
among Chriftians the temporall, and fpirituall power
do ftill remaine two diftinct fupreme powers, *for that*
the Mediateur betwixt God and men Chrift Iefus *hath*
alfo by proper actions, and diftinct dignities diftinguifhed
either

c *In epst. ad*
Michaelem;
Imp. *Cum ad*
verum dist. 96.

either power, as *Pope Nicholas* the firſt doth well affirme c, yet they are ſo vnited, and conioyned together among Chriſtians, that temporall authoritie and ſpirituall authoritie, temporall authoritie, and ſpirituall ſubiection, temporall ſubiection and ſpirituall ſubiection (to omit ſpirituall authoritie and temporall ſubiection) may be vnited and conioined, at one or diuerſe times, in one and the ſelfe ſame Chriſtian man: by reaſon of which vnion and coniunction the ſame Chriſtian man may be both a temporall, and alſo a ſpirituall Prince, as we ſee in the *Pope,* who by the inſtitution of *Chriſt* is the ſupreme ſpirituall Paſtour of the Church, and by the conſent of Chriſtian Princes and people is become alſo a temporall Prince: the ſame Chriſtian man may be both a temporall Prince, and alſo a ſpirituall ſubiect, as are all Chriſtian Princes, who, as Princes, are ſupreme in temporalls, and as Chriſtians, are ſubiect in ſpirituals to the ſpirituall Paſtour of Chriſts Church ; the ſame Chriſtian man may bee both a temporall, and alſo a ſpirituall ſubiect, as are other Chriſtians whatſoeuer ; and whether the ſame man may be a ſpirituall Prince, and yet a temporall ſubiect, dependeth on that queſtion, whether and in what manner our *Sauiour Chriſt* hath exempted *Cleargie men*, and eſpecially the *Pope* from ſubiection to temporall Princes. But the queſtion betwixt me, and Card. *Bellarmine* is, whether this manner of vnion and coniunction of theſe two powers, or ſubiections in the ſame Chriſtian man, be ſufficient to make the whole Chriſtian world to be *formally* one complete and totall body, or common wealth, conſiſting of ſpirituall and temporall power, whereof the *Pope* is the ſupreme viſible head, or elſe, notwithſtanding the aforeſaid vnion and coniunction, the temporall and ſpirituall common wealth among Chriſtians doe ſtill remaine *formally* two totall and complete bodies or common wealths, the one
conſiſting

confisting onely of spirituall, and the other only of
temporall power, although *materially*, and accidentally vnited in one subiect, in that manner as I haue
now declared.

4. *Thirdly,* I doe also make no question, but that,
as the world containing both Chriltians and infidels,
and therefore confisting of spirituall and temporall
power, may be called one complete, and totall body
or kingdome, whereof God onely is the chiefe head
and King , although in *the same* totall body or kingdome, but not of the fame totall body or Kingdome, there be many supreme visible heads and Gouernours, and consequently being *(supreme*, they doe
not depend one of the other, in fo much that neither
the temporall power of *Infidell Princes* is subiect to
the spirituall power of the *Pope*, nor the spirituall
power of the *Pope* is subiect to the temporall power
of *Infidell Princes*, but both of them are subiect immediately to God alone the inuisible head and King of
them both, in regard of whom they make one totall
body or kingdome, although the temporall power
alone being compared to the uisible heads on earth,
doth actually make diuerfe totall and complete earthly kingdomes : So also I make no question, but that
the whole Chriftian world, confisting of temporall
and spirituall power, being compared to Chrift the
invisible head thereof, who, at leaft wife as he is God,
is King of Kings, and Lord of Lords both temporall
and spirituall, doth make one totall bodie, Kingdom,
or Common-wealth, contayning in it both the
earthly kingdomes of Chriftians, and the spirituall
kingdome of Chrift ; neither of this can there in my
iudgement be made any question.

5   But the question betwixt me and *Card: Bellarmine* is, whether the temporall & spirituall power
among Chriftians, or the Chriftian world confisting
of both powers, not as they are referred to Chrift,
who,

who, at leaſt wiſe as he is God, is the inviſible head of both powers (I ſay at leaſt wiſe as he is God, for that it is a controuerſie betwixt the Diuines and Canoniſts, whether Chriſt as man be only a ſpirituall, or alſo a temporall King) but as they haue relation to their viſible heads here on earth, doe make one totall and compleat bodie, or common-wealth, conſiſting of temporall and ſpirituall power, whereof the *Pope* is the ſupreme viſible head, and Chriſtian Kings are not ſupreme, but depending on him not onely in ſpiritualls, but alſo in temporalls ; or whether the temporall and ſpirituall power among Chriſtians doe truly, properly, and formally make two entire and complete bodies, Kingdoms, or Common-wealths, to wit, the earthly kingdoms of this Chriſtian world, conſiſting only of temporall power, whereof temporall Princes are the ſupreme viſible heads, and therefore in temporalls ſubieƈt to no other viſible head here on earth, and the ſpirituall kingdom and myſticall body of Chriſt, conſiſting onely of ſpirituall power, whereof the *Pope* onely is the ſupreme viſible head, Prince, and Paſtour, and conſequently in ſpiritualls ſubieƈt to no other viſible head or Superiour on earth. This is the true ſtate of the queſtion.

6   Concerning which queſtion there is a great controuerſie betwixt the Canoniſts, and Diuines. For the Canoniſts ſuppoſing Chriſt our Sauiour to bee, not onely a ſpirituall, but alſo a temporall King, and to haue directly and properly both temporall and ſpirituall power, ouer the whole world, and that hee gaue this power to his Generall Vicar here on earth *S. Peter* and his Succeſſors, doe conſequently affirme, that the whole world, but eſpecially which is Chriſtian, conſiſting of ſpirituall and temporall power doth make one entire or totall body, whereof the *Pope*, being by the inſtitution of *Chriſt* not onely a ſpirituall, but alſo a temporall Monarch, is the ſupreme

preme vifible head, to whom all Princes, especially who are Chriftians,are fubiect not only in fpiritualls, but alfo in temporalls. But contrariwife the Diuines, who doe hold, that Chrift as man, was not a temporal[l], but only a fpirituall King, and although hee had directly both temporall and fpirituall power, yet that he gaue to *S. Peter* and his Succeffors onely the keyes of the kingdome of heauen,and not of earthly kingdomes, and only fpirituall not temporall authoritie, are confequently bound to maintaine that the temporall and fpirituall power, as they are referred to the vifible heads here on earth, doe not truly, properly, and formally make one totall and entire body, or kingdome, whereof the *Pope* is the fupreme vifible head, but two totall and entire bodies or kingdomes but vnited in fubiect, as I declared before, to wit, earthly kingdomes, confifting only of temporall authoritie, whereof temporall Princes only are the fupreme vifible heads, and the fpirituall kingdome, the myfticall body, or the Church of Chrift, confifting only of fpirituall power, whereof the *Pope* is the fupreme vifible head, Prince, and Paftour.

7 Now what is the opinion of Card: *Bellarmine* touching this point, for that he fpeaketh fo contrarie to his owne principles,truly I can not tell. For although he adhereth to the Diuines, and impugneth the Canonifts, in that they hold the *Pope* to be not only a fpirituall,but alfo a temporall Monarch of the world,and to haue directly power in temporalls, yet contrarie to this his doctrine, as you fhall fee in the next chapter, he doth in expreffe words, whatfoeuer his meaning is,affirme, that the temporall and fpirituall power doe make one totall and entire bodie, Familie, Cittie, Kingdome, or Common-wealth, whereof the *Pope* is the fupreme vifible head: yea he is fo confident in this his affertion, that he feareth not to auerre, [d] *that it is againft the Catholike faith* to

d in his Schulc-
kenius cap. 5.
pag.195.

fay, that the Ecclefiasticall and ciuill power are not parts
of one and the fame Common-wealth, but that they make
altogether two common-wealths, vnleffe this diftinction
and explication be added, to wit, that the Ecclefiaficall
and ciuill power doe make one totall common-wealth
(which^e afterwards he calleth, the familie, cittie, Kingdome, myfticall bodie, and Church of Chrift) and
two partiall, which are indeed diftinct by acts, offices, dignities, and ends, but connected betweene themfelues, and
one fubordained to the other. But how weakely and
contrarie to his owne principles *Card: Bellarmine* proueth this vnion and fubordination of the temporall
and fpirituall power, you fhall forthwith perceiue.

e *Cap.7.p.287. & pag.340.*

Chap. 2. *Wherein the argument of Card.* Bellarmine *taken from the authoritie of*
S. Paul Rom. 12. wee being many
are one body in Chrift, *is exa-*
mined.

1. AND to begin firft with the *vnion*; *Card. Bel-*
larmine bringeth two arguments to proue,
that the ciuill and fpirituall power doe make one
bodie or common-wealth among Chriftians. The
firft is taken from the authoritie of *S. Paul* Rom: 12.
and 1 Cor: 12. where hee affirmeth, *that wee being*
many are one body in Chrift: from whence *Card: Bel-*
larmine concludeth, ^a that *Kings and Bifhops, Clerkes*
and Laikes doe not make two common-wealths, but one,
to wit, the Church.

2. To this argument I anfwered in my ^b*Apologie,*
that the meaning of *S. Paul* in thofe places is, that
all Chriftians, both Kings and Bifhops, Clerkes and
Laikes, as they are by Baptifme regenerate in Chrift,
doe truly, properly, and formally make one bodie,
one houfe, one cittie, one communitie or common-
wealth,

a *Lib.5.de Rom. Pont:cap.7.*

b *Num:83. 89.166.*

Y 2

c *Lib.3. de Ecclesia cap 2.*

wealth, to wit, the spirituall kingdome, the mysticall body, or the Church of Christ, which *Card. Bellarmine* defineth ᶜ to be, a *companie of men vnited together by the profession of the same Christian faith and Communion of the same Sacraments vnder the gouernment of lawfull Pastours, and especially of one Romane Bishop Christ his Vicar in earth.* But S. *Paul* doth not say, that the temporall and spirituall power doe make one *onely* bodie, communitie or common-wealth, and not also two, or that Kings and Bishops, Clerkes and Laikes, not considered as Christians or regenerate in Christ by baptisme, but as by their naturall birth or ciuil conuersation they are subiect to temporal Princes, which subiection Baptisme doth not take away, doe not also truely, properly and formally make also another politike bodie, another citie, another communitie or common-wealth, to wit, the earthly Kingdomes of the Christian world.

3. Wherefore it is not true, that Kings and Bishops, Clearkes and Laikes considered diuerse waies do not make diuerse kingdoms or common-wealths, but one onely, as *Card. Bellarmine* concludeth out of *S. Paul?* for as by Baptisme they are regenerate in *Christ*, and subiect in spirituals to *Christ* his vicegerent in earth, they make one body, or common-wealth, which is the spirituall kingdome and Church of *Christ*, and this onely doth signifie S. *Paul* by those words, *we being many are one body in Christ*, but S. *Paul* doth not denie, that all Christians, as by their naturall birth or ciuill conuersation they are subiect to Secular *Princes* in temporall causes, which subiection Baptisme doth not take away, doe also truely, properly and formally make another body or common-wealth, which are the earthly kingdomes of the Christian world. *Cleargie men,* saith Card. *Bellarmine* himselfe, ᵈ *besides that they are Cleargie men, are also citizens and certaine parts of the ciuill common-wealth,* and

d *Lib. de Clericis cap. 28.*

againe,

againe, e *if one,* faith he, *confider the companie of Lay-*   e *Ibid.cap.* 30.
men, not as they are Chriſtians, but as they are Citizens, or
after any other manner, that companie cannot bee called
the Church, and confequently they muſt bee another
common-wealth, and therefore the ciuill and Eccleſiaſticall power, or Clerkes or Laikes, in whom the
Eccleſiaſticall and ciuill power doe reſide, being conſidered diuerſe waies, doe not truely, properly and
formally make one only body, but two diſtinct & ſeuerall bodies or common-wealths, although materially and accidentally vnited in that maner as I declared before, f and prefently will declare more at   f *Cap.1.nn.3.*
large.

4. And whereas *Card. Bellarmine* affirmeth, *that*
although the temporall and ſpirituall power doe make two
partiall common-wealths, yet they doe alſo make one entire
and totall commonwealth, which is the Church of Chriſt,
whereof the Pope is the ſupreme viſible head, and to affirme
the contrary, is, faith he, *againſt the Catholike faith,* hee
doth heerein both ſpeake contrarie to his owne principles, and to that which hee knoweth to bee the Catholike faith, and hee muſt alſo of neceſſitie fall into
the *Canoniſts* opinion, which he before g pretended to   g *Lib.5. de Ro.*
confute concerning the *Popes* ſpirituall and temporall   *Pont.a cap.2.*
Monarchie ouer the whole Chriſtian world. For if
the Church of Chriſt be one totall body or common-
wealth compounded of Eccleſiaſtical and ciuill power, as a man is compounded of ſoule and body (for
this is that ſimilitude which ſo much pleaſeth Card.
Bellarmine, and is therefore ſo often inculcated by
him) it muſt neceſſarily follow, that the *Pope* as *Pope,*
in whom, according to his other grounds, all the power of the Church doth reſide, muſt haue truly, properly, and formally both temporall and Eccleſiaſticall power, as a man who is compounded of ſoule
and bodie, hath truely, properly and formally in him
both the ſoule and bodie, and all the powers and faculties

culties of them both : And what elſe is this, I pray
you, then to maintaine with the *Canoniſts*, that the
Pope as Pope is both a temporall and ſpirituall Monarch, and that hee hath truely,properly and formally both ciuill and ſpirituall authority : And yet Card.
Bellarmine in other places doth expreſſely affirme,
that the *Pope* as *Pope* hath onely ſpirituall and not
temporall power.

   5 *The Diuines,* ſaith he, [h] *doe giue to the Pope temporall and ſpirituall power onely in the Dominions of the
Church, which power in the patrimonie of S.* Peter *Pope*
Innocent *in cap. per venerabilem doth call a full power ;
ouer other Chriſtian Prouinces they doe giue to the Pope
onely a ſpirituall power, which of it ſelfe and properly doth
regard ſpirituall things, but temporall things it doth regard
as they are ſubordained to ſpirituall. And therefore when
we ſpeake properly, we ſay that the Pope hath power in temporals, but not that he hath temporall power, as he is Pope.*
Now how theſe two can ſtand together, that the ſpirituall and temporall power among Chriſtians doe
make one entire and totall body, whereof the *Pope* is
the ſupreme viſible head, as the body and ſoule doe
make one man, and yet that the *Pope,* as *Pope,* ſhall
haue no temporall power, which in it ſelfe is temporall, but onely ſpirituall, athough in ſome caſes extended to temporall things, ſeeing that theſe two
powers doe truely compoſe the Church of *Chriſt,* and
conſequently both of them are truly and really in the
Church which they compound, and ſo likewiſe in the
Pope, in whom all the power of the Church doth reſide, I remit to the iudgement of any ſenſible man.
   5. Beſides what a more flat contradiction can
there be, then this, to ſay, *that the ciuill and ſpirituall
power among Chriſtians doe compound indeede two partiall, but one entire and totall common-wealth, which is the*
Church *of Chriſt, or Chriſtian common-wealth,* as hee
heere affirmeth, [i] and withall, *that the Church of Chriſt*
or

or the Christian common-wealth is compounded onely of
spirituall authoritie, as a little beneath hee affirmeth
in these words: k *That which my Aduersarie* Widdrington *saith, that the mysticall bodie, Church, or Chri-*
stian common-wealth is compounded of spirituall authority
alone, is true in this sense, that to compound the Christian
common-wealth there is not necessary a power, which is for-
mally ciuill, but yet there is necessarie a power, which is so
formally spirituall, that it is also vertually ciuill &c. For
how can the Church of Christ be compounded of ciuill and spirituall power, which are formally two distinct powers, and yet the Church not haue power
which is formally ciuill, but onely spirituall ? Neuerthelesse I doe not intend to denie, that the spirituall
or Ecclesiasticall power among Christians may in this
sense be called vertually ciuill or temporall, because it
may for the spirituall good command, and compell
spiritually temporall Princes to vse their temporall power, for this were onely to contend about words, but
that the Church of Christ, whereof the Pope is head,
is truely, properly and formally compounded of ciuil
and spiritualll power, this I say is both vntrue, and
also flat contrarie to Card. *Bellarmines* own grounds;
but whether the spiritual power of the church may be
called vertually ciuill or temporal, for that it may also
constraine and punish temporall Princes *temporally,*
or vse temporall and ciuill authoritie, in case the
temporall Prince for the spirituall good will not vse
it, this is the maine question betwixt mee and Card.
Bellarmine.

7. To conclude therefore, this answere I doe
freely grant : that *Kings* and *Bishops, Clearks* and *La-*
icks, as by baptisme they are regenerate in *Christ,* doe
truely, properly, and formally, make one entire and
totall body, which is the spirituall kingdome, and
Church of *Christ,* whereof the *Pope* is the supreme visible head : but I vtterly deny, that this spirituall
kingdome,

d In his
Schulckenius
cap.5.p.203.

kingdome, or Church of Chrift is compounded of
fpirituall and temporall, but onely of fpirituall, or
Ecclefiafticall 'power: or that *Clearks* and *Laicks*, as
they are citizens, or by their naturall birth are fubiect
in temporall affaires to temporall Princes doe compound this Church of *Chrift*, but onely the earthly
kingdomes of the Chriftian world, which are onely
compounded of ciuill and temporall authority. In
which Chriftian world, or Chriftian common-wealth,
(taking them for an *aggregatum per accidens*, including
both the fpirituall kingdome of *Chrift*, whereof the
Pope is head, and alfo earthly kingdomes, whereof
Chriftian Princes are the onely vifible heads, for the
Church of *Chrift* is feldome times taken in this fenfe)
there is but one totall or intire Catholike Church: yet
there be many intire temporall kingdomes or common-wealths, as of Englifh, French, Spanifh, which
haue their feuerall Princes, Lawes, and gouernments,
and haue no other communion then in friendfhip
and amitie: Yea, & the Catholike Church is one totall
body, or common-wealth in Chriftian and Infidell
kingdomes. And alfo in one particular Chriftian
kingdome there be two diftinct totall bodies, or common-wealths, to wit, the temporall, confifting of ciuill power, and the Ecclefiafticall, confifting of fpirituall: wherein as there bee two diftinct communions, the one fpirituall in things belonging to grace,
and the other temporall in things belonging to nature. So alfo their be two excommunications, the one
in fpirituals; wherein thofe that be excommunicated
by the Church, doe not participate, and the other
in temporalls; whereof thofe, who be excommunicated, or made out-lawes by temporall Princes, are
not partakers; in fo much that they, who are depriued of one of thefe communions, are not thereby
depriued of the other, for an out-law may be a member of the Church, and be partaker of fpirituall communion:

munion : and he, who by Excommunication is depriued of Ecclefiafticall communion, may bee a
member of the ciuill common-wealth, as Heathens
and Publicans were, and not therefore to be excluded
from ciuill focietie and conuerfation.

8. Wherefore although the temporall and fpirituall power among Chriftians, as they are referred to
the vifible heads thereof, doe truely, properly, and
formally make diuerfe totall bodies, or common-
wealths, which neuerthelefte ought both to confpire
in league & friendfhip, to bring both Princes and fubiects to life euerlafting : yet they are not like to two
confederate Cities or Kingdomes, which are onely
vnited in league and amity, and haue no ciuill communion one with the other, neither is the fame man
a citizen of both Cities, or a fubiect of both Kingdomes; but the temporall and fpirituall power are fo
vnited among Chriftians, that the fame man, who
by ciuill conuerfation, or naturall birth is a citizen,
part, and member of the temporall City, Kingdome,
or Common-wealth, and confequently fubiect to
her Lawes, is alfo by baptifme or fpirituall regenera-
tion made a citizen, part, or member of the fpirituall Citie, Kingdome, or Cōmon-wealth, which is the
Church of Chrift, and confequently is alfo fubiect
to her Lawes. So that although the vnion, and communion of earthly Kingdomes, and the fpirituall
kingdome of *Chrift* bee greater among Chriftians,
then of two confederate Cities or temporall kingdomes, yet this vnion and communion being onely
material, accidentall, and in fubiect (as Muficke and
Phyficke are vnited in one man, by reafon whereof
the fame man is both a Mufician and a Phyfician,
and confequently fubiect to the precepts and directions of either art) is not fufficient to caufe them to
make truely properly, and formally one totall body,
kingdome, or common-wealth, whereof the *Pop.*

Z   is

l *cap. 1. nu. 4.*

is head : as neither the vnion of two accidents in one subiect is sufficient to cause them to make truely, properly, and formally, one entire & totall accidentall. cópound. Neuerthelesse I do not deny, as I obserued before. but that the temporal & spiritual power, earthly kingdomes, and the spiritual kingdome of *Christ*, as they are referred to *Christ* : who, at leastwise as God, is the head of them both, doe make one totall body, whereof *Christ* onely is the head, which may be called the Christian world, consisting of ciuill and spirituall power : but in this manner neither the Pope nor temporall Princes are the head, but onely parts and members of this totall body, as beneath ᵐ I will declare more at large.

Chap. 3. *Wherein the authoritie of* S. Gregorie Nazianzen, *comparing the temporall and spirituall power to the body and soule in man, is declared.*

a *Lib. 5. de Rom. Pont. c. 6.*

1.   **T**He *second argument*, which *Card. Bellarmine* bringeth to proue, that the ciuill and spirituall power among Christians doe make one totall body, or common-wealth, is taken from the authority of S. *Gregory Nazianzene*, who compareth the spirituall and temporall power among Christians to the soule and body of man. From which similitude *Card. Bellarmine* argueth in this manner ᵃ. *These two powers in the Church,* saith hee, *are like to the spirit and body in a man. For the body & the spirit are as it were two common-wealths, which may be found diuided and vnited. The body is found without the spirit in beasts, the spirit is found without the body in Angels, the body and spirit are both vnited in man, and doe make one person. So likewise, the ciuill and spirituall power are sometimes found diuided, as long since in the Apostles time, sometimes vnited as now,*

and

and when they are vnited they make one body, or common wealth.

2. To this argument I answered in my *Apologie* [b], that from the words of S. *Gregorie Nazianzene* onely these two things can be gathered. The *first*, that the spirituall power is more worthy, and more noble then the temporall, and that therefore the temporall must in worthinesse yeeld and giue place to the spirituall. The *second* is, that Christian Princes, although in temporalls, and in things belonging to ciuill gouernment they are supreme on earth, and therefore subiect to none, yet in that they are Christians, they are subiect in spirituals, and in things belonging to Christian Religion to the command of spirituall Pastours of the flocke of *Christ.* For these bee the expresse wordes, which he vsed to the Christian President : *For the law of Christ doth make you also subiect to my power and authoritie, for we also haue authoritie to command, I add also, a more noble, and more perfect, vnlesse it be meete, that the spirit do submit her power to the flesh , and heauenly things doe giue place to earthly.* From which words this onely can be inferred, that the spirituall power is more noble, then the temporall, and that all Christian Princes and Magistrates, as they are the sheepe of *Christ*, are in spirituall things subiect to the spirituall Pastours of the Church, which all Catholikes will freely grant. But that the temporall and spirituall power among Christians, as they are referred to the supreme visible heads here on earth, do make one totall body or common wealth, as the soule and body do make one man, or that the temporall power among Christians, as it is temporall (for this much doth signifie the temporall and spirituall power taking them *in abstracto*)or which is all one, that temporall Princes are in meere temporall causes subiect to spirituall Pastours, cannot with any shew of probabilitie bee gathered out of those words of S. *Gregorie Nazianzene.*

b *num.* 139. 140.

3. Where-

3. Wherefore the vnion of the temporall and spirituall power among Christians is nothing like to the
vnion of the body and soule in man, for that the body is a substantiall matter, and the soule a substantiall
forme, and therefore being vnited they make one substantiall compound, which is called man; who therefore hath in him actually, properly, and formally
both body and soule, as euery compound hath in him
the parts, whereof it is compounded, but the ciuill and
spirituall power are not among Christians vnited; as
two parts, compounding really and actually one totall body, which is the Church of *Christ*, whereof the
Pope is head, for that, according to Card. *Bellarmines*
owne doctrine, the Church of *Christ*, whereof the
Pope is head, is compounded only of spirituall power,
and not of ciuill power, as ciuill is distinguished from
spirituall, but ciuill and spirituall power, ciuill power
and spirituall subiection, ciuill subiection and spirituall subiection, (to omit now spirituall power and ciuill subiection) are only vnited among Christians, as
two accidents, for example, Musike and Phisike, are
vnited in one man, which vnion, being only accidentall, and in subiect, is not sufficient to cause the temporall and spirituall power to make truely, properly
and formally one body, whereof the *Pope* is head, but
only to make the same man, either to haue in him
both temporall and spirituall power, or temporall
power, and spirituall subiection, or both temporall
subiection and spirituall subiection,)to omit now spirituall power and temporall subiection) and consequently, the same man to bee guided, directed, and
gouerned in temporall things by the lawes, precepts
and directions of the temporall power, and in spirituall things by the lawes, precepts, and directions of the
spirituall power: As the vnion of Musike and Phisike
in one man, although it be only materiall, accidentall, and in subiect, yet it maketh the same man to be
both

both a Mufician, and a Phyfitian , and as he is a Mufitian , to be guided and directed by the lawes and precepts of Muficke,and as a Phifitian by the rules & precepts of phifike , but it doth not make Mufike to be guided and directed by Phyfike, or a Muficion, as he is a Mufician, to be guided and directed by a Phyfition, as he is a Phyfitian : So likewife the aforefaid vnion of temporall and fpirituall power,of temporall power and fpirituall fubiection &c. in one man, doth not make the temporall power to be fubiect to the fpirituall, or a temporall Prince, as hee is a temporall Prince, or which is all one, in temporall caufes, to bee guided, directed, and gouerned by the fpirituall power, as it is fpirituall : But of this fimilitude of the foule and body wee fhall haue occafion to treat againe beneath [c].   c *Cap.* 8.

4. Pardon me, *good Reader*, that fometimes I repeate the fame things fomewhat often ; it is not to make my booke the bigger , and to fill it vp with idle repetitions of the fame things , as my *Aduerfaries*, to difgrace me, are pleafed to lay to my charge, not confidering that they themfelues do often times commit the like , but it is onely to cleere thy vnderftanding, and to make thee throughly comprehend the difficultie, and in what manner the temporall and fpirituall power are vnited and fubordained among Chriftians, confidering that my *Aduerfaries*, to prooue the *Popes* power to depofe Princes, to difpofe of all temporalls , and to punifh temporally by way of conftraint, doe fo often inculcate this vnion and fubordination , as a principall ground , whereon the *Popes* power in temporalls doth depend. And thus you haue feene, how weakely Card. *Bellarmine*, and difagreeably to his owne principles , hath laboured to proue, that the temporall and fpirituall power among Chriftians doe make one totall body , or common wealth, whereof the *Pope* is head : now you fhall fee,

Z 3   how

how weakely also, and not conformably to his owne doctrine, he endeauoureth to proue, that the temporall power among Christians is subiect and subordained to the spirituall.

Chap. 4. *Wherein the true state of the question, concerning the subiection and subordination of the temporall power among Christians to the spirituall is propounded, and the different opinions of Catholikes touching this point are rehearsed.*

1.   F*Irst* therefore, that you may perceiue the true state of the question, and wherein I doe agree with *Card: Bellarmine*, and wherein we differ, I doe agree with him in this, that Christian Princes, in whom the supreme temporall power doth reside, being the sheepe of Christ, no lesse then inferiour persons, are subiect to the supreme visible Pastour of the Church of Christ : but the question is, in what things, and also in what manner they are subiect. *Secondly,* we also agree in this, that Christian Princes are in spirituall things, or which doe belong to Christian faith and Religion, subiect not onely to the directiue, or commanding power, but also in spirituall punishments to the coerciue or punishing power of spirituall Pastors, in such sort, that Christian Princes are not onely bound to obey the command of their spirituall Pastors, in things which doe concerne Christian faith and religion, but also, if they be disobedient, they may with spirituall punishments be punished and compelled therevnto. *Thirdly,* we doe also agree in this, that Christian Princes are bound to obey the commanding power of spirituall Pastours, not only in those things, which of their owne nature are

Eccle-

Ecclesiasticall or spirituall, but also in things temporall, when *by accident* they become spirituall; in so much that a spirituall Pastor hath authoritie to command a temporall Prince to vse or not vse his temporall power, when it is necessarie or hurtfull to Catholike faith and religion, but this is nothing else, then that temporall Princes in things spirituall (for whether they be *per se*, and of *their owne nature*, or onely by *accident* spirituall, it little importeth) are subiect to the commanding power of spirituall Pastors, as likewise all temporall causes and crimes, whether of *their owne nature*, or onely by *accident* they become temporall, are subiect to the commanding and coerciue power of temporall Princes.

2   But the controuersie betwixt me and Card: *Bellarmine* is concerning two things; the first is, concerning the commanding power, to wit, whether temporall Princes are subiect to the commanding power of spirituall Pastors, not onely in things spirituall, and in temporall, when they become spirituall, but also in meere temporall things; for this is properly temporall power (taking temporall power in *abstracto*) to be subiect to the spirituall For as a *Musician* can not truly be said to be subiect, as he is a Musician, and in all things belonging to Musicke, to a Physition as he is a Physition, for that Musicke is not *per se*, and of it owne nature referred to Physicke, and if Musicke were *per se*, and of it owne nature subiect to Physicke, a Musician, as he is a Musician, and in all things belonging to Musicke, should be subiect to a Physician, as he is a Physician: for which cause a Shipwright, as he is a Shipwright, hath intrinsecall reference to a Nauigator, for that the Art of making ships is *per se*, and of it owne nature ordayned for nauigation; So also if the temporall power among Christian be *per se*, and of it owne nature subiect to the spirituall power, it must follow, that temporall

Z 4   Princes,

Princes,who are Chriftians,are, as they are temporall
Princes, and in all things belonging to temporall
power,fubiect to fpirituall Paftours, as they are fpirituall Paftours: And if temporall Princes, who be
Chriftians, are not fubiect, as they are temporall
Princes, to fpirituall Paftors,as they are fpirituall Paftors,the temporall power among Chriftians is not
per fe, and of it owne nature fubiect to the fpirituall
power.

3   The _fecond_ thing, which is in controuerfie betwixt me, and _Card._ B _ellarmine,_ is concerning the _co-_
erciue power of fpirituall Paftors,to wit,whether temporall Princes are fubiect to the coerciue power of
fpirituall Paftors in fuch fort, that fpirituall _Paftors,_
(efpecially the _Pope,_ who is the fupreme _Paftour_ of
all Chriftians) haue by the inftitution of _Chrift_ authoritie, to depriue temporall _Princes_ of their Kingdomes,to difpofe of all their temporalls, and to punifh them temporally, or with all kinde of temporall
punifhments, in cafe they will not obey their iuft
command. And this is the maine point, and principall fcope, at which both the Canonifts, who hold
that the _Pope_ hath directly power in temporals _in ha-_
bit, although _the vfe_ they haue committed to temporall _Princes,_ and alfo the Diuines, who hold that hee
hath onely indirectly, that is, in order to fpirituall
good, power in temporalls, doe chiefly aime. Now
concerning thefe two points, there be three different
opinions of Catholikes.

4   The _firft_ opinion is of the Canonifts, who
holding, that the Church of _Chrift,_ whereof the _Pope_
is the fupreme vifible head, doth confift both of temporall and fpirituall power, doe confequently hold,
that all Chriftian Princes, not only as they are Chriftians, but alfo as they are temporall Princes, are in
all temporall caufes fubiect to the _commanding_ power,
and in all temporall punifhments fubiect alfo to the

coerciue

coercine power of the *Pope*, whom they make the supreme, both temporall and spirituall Monarch of the world, and to haue directly both temporall and spirituall power, although the vse, exercise, and execution of his temporall power, he hath out of the territories of the Church, committed to Secular Princes, as to his *Vice-Royes*, *Vicegerents*, or *Deputies*: and this doctrine some Lawyers held to be so certaine, that they were not afraid to condemne the contrarie as *hereticall*, for which they are worthily taxed by *Couerruuias*[d] of great *temeritie*; But with this opinion, for that it is commonly reiected by all Diuines, and confuted also by *Card: Bellarmine* himselfe[e], I will not at this time intermeddle.

5 The *second* opinion is of many Schoole-Diuines especially of these later times, who although they seeme greatly to mislike the Canonists opinion, in that the Canonists hold the *Pope*, as *Pope*, to haue directly, not only spirituall, but also temporall power, and to be both a temporall Monarch, and also a spirituall Prince and Pastour of the whole Christian world, yet in effect they doe giue as full and ample authoritie to the *Pope* ouer Christian Princes, as the Canonists do; for whatsoeuer the Canonists affirme, that the *Pope* can directly effect by his temporall power, the same doe the Diuines affirme, that he can effect indirectly, and in order to spirituall good by his spirituall power: And therefore, although they will not grant, that the *Pope* hath *formally* temporall power, but only spirituall, yet they grant, that this spirituall power of the *Pope* is *virtually*, and in effect temporall; and that therefore the *Pope* by his spirituall power can in order to spirituall good depriue temporall Princes of their kingdomes, dispose of all their temporalls, punish them with all kinde of temporall punishments, and finally whatsoeuer temporall Princes can by their temporall power doe for the

d *In Regula,*
peccati. 2 part.
Relect. §. 9.
num. 7.
e *Lib. 5. de*
Rom. Pont.
a *cap. 2.*

temporall good, they affirme that the *Pope* by his
spirituall power can doe for the spirituall good. Yea
some of them doe so extend this spirituall good and
spirituall harme, taking spirituall harme, not only for
spirituall crimes, as *heresie, Apostacie,* and such like,
but also for all temporall crimes, as are *drunkennesse,
fornication,* and the like, that they giue a more ample
power to the *Pope,* to depriue Princes of their kingdomes, then by temporall lawes is vsually granted to
temporall Princes to depriue their subiects of their
lands, who for whoredome, drunkennesse, and many
other temporall crimes, can not vsually by the lawes
of any Christian kingdome bee depriued of their
lands and possessions.

   6. The *third* opinion is of many other learned Catholikes both Diuines and Lawyers whom I cited be-
f *Part. 1. per
totum.* fore, f who although they agree with the second opinion in this, that the *Pope* hath power to command
temporall Princes in spirituals, but not in meere temporals, and to punish them with spirituall punishments, when they refuse to obey his iust command,
yet that the *Pope* hath any *coerciue* power (call it spirituall or temporall, for in effect it is truely temporall) to inflict temporall punishments, to dispose of
temporals for the spirituall good, or to depriue temporall Princes of their temporall dominions, they vtterly denie, affirming, that onely Excommunication,
or some such like spirituall punishment, is the last, to
which the *Popes coerciue* power can extend : And this
their doctrine, which Card. *Bellarmine,* and some few
others of his *Society,* haue presumed to condeme as altogether *improbable,* yea and wholly repugnant to
Catholike faith, I haue taken vpon me to maintaine, as
neither repugnant to Catholike faith or religion, nor
preiudiciall to eternall saluation, and that therefore it
may be defended by any Catholike without any note
of *heresie, errour* or *temerity.*

                            7. These

7. These bee the different opinions of Catholikes concerning the subiection of the temporall power to the spirituall, wherby you see, that althogh all Catholikes doe grant, that temporall Princes, who are somtimes called temporall powers, are subiect to the spirituall Pastour in things spirituall, and in temporall when they become spirituall, yet all doe not grant, that the temporall power it selfe, euen among Christians, is *per se*, and of it owne nature subiect to the spirituall, nor that the *Pope*, as *Pope*, hath any coerciue power to constraine and punish with temporall punishments, but onely with spirituall; Neither doth it follow, that becaufe Christian Princes are subiect to the *Pope*, therefore they are subiect in all things, and in all manner of subiection, but onely in that sort, as *Christ* hath giuen him power both to command & punish: As children are subiect to their Parents, seruants to their Masters, wiues to their husbands, yet they are not bound to obey them, but in those things, wherein they haue power to command, nor to be punished by them, but in that sort, as the temporall common-wealth, whereof they are members, hath expressely or couertly giuen them leaue to punish; and the reafon is, for that they are not *Superiours* in an abfolute and indefinite, but onely in a limited and determinate manner.

8. Now what opinion Card. *Bellarmine* doth follow, whether of the Diuines, or of the Canonists, truly I cannot as yet well vnderstand. For although he seeme to disallow the Canonists doctrine, which at large he confuteth in his controuersies, yet to prooue the Popes power to depose Princes, and to difpose of temporals in order to spirituall good, hee laieth fuch grounds, concerning the vnion and fubordination of the temporall and spirituall power among Christians, which doe cleerely confirme the Canonists doctrine. For concerning the vnion of these two powers, hee

A a 2   affirmeth,

affirmeth, as you haue seene, that the temporall 'and spirituall power, the kingdome of *Christ*, and the kingdomes of this world, when they are Christian, doe make one totall body, which is the Christian common-wealth and Church of Christ, whereof the *Pope* is head; from whence it necessarily followeth, that the *Pope*, in whom all the power of the Church doth reside, must haue truely, properly and formally both ciuill and spirituall power, which is the Canonists opinion, and not onely spirituall power, which is not *formally*, but onely *vertually* ciuill, which the Diuines, and alfo Card. *Bellarmine* in places doe affirme. And now concerning the subiection and subordination of these two powers, he affirmeth, that the temporall power among Christians, not onely as it is Christian, but alfo as it is temporall, is subiect to the Ecclesiasticall, as it is Ecclesiasticall, or which is all one, that the temporall power it felfe among Christians is *per se*, and of it owne nature subiect to the spirituall : from whence it cleerely followeth as before I shewed by the examples of Musike and Physike, Christian Princes not onely in spirituals and in temporals, when they become spirituals, which is in order to spirituall good, but alfo in meere temporall caufes, are subiect to spirituall Paftours, which is the Canonists opinion, and which Card. *Bellarmine* in other places doth disprooue.

   9. But how vnfoundly Card. *Bellarmine*, and not conformably to his owne grounds laboreth to proue, that the temporall power it felfe among Christians, as it is temporall, is subiect to the spirituall, as it is spirituall, you shall anone perceiue. For six principall arguments I doe finde in Card. *Bellarmine*, by which he endeauoureth to conuince, that the temporal power it felfe among Christians, as it is temporall, is subiect and subordained to the spirituall, as it is spirituall, or, which I take for all one, that the temporall power among

among Christians is *per se*, and of it owne nature, suppo-
posing the institution of *Christ*, subiect and subordained to the spirituall ; which arguments of *Card. Bellarmine* I thinke it fit to examine in this place, toge her
with the Replyes, which he either in his booke against
D. *Barclay*, or in his *Schulckenius* against mee hath
brought to confirme the same, that thereby the Reader may fully vnderstand, in what manner the temporall power is subiect to the spirituall , and how strong
or weake a proofe is the subiection or subordination
of these two powers, which is by Mr. *Fitzherbert* suppo-
posed to be so inuinsible a ground, to conclude from
thence, that the *Pope*, as *Pope*, hath power, in order to
spirituall good, to dispose of all temporalls, to depose
temporall Princes, and to punish by way of coercion
with all kinde of temporall punishments.

Chap. 5. *Wherein is examined Card.* Bellar-
mines *first argument taken from the
ends of the temporall and spirituall
power.*

1. THe *first* argument, which *Card. Bellarmine* affirmeth ᵃ to *demonstrate, that the temporall power
among Christians, not only as it is Christian, but also as it is
ciuill,* or *temporall, is subiect to the Ecclesiasticall, as it is
Ecclesiasticall,* is taken from the ends of both the powers. For *a temporall end,* saith he, *is subordained to a spirituall end, as it is manifest , because temporall felicitie is
not absolutely the last end , and therefore it ought to bee referred to eternall felicitie : but it is apparant out of Aristotle,* 1 Ethic. cap. 1. *that faculties, or powers are so subordained, as their ends are subordained.*

2. To this argument I answered in my *Apologie* b,
" that not euery temporall end is *per se*, and of it owne
" nature ordained, or subordained to a spirituall end

a *Lib.* 5. *de
Rom Pont. c.* 7.

b *Num.*162.*&
seq.*

A a 2   " (speaking

"(speaking of create ends, and not of God almigh-
"ty, who is the beginning and end of all things) but
"it is only by *accident*, or accidentally by man, who
"worketh for an end, ordained to a spirituall end.
" And therefore although temporall good, or felicity
" be not absolutely the last end of man, yet it is the
last end of the temporall power it selfe, which is in
"man. For euery power, as it is a power, hath for
" her last end, her act or worke, as euery science hath
" of it owne nature for her last end the knowledge of
" her obiect, and euery art the effecting of her work,
" (as the last end of naturall philosophie is to know
" the secrets of nature, and of Phisike to cure and pre-
"serue the body from diseases) although man him-
"selfe, in whom that power, art, or science doth re-
"side, doth intend a farther end. Whereupon S. Au-
"stin doth well affirme, *that the will to see hath no other*

c *Lib.* 11. *de Trin. cap.* 6.

" *end then seeing: The will*, saith he, *c to see hath seeing*
" *for her end, and the will to see this thing hath for her end*
" *the seeing of this thing: The will therefore to see a skarre*
" *doth desire her end, that is, the seeing of a skarre, and no*
"*further doth appertaine to her.* Wherefore, as the
"Philosophers do distinguish betwixt the last end of
" any art or worke, and the last end of the artificer, or
" worker, so we also ought to distinguish betwixt the
"last end of the power it selfe, and of him, in whom
"the power doth reside. It is called the last end of the
"worke, for that the worke is in that lastly ended,
" and not the last end of the worker, for that the wor-
"ker doth not referre all that is his to that end, as a
"thing to be desired and loued aboue all things.

   3. I grant therefore that the end of a Christian
" Prince, who hath temporall power, is spirituall and
" eternall felicitie, to which Christians ought to refer
" all their actions, and the vse not only of the Eccle-
"siasticall, but also of the ciuill power, but withall I
" affirme, that the last end, which the ciuill power hath

                 " per

" *per se,* and of it owne nature, is only temporall peace
" and quietnesse, in the getting and conseruing wher-
" of of it owne nature it doth lastly rest. And there-
" fore for this reason it is not necessary, that the ciuill
" power it selfe be *per se,* and of it owne nature subor-
" dained to the Ecclesiasticall, but onely accidentally
" and by the intention of him, who referreth tempo-
" rall peace to eternall felicitie in that maner as I haue
" declared. To that assertion of *Aristotle,* powers
" are so subordained as their ends are subordained (al-
" though in that place hee rather saith, that ends are
" subordained, as powers are subordained) I answer-
" ed, that it is to be vnderstood of those ends, which
" powers haue of their owne nature, and not of the
" ends of the men, in whom the powers doe reside.
Thus I answered in my *Apologie.*

4. Now you shall see how insufficiently *Card. Bellarmine* in his *Schulckenius* replyeth to this answere. *I
answere* saith he, [d] *that not euery temporall or corporall end
is subordained* per se, *and of it owne nature to a spirituall
end, my* Aduersary Widdrington *doth say, but hee doth
not proue.* But *first,* who knoweth not, that it doth not
appertaine to the Answerer to proue, for to this the opponent only is tyed, and for the Answearer it sufficeth
by granting, denying, or distinguishing for him to
answere.

5. *Secondly,* I did not conceiue, that this assertion, being so cleere and manifest of it selfe, needed a-
ny proofe at all, and therefore I little thought, that a-
ny learned man would euer deny the same: for that,
according to the knowne principles of Philosophy
and Diuinitie, no naturall thing can intrinsically, and
of it own nature be referred to a thing, which is supernaturall and aboue the course of nature ; and therefore betwixt naturall and supernaturall things, there
can be no naturall subordination. Now that temporall peace in a temporall common-wealth is a naturall
thing

d *Pag.* 329.
ad num. 162.

thing, and eternall felicitie, which confifteth in the cleere vifion and fruition of almighty God, is fupernaturall, and goeth beyond the bounds, limits, and order of nature, no man can make any doubt; and therefore temporall peace cannot of it owne nature be referred to eternall felicity; but onely by the will and intention of man, who by the helpe of fupernaturall light and grace doth referre it, direct it, and eleuate it to that fupernaturall end.

6. And for this caufe alfo it is very cleere, that temporall power cannot of it owne nature bee referred to true fpirituall and Ecclefiafticall power, for that it is fupernatural, and giuen onely by *God*, as he is the Author, not of nature, but of fupernaturall grace. Yea out of Card. *Bellarmines* owne grounds it may be cleerely conuinced, that the temporall power among Chriftians is not of it own nature fubiect, and fubordained to the fpirituall power, and confequently, that temporall peace, which is the end of temporall power, is not of it own nature referred or ordained to eternal felicity, which is the laft create end of the fpiritual power, for that according to *Ariftotle* [e], *ends are fo*

fubordained, as their powers are fubordained. His firft ground is, for that in his *Controuerfies* he affirmeth [f], *that in Infidels there is true ciuill powtr without any order, or relation to any true fpirituall, or Ecclefiafticall power,* and confequently in Infidels the ciuill power is not fubiect or fubordained to the fpirituall, for where there is no order, or relation, there can be no fubiection, or fubordination, for that fubiection and fubordination doth necelfarily imply an order, relation, or reference to that, to which any thing is fubordained.

7. Seeing therefore that Chriftian Religion doth not take away true ciuill power, as *Card. Bellarmine* himfelfe alfo in another place affirmeth [g], neither

is the true nature, or any intrinfecall propertie of the ciuil power changed or altered, for that it is in a Chriftian,

ſtian, or an Infidell, in this ſubieƈt, or in that, it neceſſarily followeth, that if true ciuill power bee not of it
own nature ſubieƈt, or ſubordained in Infidels to true
ſpirituall, or Eccleſiaſtical power, it is not alſo in Chriſtians *per ſe,* and of it own nature ſubieƈt or ſubordained to true ſpirituall or Eccleſiaſticall power. This
onely alteration hath ciuill power for being in this
ſubieƈt, or in that, in Infidels, or in Chriſtians, that
Chriſtians ought, according to the true grounds of
Chriſtian Religion, referre it by the aide of true ſupernaturall faith to a true ſupernaturall end, to which
Infidels, who want true ſupernaturall faith, cannot referre it : but this alteration is extrinſecall or accidentall, not intrinſecall or eſſentiall, neither doth it proceed from the nature of the ciuill power it ſelfe, but
from the wil & intention of him, in whom true ciuill
power doth reſide. As likewiſe the nature or intrinſecall properties of other accidents, as of Muſick, Phy-
ſick, and ſuch like, are not altered, or changed by the
changing or altering of their ſubieƈts, & for that they
are in Chriſtians, or in Infidels, although a Chriſtian
Muſician will refer & ordaine his Muſick to the true
worſhip of God, & an Infidel to the honor of his Idol.

     8. The ſecond ground, which *Card. Bellarmine*
layeth to prooue, that the temporall power among
Chriſtians is not *per ſe,* and of it owne nature ſubieƈt to the ſpirituall power, is, for that in his *Schulcke-*
nius he affirmeth [h], *That among the Heathen Romanes,*
the ciuill power was ſubiect to the ſpiritual power of a falſe
religion: and a little beneath, *if the ciuill power,* ſaith
he, *be ioyned with a falſe Eccleſiaſticall power, that is of*
a falſe Religion, as it was in the Heathen Romane Com-
mon-wealth, then it is actually ſubordained to a falſe Ec-
cleſiaſticall power, and if it bee ioyned with a true Ec-
cleſiaſticall power, as in the Chriſtian and Catholike
Church, then it is actually ſubordained to a true Eccleſi-
aſticall power. Now what Philoſopher, or Diuine

[h] *Pag.* 276. *ad*
nu. 140.

will affirme that a true ciuill power is *per fe*, and of it owne nature actually ordained, fubordained, or referred to a falfe Ecclefiafticall power, that is of a falfe Religion, or to the worfhipping of falfe Gods. Therfore this fubiection, fubordination, or relation of true ciuill power to the fpirituall, proceedeth from the intention of him, in whom the ciuill power doth refide, who according to his faith and religion (bee it true or falfe) referreth his true ciuill power to a true or falfe Religion, to a true or falfe worfhipping of God, and not from the nature, or any intrinfecal propertie of the true ciuill power it felfe, which, as it is the fame in Infidels and Chriftians, or in whatfoeuer fubiect it be: fo alfo of it own nature hath the fame end as well in Infidels as in Chriftians, to wit, temporall peace, to which of it owne nature it is alwaies referred. And therefore I doe not onely fay : but alfo I doe cleerely prooue, and that out of Card. *Bellarmines* owne grounds, to which neuerthelelfe I being only an anfwerer, and not an opponent, was not tied, that neither the ciuil power, being only a naturall power, nor the end of ciuill power, which is temporal peace, being onely a naturall end, is *per fe*, and of it owne nature fubiect, or fubordained to a true fupernaturall power or end, but onely by the intenfion of him, in whom the ciuill power doth refide.

9. Now you fhal fee how wel D. *Schulckenius* proueth the contrarie. *But wee prooue the contrary*, faith he, ⁱ *becaufe the end of the fpirituall common-wealth is euerlafting faluation, which is the laft end ; the end of the temporall common-wealth is the peace of the Citie, or Kingdome, which is not the laft end, but a mediate end. But all ends are fubordained* per fe, *and of their owne nature to the laft end, and in vertue of it they doe mooue, as all efficient caufes are fubordained* per fe, *and of their owne nature to the firft efficient caufe, and in vertue of it they worke whatfoeuer they doe worke. See S.* Thomas 1*a.* 2*a. q.* 1. *ar.* 6.

i *Pag.* 329. *ad nu.* 162.

10 But

10. But to this argument I answered before, that the last create end of the spirituall common-wealth, which is a companie of men vnited by Baptisme, in that manner as I declared before, is eternal saluation, to which they ought to referre all their powers both temporall and spirituall, and all their actions both in generall and particular: but I denied, that the last end of the temporall power it selfe, although it bee con-ioyned in one & the selfe same subiect with true spiri-tuall power, is eternall saluation, but onely temporall peace in the common-wealth, to which of it owne nature it is onely referred, as to her last end, although by the intention of him, in whom true ciuill and spi-rituall power doth reside, it ought to bee referred to eternall saluation, as to the last end of a Christian man, but not as to the last end, which the temporall power it selfe hath *per se*, and of it owne nature. Nei-ther hath D. *Schulckenius* proued the contrary, but ra-ther in his *Reply* to my answere hee in expresse words confirmeth what I haue said. For in his answere to the authority, which I brought out of S. *Augustine*, hee affirmeth, *That the last end of one particular will, power, or science is their act or operation*, and therefore it cannot of it owne nature be referred to eternall salua-tion, as to the last end, vnlesse D. *Schulckenius* will admit, that the same particular power hath of it owne nature two last ends, or a later end then the last, which implieth a manifest contradiction; but it must onely be referred extrinsecally to eternall saluation by the intention of him, in whom the particular power doth reside.

11 True it is, *That all create ends are subordained per se, and of their nature to that end, which is simply and absolutely the last end, and doe moue in vertue thereof, as all efficient causes are subordained per se, and of their owne nature to that, which is simply and absolutely the first efficient cause, and in vertue thereof they doe worke what-*

B b 2   *soeuer*

soeuer they do worke : But this efficient and finall cause
of all created things is not the eternall saluation of
men, but God amighty, who is *Alpha* & *Omega, prin-*
cipium & *finis,* the beginning and end of all created
things, both naturall and supernaturall, both vnrea-
sonable and reasonable, of accidents and substances,
of all powers and of all things wherein powers doe
reside, and who is glorified not onely by the eternall
saluation, but also by the eternall damnation of men.
God alone is simply and absolutely the last end of all
created things, to whome all naturall things are of
their owne nature lastly referred, as to the first Authour and last end of nature, and supernaturall
things, as to the first Authour and last end of grace
and glory : Neither can naturall things of their owne
nature be referred to any supernaturall create end, as
is eternall saluation, but onely by the will and intention of him : who by the helpe of supernatural grace
shall referre and eleuate them aboue their nature to a
supernaturall end.   Neither doth S. *Thomas* in that
place affirme the contrary, but rather most cleerely
confirmeth, what I haue said : for there he only dis-
puteth, how euery man by his wil,intention, and desire, referreth all good things, which hee desireth to
the last end.

12. Marke now, I beseech you, D. *Schulckenius*
his second proofe, which is no whit better then the

k *Pag.* 330.

former. *Moreouer is not the body,* saith he[k], *per se, or*
of it owne nature for the soule ? why then are not corporall
things, per se, or of their owne nature for spirituall things?
And whereas my Aduersarie Widdrington *seemeth to*
say, that euery temporall end is per accidens, *or acciden-*
tally referred to a spirituall end : as by man, who worketh
for an end, it is ordained to a spirituall end, it is altoge-
ther false. For oftentimes wicked men doe ordaine spiri-
tuall things to temporall, of whom the Apostle *saith,*
whose God is their belly : *and by this a temporall end is*
per

per se, *and of it owne nature alwaies ordained to a spiritu-* *all end, but by accident and against nature by the wicked-* *nesse of humane intention sometimes a spirituall end is or-* *dained to a temporall.*

13. The reason why the body is *per se,* and of it owne nature for the soule or spirit, and yet the temporall power, or the end thereof, is not *per se,* and of it owne nature referred to the spirituall power, or the end thereof, I did declare in my *Apologie*[1], which D. *Schulckenius* also did relate a little before, [m] *because the bodie and soule doe compound one substantiall thing consi-* *sting of two essentiall parts, whereof the bodie is the mat-* *ter,* as the Philosophers doe call it, *and the soule the* *forme; and this is the reason, why the body is* per se, *and of* *it owne nature, for the soule and subiect are subordained to* *it;* for that all Philosophers doe grant, that euery matter is *per se,* and of it owne nature for the substantiall forme, wherewith it maketh one essentiall compound; *but the temporall and spirituall powers doe not* *make one totall bodie* or common-wealth; *whereof the* *temporall power is insteed of the matter, and the spirituall* *insteede of the forme.* And therefore D. *Schulckenius* had small reason to make that interrogation, seeing that hee himselfe did a little before set downe this my reason, which doth fully satisfie the aforesaid demand.

14 Neither did I say, as *D. Schulckenius* here affirmeth me to say, although a little before, as you haue seene [n], he related my words otherwise, *that* *euery temporall end* is *per accidens,* or accidentally *re-* *ferred to a spirituall end,* but I only affirmed, *that not* *euery temporall end,* and in particular *temporall peace* among Christians, which is the last end of the ciuill power it selfe, *is not* per se, *and of it owne nature ordai-* *ned to eternal saluation,* which is the last end of the spirituall power, but onely *per accidens,* or accidentally, as by the will and intention of a Christian man,

it is ordained to eternall faluation, which is a fupernaturall end, and therefore not proportionate to the
nature of any ciuill or naturall power. And although
I had faid, that euery temporall end is *per accidens*
referred to a fpirituall end, yet *D: Schulckenius* could
not but perceiue by the whole fcope of my words,
that my meaning was to fay, that euery temporall
end, which is referred to a fpirituall end, is not *per fe,*
and of it owne nature referred to that fpirituall end,
but *per accidens,* and extrinfecally by the will and intention of man, who referreth it to that fpirituall
end. for no man can bee fo ignorant as to imagine,
that Chriftians doe alwaies referre and ordaine all
temporall ends to the eternall faluation of their
foules.

15   True it is, that all naturall things belonging
to man are of fuch a nature, as that by the intention
of man they may be ordained to good or bad ends,
and temporall peace, which is a naturall end, may by
the will of man, being aided with fupernaturall grace,
be referred and eleuated to eternall felicitie, which is
a fupernaturall end; and this is agreeable to reafon,
and to the nature of man, as he is a reafonable creature, or led by reafon, to ordaine, referre, and eleuate
all naturall things, which are in his power, when by
the helpe of grace he is able fo to doe, to true fupernaturall ends, and to eternall felicitie, for which hee
was created, and to doe otherwife were againft reafon, and againft the nature of man, as hee is endued
with reafon : But that naturall powers, or ends, fhould
be *per fe,* and of their owne nature *actually* referred,
and eleuated to fupernaturall powers or ends, much
leffe fupernaturall powers or ends, fhould be referred
and depreffed to naturall powers or vicious ends, but
only by the good or wicked intention of a man, in
whofe power it is to ordaine a good thing to a bad
end, a naturall power to a fupernaturall, and contrariwife,

riwiie, this truly I thinke no man of any learning can conceiue, and before I haue clearely proued, that it is altogether falfe.

16 *Laftly*, to thofe words, which I alledged out of *S. Auftin*, and to the reft which follow in my An-fwer, *D. Shulckenius* replyeth in this manner : *I an-fwer firft*, faith he °, *It is true, that the laft end of one* o *Pag.* 332. *particular will, power, or science is their act , but it is not true, that the laft end of one particular will, power, or sci-ence is not referred* per fe *and of their owne nature to that end, which is simply the laft end, but onely by accident by the intention of him, who hath that will, power, or science. And this not only* S. Thomas *in the place cited doth teach, but alfo* S. Auftin *in the place alledged by* Widdrington, *to wit,* lib. 11. de Trinit. cap. 6. *All thefe,* faith S. Au-ftin, *and fuch like wills haue firft their ends, which are referred to the end of that will, whereby we are willing to liue happily.* Thus S. Auftin, *who, when he fubioyneth,* the will therefore to fee a skar doth defire hir end, to wit, the feeing of a skar, and farther doth not apper-taine to hir, *he signifieth indeed, that the feeing of a skar is the laft end of the will to fee a skar, but hee doth not deny, that the feeing of a skar is* per fe, *and of it owne nature referred to a higher end of a higher will, and that to an other, vntill we come to that end, which is* fimply the laft end. *For all good ends are of their owne nature refer-red to that end, which is* fimply *the laft end, and as ends are of their owne nature fubordained one to an other, fo alfo it is neceffarie, that wills, powers, or fciences be fub-ordained. As for example, (to perfift in* S. Auftins *ex-ample) a man hath many wills, one to fee a skar, an other, by feeing the skar to finde the wound ; the third, by fin-ding the wound, to convince and correct him, who did inflict the wound ; the fourth, by correcting him to heale the wound of his foule ; the fift, by this act of charitie to me-rit life euerlafting ; it is certaine, that euery one of thefe wills haue their proper end, neither any thing farther doth*

appertaine

appertaine to them, but it is also certaine, that the end of the first will is referred to the end of the second will, and the first will it selfe subordained to the second, and so in order. Thus *D. Schulckenius.*

17 But truly in my opinion *D. Schulckenius* doth in this Reply both plainly contradict himselfe, and also clearely confirme my Answer. And *first* no man can make any doubt, but that all wills, powers, sciences, ends, and things whatsoeuer are *per se*, and of their owne nature referred to that, which is *simply* the last end ; but that, which is *simply* the last end of all things, is not the eternall felicitie of any creature, but *God almightie*, who alone is *simply* the efficient and finall cause of all things, and *made all things*, both heauen and hell, *for himselfe*, Prouerb. 16. and who is glorified not only in the eternall saluation, but also in the eternall damnation both of Men and Angells: And this *D. Schulckenius* can not deny, and he might haue seene the same confirmed by *S. Thomas* in the same question cited by him *ar.* 8. but more expressely 1ª. *part. q.* 44. *ar.* 4. where he proueth, that becaufe *God* almightie is the first efficient caufe of all things, he must of neceffitie be also the last end of all things: and by *S. Auftin* also in infinite places.

18. *Secondly*, whereas D. *Schulckenius* affirmeth, *that the last end of one particular will, power, or science is their act*, and withall, *that this last end is* per *se, and of it owne nature referred to a further create end*, (whereof only he speaketh) and confequently that particular will or power must also be referred to that farther end, and so it must be referred to a farther end then to the last, he cleerely contradicteth himselfe. For how can any act be *per se*, and of it owne nature be the last end of one particular will, power or science, and yet this last end bee *per se*, and of it owne nature referred to a farther end, seeing that according to the approoued grounds of philofophie, which kinde of arguing the Logicians

Logicians call *Sorites*, or *à primo ad vltimum*, *an argument from the firft to the laft*, euery particular will, power or fcience, which is *per fe*, and of it owne nature referred to any particular end, is alfo referred to all thofe ends, to which that particular end is *per fe*, and of it owne nature referred ? As for example, if any particular will be *per fe*, and of it owne nature referred to the feeing of a skar, and the feeing of a skarre bee *per fe*, and of it owne nature referred to the finding out of the wound, and the finding out of the wound be *per fe*, and of it owne nature referred to the correcting of him who did inflict the wound &c. then *à primo ad vltimum*, *from the firft to the laft*, the will to fee a skarre muft *per fe*, and and of it owne nature bee referred to the correcting of him, who did inflict the wound &c. Wherefore if the feeing of a skarre bee the laft end of the will to fee a skarre, as D. *Schulckenius* heere affirmeth, it cannot *per fe*, and of it owne nature bee referred to a farther end, vnleffe hee will grant, that the fame will fhall haue *per fe* a farther end, then the laft, which is a flat contradiction ; but if it be referred to a farther end, it is onely by *accident*, and extrinfecally by the intention of the feer, who referreth the feeing of a skarre to a farther end, then it hath of it owne nature. Neither doth S. *Thomas*, or S. *Auftin* affirme the contrary, but confirme what I haue fayd.

19. For although S. *Auftin* doth affirme, *that all thefe & fuch like wils haue their proper ends, which are referred to the end of that will, wherby we defire to liue happily, and to come to that life, which is not referred to any other thing, but it doth of it felfe fatisfie the Louer*, yet he doth not fay, that thefe proper ends, are *per fe*, and of their owne nature referred to euerlafting happineffe, but he doth rather in expreffe words fay, that they are by fome particular will, or intention of man referred to euerlafting happineffe. And therefore he concludeth,

C c deth,

deth, *that all wils are well connected together, if that will be good, whereunto all the rest be referred, but if that bee bad, all the other wils are bad.* So that S. *Austin* cannot be so vnderstood, that all those wils are *per se,* and of their owne nature referred to a good, or to a bad will, for that a will, which of it owne nature is good, can not of it owne nature be referred to a bad will, or to a bad end. And therefore when S. *Austin* saith, *that the will to see a skarre hath for her proper end the seeing of a skarre, and no farther appertaineth to her,* hee vnderstandeth of the last end, which the will to see a skar hath *per se,* and of it owne nature, and when he saith, *that it may be referred to a farther end, good or bad,* he vnderstandeth of a farther end, not which it hath of *it owne nature,* but which it hath by some other will or intention, which may be good or bad, according as it referreth all the other wils to a good or bad end.

20. Moreouer those examples, which D. *Schulckenius* bringeth in the end of his *Reply,* doe most cleerly confirme my answer, and confute his owne *Reply.* For if a man haue many wils, one to see a skarre, another by seeing the skar to prooue the wound, the third by prouing the wound to correct him who inflicted the wound and so foorth, it is certaine, that the seeing of the skarre is not *per se,* and of it owne nature referred and ordained to prooue the wound, and to correct him, who did inflict the wound, but onely by the will and intention of the seer, who referreth it to those ends, in whose choice it is to refer the seeing of a skar to other ends : neither is their any naturall or necessary connexion betwixt the seeing of the skar, the proouing of the wound, and the correcting of him, who did inflict it : for that a skar may be seene for many other ends, and not at all for those. Besides, it is repugnant to the course of nature, that the seeing of a skar, which is a naturall thing, should be *per se,* and of it own nature referred & ordained to the euerlasting

happinesse

happinesse of man, which is a thing aboue nature, and
beyond the course of naturall things, and therefore it
is only *by accident*, and extrinsecally by the intention
and will of man referred and ordained to that supernaturall end. And thus you see, that I haue not only
clearely answered to this *first argument* of Card. *Bellarmine*, which had been sufficient for me, who tooke
vpon mee only to answere, and not to proue, but also
haue clearely prooued, that although eternall felicitie,
be the last create end of man, yet temporall peace,
and not eternall felicitie is the last create end, to which
temporall power euen among Christians is *per se*, and
of it owne nature referred.

21. Neuerthelesse, I will go a little farther with
Card. Bellarmine, and grant him for Disputation sake,
which hitherto he hath not in my iudgement so much
as *probably* proued, that thereby the weakenesse also of
this his first pretended demonstration may the more
easily appeare; to wit, that not only the Ecclesiasticall,
but also the ciuill power among Christians is *per se*;
and of it owne nature, and not only by the will and intention of Christian men referred to the true eternall
saluation of man, as to the last end not only of man,
but of the ciuill power it selfe, yet it can not therefore
from hence by any necessarie consequence bee inferred, that the ciuill power among Christians is *per se*;
and of it owne nature subiect and subordained to the
spirituall power, or that the end of the ciuill power is
subordained to the end of the spirituall power, but at
the most, that both of them haue one & the selfe same
last end, to wit, the eternall felicitie of man, to which
the spirituall power leadeth Christian men by spirituall
meanes, to wit, by spirituall directions, lawes, and punishments, and the ciuill power by ciuill meanes, directions, lawes, and punishments: And therefore there
is no subordination of ends, betwixt the ends of the
spirituall and temporall power, and consequently no

subordina

subordination of powers, but they haue both one laſt
end, to wit, euerlaſting happineſſe, although diuerſe
waies, or meanes to attaine thereunto, not much vnlike diuerſe lines in a circle, which doe end all in one
center, and yet one line is not ſubordained to another,
although all of them doe tend by diuerſe waies to the
ſame center. And therefore by this firſt argument
Card. Bellarmine hath not ſufficiently proued, that the
ciuill power among Chriſtians is *per ſe*, and of it owne
nature ſubordained to the ſpirituall, or the proper end
of the ciuil power, which is her act tending to teporall
peace, ſubordained to the proper end of the ſpirituall
power, which is alſo her act tending laſtly to euerlaſting happineſſe ; although I ſhould grant him, that
both of them haue *per ſe*, and of their owne nature one
and the ſelfe ſame laſt end, which is the eternall ſaluation of man, in whom thoſe powers doe reſide. And
therefore D. *Schulckenius* perceiuing belike the ſufficiencie of my anſwere, and the weakneſſe of his owne
Reply, flieth to a ſecond *Reply*, which neuertheleſſe is
as inſufficient as the former.

P *Pag.* 333.   22. But *although we ſhould grant*, ſaith her, *to Widdring-*
ton, that the end of the ciuill power is not referred per ſe,
and of it owne nature to the end of the ſpirituall, but onely by
the intention of the Prince, in whom the ciuill power doth re-
ſide, yet the argument which Card. Bellarmine *brought*
from the ſubiection of the temporall power to the ſpirituall, to
proue that the ſpirituall Prince could not onely command
temporall Princes, but alſo diſpoſe of temporalls in order to
ſpirituall good, would be moſt ſtrong and good. For a Chri-
ſtian temporall Prince ought to referre the publike peace,
which is the end of ciuill power, to the eternall peace and fe-
licitie of himſelfe and of his people, which is the end of the
ſpirituall power. And therefore hee ought to ſubiect and
ſubordaine the end of his power to the end of the power of the
ſpirituall Prince. But as he ought to ſubiect and ſubordaine
end to end, ſo alſo power to power. Wherefore hee ought not
to

to take it in ill part, if he be truly a Christian Prince, that the Pope *by his spirituall power direct, and correct the ciuill power, and that so the sword be vnder the sword, and in the Christian common wealth there be order, peace, and quietnesse, whiles Superiours do rule inferiours, and inferiours be subiect to Superiours.*

23. But in this Reply there lie hidden some cunning equiuocations, and the most that it proueth, as oftentimes heretofore I haue signified, is, that the temporall power or sword, or rather temporall Princes who haue temporall power, and beare the temporall sword, are in spirituall causes) whether of their owne nature, or by some accidentall circumstance they become spirituall) to the spirituall or Ecclesiasticall power, by which they are to be directed & corrected, not in meere temporals, but only in spirituals, not by temporall lawes, or with temporall punishments, which doe belong onely to the temporall power, but only by Ecclesiasticall lawes or directions, and with Ecclesiasticall or spirituall punishments or corrections, which onely do appertaine to the Ecclesiasticall or spirituall power.

24. True it is, that eternall saluation is the last create end not only of the spirituall, but also of the temporall power among Christians, seeing that all Christian Princes are bound by the law of Christ to referre their temporall power, and the vse thereof, not onely to temporall peace in the common weath, which is the last end, which temporall power hath *per se,* and of it owne nature, but also to the eternall peace and felicity of themselues, and of their people ; And therefore there is here no subordination of ends betwixt the temporall power and the spirituall, and consequently in this respect no subordination of powers, as D. *Schulckenius* doth here from thence inferre, but aswell the ciuill power among Christians, as the spirituall, haue one and the selfe same last end (whether it bee intrinsecall

trinfecall to one power, and extrinfecall to the other, or intrinfecall to both as I declared before) to which the temporall power by temporall lawes, directions, and corrections, and the spirituall power by spirituall lawes, directions, and corrections or punishments are by the law of Christ bound to direct, and lead all Christians.

25. Whereupon *S.* Thomas, or whosoeuer bee the Authour of that booke de Regimine Principum doth well affirme, *q that the end which a King ought principally to intend in himselfe, and in his subiects, is eternall happinesse, which doth consist in the seeing of God, and because this seeing of God is the most perfect good of all, it ought to moue exceedingly a King and euery Lord, that their subiects may attaine to this end.* Therefore, when Kings, saith *S. Austin,* ʳ *in the time of the Apostles did not serue our Lord, then impieties could not be forbidden by lawes, but rather exercised. But afterwards, when that began to be fulfilled which is written,* ſ *And all the Kinges of the earth shall adore him, all nations shall serue him, What sober minded man can say to Kings, Doe not you regard by whom the Church of your Lord is defended or impugned in your kingdome, that it doth not appertaine to you, who will be religious or sacrilegious in your kingdome, to whom it can not be said, that it doth not appertaine to you, who will bee chaft, or wanton in your kingdome.*

27. Wherefore if a Christian Prince should by his lawes, or otherwise, withdraw his subiects from the attaining to eternall saluation, should impugne not defend the Church, command not forbid impieties, hee should greatly offend God and the Church, and ought not to take it in ill part, that hee should be therefore corrected by the chiefe Pastour of the Church, to whom he is subiect in spiritualls, with Ecclesiasticall and spirituall punishments, which only doe belong to the spirituall power. But if the Pastour of the Church should take vpon him to correct such a Prince by way

way of coercion and constraint with temporall punishments, which kinde of correction doth passe the limits of his spirituall power, then the Prince may iustly take it in ill part, for this were to vsurpe temporall Iurisdiction, which is proper only to a temporall Prince, and not to obserue due order, but to make a confusion betwixt sword and sword, betwixt the spirituall and temporall power, which temporall power is only in spirituall corrections, and not in temporall punishments subiect to the constraint of the temporall power.

28   And therefore well said our most learned Countryman Alexander of Hales ᵗ cited by me before, *that the subiection of Kings and Emperours to the Pope is in spirituall not corporall punishment, according as it is said* 2ª. *q. 7. that it belongeth to Kings to exercise corporall punishment, and to Priests to vse spirituall correction. Whereupon* S. Ambrose *did excommunicate the Emperour* Arcadius, *and did forbid him to enter into the Church. For as an earthly Iudge not without cause beareth the sword, as it is said* Rom: 13. *so Priests doe not without cause receiue the keyes of the Church; he beareth the sword to the punishment of malefactors and commendation of the good, these haue keyes to the excluding of excommunicated persons, and reconciling of them who are penitent. Expound therefore;* A King is to be punished only by God, *that is, with materiall punishment,* and againe, A King hath no man to iudge his doings, *that is, to inflict corporall punishment.* and a little beneath, *A King,* saith Alexander, *doth excell,* 1. Pet: 2. *true it is in his order, to wit, to inflict corporall punishment, with which punishment, if he offend, he hath none to punish him but only God.* what can be spoken more plainly.

t 3. part. q 40. memb. 5. q. 4.

29   And by this you easily see the weaknes of *D. Schulckenius* his argument, and how cunningly with generall and ambiguous words he would delude his Reader. *A temporall Prince,* saith he, *ought to refer*
                                                            publike

publike peace to the eternall peace and felicitie of him selfe and of his people, which is the end of the spirituall power. And what then? *And as hee ought to subiect temporall peace to eternall peace, so he ought to subiect his temporall power to the spirituall power.* But how, in what manner, in what causes, in what punishments temporall power ought to bee subiect to spirituall power *D. Schulc.* cunningly concealeth. Temporall power to be subiect to spirituall, if wee will speake properly, and in *abstracto,* doth signifie, that a temporall Prince is in all temporall affaires subiect to the spirituall power of spirituall Pastors. And if by those generall words *D. Schulckenius* meaneth this, he falleth into the *Canonists* opinion, whose doctrine in this point learned *Victoria* [u] is not afraid to condemn *as manifestly false,* and *who being poore themselues in learning and riches to flatter the Pope gaue him this direct power and dominion in temporalls.* For the truth is, that temporall Princes in temporall affaires are not subiect to any besides God alone, which is the receiued doctrine of the ancient Fathers. The sense therefore of that proposition must be, that temporall Princes are in spiritualls, but not in temporalls subiect to the spirituall power of the *Pope.* But what then? *wherefore he ought not to take it in ill part, if he be truly a Christian Prince, that the Pope by his spirituall power direct, and correct the ciuill power* &c. Still you see he speaketh ambiguously, and in generall words, the sense whereof if hee had declared, you would presently haue perceiued the weaknesse of his argument: for if he meane, that therefore a temporall Prince ought to be directed in spiritualls, and in things belonging to Christian Religion, and corrected with spirituall punishments by the *Pope,* this I easily grant him, and so he proueth nothing against me, but if hee meane, that therefore a temporall Prince ought to be directed by the *Pope* in temporalls, and corrected by him

with

u *in Relect.* 1. *de potest. Eccles. num.* 2. *& 3.*

with temporall punishments, this consequence I vtterly denie, for this were to confound all good order,
and to vsurpe temporall Iurisdiction, as I declared
before. And thus much concerning *Card: Bellarmines* first argument, my answer, and *D. Schulckenius*
his Reply to the same.

Chap. 6. *Wherein is examined the second argu-
gument taken from the vnion of
Kings, and Bishops, Clerkes and Laikes
in one Church.*

1.   THe *second* argument, which *Card: Bellar-
mine* bringeth [a] to proue, that the *ciuill power*   a *Lib. 5. de
Rom. Pont.
cap. 7.*
*among Christians not onely as it is Christian, but also as it
is ciuill, is subiect to the Ecclesiasticall, as it is Ecclesiasticall,* is this: *Kings and Bishops, Clerkes and Laikes doe
not make two common-wealths but one, to wit, one Church.
Rom: 12. & 1.Cor.12. but in euery bodie the members
are connected, and one dependeth on the other, but it can
not rightly be said, that spirituall things doe depend vpon
temporall, therefore temporall things doe depend vpon spirituall, and are subiect to them.*
    2   To the *Maior* proposition of this argument
I answered before [b], that Kings and Bishops, Clearkes   b *Cap. 2.*
and Laikes, being diuerse waies considered, doe
make two totall, and not onely one totall body or
common-wealth. For as they are referred to the Ecclesiasticall or spirituall power of the chiefe visible Pastour, to whom all Christians are subiect in spirituals,
they make one totall body or common-wealth, to
wit, the Catholike Church, which is the spirituall
Kingdome and mysticall body of Christ, but as they
are referred to the ciuill power of temporall Princes,
to whom all inferiour Clerkes and Laikes are subiect
in temporals, as all members are subiect to the head,
        D d   they

they make another body or common-wealth, to wit, earthly kingdomes, as before I declared more at large. And this is sufficient to shew the weaknesse of this *second argument*, the *Maior* proposition thereof being cleerely false.

3. But to declare more fully the insufficiencie thereof, and to shew most plainely, that not onely his *Maior* proposition, as I haue prooued before, but also his *Misor* is apparantly false, I answer *secondly* with D. *Barclay* to his *Minor*, that although in euery "body the members are vnited and connected ei-"ther immediately, or mediately to the head, vpon "whom they all depend, yet that in euery body all "the members doe depend one vpon the other, there "is no man so ignorant that will affirme : for neither "one foote doth depend vpon the other, nor one "arme vpon the other, nor one shoulder vpon the o-"ther, but they are connected to some third either "immediately by themselues, or to other members, "to which they adhere. May it not, I pray you, by "the same manner of arguing, and by the very same "argument be concluded thus : The armes of euery "man are members of one body, but in euery bodie "the members are connected, and depending one "vpon the other, but it cannot rightly bee said that "the right arme doth depend vpon the left, therfore "the left arme of euerie man doth depend vpon the "right, and is subiect vnto it. Who would not skorn "such foolish arguments?

c *In Tract.
contra Barcl.
cap. 14.*

4. To this answer *Card. Bellarmine* c replieth in this manner. *That which I sayd, that the members of the same body are connected, and that one doth depend vpon another, I vnderstood of members of a diuerse kinde, as is a finger, a hand, an arme, a shoulder and a head, and not of members of the same kinde, as are two hands, two feet, two eyes, two eares. For the ciuill and Ecclesiasticall power, whereof we speake, are of a diuerse kinde, as it is manifest,*
and

and words are to bee vnderftood according to the matter,
which is treated of, otherwife there could not bee any de-
monftration fo certaine, againft which there could not bee
brought fome cauill. Therefore Kingly power, which is
principall in his kinde, if it compound one body with the Ec-
clefiafticall power, which alfo in his kinde is principall, muft
of neceffitie be either fubiect, or fuperiour, leaft that in one
bodie there be two heads ; and feeing that it is manifeft e-
nough, that the Pope is head of the Church in fteede of
Chrift, it doth plainely follow, that a King muft either bee
no member of this body, or elfe hee muft bee fubiect to the
Pope, and in the fame manner the ciuill power, which doth
chiefely refide in the King, muft either bee fubiect to the
fpirituall, which doth chiefely refide in the Pope, or elfe it
muft remaine out of the Church ; in that manner as a fin-
ger cannot be in the body, which doth not depend vpon the
hand, nor a hand, which doth not depend vpon the arme,
nor an arme, which doth not depend vpon the fhoulder, nor
a fhoulder, which doth not depend vpon the head.

5. *But that, which* Barclay *faith a little after, that*
the fpirituall and ciuill power are as two fhoulders in a body,
whereof neither is fubiect to the other, but both of them are
fubiect to one head, which is Chrift, is not onely falfe, be-
caufe thofe powers are not of the fame kinde ; that they may
be compared to two fhoulders, but alfo it appertaines to the
herefie of this time. *For what doe the heretikes of this*
time more endeauour to perfwade the people, then that the
Pope is not the vifible head of the body of the Church, vn-
to whom all Chriftians, if they will be faued, muft bee fub-
iect ? But this Barclay *of his owne accord doth grant them,*
who neuerthelefe in all his booke doth make himfelfe a Ca-
tholike: Therefore the fpirituall and ciuill power are not
well compared to two fhoulders, but they ought either to
bee compared to the fpirit and flefh, as did S. Gregorie
Nazianzene *in the place often cited compare them, or elfe*
to the fhoulder and head, to wit, principall members, wher-
of neuerthelefe the one, although of it felfe very ftrong and

potent,

potent, ought to bee directed and gouerned by the other, which is superiour.

6 But this *Reply* of Card: *Bellarmine*, although at the firſt ſight may ſeeme eſpecially to the vnlearned to haue in it ſome ſhew of *probabilitie*, yet to the iudicious Reader, who will be pleaſed to examine it more exactly, it will clearely appeare, to be in very deede very vnſound and fallacious, to *D. Barclay* very iniurious, to Catholike religion very ſcandalous, and in very truth to haue in it no *probabilitie at all*, as Mr. *Iohn Barclay* in his anſwer to Card. *Bellarmine* hath moſt clearely conuinced. And firſt, whereas Card. *Bellarmine* affirmeth, *that when he ſaid, that members of the ſame body are depending one vpon the other, he vnderſtood of members of a diuers kinde, as is a finger, a hand, an arme, a ſhoulder, a head, and not of members of the ſame kind, as are two hauds, two feet &c.* "Mr. *Barclay* replyeth, that it is vntrue, that mem-"bers of a diuerſe kind are depending one vpon the "other, as the hand doth not depend vpon the foot, "the liuer vpon the lights, the ſplene vpon the ſhoul-"ders, &c.

7 " And as for thoſe examples, which Card. *Bel-*"*larmine* doth bring, hee vſeth therein great deceipt, "for neither doth the finger for that cauſe depend "vpon the hand, nor the hand vpon the arme, nor "the arme vpon the ſhoulder, for that they are mem-"bers of one body, but for that by order of nature "the finger cannot conſiſt, or bee of it ſelfe without "the hand, nor the hand without the arme, nor the "arme without the ſhoulder ; Neuertheleſſe many "members of the ſame body alſo of a diuerſe kinde "can well conſiſt one without the other, as the eye "without the eare, the ſhoulder without the foot, the "noſe without the eie &c as likewiſe theſe two mem-"bers, whereof we now treate of the Chriſtian com-"mon-wealth, not onely may, but alſo did actually,
"as

d *Cap.*14.§. 2°.

" as *Card. Bellarmine* himselfe confesseth, ^e in the A-
" Apostles time consist one without the other. And
if this proposition of *Card. Bellarmine* be true, that the
members of one body, if they bee of a diuerse kinde
must depend one vpon the other, hee must acknowledge, that in one kingdome the Musician must depend vpon the Physician, or the Physician vpon the
Musician, the Shooe-maker vpon the Taylor, or the
Taylor vpon the Shooe-maker, the Lord Chamberlaine vpon the Lord Treasurer, or the Lord Treasurer vpon the Lord Chamberlaine, to omit infinite o
ther such like trades and dignities, all which are mem
bers of the same bodie or Kingdome, whereas it is too
too manifest, that they are not subiect, or depend one
vpon the other, but either immediately vpon the
King, or vpon those Magistrates, whom the King
shall appoint.

e *Lib.* 5. de
Rem. Pont. c. 6.

8. *Secondly*, whereas *Card. Bellarmine affirmeth,
that it is manifest enough, that the Pope is head of the
Church in place of Christ, from whence it doth clearely
follow, that a King must either be no member of this body,*
" *or else he must be subiect to the Pope*, Mr. *Barclay* re-
" plyeth, *that* Card. Bellarmine *doth cunningly equiuo-*
" *cate in that word,* [Church]. For the *Pope* indeed is
" head of the *Church*, that is of *Ecclesiasticall things*, or
" of *Christians*, as they are *Christians*, in so much that
" a *King* cannot be a member of the *Church* being ta-
" ken in this manner, but hee must be subiect to the
" *Pope*. But if by the *Church* hee vnderstand both
" powers, ciuill and Ecclesiasticall, which are among
" Christians, both Lay-men and Cleargiemen, who
" are ioyned by one linke of faith, he is altogether de-
" ceiued. For the *Pope* is not the head of ciuill things :
" and therfore in vaine doth *Card. Bellarmine* affirme,
" *that Kingly power must of necessitie be either subiect or*
" *superiour, least that there be two heades in one bodie.*
" For taking the *Church* in that sense, as it compre-

    " hendeth

"hendeth ciuill and spirituall power, the *Church* hath
"*Christ* only for the head, and the *Pope* and *Kings* for
"chiefe members, who also in an other respect are
"ministeriall heades vnder *Christ*, the *King* of ciuill
"gouernment, and the *Pope* of spirituall. Besides,
"*Card. Bellarmine* doth now change his *medium*, as
"the Logicians call it: His argument, which he tooke
"vpon him to defend, was this: *They are members of*
"*one body, therefore one dependeth vpon the other ;*now
"his argument proceedeth thus; *Members doe depend*
"*vpon the head, the* Pope *is head of the Church, therefore*
"*Kings, who are members of the Church, doe depend vpon*
"*the Pope,* which are two distinct arguments, yet both
of them fallacious, and insufficient to proue, that the
temporall power it selfe, or which is all one, that temporall Kings in temporall causes are subiect to the
Pope, as you haue seene before.

9. *Thirdly,* whereas *Card. Bellarmine* affirmeth, *that*
the assertion of D. Barclay *comparing these two powers to*
two shoulders of the Church, which are connected to one
head, who is Christ, *doth appertaine to the heresie of this*
time, which affirmeth, that the Pope *is not the visible head*
of the Church, and that D. *Barclay doth of his owne ac-*
"*cord grant thus much,* M. *Iohn Barclay* answereth, that
"*Card. Bellarmine* doth in this both slander D. *Bar-*
"*clay,* and also maketh the *Church* and *Pope* odious
"to *Princes.* For what Protestant reading this may
"not with very good reason conclude, that Catho-
"likes, according to Card. *Bellarmines* doctrin, when
"they say, that the *Pope* is the visible head of the
" Church, and that this is a point of Catholike-faith,
"doe vnderstand, that he is head and Gouernour not
"onely in Ecclesiasticall, but also in ciuill causes?
"what wise men of this world will not relate these say-
"ings to Princes? and what Prince can without in-
"dignation here them. Neither did D. *Barclay* euer
"make any doubt, but that the *Pope Christs* Vicar in
"earth

" earth was head in Ecclesiasticall causes, neither did
" Catholike faith euer teach, that he was head in ciuill
" causes. Only *Christ* is head of Popes and Kings, the
" chiefe head I say of the Church. Whereupon S.
" *Austin* doth affirme, [f] *that an excommunicated person is*
" *out of the Church, and out of the body, whereof Christ is*
" *the head.*

10 And therefore that similitude betweene the
soule and body compounding one man, and the spirituall and ciuill power compounding one Church , or
rather one Christian common wealth , or Christian
world, is no fit similitude , and it is wrongfully ascri-
bed to S. *Gregorie Nazianzene* by *Card. Bellarmine* , as
I shewed before [g] , for that the soule is as the forme,
and the body as the matter, compounding one essentiall thing, which is man, but the ciuill power is not as
the matter, nor the spirituall as the forme compounding one essentiall body , which is the Church of
Christ : but if we will haue them to compound one totall body, which is the Church, taking the Church for
the Christian world consisting both of the temporal
and spirituall power, which are in Christians, whereof
Christ or God, and not the *Pope* is the head, they are
onely *integrall*, to vse the termes of Philosophers, and
not *essentiall* parts , neither doe they compound one
essentiall , but only one *integrall* compound, in which
kinde of compound it is not necessary, that one part
doth depend vpon the other, as hath beene now conuinced ; but all must of necessitie depend vpon the
head , although in an *essentiall* compound one part
must of necessitie depend vpon the other, for that
in such a compound one part must bee as the matter
and the other as the forme, as I declared before.

11. Wherefore the spirituall and ciuill power in
the *Church*, taking the *Church* for the Christian world
containing in it both powers, or which is all one, for
the company of all Christians , in whome are both
　　　　　　　　　　　　　　　　　powers,

f *In serm. de
remiss pec. &
refertur* I. q. I.
can. Vt cui
denter,

g *Cap.* 3.

powers, or both subiections, are not like to the soule
and body, which are essentiall parts of man : but
they are as two shoulders, or two sides, which are only *integrall* parts of mans body : both which powers,
although each of them in their kinde bee a visible
head, the one of temporals, the other of spirituals,
and in that respect doe *formally* make two totall bodies, to wit, earthly kingdomes, whereof temporall
Princes are the head, and the spirituall kingdome, or
Church of *Christ,* whereof the *Pope* is the chiefe visible head, yet they are connected to one celestiall and
inuisible head which is *Christ,* in which respect they
make one totall body, whereof *Christ* onely and not
the *Pope* is head, which may bee called the Christian
world, consisting of earthly kingdomes, and the spirituall kingdome, or Church of Christ.

  "   12.   Neither is it true, that these two powers be
  " of so diuerse a kinde, that they cannot be well com-
  " pared to two shoulders, for both of them are pow-
  " ers, and in that respect of the same kinde, and as
  " powers they are compared to two shoulders. And
  " why may they not bee aptly compared to two
  " shoulders, seeing that there is nothing more strong
  " and more neere to the head in the Christian com-
  " mon-wealth ? Neither is it materiall, that one is a
  " more strong shoulder then the other ; for in mans
  " body the right arme is stronger then the left, and
  " yet one is not more an arme then the other. May
not, I pray you, two pillars of a diuerse kinde, one
of brasse, the other of marble, bee aptly compared
one with the other, in that both of them are pillars.
The temporall and the ciuill power, or Kings as
Kings, and hauing temporall authoritie, and Bishops
as Bishops, and hauing spirituall power, are as two visible pillars which doe sustaine the edifice of the Christian world, or common-wealth, the one in temporalls, the other in spirituals, they are as two shoulders,
which

which as in mans body are next vnder the head, and all the other inferiour members doe depend vpon them ; so also they are next vnder God the head of both, and all other inferiour members of the Chri-ſtian world doe depend vpon them ; nay being compared to the inferiour members of the Chriſtian world, they are also as two viſible and miniſteriall heads ; from whence, as from the head of mans body, which is the roote, beginning, and foundation of all ſenſe and motion in all the inferiour parts, all ſpirituall and temporall directions, Lawes, and puniſhments doe proceed.

13. And truely if D. *Barclay* muſt bee taxed of *hereſie,* for *comparing the temporall and ſpirituall power in the Church,*or Chriſtian world (for now the *Church* and Chriſtian world which conſiſteth of both powers, is taken for all one) *to two ſhoulders,* and for affirming, *that Chriſt only is the chiefe celeſtial and inviſible head of both theſe powers, and that Kings and Popes are two miniſteriall heads thereof* (although both of them are also principall in their owne kinde, and in the nature of a viſible head) then muſt *Hugo* de *S. Victore* be taxed of *hereſie,* when he compareth [i] theſe two powers *to two ſides,* affirming, *that Lay-men, who haue care of earthly things are the left ſide of this body, and Clergie men, who do miniſter ſpirituall things are the right, and that earthly power hath the King for the head, and the ſpirituall hath the Pope for head :* Lo heere two ſides (and conſequently two ſhoulders) and two viſible heads, wherof *Chriſt* is the principal and inuiſible head.

14. Then muſt *Thomas Waldenſis* our learned Country-man be taxed of *hereſie,* when after hee had related the aforeſaid words of *Hugo,* hee concludeth thus [k] : *Behold two powers, and two heads of power :* and beneath *Likewiſe,* ſaith he, *neither Kingly power, which by the ring of faith or ſidelitie is eſpouſed to the king-*

i Lib. 2. de Sa-ram. p. 2. ca. 3.

k Lib. 2. declr. ſid. art. 3. ca. 7 S

E e   *dome,*

dome, is reduced to any man authoritatiuely aboue the King besides Christ: and therefore the *Pope* is not head of the *King*, or *Kingdome* in temporalls. Then must *S. Fulgentius* be taxed of *heresie*, when he affirmeth [l], *that in the Church none is more principall then a Bishop, and in the Christian world none more eminent then the Emperour.* Then must *S. Ignatius* be taxed of *heresie*, when hee affirmeth [m], *That no man is more excellent then a King, nor any man is like to him in all created things, neither any one is greater then a Bishoppe in the Church.* Then must *S. Chrysostome, Theophylact,* and *Oecumenius* bee taxed of *heresie,* when they affirme [n], *That whosoeuer hee bee, whether he be a Monke, a Priest, or an Apostle, he is according to S. Paul subiect to temporall Princes*; as likewise Pope *Pelagius* the first, who affirmeth [o], *That Popes also according to the command of holy Scriptures were subiect to Kings.*

15. Then must the ancient Glosse of the *Canon Law* [p], related and approued by *Cardinall Cusanus* [q], (which Glosse *Card. Bellarmine* [r], with small respect to antiquity, doth shamefully *call a doting old woman, and which perchance is abolished for ouermuch old age*) be taxed of *heresie,* affirming, *That as the Pope is Father of the Emperour in spirituall*; *so the Emperour is the Popes Father in temporalls.* Then must *Pope Innocent* the fourth bee taxed of *heresie,* when hee affirmeth [ſ], *That the Emperour is Superiour to all both Church-men and Lay-men in temporalls.* Then must *Hugo Cardinall* related by *Lupoldus* of *Babenberg* be taxed of *heresie,* when he affirmeth [t], *That the Emperour hath power in temporalls from God alone, and that in them he is not subiect to the Pope.* Then must *Ioannes Driedo* be taxed of *heresie,* when hee affirmeth [u], *That the Pope, and the Emperour are not in the Church as two subordinate Iudges, so that one receiueth his iurisdiction from the other: but they are as two Gouernours, who are the Ministers of one God deputed to diuerse offices, so that the*

                              Emperour

l *In lib. de veritate praedest. & gratia.*

m *In Epist. ad Smyrnenses.*

n *Ad Rom.* 13.

o *Apud.* Bininum *tom.* 2. *Concil. pag.* 633 p *In cap.* Adrianus *dist.* 63. q *Lib.* 3. *de* Concord. Cath. *cap.* 3. r *In Tract. con̄tr.* Barcl. *ca.* 13. 16

ſ *Super ca.* Nouerit de sent. excom.

t *De iure regni & Imperij cap.* 9 *in principio.*

u *Lib.* 2. *de libert. Christiana cap.* 2.

Emperour is chiefe ouer Secular causes, and persons for the peaceable liuing in this world, and the Pope ouer spiritualls for the aduantage of Christian faith and charitie. Then must many of the ancient *Fathers* be taxed of heresie, when they affirme, ˣ *that Kings and Emperors are next vnder God, and inferiour to God alone* ; as likewise infinite other Catholike writers, who with *Hector Pintus* doe affirme, ʸ *that Kings in temporalls haue no Superiour, although in spiritualls they are subiect to Priests.*

16   But to these and such like pittifull shifts and extremities are sometimes driuen men otherwise very learned, when they are not afraid by clamours, slanders, and threatnings, rather then by force of reason, to thrust vpon the Christian world their owne vncertaine opinions for infallible grounds of the Catholike faith, and rather then they will seeme to haue been too rash in their Censures, or not so sound in their iudgements, they care not, although with palpable sophismes, so that they may in regard of their authoritie any way blinde the eyes of the vnlearned Reader with their cunning and ambiguous speeches, to maintaine what they haue once begun, and with no small scandall to Catholike religion, and great hurt to their owne soules, and which also in the end will turne to their owne discredit, to impeach those Catholikes of *disobedience, heresie,* or *errour,* who shall impugne their new pretended faith and doctrine, as being no point of the true, ancient, Catholike, and Apostolike faith, nor grounded vpon any one certaine authoritie or argument taken either from the testimonie of holy Scriptures, ancient Fathers, decrees of Councells, practise of the primitiue Church, or any one Theologicall reason, wherevpon any one of the most learnedst of them all dare rely.

17   For which cause they are so often enforced to vse so great equiuocation and ambiguitie of words

in

in their arguments and answers, not declaring in
what sense they take such ambiguous words : as in
this question, concerning the temporall power compounding the Church, and being subiect therevnto,
in one proposition they will seeme to take temporall
power *formally* and in *abstracto,* signifying temporall
Princes *formally,* as they haue temporall power, and
in an other they will take it *materially,* and in *concreto,*
for temporall Princes, who indeed haue temporall
power, but not as they haue temporall power ; In
one proposition they will seeme to take the Church
formally, as it signifieth the spirituall kingdome of
Christ, and consisteth only of spirituall power, and in
an other they will take it *materially* for all Christian
men, or for the Christian world, as it is compounded
both of temporall and spirituall power, and contay-
neth both the spirituall kingdome of *Christ,* and the
earthly kingdomes of the Christian world. So likewise they will not insist vpon any one authoritie of
holy *Scriptures,* any one decree of *Pope* or *Councell,*
or any one Theologicall reason, as vpon a firme, sure,
and infallible ground of their new pretended faith,
which if they would doe, this controuersie would be
quickly at end, but from one place of holy Scripture
they flie to an other, from the new Testament to the
ould, from one Councell to an other, and from one
Theologicall reason to an other, and when all their
arguments be answered, then with clamours, slanders, and forbidding of the bookes which are written
against them, but not declaring why, or for what
cause they are forbidden, or what erroneous doctrine is contayned in them, they will make the matter cleare. But truth and plaine dealing in the end
will preuaile, neither will violence, but reason satisfie
mens vnderstandings, and this their violent, shuffling,
and vnsincere proceeding doth plainly shew, that
they distrust their cause. And thus much concerning the second argument.

Chap. 7. *Wherein the third argument, which is taken from the changing of temporall gouernment, when it hindereth the ſpirituall good, is examined.*

1.　THe third argument, which *Card. Bellarmine* bringeth to proue, *that the ciuill power among Chriſtians, not only as it is Chriſtian, but alſo as it is ciuill, is ſubiect, and ſubordained to the Eccleſiaſticall as it is Eccleſiaſticall,* is this : *Thirdly,* ſaith he, [a] *if the temporall gouernment hinder the ſpirituall good, the Prince, according to the opinion of all men, is bound to change that manner of gouernment, euen with the hinderance of temporall good, therefore it is a ſigne that the temporall power is ſubiect to the ſpirituall.*

2　*Neither doth he ſatisfie, that ſhould anſwer, that a Prince is bound to change that manner of his gouernment, not for the ſubordination to the ſpirituall power, but onely for order of charitie, by which wee are bound to preferre greater goods before leſſer. For in regard of the order of charitie, one common-wealth is not bound to ſuffer detriment, that an other common-wealth more noble doe not ſuffer the like detriment. And one priuate man, who is bound to giue all his goods for the conſeruation of his owne common-wealth, is not bound to doe the like for an other common-wealth, although the more noble. Seeing therefore that the temporall common-wealth is bound to ſuffer detriment for the ſpirituall common-wealth, it is a ſigne that they are not two diuerſe common-wealths, but parts of one and the ſame common-wealth, and one ſubiect to the other.*

3.　*Neither alſo is it of force, if one ſhould ſay, that a temporall Prince is bound to ſuffer detriment for the ſpirituall good, not in regard of any ſubiection of the temporall commonwealth to the ſpirituall common wealth, but becauſe*

　　　　　other-

a *Lib.* 5. *de Rom: Pont. cap:* 7.

otherwise he should hurt his subiects, to whom it is hurtfull to loose spiritualls for temporalls. For although those men, who are not his subiects, but are of an other kingdome, should suffer any notable hurt in spiritualls, for the gouernment in temporalls of some Christian King, he is bound to change his manner of gouernment, whereof no other reason can be giuen, but that they are members of the same body, and one subiect to the other.

4. By this argument *Card. Bellarmine*, as you see, laboureth to proue two things, the *one* is, that not onely Lay-men, and Cleargie-men doe make one totall body, which is the Church of *Christ*, whereof the *Pope* is head, for of this no Catholike maketh any doubt, but also that the temporall & spirituall power themselues, or which is all one, the temporall and spirituall common wealth, as they consist of temporall and spirituall power, are parts of this totall body called the *Church* of *Christ*, whereof the *Pope* is the supreme visible head. The *second* is, that not onely temporall Princes are in spirituals subiect to the supreme spirituall Pastour, but also, that the temporall power it selfe, as it is temporall, is among Christians subiect to the spirituall power, as it is spirituall, and consequently, that temporall Princes not onely in spiritualls, but also in all temporalls are subiect to the spirituall power. But neither of these can bee rightly concluded from this argument, as I shewed in my *Apolo-*
"*gie* [b], where I denied the consequence of this *third*
"*argument*, speaking of subiection and subordination
"*per se*, and of it owne nature. For if temporall go-
"uernment doe hinder spirituall good, the temporall
"Prince is bound to change that manner of gouern-
"ment euen with detriment of temporall good, not
"for that the temporall power is *per se*, and of it owne
"nature subiect to the spirituall, as though of the tem-
"porall and spirituall power were made *formally* one
"politike body, but for both the reasons alledged by
Card.

b *Num.* 160. & *seq.*

" Card. *Bellarmine,* which he did not sufficiently con-
" fute in his *Replyes.*

5. The *first reason is for the order of charitie, by which*
" *we are bound to prefer greater goods before lesser.* To
" the *Reply,* which Card. *Bellarmine* made to the con-
" trarie, I answered thus, that although for the order
" of charity one common wealth is not bound to suf-
" fer detriment, that an other common wealth more
" noble doe not suffer the like detriment, yet in case
" that both common wealths bee subiect to one
" Prince, or that the Prince of the lesse noble comon
" wealth be also a subiect of the more noble, then that
" Prince is bound for order of charitie, all other things
" being alike , to preferre the more noble common-
" wealth before the lesse noble. And although one
" priuate man, who is bound to giue all his goods for
" the conseruation of his owne common-wealth, bee
" not bound to doe the like for an other common-
" wealth, although the more noble , yet in case that
" the same priuate man should at the same time bee a
" Citizen of both common-wealths, if he be bound to
" giue all his goods for the conseruation of the lesse
" noble common wealth, whereof he is a Citizen, he
" is much more bound for the same order of charitie,
" to giue all his goods for the conseruation of the more
" noble common wealth , to which also he is subiect.
" And this is the very case in this present question.
" For the spirituall and ciuill power, and the common
" wealths which they compound, are so vnited and
" connected among Christians , that euery Christian
" is a Citizen of both common wealths, and both com-
" mon wealths may be subiect to the same Prince, as
" appeareth in the *Pope,* who is the spirituall Prince
" or Pastour of the whole Christian world , and also a
" temporall Prince of some Prouinces thereof.

6. The *second reason,* for which a temporall Prince
" is bound to change the manner of his gouernment
" in

"in the aforesaid case, is, *for that otherwise he should*
"*hurt his subiects, to whom it is hurtfull to loose greater*
"*goods for the lesser, that is spirituall goods for temporall.*
"To the *Reply*, which Card. *Bellarmine* made to the
"contrary, *I answered*, that the reason wherefore a
"temporall Prince is bound to change his manner of
"gouernment, if it be greatly hurtfull to the spirituall
"good not only of his owne subiects, but also of the
"subiects of another Kingdome, is not for that the
"temporall power is *per se*, and of it owne nature sub-
"iect to the spirituall, or for that both of them are
"parts of one, and the same totall common wealth,
"but because both the King, and also those subiects
"of an other temporall kingdome, are also members
"of the same mysticall body of *Christ*, and Cittizens
"of the same spirituall Kingdome, and therefore that
"King least that he should greatly preiudice in spiri-
"tualls the kingdome of *Christ*, whereof he is a Citi-
"zen, by his temporall gouernment, is bound to
"change that manner of gouernment. Thus I an-
"swered in my *Apologie.*

7. Now you shall see how cunningly D. *Schulckenius* would shift of this answere. To the first part of

c *Pag.* 339.

my answere he replyeth thus: ᶜ *Heere I see nothing that
needeth any answere sauing that* [as though of the temporall and spirituall power were formally made one
politike body] *For my* Aduersary Widdrington *doth
grant the antecedent. of* Card. Bellarmines *argument,
and denieth the consequence, and for this cause he doth deny it, for that of the temporall and spirituall power is not
made* formally one politike body, *and therefore one
power is not* per se *subiect to the other. But what man that
is well in his wits did euer say,* that of the temporall and
spirituall power is made formally one politike body?
*For although Cleargie men are Cittizens of the ciuill com-
mon wealth, as they liue together with the Cittizens of that
common wealth, and do buy, sell, and doe other things according*

cording to the lawes of that common-wealth, yet because they are exempted from the power of the politike Prince, and doe obserue his lawes not by force of the law, but by force of reason, they cannot properly and formally, but onely materially be called parts of the ciuill common-wealth.

8. *Adde also that if the Ecclesiasticall and ciuill power should make one politike body, the Ecclesiasticall should either be superiour, or subiect to the ciuill, superiour it could not be, for that the King is head of the politike body, neither could it be subiect, for that a superiour power ought not to be subiect to an inferiour. And besides (as it hath beene sayd) Cleargie men are exempted from the power of a politike Prince, and therefore the Ecclesiasticall and ciuill power doe not make properly and formally one politike body. But my* Aduersarie *doth faine absurd opinions, which hee may refell. That which* Card. Bellarmine *saith, is, that the spirituall and temporall power, that is, Bishops, Kings, and their subiects, Clerkes and Laikes doe make one Church, one Christian common-wealth, one people, one kingdome, or mysticall body of Christ, wherein all things are well ordered and disposed, and therefore superiour things doe rule inferiour things, and inferiour things are subiect to superiour things. Let my Aduersarie* Widdrington *ouerthrow this, and then let him deny the consequence of* Card. Bellarmines *argument. Thus* D. *Schulckenius.*

9. But how vnsound, cunning, and insufficient, is this *Reply* of D. *Schulckenius,* and also repugnant to his owne grounds, you shall presently perceiue. And *first* when I denied, *that the spirituall and temporall power doe make formally one politike body,* by *a politike body* I did not vnderstand, as it distinguished and contra- diuided to a *spirituall body,* but as it is distinguished from a *naturall body,* and comprehendeth in generall all politike gouernments, whether they be temporall, spirituall, or mixt, in which sense not onely earthly kingdomes compounded of temporall power, but

also

also the spirituall kingdome , mysticall body or
Church of Chrift confifting onely of spirituall power
is a *politike body.* Wherefore by the name of a *politike
body* I vnderftood a common-wealth in generall, whether it were temporall, spirituall, or mixt of both, as
any man, who is not defirous to cauill, may eafily
perceiue by all thofe anfwers and affertions, which I
did fo often inculcate concerning the vnion and coniunction of thefe two powers. So that my meaning
in that place onely was to deny, that the temporall
and spirituall power, as they are referred to the vifible
heads and fubiects of both powers, doe make *formally one totall common-wealth*, but onely *materially*, for
that the fame Chriftian men , who haue temporall
power or temporall fubiection, doe make one spirituall Kingdome or Church of Chrift, but not *formally*,
as they haue temporall power, or temporall fubiection, for fo they make onely temporall and earthly
kingdomes, but *formally* as they haue temporall and
spirituall power, temporall and spirituall fubiection,
and are referred to the vifible heads thereof, they
make two totall bodies or common-wealths, as before
I haue declared more at large.

10. *Secondly*, although it be true, that temporall
and spirituall power, that is, *Kings and Bishops, Clerks
and Laikes*, as D. *Schulckenius* expoundeth thofe
words (which neuertheleffe is a very improper accep-
tion of thofe words, for that temporall and spirituall
power in *abstracto* doth fignifie Kings and Bifhops,
Clerkes and Laikes as they haue temporall and spirituall power) *doe make one Church, one Christian common-wealth, one people, one kingdome or mysticall body of
Christ*, yet this was not all that, which *Card. Bellarmine* affirmed, for *Card. Bellarmine* affirmed another
thing, which I pretended to impugne, and which D.
Schulckenius cunningly concealeth, to wit, that *Kings
and Bishops, Clerkes and Laikes doe not make two com-*
mon-

mon-wealths, but one ; This was that which I impugned, [*not two common-wealths, but one*] I neuer denied
that they did make one common-wealth, to wit, the
Church of Chrift,but withall I affirmed,that they did
make alfo two, to wit the earthly kingdomes alfo of
this Chriftian world : So that I did not inuent, or
faine abfurd opinions to confute them, as D. *Schulckenius* vntruely affirmeth, but I haue cleerely fhewed,
and that out of (*ard. Bellarmines,* or D. *Schulckenius*
his owne grounds, as before you haue feene more at
large, ᵈthat the temporall and fpirituall power doe
make *formally* two totall bodies or common-wealths,
and that Kings and Bifhops, Clerkes and Laikes diuerfe wayes confidered are parts and members of
them both.

ᵈ *Cap.1.2.3.*

11. *Thirdly,* although I had taken a *politike bodie*
for a temporall common-wealth, as in very truth I
did not, but onely for a common-wealth in generall,
as a *politike bodie* is diftinguifhed from a *naturall bodie,*
yet I might be very well in my wits,and neuerthelefe
haue affirmed, that the temporall and fpirituall power
doe in the like manner, and for the fame caufe make
formally one temporal common-wealth,for the which
D. *Schulckenius* doth heere affirme, *that temporall and
fpirituall power doe make* formally *one fpirituall bodie or
common-wealth.* For the reafon why he affirmeth,that
the temporall and fpirituall power doe make *formally*
one Ecclefiafticall or fpirituall common-wealth, is,
for that *Kings and Bifhops, Clerkes and Laikes are members of the fpirituall kingdome of Chrift, and fubiect to
the fpirituall power of the fupreme fpirituall Paftor,*which
reafon, if it be of force, doth alfo conclude, that the
temporall and fpirituall power may in like manner be
fayd to make *formally* one temporal common-wealth,
for that *Kings and Bifhops, Clerkes and Laikes, are alfo
true members and parts of the temporall common-wealth,*
and therfore they are either temporall Princes them-

selues,or subiect in temporals,to the temporal power of temporal Princes. And therfore the reason,why D. Schulckenius doth here affirm,*That the temporall and spirituall power do not make formally one politicke or temporal body*,is,as you haue seen; for that *the Clergie are exempted from the power of a politicke Prince,and do obserue his Lawes not by force of the Law ; but by force of reason,* and therefore, saith he,*they cannot properly and formally,but onely materially be called a part of the politicke common-wealth*. From whence it cleerly followeth , that if a man may be well in his wits, and yet affirme, that *Cleargie men are true parts, members, and subiects of the temporall common wealth*, and consequently are not exempted from temporall subiection ; but doe owe true fidelitie and allegiance to temporall Princes, hee may also bee well in his wits, and yet affirme according to D. Shulckenius his reason , that of the temporall and spirituall power, that is, of *Kings and Bishops, Clerkes and Laikes is made properly and formally one politike body, or temporall common-wealth*.

 12. And dare D. *Schulckenius*,trow you,presume to say that S.*Chrysostom,Theophylact,Oecumenius,*[*]and those others whom partly I did cite before[e],and partly I will beneath [f], were not well in their wits, when they affirmed,*That whether he be a Monke, or a Priest, or an Apostle, he is according to S.Paul, subiect to temporall Princes*. Or dare he presume to say, that *Dominicus Sotus, Franciscus Victoria,Medina, Sayrus,Valentia,* and innumerable other Diuines cited by *Sayrus* [g],and also by *Salas* [h] the Iesuite, whose opinion hee approoueth and withall affirmeth,*That some few moderne Diuines doe hold the contrary* , were not well in their wits, when they taught, *that Cleargie men are directly subiect to the ciuill Lawes, which are not repugnant to their state, nor to Ecclesiasticall Lawes , or Canons,* and that *Kings are Lords of Cleargie men, and that Cleargie men are bound to come at their call, and as Subiects to sweare alle-*

geance

* Ad Rom.13.
e Cap.6.
f Cap.12.

g Lib. 3. Thesauri c.4.nu.16
h Disp.14.de Legibus sect.8.

ance and obedience to them, as *Salas* in expreſſe words
affirmeth ; and *that Cleargie men are not exempted from
secular power concerning the directiue*, *or commanding
force thereof, in ciuill Lawes, which are profitable to the
good state of the common-wealth*, which are the expreſſe
words of *Gregorius de Valentia, tom.* 3. *diſp.* 9. *q.* 5.
punc. 3.

13   And to conclude, dare D. *Schulckenius* preſume to ſay, that *Cardinall Bellarmine* was not well in
his wits, when hee wrote, ⁱ *That Cleargie men are not in
any manner exempted from the obligation of ciuill Lawes,
which are not repugnant to holy Canons, or to the office of
their Clergie*, although in the laſt Editions of his
Booke, he hath left out thoſe words [*in any manner*]
not alleaging any cauſe wherefore. And therefore although Cleargie men are by the Eccleſiaſtical Lawes,
and priuiledges of temporall Princes, exempted from
the tribunalls of ſecular Magiſtrates, and from paying of certaine tributes, and perſonall ſeruices : yet to
ſay that they are exempted wholly from temporall
ſubiection, and that they are not ſubiect to the directiue power of the ciuil Lawes, nor can truely and properly commit treaſons againſt any temporall Prince,
for that they owe not true fidelitie, allegiance, and
ciuill ſubiection to any temporall Prince (as ſome
few Ieſuites of theſe latter times haue not feared to a
uerre, whoſe opinion Card. *Bellarmine* now, contrarie to his ancient doctrine, which for many yeeres together he publikely maintained, doth now ſeeme to
follow) is repugnant in my iudgement both to holy
Scriptures ſo expounded by the ancient Fathers, to
the common opinion of the Schoole Diuines, and
once alſo of Card. *Bellarmine* himſelfe, at which
time I thinke D. *Schulckenius* will not ſay, that he was
not wel in his wits, and alſo to the practiſe both of the
primitiue Church, and of all Chriſtian Kingdomes
euen to theſe dayes, and it is a doctrine newly broa-

F f 3   ched

i *Lib.* 1. *de
Clericis cap.*
28. *propos.* 2a.

ched in the Christian world without sufficient proofe,
scandalous to Catholike Religion, iniurious to Chri-
an Princes, and odious to the pious eares of all faithfull and well affected Subiects.

14.   The *other reason,* which D. *Schulckenius* al-
legeth, why *Kings and Bishops, Clearkes and Laicks doe
not make* properly and formally *one politike body or temporall common-wealth,* (for to say that temporall and
spirituall power *in abstracto* doe make *formally* either
one temporal, or one spiritual cómon-wealth, is very
vntrue and repugnant-to his owne grounds, as I haue
shewed before, vnlesse we will speake very improperly) to wit, for that Cleargie men *are superiour and not
subiect,* is as insufficient as the former ; for that temporall Princes are in temporalls superiour, and haue
preheminence not onely ouer Lay-men, but also o-
uer Cleargy men. And therefore the temporall, and
spirituall power, or Kings and Bishops, Clearkes and
Laikes, as they are referred to the visible heads heere
on earth, doe neither make one politike or temporall
body, nor one spirituall or Ecclesiasticall body, nor
one total common-wealth consisting of both powers,
whereof the *Pope* is head, but they doe make *formally,*
and *properly* two totall bodies or common-wealths, to
wit, the spirituall kingdome of *Christ*, which consisteth onely of spirituall power, and the earthly kingdomes of this Christian world, which consisteth onely of temporall and ciuill authority, both which bodies are commonly signified by the name of the
Christian world, or Christian common-wealth, wherin all things are well ordered, and rightly disposed,
and therefore superiours are aboue inferiours, and inferiours are subiect to superiours ; but in temporall
causes temporall power, whereof temporal Princes
are the head, hath the preheminence not only ouer
Lay-men, but also ouer Cleargy-men, and in spirituall causes the spirituall power, whereof the *Pope* is
head,

head, is superiour, and to confound these two powers,
were to breake all good order, as before I also declared. And therfore for good reason I granted the
antecedent proposition of *Card. Bellarmines* argument, and denied his consequence.

15. But *fourthly* obserue, *good Reader*, another
palpable vntruth, which D. *Schulckenius* in this place
affirmeth. *Card. Bellarmine*, as you haue seene, ende-
uoured by his third argument to proue, that the temporall power as it is temporall, is among Christians
subiect to the spirituall power, as it is spirituall ; and
his argument was this : *If the temporall gouernment
hinder the spirituall good, the Prince is bound to change
that manner of gouernment, euen with the hinderance of
the temporall good, therefore it is a signe that the temporall
power is subiect to the spirituall..* The antecedent proposition I did grant, and I denied his consequence.
Now D. *Schulckenius* affirmeth, *that for this cause I
denyed his consequence, for that of the temporall and spirituall power is not made formally one politike body*, which
is very vntrue. For although I should acknowledge,
as in very deede I doe, that the temporall and spirituall power, as they are referred to Christ the invisible
and celestiall head, doe make *properly* and *formally*
one totall body, or common-wealth, consisting of
both powers, which may be called the Christian common wealth, but more properly the Christian world,
yet I would and doe denie his consequence : and the
reason hereof I alledged before, for that they are not
essentiall parts of this totall bodie, as the bodie & soule
are of man, but *integrall* parts, as two shou'ders, two
sides, hands, feete, eyes, eares, &c. are *integrall* parts of
mans bodie, and doe not make an *essentiall*, but an *integrall* compound, in which kinde of compound it is
not necessarie, as I shewed before [k], that one part bee
subiect to an other, but it sufficeth that both be subiect to the head. And although I should also grant,

k *Cap. 6. nu. 6.*
10.

as

as I doe, that *temporall and spirituall power* doe make
formally one politike bodie , or temporall common
wealth, taking *temporall and spirituall power* in that improper fenfe, as is declared by *D. Schulckeniu,*to wit,
for *Kings* and *Bishops, Clerks* and *Laikes,* who diuerfe
waies confidered, doe make *properly,* and *formally* not
onely a fpirituall, but alfo a politike bodie or temporall common-wealth :   yet I fhould and do notwithftanding denie his confequence,for thofe two caufes,
which Card.*Bellarmine* did in his *Replyes* alledge,but,
as you haue feene,not fufficiently confute.

16   And truly if this argument of Card. *Bellar-*
mine were of force, it would in my opinion convince,
that not only the temporall power among Chriftians
is fubiect to thefpirituall power of the *Pope ,.* but alfo
that the temporall power among infidell Princes is
alfo fubiect to the *Popes* fpirituall authoritie , which
neuerthelefle Card. *Bellarmine* doth denie; for if the
temporall gouernment of an infidell Prince doe hurt
and hinder the fpirituall good of Chriftian Religion,
he is bound to change that manner of gouernment
euen with the hinderance of temporall good , therefore I might conclude with Card. *Bellarmine,*that it is
a figne that the temporall power of an heathen
Prince is fubiect to the fpirituall power of Chriftian
religion.   And therefore as the changing of temporall gouernment among infidells, when it hindereth
the fpirituall good of Chriftian religion, is no probable figne of any fubiection *per fe* of their temporall
power to the *Popes* fpirituall authoritie, but onely of a
bond of charitie, whereby all men are by the law of
God and nature bound not to hinder true fpirituall
good for a temporall commoditie, fo alfo among
Chriftians it is no probable figne of any fubiection
or fubordination of the temporall power to the fpirituall, but at the moft of a greater bond of charitie,
whereby Chriftians not only by the law of God and
                                                  nature,

nature, but alfo by the bond of Chriftian religion, which they profeffe, are obliged not to hinder the fpirituall good thereof for a temporall commoditie.

17   Now you fhall fee, how infufficiently alfo *D. Schulckenius* replyeth to thofe two anfwers, which I made to Card. *Bellarmines Replyes,* wherein are alledged the caufes, why I denyed the *confequence* of his argument, and why a temporall Prince is bound to change the manner of his temporall gouernment, when it hindereth the fpirituall good.   And *firft* to my *firft* anfwer *D. Schulckenius* replyeth thus : [1] that by my anfwer *it is clearely gathered, that I fay nothing in this place, which maketh to the ouerthrowing of* Card. Bellarmines *argument.   For I confeffe,* faith he, *that a Prince of a leffe noble common-wealth is not bound to fuffer any detriment onely for the order of charitie, that an other common-wealth more noble doe not fuffer the like, vnleffe either hee bee fubiect to the Prince of that noble common-wealth, or vnleffe one hath both the common wealths fubiect to him.   Therefore I am conftrained,* faith he, *to confeffe, that the principall reafon, why a temporall Prince ought to fuffer detriment in temporalls, left that the fpirituall good be hindered, is not the order of charitie, but the fubiection of the temporall common wealth to the fpirituall, when they concurre to make one Chriftian common-wealth, or one myfticall bodie of Chrift. Therefore I haue not,* faith hee, *confuted* Card: Bellarmines *argument, but haue yeelded vp the bucklers, yea and alfo haue confirmed it.*

1 *Pag.* 341.

18   But truly it is ftrange to fee, with what boldneffe, men otherwife learned, dare aduenture to auouch fuch groffe and palpable vntruths, and when their anfwers are cleane ouerthrowne, to brag not only of the victorie, but alfo that their *Aduerfarie* hath granted, and confirmed their anfwers.   For obferue, *good Reader,* how vntrue and fraudulent this anfwer is. I affirmed, as you haue feene, that the reafon, why a

Gg   tempo-

temporall Christian Prince is bound to change his manner of gouernment, if it hinder the spirituall good, is not, for that the temporall power is *per se*, and of it owne nature subiect to the spirituall, as Card. *Bellarmine* pretended, but because he being a Christian Prince, to whom especially, more then to a Heathen, it doth belong to haue care of true spirituall good, which Christian Religion ought chiefly to intend, is by the order of charitie, and not for any intrinsecall subiection, or subordination of the temporall power to the spirituall, bound to preferre, *cæteris paribus*, the spirituall good before the temporall. And whereas *Card. Bellarmine* replyed, *that for the order of charitie one common wealth, although the lesse noble, is not bound to suffer detriment, that an other common wealth more noble do not suffer the like detriment ; and one priuate man, who is bound to giue all his goods for the preseruation of his owne common wealth, is not likewise bound to doe the like for an other common wealth although more noble ; Seeing therefore that a temporall common-wealth is bound to suffer damage for the spirituall, it is a signe, that they are not two diuerse common-wealths, but parts of one and the selfe same common wealth, and one subiect to another.*

12. To this *Reply* I answered, by shewing the disparitie betwixt one temporall common-wealth compared to an other, and a temporall common-wealth compared to the spirituall common wealth : because the same Prince, or subiect of one temporall common wealth is seldome, or neuer, a Prince or subiect of the other, and therefore the order of charitie requireth, that both the Prince and subiect ought to prefer the temporall good of their owne common wealth, before the temporall good of an other more noble common wealth : As also a man lesse noble ought in charitie to prefer, if other things be alike, his own temporall good before the temporall good of an other man more noble. But if it should so fall out, that the same

man

man were Prince of both common wealths, or the
fame priuate man were a part and member of both
common wealths, in this cafe the order of charitie
would require, that he, who is member, or hath charge
of both common-wealths, fhould preferre, if other
things be alike, the temporall good of the more noble
common wealth before the temporall good of the leffe
noble, not by reafon of any fubiection of one common wealth to the other, but becaufe both common-
wealths are fubiect to the fame Prince , or the fame
priuate man is fubiect to both common wealths, and
therefore they ought with due refpect and order of
charitie to haue care of both, and to preferre the more
worthy common wealth before the leffe worthy.

20. As likewife if one man hath diuerfe trades, one
more noble, an other leffe noble, one more profitable, and other leffe profitable , if in cafe he fhould bee
compelled to loofe, or preiudice one of his trades, the
order of charitie would require, that hee fhould rather
loofe, or preiudice the leffe noble, then the more noble, the leffe profitable, then the more profitable trade,
neither from hence could it bee gathered , that one
trade were fubiect, or fubordained to another, but only that both trades were fubiect to one man. So likwife
if a man were conftrained to loofe either his eye or his
finger , the order of charitie would require that hee
fhould preferre the eye before the finger, for that the
eye is a more noble, a more neceffarie , a more profitable part of the body then the finger , and yet from
hence we cannot well conclude, that therefore the finger is fubiect or fubordained to the eye, but that both
are parts and members of the body of the fame man,
who therefore by order of charitie ought with due order and refpect to haue a care of the whole body and
euery part thereof , and to preferre the more worthy,
neceffary or profitable before the leffe worthy, neceffarie or profitable member. And this I faid was the

plaine cafe of the temporall power among Chriftians
compared to the fpirituall, for that the Ecclefiafticall
and ciuill power, temporall power and fpirituall fubiection &c. are among Chriftians fo vnited in one
fubiect, that the fame Chriftian man is a part, member, and Citizen both of the temporall, and alfo of the
fpirituall common wealth, and both common wealths
may be fubiect to the fame Prince, as appeareth in the
Pope, and therefore the order of charitie doth require, that euery Chriftian man ought to preferre the
fpirituall good, and fpirituall common wealth, before
the temporall good and the temporall common-
wealth, not for that the temporall power, or common
wealth is fubiect to the fpirituall, but for that all Chriftian Princes and people are parts, members, and Citizens of both common wealths, and the fpirituall is
farre more noble, and worthy, and therefore if other
things be alike, to bee preferred before the temporall, by them who are parts and members of them
both.

   2 1.   Now D. *Schulckenius* would cunningly *forfooth*
make the Reader beleeue, that I fay the very fame
that Card. *Bellarmine* doth, and that I doe not by my
anfwere ouerthrow, but confirme Card. *Bellarmines*
Reply : *for that I am enforced,* faith he, *to confeffe that*
the chiefe caufe, why a temporall Prince ought to fuffer da-
mage in temporalls, leaft the fpirituall good fhould be hindere
ed, is not the order of charitie, but the fubiection of the
temporall power to the fpirituall, when they make one fpir-
tuall common wealth, or myfticall body of Chrift, which
neuertheleffe, as you haue feene, is apparantly vntrue.
For although I doe indeed alledge fubiection for a
caufe, why the order of charitie doth require, that a
temporall Chriftian Prince ought to preferre the fpirituall good before the temporall, by which word
[*fubiection*] D. *Schulckenius* taketh occafion to delude
his *Reader,* yet I doe not alledge that manner of *fub-*
iection,

iection, which Card. *Bellarmine* doth , as D. *Schulcke-*
nius vntruly affirmeth,to wit , *the subiection of the tem-*
porall power to the spirituall , *or of the temporall common*
wealth to the spirituall , *taking temporall common-wealth*
properly as it confisteth of *temporall power and tempo-*
rall subiection, but the fubiection of both common-
wealths to one Prince,or the fubiection of all Chriftians to both common wealths, to bee the caufe, why
the order of charitie requireth, that a Chriftian Prince
is bound to change his manner of gouernment,when
it hindereth the fpirituall good.

    22. Belike D. *Schulckenius* would inferre , that be-
caufe the *Pope* is Lord of *Ancona* , and *Ferrara* , and
ought to prefer *cæteris paribus* the good of the one before the other,therefore the State of Ancona is fubiect to the State of Ferrara,or contrariwife,or becaufe
the *King* of *Spaine* is *King* of *Naples* and *Duke* of *Millan,* therefore the *State* of *Millan* is fubiect to *Naples,*
or becaufe a man hath two trades, and ought to preferre the one before the other, therefore the one is
fubiect to the other, or becaufe one man is a Cittizen
of two cities, therefore one of thofe cities is fubiect to
the other, or becaufe the eyes and eares are parts and
members of the fame body of man, who ought therefore by order of charity to preferre the good of the
more worthy and neceffary member before the good
of the leffe worthie and leffe neceffarie, therefore the
eares are fubiect to the eyes or contrariwife. I euer
affirmed,that the temporall power among Chriftians
is not *per se,* and of it owne nature fubiect to the fpirituall, and that they doe not *properly and formally,* as
they are referred to the vifible heads heere on earth,
make one totall, but two totall common-wealths, although the fame Chriftian man being confidered diuerfe waies, is a part and member of both common-
wealths, and as in fpirituall caufes he is fubiect to the
Ecclefiafticall power, which onely doth *properly* and

          Gg 3   *formally*

formally make the spirituall, or Ecclesiasticall common-wealth, so in temporall causes hee is subiect to
the ciuill power, which onely doth *properly* and *formally* make the temporall or earthly kingdomes of
this Christian world, and because the spirituall common-wealth and good thereof is the more noble and
more worthy, therefore the same Christian man, be
ing a member and citizen of both common-wealths,
ought to preferre, if other things be alike, the spirituall good before temporall, and not for any subiection
of the temporall power, or commonwealth to the spirituall. But when men are not disposed to deale sincerely for truthes sake, but are resolued to defend *per
fas & nefas,* what they haue once taken in hand to
maintaine, and doe not fight for truth, but for credit,
they little regard what they say, so that with cunning & smooth words they may colour their sayings
in such sort, as that they may blind, dazel or confound
the vnderstanding of the Reader. And thus much
concerning *Card. Bellarmines* first *Reply.*

23. Now to the answer, which I made to Card.
Bellarmines second *Reply,* by which hee pretended to
prooue the subiection of the temporall power to the
spirituall, D. *Schulckenius* m *Pag.343.* ^m replieth in this manner.
I answer that my Aduersary Widdrington *saith nothing,
which doth weaken* Card. Bellarmines *argument. That
which* Card. Bellarmine *did assume, to wit, that a temporall Prince is bound to change his manner of gouernment,
not onely, least that hee should hurt in spirituals his owne
subiects, but also least that he should hurt other Christians,
my Aduersarie* Widdrington *doth grant. And in this af-
sumption, or antecedent proposition all the force of* Card.
Bellarmines *argument doth consist. Besides, when* Widdrington *denyeth, that the temporall power is per se subiect to the spirituall, or that both of them bee parts of one,
and the selfe same Christian common-wealth, and afterwards granteth, that a temporall King, and those, who are
ciuilly*

*ciuilly subiect vnto him, are members of the mysticall body,
and Citizens of the same spirituall Kingdome, he doth manifestly contradict himselfe.* For what else is this, that
*Christian Kings and their Subiects are members of the
same mysticall body of Christ, and Citizens of the same spirituall Kingdome,* I say, what else is this, then that Chri-
*stian Kings, and their Lay-Subiects are parts of the Chri-
stian common-wealth?* For the *Christian common-wealth,
and the mysticall bodie of Christ, and the spirituall Kingdome of Christ are altogether the same:* of which common-
wealth *Kings with Laikes, Bishops with Clerks are parts,*
as oftentimes hath beene sayd. In which *Christian com-
wealth, and mysticall body, and Kingdome of Christ all
things are so well disposed and ordered, that temporall
things doe serue spirituall, and ciuill power is subiect to
Ecclesiasticall,* which conclusion my *Aduersarie* Widdrington *hath many waies attempted to ouerthrow,* but he
was not able. And he was not able not onely to ouerthrow
the conclusion, but also he hath not beene able to weaken at
all with any probable answer the first *argument* which
Card. Bellarmine *brought to prooue this conclusion,* which
the Readers will easily perceiue, if without perturbation
of minde they will consider that which hath beene sayd
by vs.

24   But this *Reply* of D. *Schulckenius* is as fraudulent, and insufficient, as the former : for in effect it is
only a repetition of his former *Reply,* to which I haue
already answered , besides some fraudulent dealing,
which he hath vsed herein. And *first* it is very true,
that I granted the antecedent proposition of this second *Reply* of Card. Bellarmine, *but that all the force
of Card. Bellarmines argument doth consist in the antecedent proposition, or assumption,* as D. *Schulckenius* affirmeth, is very vntrue, and I wonder, that D. *Schulckenius* is not ashamed with such boldnesse to affirme the
same. The Antecedent proposition was, *that a Christian Prince is bound to change the manner of his temporal
gouerment,*

*gouernment, if it hurt the spirituall good, not onely of his
owne Subiects, but also of the Subiects of other Christian
Princes*, and this propofition I did willingly grant
him, but the force of his argument did not confift
only in this *antecedent propofition,* as *D. Schulckenius*
vntruly affirmeth, but in the *confequence*, which hee
inferred from this antecedent propofition, or if wee
will reduce his argument to a fyllogifticall forme, in
his *Minor propofition,* or *affumption,* which was this,
but of this, to wit, that a Chriftian Prince is bound to
change the manner of his temporall gouernment in
the cafe aforefaid, *no other reafon can be giuen, but that
both powers are members of the fame body, and one power
or body fubiect to the other.* And this *confequence, affumption,* or *Minor* propofition, wherein the whole
force of his argument did confift, I vtterly denyed,
and I alledged, as you haue feene, an other plaine and
perfpicuous reafon, why a Chriftian Prince in the cafe
aforefaid is bound to change the manner of his temporall gouernment, to wit, not for that temporall
power is *per fe* fubiect to the fpirituall, or for that
they make one totall bodie, or common-wealth, confifting of temporall and fpirituall power, but for that
all Chriftians, both Princes and fubiects, are parts
and members not onely of the temporall, but alfo of
the fpiritual common-wealth, for which caufe a Chriftian Prince is bound to change the manner of his
temporall gouernment, when it is hurtfull to the fpirituall good of the Church, or fpirituall kingdome of
Chrift, whereof he is a true part and member, as I declared before.

25. *Secondly,* it is very vntrue, *that I doe any waie
contradict my felfe,* as D. *Schulckenius* affirmeth, *firft in
denying that temporall power is* per fe *fubiect to the fpirituall, or that both of them are parts of one and the felfe-
fame Chriftian common-wealth or Church of Chrift, and
afterwards in granting, that temporall Kings, and their*
fubiects,

subiects, are members of the *same spirituall kingdome or Church of Chrift.* For thefe propofitions, *temporall power is not* per fe, *fubiect to fpirituall power, and temporall Princes are fubiect to fpirituall power,* are not repugnant or contradictorie one to the other, as neither thefe propofitions are contradictory, *Temporall power and fpirituall power, are not parts of the fpirituall kingdome or Church of Chrift, and temporall Princes are parts of the fpirituall kingdome or Church of Chrift.* For *contradiction* according to *Ariftotle* n, *is an affirming and denying of the fame thing, and in the fame manner:* But there is no man fo ignorant that will affirme that the fame thing, and in the fame manner is affirmed and denied in the aforefaid propofitions: for the fubiect of the firft propofitions, is temporall power *in abftracto,* and it is taken *formally,* and in the fecond propofitions it is temporall power *in concreto,* and it is taken onely *materially,* and hath this fenfe, that temporall Princes, who haue both temporall power, and alfo fpirituall fubiection, are indeed fubiect to the fpirituall power, and are parts and members of the fpirituall kingdome of Chrift, but not *formally,* as they haue temporall power, but onely *materially,* who haue temporall power, but *formally* as they haue fpiritual fubiection. But D. *Schulckenius* doth manifeftly contradict himfelfe, as I plainely fhewed before o, firft affirming, *That the Church of Chrift is compounded of temporall and fpirituall power,* which are *formally* two diftinct powers, as he himfelfe alfo confeffeth, and afterwards in denying, *that it is compounded of temporall, or ciuill power,* which is formally *ciuill.*

26. But marke now *good Reader,* what fraude D. *Schulckenius* vfeth in prouing, that I doe manifeftly contradict my felfe. He would feeme to his Reader to proue, that I affirme and deny one and the felfe fame thing: for this he taketh vpon him to proue, and yet he proueth nothing elfe, but that which I haue alwaies

H h

waies

n *Lib.* 1. *de* Interp. *cap.* 4.

o *Cap.* 2.

waies affirmed, and neuer denied, to wit, that Chriftian Kings, and their fubiects are parts and members
of the Church, and fubiect to the fpirituall power
thereof, but the contradiction, which hee pretended
to proue, he doth not proue at all, nor make any fhew
of proofe thereof, to wit, that it is all one to fay, that
Chriftian Princes and their fubiects are parts and
members of the Church, and fubiect to her fpirituall
power, which I alwaies granted, and that the temporall and fpirituall power doe compound the Church,
or that the temporall power it felfe is *per fe,* fubiect to
the fpirituall power of the Church, which I euer denied, and out of Card. *Bellarmines* owne grounds
haue cleerely proued the contrary, and haue plainely
fhewed, that temporall power doth only compound
a temporall or ciuill body or common-wealth, *whereof the King is head,* as D. *Schulckenius* doth heere exprefly affirme, and that the Church of *Chrift* his myfticall body, and fpirituall Kingdome, or Chriftian
common-wealth (taking the Chriftian common-
wealth for the Church onely, and not for the Chriftian world, as it containeth temporall and fpirituall
power) is compounded onely of fpirituall, and not
of temporall power. In which Church of Chrift, and
alfo Chriftian world, all things are fo well ordered
and difpofed, that temporall things ought by the intention of good Chriftians, to ferue fpirituall things,
and temporall Princes, although in fpiritualls they
are fubiect to the fpirituall power of the Church, yet
in temporalls, or as they haue temporall power, they
are not fubiect but fupreame, and confequently the
temporall power it felfe fpeaking *properly* and *for-*
mally, is not fubiect to the fpirituall, nor dooth
compound the fpirituall kingdome or Church of
Chrift. And therefore I haue not onely weakened,
but alfo quite ouerthrowne, and that out of his owne
grounds this conclufion of Card. *Bellarmine,* and all
thofe

thofe three arguments, which he brought to confirme the fame, as any iudicious Reader, who will duly examine both our writings, will eafily perceiue.

Chap. 8. *Wherein is examined the fourth argument, taken from the authoritie of S. Gregorie Nazianzene, comparing the temporall and fpirituall power among Chriftians, to the body and foule in man.*

1.   **T**HE *fourth argument,* which Card. *Bellarmine* bringeth to prooue this fubiection of of the temporall power among Chriftians, to the fpirituall power of the Church, is taken from the authoritie of S. *Gregorie Nazianzene, who compareth the temporall and fpirituall power among Chriftians to the body and foule in man :* yea, and alfo affirmeth, *that temporall Magiftrates are fubiect to fpirituall Paftors.* And this fimilitude doth fo greatly pleafe Card. *Bellarmines* conceit, that when hee hath any fit occafion, he fpareth not to inculcate it, as a very ftrong argument, and fit fimilitude to proue, that the temporall power among Chriftians is *per fe,* and of it owne nature fubiect to the fpirituall, as the body in man is *per fe,* fubiect to the foule. *For as the fpirit and flefh,* faith he [a], *are in man, fo are the fpirituall and temporall power in the Church. For the fpirit and flefh are as it were two common-wealths, which may be found feparated, and alfo vnited. The flefh hath fenfe and appetite, to which are anfwerable their acts and proper obiects, and of all which the immediate end is the health & good conftitution of the body. The fpirit hath vnderftanding and wil, and acts and proportionate obiects, and for her end the health and perfection of the foule. The flefh is found without the fpirit in beafts, the fpirit is found without the flefh in Angels.*

a *Lib.* 5. *de Rō. pont. cap.* 6.

2   *Whereby it is manifest, that neither of them is precisely for the other. The flesh also is found vnited to the spirit in man, where because they make one person, they haue necessarily subordination and connexion. For the flesh is subiect, the spirit is superiour, and although the spirit doth not intermeddle hir selfe with the actions of the flesh, but doth suffer the flesh to exercise all hir actions, as shee doth exercise in beasts, yet when they doe hurt the end of the spirit, the spirit doth command the flesh, and doth punish hir, and if it be needfull, doth appoint fastings, and also other afflictions, euen with some detriment, and weakning of the bodie, and doth compell the tongue not to speake, the eyes not to see, &c. In like manner if any action of the flesh, yea and death it selfe, be necessarie to obtaine the end of the spirit, the spirit hath power to command the flesh to expose hir seife and all hirs, as wee see in Martyrs.*

3   *Euen so the ciuill power hath hir Princes, lawes, iudgements &c. and likewise the Ecclesiasticall hath hir Bishops, Canons, iudgements. The ciuill hath for hir end temporall peace, the spirituall euerlasting saluation. They are sometimes found separated, as long since in the time of the Apostles, sometimes vnited as now. And when they are vnited, they make one bodie, and therefore they ought to be connected, and the inferiour subiect, and subordained to the superiour. Therefore the spirituall power doth not intermeddle hir selfe with temporall affaires, but doth suffer all things to proceed, as before they were vnited, so that they be not hurtfull to the spirituall end, or not necessarie to the attayning therevnto. But if any such thing doe happen, the spirituall power may and ought to compell the temporall by all manner, and waies, which shall seeme necessarie therevnto.*

4   Thus you see, that *Card: Bellarmine* hath made here a plausible discourse, but truly more beseeming, as I will most clearely convince, a cunning oratour, who with fine, and wittie conceipts seeketh

rather

rather to pleafe curious eares, then a found Diuine, who with fubftantial arguments, and forcible proofes fhould endeauour to convince the vnderftanding of iudicious men, efpecially in fuch points, as are pretended to belong to Catholike faith, and eternall faluation. For neither is the temporall and fpirituall power among Chriftians well compared to the body, and foule of man, either in vnion, or in fubiection, and befides, although it were in all things a fit fimilitude, yet it doth not any way proue that, which Card. *Bellarmine* pretendeth to proue thereby, but it doth clearely and directly, as you fhall fee, convince the flat contrarie.

5 For *firft*, as I fhewed before [b] out of Card. *Bellarmines* owne grounds, the temporall and fpirituall power, as they are referred to their vifible heads here on earth, doe not make *properly* and *formally* one totall bodie, or common-wealth, which is the fpirituall kingdome, or Church of Chrift, but they doe make *properly*, and *formally* two totall bodies, or common wealths, to wit, earthly kingdomes, or a temporall, and ciuill bodie, *whereof the King is head*, as D. *Schulckenius* expreffely affirmeth [c], and the fpirituall kingdome, myfticall bodie, or Church of CHRIST, whereof the *Pope* is head, and *which* as D. *Schulckenius* alfo affirmeth, [d] *is onely compounded of fpirituall power.* Seeing therefore, that the reafon why Card. *Bellarmine* affirmeth, that temporall power among Chriftians is fubiect to the fpirituall, is for that they do make one totall bodie, or common-wealth, as the bodie and foule doe make one man, and confequently the temporall power muft be fubiect to the fpirituall, as the bodie is fubiect to the foule of man, and as I haue clearely proued, there is no fuch vnion of the temporall and fpirituall power to make one totall bodie confifting of both powers, which is the fpirituall kingdome or Church of CHRIST, it is manifeft, that

b *Cap.* 2. 3.

c *Pag.* 339.

d *Pag.* 203.

Hh 3   Card.

Card *Bellarmines* argument drawne from this similitude of the soule and bodie, being grounded vpon
this vnion of the temporall and spirituall power, compounding one totall bodie, hath no sure ground, or
foundation at all.

6   *Secondly*, although I doe willingly grant, as
e *Cap.* I. you haue seene before e, that not onely the temporall
and spirituall power among Christians, as they are
referred not to their visible heads here on earth, but
to C H R I S T the invisible head of them both, doe
make one totall bodie, or common-wealth, consisting
actually of both powers, which may bee called the
Christian world (in which sense the Christian common wealth is vsually taken, but the Church of
CHRIST, and especially the spirituall kingdome of
CHRIST is seldome taken in that sense) but also the
whole world, consisting of Christians, and Infidells,
may in that manner be called one totall bodie, whereof CHRIST, at least wise, as he is G O D, is the invisible, and celestiall head, neuerthelesse this similitude
of the soule and bodie vnited in one man doth nothing auaile to proue the subiection of the temporall
power to the spirituall, both vnited in one totall bodie, whereof C H R I S T onely, and no earthly creature is the head. For the reason, why the bodie in
man is subiect to the soule, is becaufe the bodie and
soule doe make one *essentiall* compound, as the Philosophers doe call it, whereof the bodie is the matter,
and the soule is the forme, and consequently the bodie must of necessitie, and by a naturall sequele, be
subiect to the soule, as euery matter is *per se* and of it
own nature subiect to the form, with which it maketh
one *essentiall* compound, but the temporal & spiritual
power or earthly Kingdomes, and the spirituall kingdome of Christ, as they make one totall body, wherof
Christ onely is the head, doe not make one *essentiall*
compound, whereof one is as the matter, and the o-
ther

ther as the forme, but they doe make one *integrall*
compound, as the Philofophers doe call it, in that
manner as the bodie of man is compounded of eyes,
eares, tongue, hands, feete, which are called by the
Philofophers *integrall*, and not *effentiall* parts of mans
bodie; but in an *integrall* compound, it is not necelfa-
ry, as I fhewed before f, that one part be fubiect to a-   f *Cap.6.nu:10.*
nother, although all muft be fubiect to the head, as it
is apparant in the eyes, eares, tongue, hands, and feet
of mans bodie, whereof none is fubiect one to the o-
ther, although all be fubiect to the head. Seeing
therefore that the temporall and fpirituall power are
onely *integrall* parts of the totall body, whereof *Chrift*
onely is the head, it is euident that from hence no
probable argument can be drawne to proue, that the
temporall power is fubiect to the fpirituall, but that
both of them are vnited and fubiect to *Chrift* the inui-
fible head of them both.

7. *Thirdly*, although I fhould alfo grant, that this
were a fit fimilitude in all things, and that the temporall power is fubiect to the fpirituall in that manner as
the body is fubiect to the foule of man, yet this manner of fubiection would nothing auaile to proue, that
the fpirituall power could either directly, or indirectly difpofe of temporalls, depriue temporall Princes of
their temporall liues or dominions, vfe temporall punifhments, or exercife any temporall action, but it is
rather a very fit fimilitude to conuince the flat contrary. For as I will eafily grant, that the foule hath
power to command, or forbid the body to exercife a-
ny corporall action, when it is necefsarie or hurtfull to
the end not onely of the foule but alfo of the body,
(which lalt claufe Card. *Bellarmine* cunningly omitteth, for that it fauoureth, as you fhall fee, the Popes
direct power to command temporalls) as to fee, to
heare, to fpeake, and fuch like actions, which are fubiect to the command of mans will, I fay, *which are fub-*
iect

iect to the command of mans will, for that there be many corporall actions, which are not in the power of mans will to command, as are all the actions of the nutritiue, vegetatiue and generatiue powers ; But if the body by any let, or hinderance can not, or (if it were possible) would not doe that corporall action, which the soule would willingly haue the body to doe, as to fee, to heare, to fpeake, or to goe, the foule hath no power of her felfe either directly, or indirectly, that is, either for the good of the body, or for the good of the foule, to do that corporall action, as to fee, heare, fpeake, or goe, without the concurrence of the body it felfe.

8. Neither hath the foule any power to inflict any corporal punifhment by way of *coercion* or conftraint, that is, to punifh actually with corporall punifhment any member of the body without the concurrence of fome one or other member thereof, but onely by the way of *command*, that is, to command fome one member to punifh it felfe ; or an other member, as the hands, feete, or head, to put themfelues into fire or water, or the hands, to whip the fhoulders, to clofe thy eye-lids, to ftop the eares, not to put meate into the mouth, and fuch like, which if the bodily member by any let, or hinderance can not, or, *if it were poffible*, would not doe, the foule hath done all that is in her power to doe, for that fhe cannot of her felfe doe any corporall action, without the concurrence of fome corporall member, but the moft that fhe can doe concerning any corporall action or punifhment, is to command the body to concurre with her to the doing of that corporall action, or punifhment. I faid [*if it were poffible*] for that there is fuch a naturall, neceffarie, and intrinfecall fubiection of the body to the foule, that the body cannot refift the effectuall command of the foule in thofe things which are fubiect to her command, and therefore I faid, that *if it were poffi-ble,*

ble, that the body could refist the command of the
foule, yet the foule of her felfe hath not power to exercife any corporall action without the conçurrance of a
corporall organ : which manner of fubiection is not
betweene the temporall and fpirituall power, for that
this fubiection being in diuerfe perfons hauing free
will, is free and voluntarie, and therefore the command may be refifted, but the former being of the
body to the foule, making one only perfon, who hath
free will, is neceffarie and naturall, and therefore can
not be refifted.

9. In the like manner I will eafily grant, that the
temporall power is fubiect to the fpirituall, or rather
that temporall Princes, who haue temporall power,
but not as they haue temporall power, are fubiect to
fpirituall Paftours, who haue fpirituall power, in fuch
fort, that the fpirituall Paftour hath power to command the temporall Prince to do thofe temporal actions belonging to his temporall power, which are neceffarie to the end of the fpirituall power, and to forbid him thofe actions belonging to his temporall
power, which are repugnant to the end of the fpirituall power, which is eternall faluation, which if hee refufe to doe, and will not obey the command of the
fpirituall Paftour, the fpirituall Paftour can not by
vertue only of his fpirituall power exercife any temporall; or ciuill action, belonging to the temporall, or
ciuill power, without the confent, or concurrance of
the temporall power: Neither can the fpirituall Paftor
inflict any temporall, or ciuill punifhment by way of
coercion, conftraint, or compulfion, that is, punifh
actually with any temporall, or ciuill punifhment
without the confent, & concurrance of the temporall,
or ciuill power, but only by the way of *command*, that
is, he hath power to command the temporall Prince,
who only hath fupreme temporall authoritie, to punifh himfelfe, or his fubiects with temporall, or ciuill

Ii   punifh-punishments, if they vse their temporals to the hurt, and preiudice of the spirituall power, or the end therof? although I doe willingly grant, that the spirituall Pastour hath power to punish the temporall Prince, or his subiects, with spirituall punishments, not onely by the way of *command*, but also of *coercion* and constraint, that is, to punish them actually, whether they will or no, with spirituall punishments, when they shall refuse to obey his iust command, for that this manner of punishing by way of *coercion* doth not exceede the limits of the spirituall *coercine* power.

10. Now if my *Aduersaries* demand of mee, why the spirituall power may of her selfe command temporall actions, and yet neither *directly*, nor *indirectly*, that is, neither for temporall, nor spirituall good, exercise temporall actions, may command ciuill punishments, when they are necessarie to the end of the spirituall power, and yet neither *directly*, nor indirectly punish actually with ciuill punishments without the concurrance of the spirituall power, I answer them by their owne similitude, which pleaseth them so much; for the same reason, that the soule hath power of her selfe to command bodily actions, and yet neither *directly*, nor indirectly, that is, neither for the good of the body, nor of the soule, to doe of her selfe alone any bodily action, hath power to command bodily punishments, and yet of her selfe hath not power to inflict any bodily punishment, without the concurrance of the bodie it selfe. And thus you see, that this similitude, of which Card. *Bellarmine*, and his followers doe make so great account, is no fit similitude to prooue their doctrine, but rather to confirme ours, and that from this similitude no probable argument can be drawen to prooue, that the spirituall Pastour hath power either *directly* or *indirectly* to dispose of temporals, to depose temporall Princes, or to punish temporally by way of *coercion* or constraint.

11. But

11. But *fourthly*, although the temporall and spirituall power were aptly compared by Card. *Bellarmine* to the bodie and soule, yet it would prooue two things more then he, as I suppose, would willingly admit ; The *first* is, that the temporall power can exercise no temporall action without the concurrance and assistance of the spirituall power, as the body can doe no corporall action, vnlesse the soule also, as an efficient cause thereof, doe concurre thereunto ; For this is a cleere and approoued principle in philosophie, that the soule is cause of all motions in the body, according to that common definition or description of the soule assigned by *Aristotle* [g] ; *Anima id est, quo visimus, & sentimus, & mouemur, & intelligimus primo. The soule is that, whereby we first or principally liue, and haue sense, and are mooued, and doe vnderstand.*

g 2. De Anima tex. 24.

12. The *second* is, that the spirituall power may command or forbid the ciuill power to exercise ciuill actions, not onely when they are necessarie, or hurtfull to the end of the spirituall power, which is the health of the soule, but also when they are necessarie or hurtfull to the end of the temporall power, which is temporall peace, as the soule hath power to command or forbid the bodie to exercise bodily actions, as to see, heare, speake &c. not onely when they are necessary, or hurtfull to the end, and good of the soule, which is spirituall life and health, but also when they are necessarie or hurtfull to the good of the body, which is bodily health and life. And therefore Card. *Bellarmine* declaring this similitude of the spirit and flesh doth only affirme, that the spirit doth command the flesh, when her actions are hurtfull to the end of the spirit, but cunningly omitteth, that the spirit also doth command the flesh, when her actions are necessarie, or hurtfull to the end of the flesh, least the *Reader* should presently perceiue therby the disparity of this similitude, or else from thence inferre, that in

I i 2   the

the same manner the spirituall power may command the temporall power not onely in order to spirituall good, but also in order to temporall good, which is the Canonist, doctrine, and which *Card. Bellarmine* doth at large impugne.

13. *Lastly*, in what manner S. *Gregory Nazianzene* did compare the temporall and spirituall power, or rather temporall and spirituall Princes to the bodie and soule, I haue sufficiently declared before [h] to wit, not in the manner of their vnion or subiection, but onely in nobility, and in that temporall Princes are in as excellent and worthy manner subiect to temporall Princes, as spirituall things are more excellent and worthy then temporall. So that neither from the authority of S. *Gregorie Nazianzene*, nor from the similitude it selfe of the bodie and soule, as it is declared and vrged by Card. *Bellarmine*, can it with any probabilitie be gathered, that the spirituall power can of her selfe exercise any temporall action belonging to the ciuill power, without the concurrance of the ciuill power, although it be necessarie to the end of the spirituall power, as the soule cannot of her selfe without the concurrance of the bodie exercise any bodily action, although it be necessarie to the end, not onely of the body, but also of the soule. And therefore I maruell, that Card. *Bellarmine* could bee so much ouerseene, as to vrge and repeat so often this similitude of the soule and body to prooue the *Popes* power to depose, and to dispose of all temporals, which is so flat against him, and which, if it were a fit similitude, doth rather confirme the doctrine of the Canonists, whom Card. *Bellarmine* taketh vpon him to confute, then his owne opinon. But the truth is, that it confirmeth neither, for that, as I declared before, [i] the temporall and spirituall power, or the temporal and spirituall Common-wealth are not parts compounding one totall Body or Common-wealth,

h *Cap.3.*

i *Cap.2.3.*

as

as the bodie and foule doe compound a perfect man.

Chap. 9. *Wherein the fift argument to proue the ſubiection of the temporall power to the ſpirituall, taken from the authoritie of* S. Bernard *and* Pope Boniface *the eight, is examined.*

1.   THe *fift argument, which* Car. *Bellarmine* bringeth ᵃ to proue the ſubiection of the temporall power among Chriſtians to the ſpirituall, is taken from the authoritie of S. *Bernard Lib.* 4. *de conſiderat.* and *Pope Boniface* the eight, in the *Extrauagant,* *Vnam Sanctam, who doth imitate,* ſaith Card. *Bellarmine,* S. *Bernards words.* The words of S. *Bernard* to *Pope Eugenius* are theſe. *Why doſt thou againe attempt to vſurpe, or vſe* ᵇ *the ſword, which once thou waſt commanded to put vp into the ſcabbard? which neuertheleſſe hee that denieth to be thine, doth ſeeme to me not ſufficiently to haue conſidered the ſpeech of our Lord ſaying,* Returne thy ſword into the ſcabbard. *Therefore it is alſo thine, to be drawne forth perchance at thy becke* ᶜ*, or direction, although not with thy hand. Otherwiſe if alſo it doth in no maner appertaine to thee, when the* Apoſtles *ſaid,* Behold to ſwords heere, *our* Lord had not anſwered, It is enough, *but it is too much. Therefore both the ſpirituall, and the materiall ſword doe belong to the Church, but the materiall is indeed to bee exerciſed, or drawne forth for the Church; but the ſpirituall alſo by the Church: the ſpirituall with the hand of the Prieſt, the materiall with the hand of the Souldier, but indeed at the becke, or direction, of the Prieſt, and at the command of the Emperour.*

2.   The pricipall words of *Pope Boniface,* beſides thoſe which hee doth imitate out of S *Bernard* are, *That in the Catholike, and Apoſtolike Church, whereof*

a *Lib.* 5. *de Rom. Pont. c.* 7.

b Vſurpare.

c Nutu tuo.

Chriſt is the head, and S.Peter *his Vicar, and in her pow-*
er there be two ſwords, the ſpirituall, and the temporall, as
we are inſtructed by thoſe words of the Goſpell, Behold
heere; *that is in the Church,* two ſwords, *&c. And*
that the ſword muſt be vnder the ſword, the temporall au-
thoritie ſubiect to the ſpirituall power. For the ſpirituall,
the truth ſo witneſſing, hath to inſtruct the earthly power,
and to iudge if it be not good. So of the Church, and of the
Eccleſiaſticall power, the propheſie of Ieremy is verified, behold I haue appointed thee this day ouer nations and
Kingdomes, *and the reſt which follow. Therefore if the*
earthly power goeth out of the way, ſhee ſhall bee iudged
by the ſpirituall power, but if the inferionr ſpirituall power
goeth out of the way, ſhee ſhall be iudged by her ſuperiour,
but if the ſupreme goeth out of the way, ſhee can be iudged
by God alone, and not by man, according to the teſtimony of
the Apoſtle, That the ſpiritual man iudgeth all things,
and he is iudged by none. From all which Card. *Bel-*
larmine, who only relateth S. *Bernards* words, and affirmeth, that Pope *Boniface doth imitate the ſame,* doth
conclude, *that the meaning of* S. *Bernard,* and *Pope Bo-*
niface was to affirme, that both the temporall and ſpiritual
ſword are in the power of the Pope, & that the Pope hath
per ſe, *and properly the ſpirituall ſword, and becauſe the*
temporall ſword is ſubiect to the ſpirituall, therefore the
Pope may command, or forbid a King the vſe of the tem-
porall ſword, when the neceſſitie of the Church doth re-
quire it.

3.   Thus you ſee what S. *Bernard* and *Pope Boni-*
face doe affirme, and alſo that Card. *Bellarmine* inferreth, and concludeth from their words. And although
to this, which Card. *Bellarmine* inferreth from their
words, there needeth no anſwere at all, for that I doe
willingly grant all that, which he doth inferre, to wit,
that the temporall ſword is ſubiect in ſome caſes to
the *commanding* power of the *Pope,* and that the *Pope*
may *command,* or forbid a King the vſe of the temporall

rall sword, when the necessitie of the Church shall require it : seeing that the question betweene mee and Card. *Bellarmine* is not concerning the *Popes commanding* power, and whether the *Pope* may *command* a *King* to vse the temporal sword in the necessitie of the Church, as I haue oftentimes in all my Bookes expresly affirmed, but concerning the *Popes coerciue* power, and whether if a King will not vse the temporall sword at the *Popes command*, the *Pope* hath power to vse it himselfe, and may constraine a King not only with spirituall, but also with temporal compulsion, and punishment to fulfill his iust command ; Neuerthelesse, becaufe Card. *Bellarmine* hath now in his *Schulckenius*, taken some exceptions against the answere, which I made in my *Apologie* to the authortie of S. *Bernard*, and consequently of *Pope Boniface*, who, as hee faith, doth imitate S. *Bernards* words, I thinke it not amisse to set downe my *answere*, and also his *Reply*, that so the *Reader* may cleerely perceiue, whether S. *Bernard* doth fauour, or difsauour Card. *Bellarmines* opinion concerning the *Popes* power to vse the temporall sword, in cafe a temporall *King* will not vse it at the *Popes command*, and whether D. *Schulckenius* hath sufficiently confuted the *answere*, which I did make to the aforesaid authoritie of S. *Bernard*.

    4   Thus therefore I answered in my *Apologie* [d],   d *Nu. 196. & seq.*
" that the words of S. *Bernard* doe only signifie, that
" both the materiall, and the spirituall sword doe be-
" long *in some fort* to the Church, and are subiect vn-
" to hir, not for that the ciuill power is *per se*, and of
" it owne nature subiect to the Ecclesiasticall, or that
" the Church, hath by the law of God any power to
" vse the materiall sword euen in order to spirituall
" good, but becaufe Chriftian Princes, being chil-
" dren of the Church, are bound (and consequently
" the Church may *command* them, and by Ecclesia-
" sticall Cenfures compell them therevnto) in de-
                        " fence

" fence of their holy mother the Church, to vſe the
" temporall ſword. Wherfore although the Church,
"when ſhe hath preſent need, hath power to *command,*
" or forbid the vſe of the materiall ſword, or rather
" without any poſitiue, or conſtitutiue *command* of
" the Church Secular Princes are bound in that caſe
" to vſe it, yet it doth not therefore follow, that the
" Church hir ſelfe hath dominion, right, or power to
" vſe the corporall ſword, ſeeing that to *command* the
" vſe thereof, and to vſe it hir ſelfe are farre different

e *Num. 99.*

" things, as I haue ſhewed before ᵉ. yea and the very
" words of S. *Bernard* doe plainly ſhew as much.
" For otherwiſe if the Church, that is, as ſhee conſi-
" ſteth of Eccleſiaſticall power, ſhould haue the do-
" minion of the materiall ſword, and might vſe it in
" order to ſpirituall good, it might by the law of God
" be drawne forth and vſed, not only for the Church
" but alſo by the Church, not onely with the hand
" of the ſouldier, but alſo of the Prieſt, which neuer-
" theleſſe S. *Bernard* doth affirme to be againſt our
" Sauiours command, who *commanded* S. *Peter* to put
" vp his ſworde into the ſcabberd.

5   "Wherefore I doe not miſlike that very ex-
" poſition (if it be rightly vnderſtood) which Card:
" *Bellarmine* him ſelfe gathereth from thoſe words of
" S. *Bernard,* who in this very place, as you haue ſeen,
" doth affirme, that S. *Bernard,* and Pope *Boniface*
" *did by thoſe words ſignifie,* that the *Pope* hath *per ſe,*
" *and properly the ſpirituall ſword,* (as a temporall
" Prince hath *per ſe,* and *properly* the materiall ſword)
" *and becauſe the temporall power is ſubiect to the ſpiri-*
" *tuall* (not *per ſe,* but *per accidens,* to command tem-
" porall things in order to ſpirituall good, but not to
" puniſh temporally by way of *coercion,* but only ſpi-
" ritually as I haue often declared) *therefore the Pope*
" *hath power to command or forbid a King the vſe of the*
" *temporall ſword, when the neceſſitie of the Church doth*
" *require it.*

6 " Therefore the temporall fword according
"to the opinion of *S. Bernard* doth belong to the
" *Pope*, and is called *his fword*, for that, when the ne-
"ceffitie of the Church doth require, it is to bee
" drawne forth *for the Church, but not by the Church,*
" *with the hand of the fouldier, but not of the Prieſt,* at
" *the becke indeede*, or direction, *of the Prieſt, but at the*
" *command of the Emperour.* By which laſt words
" *S. Bernard* doth fignifie, that the Emperour in v-
" fing the temporall fword for the neceffitie of the
" Church is indeed to bee directed by the *Pope* (for
" that the *Pope* ought to declare, when the Church
" hath neceffitie, but the vfe it felfe of the fword doth
" immediately depend vpon the *Emperors command*,
" to whofe *command* the fouldiers in vfing the tempo-
" rall fword are immediately fubiect.
 7 " But what if the *Emperour* fhall refufe to vfe
"the temporall fword at the *Popes becke*, or direction?
" Hath therefore the *Pope*, according to *S. Bernards*
" opinion, power to draw it forth himfelfe, or can the
" *Emperour* by the *Popes* authoritie be depriued of the
" dominion thereof? No truly. But becaufe he doth
" not keepe that promife, which he hath giuen to the
" Church, and contrarie to the law of God hee doth
" not relieue the neceffities of the Church, the
" Church hath power to punifh him with Ecclefiafti-
" call and fpirituall punifhments, as I haue often faid.
" Wherefore thefe words of *S. Bernard* doe nothing
" fauour the *Popes* temporall power, or his power to
" vfe the temporall fword, but rather do directly con-
" contradict it. And this very anfwer hath *Ioannes*
" *Parifienfis* * in expreffe words &c. Thus I anfwered in my *Apologie.*
 8 Now you fhall fee, how well *D. Schulckenius*
replyeth to this my anfwer. *I anfwer*, faith hef, *that
which my Aduerfarie Widdrington firſt doth fay, that both
the fwords doe belong to the Church, hee faith well, but*

that

* *in Tract. de poteſt. Regia,& Papali cap.* 11.
f *Pag:* 386. *ad num.* 196.

*that which hee addeth , that both the fwords are fubiect
to the Church, he faith not well. For the fpirituall fword
to bee fubiect to the Church, doth fignifie no other thing,
then that the Popes power is fubiect to the Church, which
is manifeftly falfe , whereas contrariwife it is to bee faid,
that the Church is fubiect to the fpirituall fword, or to
the power of the Pope, vnleffe perchance* Widdrington
*be of opinion, that the Sheepheard is fubiect to his fheepe,
and not the fheepe to the Sheepheard.*

   9   Marke now, *good Reader*, the cunning, not to
fay, fraudulent proceeding of this man. Hitherto he
hath, as you haue feene, taken the Church, the Chriftian common-wealth, the myfticall bodie, or fpirituall kingdome of Chrift to be all one, and to be one
totall bodie, confifting both of temporall, and fpirituall power, and compareth hir to a man compounded of bodie and foule ; And may it not, I pray you,
be rightly faid, that all the powers both of bodie and
foule are fubiect to man ? and why then may it not
alfo be rightly fatd, that the fpirituall fword or power
is fubiect to the Church ? But now *forfooth* this Doctor , that hee might take an occafion to charge me
with a manifeft falfhood, will not take the Church, as
hee tooke it before for the whole myfticall bodie of
Chrift, which totall bodie includeth both the *Pope*,
and all other inferiour members thereof, in which
fenfe I did take the *Church*, when I affirmed, *that not
onely the fpirituall, but alfo the temporall fword is in
fome fort fubiect to the Church*, but hee will take
the *Church* for one part onely of this myfticall bodie, to wit, for all the members of the Church befides the *Pope*, in which fenfe the *Church* is indeed
fometimes taken, as when the *Church* is compared
with the *Pope*, and it is faid, that the *Pope* is head of
the *Church* ; but when the *Church* is compared with
Chrift, and is faid to be the myfticall bodie, and fpiri
tuall kingdome of *Chrift* , the *Church* doth include
                                     both

both the *Pope*, and all other inferiour members thereof, who iointly make one totall bodie, whereof *Chrisi* is the head. And the very like is seene in the bodie of man ; for when the bodie is compared with the head, the bodie doth not include the head, but when the bodie is compared with the foule, & said to be subiect to the foule, & that of the bodie & foule is made one man , then the bodie doth also include the head.

10. Wherefore taking the *Church*, as it doth signifie the whole myſticall body of *Chrisi*, in which ſenſe both *Card. Bellarmine* himselfe, and also *S. Bernard* in this very place doe take it, when they affirme, *that the materiall ſword is to be drawne foorth for the Church , and the ſpirituall by the Church*, it is truly said, that the ſpirituall ſword is ſubiect to the *Church*: Neither doth this ſignifie, that the *Popes* ſpirituall power is ſubiect to the *Church*, for now the *Church* is taken, as it excludeth the *Pope*, but rather that all ſpirituall power, which is in any member of the Church , is ſubiect to the whole body of the *Church* , and conſequently to the *Pope* , in whom all the power of the *Church* according to Cardinall *Bellarmines* opinion, doth reſide. And would not D. *Schulckenius* thinke , that I did cauill, if I ſhould ſay of him, as hee ſaith of mee, that he ſpake not rightly , when in this very place hee affirmeth , *that Chriſt gaue to the Church both the ſwords. For the ſpirituall ſword to be giuen to the Church doth ſignifie no other thing*, to vſe his owne words , *then that the Popes power was by Chriſt our Sauiour giuen to the Church*, which in Card. *Bellarmines* opinion is not only manifeſtly falſe, but also an *erroneous* doctrine.

11. I omit now, that the ancient *Doctours* of *Paris*, (who hould, that the whole body of the Church taken *collective*, and not including the *Pope*, which a *generall Councell* lawfully aſſembled doth repreſent, is ſuperiour to the *Pope*) would not thinke to ſpeake any falſhood at all, if they ſhould ſay , that Chriſt gaue all

the

K k 2

the power, which the Pope hath, also to the *Church,* and that the *Popes* power is subiect to the *Church,* and that it doth not therefore follow, that the Paſtour is subiect to the ſheepe, or the ſuperiour to the inferiour, but rather contrariwiſe. But in very truth this was not my meaning, when I affirmed, that both ſwords are in ſome ſort ſubiect to the *Church,* for by the name of *Church* I vnderſtood alſo the *Pope,* as I declared before

12. *Secondly, when* Widdrington *affirmeth,* ſaith D. *Schulckenius, that the ciuill power is not* per ſe *ſubiect to the Eccleſiaſticall, he doth corrupt the text of* S. Bernard, *and of Pope* Boniface *the eight. For when* S. Bernard *ſaith, that the materiall ſword is the* Popes, *and is to bee drawne forth at his becke,* and direction, *he clearely conſeſſeth, that the materiall ſword is ſubiect to the ſpirituall ſword, which Pope* Boniface *doth declare more* plainely, *when he ſaith, that the ſword muſt be vnder the ſword, and temporall authoritie ſubiect to ſpirituall power.*

13. But how ſhamefully *D. Schulckenius* accuſeth me of corrupting the text of S. *Bernard,* and Pope *Boniface,* let the Reader iudge ; ſeeing that I neither add, nor diminiſh, nor alter any one word of their text, but doe ſay the very ſame words which they doe ſay. For S. *Bernard* doth ſay, *that the materiall ſword is the* Popes, *and doth belong to the* Pope, but with this limitation, *in ſome ſort, to bee drawne foorth for the Church, but not by the Church, with the hand of the Souldier, not of the Prieſt, at the becke,* or direction, *of the Prieſt, but at the command of the Emperour :* and I alſo ſay the very ſame. But S. *Bernard* doth not ſay, that the materiall ſword is ſubiect to the ſpirituall ſword *per ſe,* but only *in ſome ſort, to be drawne forth for the Church, not by the Church* &c. From which words it is plainely gathered, that the materiall ſword, or temporall power is, according to S. *Bernard,* ſubiect to the ſpirituall, not *per ſe,* but *per accidens,* in ſpiritualls, not in temporalls, to be commanded in ſome caſe by the Prieſt, as he is a
Prieſt

Priest, but not to be drawne forth, or vsed by a Priest as he is a Priest, but as he is a temporall Prince, or a publike, or priuate souldier. In like manner I say with Pope *Boniface, that the sword is vnder the sword, and the temporall power is subiect to the spirituall,* but Pope *Boniface* doth not say, that the sword is *per se* vnder the sword, and the temporall power is *per se* subiect to spirituall authoritie, and therefore, seeing that hee doth imitate S. *Bernards* words, as Card. *Bellarmine* here affirmeth, he is to be vnderstood in that sense, as S. *Bernard* vnderstood them, to wit, that the sword is vnder the sword, *in some sort,* and the temporall power subiect to the spirituall in *some sort, to be drawne foorth, or vsed for the Church, but not by the Church* &c. as I now declared.

14. *Thirdly, when* Widdrington, *affirmeth,* saith *D. Schulckenius, that the Church hath not by the law of God power to vse the materiall sword euen in order to spirituall good, he speaketh too ambiguously. For the law of God doth not command Ecclesiasticall men to vse with their own hand the materiall sword, neither doth it so forbid them, but that it is lawfull for them in some cases to vse it also with their owne hand: But neuerthelesse according to* S. Bernards *opinion* Christ *gaue both the swordes to the* Church, *and by this he gaue her power to vse the materiall sword in that manner, as doth beseem her, to wit, by the seruice, or hands of others, in directing Secular Princes, that they draw it forth, or put it in the scabard, as it is expedient to the honour of God, and the saluation of Christian people.*

15. But my words are very plaine, and no whit ambiguous I say, that the *Church,* taking the *Church,* not *materially,* for all the members of the *Church,* but for Churchmen, *formally* as they are *Churchmen,* or, which is all one, for the *Church,* as it consisteth of Ecclesiasticall power, are according to S. *Bernards* doctrine commanded not to draw forth, or vse with their owne hands the materiall sword euen in order to spirituall

K k 3

rituall good. For S. *Bernards* words are plaine, *why
doſt thou againe attempt to vſe the ſword, which thou waſt
once,*not only counſelled, but *cōmanded to put vp into the
ſcabard* &c. But if the *Pope* becom a temporall Prince
or a Prieſt do lawfully becom a Soldier, to fight either
in his own defence, or in the defence of others, which
Chriſt did not forbid, although the Church in ſome
caſes hath forbidden it, neither I, nor S. *Bernard* doe
denie, that the Pope, as he is a temporall Prince, or a
Prieſt, as he is a lawfull Souldier, hath power to vſe
with their owne hands the materiall ſword. Neither
did S. *Bernard* euer grant, that the *Pope*, as he is *Pope,*
or a Prieſt as he is a Prieſt, or, which is all one, by his
ſpirituall, or Prieſtly authority, hath power to draw
foorth, or to vſe with his owne hands the materiall
ſword, althou gh the *Pope* by his ſptrituall power may
direct and command a temporall Prince to draw it
foorth, and vſe it, when the neceſſitie of the Church
ſhall require, which onely D. *Schulckenius* in this pa-
ragraph doth affirme.

16. *Fourthly, that is falſe,* ſaith D. *Schulckenius,*
g *which* Widdrington *affirmeth, that the materiall ſword
in that onely ſenſe doth belong to the Church, becauſe Secular Princes being children of the Church are bound to
fight in defence of the Church their mother.* For S. Bernard *doth grant much more to the Eccleſiaſticall Prince,
when he ſaith,* Therefore it is alſo thine, *to wit, the materiall ſword.* And beneath, Therefore both the ſpirituall and the materiall ſword are the Churches, but
the materiall ſword is to bee drawen foorth for the
Church, and the ſpirituall alſo by the Church, the
ſpirituall with the hand of the Prieſt, the materiall
with the hand of the Souldier, but truly at the becke,
or direction of the Prieſt, and at the command of the
Emperour. *Where* S. Bernard *doth not only ſignifie, that
Souldiers or Princes are bound to draw foorth the ſword
for the Church, but alſo at the becke,* or direction *of the*
Prieſt,

g *Pag.* 387.

Priest, that is, with subordination to the Ecclesiasticall power, as Souldiers ought to vse the sword with subordination to the command of the Emperour.

17 But anie man who readeth ouer but sleightly my answer in that place, will easily perceiue, that this is a meere cauill, and also a plaine vntruth ; for that in expresse words I doe affirme, *that Secular Princes and Souldiers are, according* to S. *Bernard,* to draw foorth, and vse the materiall sword for the necessity of the Church, at the becke, counsell, direction, yea, and command of the Priest, which is as much, as D *Schulckenius* heere affirmeth S. *Bernard* to say ; although S. *Bernard* did expressely distinguish betwixt *becke* and *command,* at the *becke,* saith he, of the Priest, but at the *command* of the Emperour ; whereby it is manifest, that S. *Bernard* did not account *becke* and *command* to be all one, and consequently, hee did not approoue the same subordination to be betwixt *Secular Princes,* and the *Priest* in vsing the materiall sword, as is betwixt *Souldiers,* and the *Emperour.* For albeit S. *Bernard* by the name of *becke* did not onely vnderstand aduise and counsell, which Christian Princes in all their weightie affaires concerning the Law of God and Christian Religion ought to demand of learned Priests, and who are skilfull in the Law of God, and Christian Religion, but also a *command* to fight, and vse the materiall sword in defence of the Church and Christian Religion, & to the obseruing of which command, Christian Princes may, as also I sayd, by Ecclesiasticall censures bee compelled, yet this *command* being a declaratiue *command,* which doth onely declare a former *command* of God, and nature, and doth not make a new bond, but onely *declare* and signifie a former obligation, may rather be called a *beckoning,* and signifying that Christian Princes are by the Law of God bound in that case to draw foorth, fight, and vse the materiall sword, then a true, proper, and

constitutiue

conſtitutiue *command*, which doth not onely *ſignifie*, but alſo *induce* a new bond or obligation.

18. And in this ſenſe not onely *Ioannes Pariſienſis*, whom I cited befoꝛe, [h] doth vnderſtand thoſe words of S. Bernard (*at the becke indeede of the Prieſt*) but alſo our learned Countri-man *Alexander of Hales*, *There is*, ſaith he, [i] *an authority to command, and an authority to beckon ; in the authority to command it doth follow*, he doth that thing by whoſe authority it is done, *but in the authority to beckon this doth not follow*. *The authoritie to command wicked men to be ſlaine is in the Emperour, but the authoritie to beckon is in the Pope and Prieſts. And this beckoning, as hath beene ſayd, is a preaching of the Law of God, and an exhorting, that Princes will obey the Law of God. Whereupon S.* Bernard *ſheweth how both the materiall and ſpirituall ſword are the Churches, and doe belong to the Church, not for as much as concerneth vſe or command, but for as much as concerneth beckoning: whereupon he ſpeaketh in this manner to* Eugenius, hee that denieth the materiall ſword to be thine, ſeemeth to me not to regard ſufficiently the word of our Lord ſaying, *Returne thy ſword into thy ſcabard*, and ſo foorth as it followeth in S. Bernard.

19. Wherefore, according to S. *Bernard*, the materiall ſword is ſubiect to the ſpirituall, not abſolutely, but in *ſome ſort* to be *beckoned*, but not to bee vſed or commanded, as *beckoning* is diſtinguiſhed from *command*, by the Prieſt, as he is a Prieſt. And therefore that *Gloſſe*, which D. Schulckenius maketh of thoſe words [*at the becke indeede of the Prieſt*] *that is*, ſaith he, *with ſubordination to the Eccleſiaſticall power, as Souldiers ought to vſe the ſword with ſubordination to the command of the Emperor*, is verie vntrue, & expreſly againſt S. *Bernards* words ; both becauſe the Emperour hath power to command the ſouldier to vſe the materiall ſword, but the Prieſt according to S. *Bernard* hath onely power to *beckon*, but not to *command* the vſe

vfe thereof, and alfo becaufe if the Souldier will not vfe the materiall fword at the Emperours command; the Emperour, as Emperour, may vfe it himfelfe, and with his owne hand, which the Prieft, as Prieft, or, which is all one, the Ecclefiafticall power, according to S. *Bernard*, cannot doe; and moreouer becaufe the Emperour, as Emperour, may compell the fouldier with temporall punifhments to vfe the materiall fword, and not onely depriue him of his power and right to vfe the fame; but alfo of his temporall life, which the Prieft, as Prieft, or the Ecclefiaftical power, cannot doe.

20. And therefore who would not maruaile to fee D. *Schulckenius* fo boldly, and in fuch publike writings to affirme, *That the queftion is not, whether the fpirituall Prince hath dominion, right, or power to vfe the materiall fword : but onely, whether the fword be vnder the fword, and whether the temporall power bee fubiect to the fpirituall. And whereas* Widdrington, faith he, *in this place confeffeth, that the Church hath power to command, or forbid in time of neceffitie the vfe of the materiall fword, from thence we doe gather that the fword is vnder the fword, and the temporall power is fubiect to the command, and prohibition of the fpirituall power, which onely* Card. Bellarmine *in that his fecond argument did intend. Wherefore* Widdrington *doth feeme to decline of fet purpofe the principall queftion. For, as wee haue often faid, the queftion is not concerning the dominion, or vfe of the materiall fword, but concerning the power to direct it, and concerning the fubiection of the materiall fword to the fpirituall. But thefe in the opinion of* S. Bernard *are moft manifeft. And for as much as appertaineth to the vfe of the materiall fword, wee affent altogether to* S. Bernard, *that it doth not befeeme Ecclefiafticall men to vfe the materiall fword, but onely the fpirituall, and thus much onely thofe words of our Sauiour doe fignifie,* Put vp thy fword into thy fcabbard, *and thofe of* S. Bernard,

Why

Why doeſt thou againe attempt to vſe the ſword, which once thou waſt commanded to put into the ſcabbard? *For heere it is not meant of the Law of God, by which Eccleſiaſticall men are abſolutely forbidden to vſe the materiall ſword; ſeeing that it is manifeſt, that in ſome caſes, and eſpecially in defence of themſelues, and of their Countrey: this is lawfull, but of the command of God, by which Cleargie men are inſtructed, and taught, that their vocation is not to fight with the materiall, but with the ſpirituall ſword.* Thus D. *Schulckenius.*

21. But it is ſtrange to ſee, how farre affection will carry the pens of learned men; In very truth I ſhould neuer haue imagined, that D. *Schulckenius,* or any other learned man, who hath read my *Apologie,* would euer haue beene ſo bold, as to affirme, *That the queſtion betwixt me, and* Card. Bellarmine *is not, whether the Pope hath power to vſe the materiall ſword, but onely whether the ſword be vnder the ſword, and the temporall power ſubiect to the command, and prohibition of the ſpirituall power, and that this only was intended by Card.* Bellarmine *in his ſecond argument.* For firſt concerning the queſtion betwixt mee, and Card. *Bellarmine* it is euident, that I haue oftentimes declared in my *Apologie,* and D. *Schulckenius* alſo ſetteth downe my words, that the true ſtate of the queſtion betwixt mee and Card. *Bellarmine,* is not concerning the Popes power to *command,* but to *diſpoſe* of temporalls, nor whether the ſword be in *any manner* whatſoeuer vnder the ſword, or the temporall power *in any ſort* ſubiect to the ſpirituall, but *in what manner* the ſword is vnder the ſword, and *after what ſort* the temporall power is ſubiect to the ſpirituall. For I haue often granted, that the ſpirituall power, or the *Pope* as *Pope,* may *command* temporalls, and the vſe of the materiall ſword, and puniſh diſobedient Princes with Eccleſiacall cenſures: but that, which I vtterly denied, was, that the ſpirituall power, or the *Pope* as *Pope* may *diſ-*

poſe

pofe of temporalls, *vfe* the materiall fword, or *punifh* difobedient Princes by taking away their liues, king-domes, or goods.

22. *Secondly,* it is alfo manifeft, that Card. *Bellar-mine* in his fecond argument did not onely intend to proue, that the temporal power is fubiect to the com-mand, and prohibition of the fpirituall power; as D. *Schulckenius* affirmeth, but alfo, that the fpirituall power may *vfe*, and difpofe of temporalls, depofe temporal Princes, and inftitute others, and conftraine or punifh with temporall punifhments. For marke, I pray you, his fecond argument : In the firft part thereof he argueth thus. *The power to vfe and difpofe of temporalls* (and confequently of the materiall fword which is a temporall thing) *is neceffary to the fpirituall end, becaufe otherwife wicked Princes might without punifhment fauour Heretickes, and ouerthrow Religion, therefore the Church hath alfo this power.* And yet D. *Schulckenius* doth not blufh to affirme, that Card. *Bellarmine* in his fecond argument did onely intend to proue, that the temporall power is fubiect to the command, and prohibition of the fpirituall power. And in the *fecond* part of his argument hee concludeth thus : *Therefore much more the fpirituall common-wealth, hath power to command the temporall common-wealth, which is fubiect vnto her, and to con-ftraine her to change her gouernment, and to depofe Princes, and to inftitute others, when fhe can not otherwife defend her fpirituall good. And in this manner are to bee vnderftood the words* of S. Bernard, *and* Pope Boni-face, *&c.* Thus Card. *Bellarmine.* So that according to Card. *Bellarmine*, S. *Bernards* words doe proue, that the *Pope* hath power not onely to *command* the materiall fword, but alfo to vfe it, vnleffe the *materiall* fword is not to be comprehended vnder the name of *temporalls.* And therefore not I, but D. *Schulckenius* doth of fet purpofe decline the difficultie, and alfo

vntruly affirmeth, that Card: *Bellarmine* did not intend to proue in his fecond argument, that the *Pope* hath power to vfe the materiall fword, but onely that the materiall fword is fubiect to the command and prohibition of the fpirituall power, feeing that Card: *Bellarmines* fecond argument doth moft clearely fhew the contrarie.

23 But marke now how clearely *D. Schulckenius* doth either contradict *S. Bernards* words and him felfe, or elfe fowly equiuocate, and confirme the anfwer which I gaue to the authoritie of *S. Bernard*. I affirmed, that *S. Bernards* words are fo to be vnderftood, that it is lawfull for Ecclefiafticall men, as they are Ecclefiafticall men, to command in fome cafes the vfe of the materiall fword, but that to vfe the materiall fword themfelues, as they are Ecclefiafticall men, they are forbidden by the expreffe command of Chrift. Now *D. Schulckenius* affirmeth [k], *that for as much as appertaineth to the vfe of the materiall fword, he affenteth altogether to S. Bernard, that it doth not befeeme Ecclefiafticall men to vfe the materiall fword, but onely the fpirituall; and thus much onely thofe words of our Sauiour doe fignifie,* Returne thy fword into the fcabbard; *and thofe of S. Bernard,* why doft thou againe attempt to vfe the fword, which once thou waft commanded to put into the fcabard? *For here it is not meant of the law of God, by which Ecclefiafticall men are abfolutely forbidden to vfe the materiall fword, feeing that it is manifeft, that in fome cafes, and efpecially in defence of themfelues and of their countrey, this is lawfull, but of the command of God, by which Cleargie men are inftructed, and taught, that their vocation is not to fight with the materiall, but with the fpirituall fword.* Thus *D. Schulckenius.*

24 But if *D. Schulckenius* meane that Ecclefiafticall men are onely for decencie, which implyeth no command, not to vfe the materiall fword, he plainly contra-

k *Pag.* 390.

contradicteth *S. Bernard,* to whom neuerthelesse hee
affirmeth altogether to assent, who expressely auerreth, that the *Pope* in *S. Peter* was not only *counsailed,*
but *commanded* not to vse the materiall sword. And
therefore *S. Bernards* words can not otherwise be vnderstood, but that Ecclesiasticall men, as they are
Ecclesiasticall men, and the *Pope,* as *Pope,* are by the
command of *Chrift* absolutely forbidden to vse the
materiall sword; for *S. Bernard* did not intend to
affirme, that Ecclesiasticall men, if they become
temporall Princes, or being considered, as they are
priuate men, or citizens, and parts, or members of the
temporall common-wealth, are by the *command* of
Chrift forbidden to vse the materiall sword, and to
fight in defence of their owne persons, or of their
Countrey.

25   Wherefore those last words of *D. Schulckenius,*
to wit, *that S. Bernards saying is to be vnderstood of the
command of God, by which Cleargie men are instructed,
and taught, that their vocation is not to fight with the
materiall, but with the spirituall sword, are somewhat
equivocall.* For if *D. Schulckenius* doe onely vnderstand of such an instruction, which implyeth no command of Chrift, but onely a certaine decencie, counsell, and aduise, for that it doth not beseeme the perfection of those men, who haue a spirituall vocation,
to fight with the materiall sword, hee plainly contradicteth himselfe, and also *S. Bernard* himselfe, for
that hee acknowledgeth *a command of God, whereby
Cleargie men are instructed* &c. but this instruction
supposeth no command of God; *S. Bernard* also he
contradicteth, who expressely speaketh of a *command,*
whereby Ecclesiasticall men are by the law of Chrift,
and not only of the Church forbidden to vse the materiall sword, which *command* of Chrift, as I said before, can bee no other, then that Ecclesiasticall men
can not, as they are Ecclesiasticall men, vse the mate-

riall fword ; for that although the Ecclefiaſticall
power doth according to *S. Bernard* and the truth,
extend to the *beckoning*, or declaratiue commanding
of the materiall fword in fome cafes, yet it doth not
extend to the vfing thereof, but this power to vfe the
materiall fword doth proceed from the law of nature,
or the ciuill power, who doe giue authoritie to euery
man, whether he be a Clerke, or Laike in cafe at leaſt
wife of neceſſitie, to vfe the materiall fword in defence of his owne perfon, or of his countrey. And
if *D. Schulckenius* only intend to fignifie thus much
by thofe laſt words of his, which in very deede can
not be otherwife vnderſtood, vnleſſe wee will make
them repugnant to themfelues, hee doth fauour, not
contradiċt, confirme and not impugne my anfwer.

 26 *Fiftly*, obferue, *good Reader*, how cunningly
D. Schulckenius would ſhift off the laſt, and principall
Anfwer, which I made to the authoritie of *S. Bernard*.
I granted, as you haue feene before, that the *Pope*, as
Pope, hath, according to *S. Bernard*, power to *beckon*,
or command the Emperour to vfe the materiall
fword, when the neceſſitie of the Church ſhall require
and to punifh him with Ecclefiaſticall punifhments,
if he ſhall refufe to obey his iuſt command, or *becke*,
and I affirmed, that this is the moſt, that can be gathered from thofe words of *S. Bernard*. But if the *Emperour* ſhould refufe to vfe the materiall fword at the
Popes command, or *becke*, I affirmed, that it could not
be inferred from that authoritie of *S. Bernard*, that
the *Pope*, as Pope, could vfe it himſelfe, or depriue the
Emperour of his temporall dominion, or power to vfe
the materiall fword ; for this were to vfe, and to difpofe of temporalls, and implyeth a power to vfe, and
draw forth the materiall fword it felfe, which *S. Bernard* expreſſely denyeth to the *Pope* : and that therefore *S. Berniards* authoritie doth nothing fauour, but
clearely contradiċt the *Popes* power, I doe not fay, to

command

command temporalls, but to *dispose* of temporalls, and
to vse temporalls, as *Ioannes Parisienfis*, and *Alexander
of Hales*, [l] *did before affirme.* Now to this my anfwere
D. *Schulckenius* replyeth [m] in this manner.

27. *Thou didst runne well, who hath hindered thee so
soone not to obey the truth? For now thou dost not follow S.
Bernard, but William Barclay, as thy Mafter. If that the
Emperour shall refufe to vfe the fword at the becke of the
Pope in great necefsitie of the Church, it is not indeed fitting for the* Pope *to vfe the materiall fword, but hee hath
power to conftraine the* Emperour, *firft with Ecclefiafticall
punifhments, and afterwards alfo by depriuing him of the
fword, as in the like cafe the Councell of* Lateran *often cited
doth teach, which one Councell is to be preferred before all
the* Barclaies, *or* Iohns *of* Paris, *all men doe thinke, who
are not mad.*

28. Is not this thinke you a trim anfwere? The
queftion betwixt me, and Card. *Bellarmine* in this
place was not concerning the *Councell of Lateran*, wherof I will treat beneath, * and plainely fhew, that, notwithftanding all the clamours of my *Aduerfaries*, the
faid *Councell* hath neither defined, or fuppofed for certaine, nay or fuppofed at all, that the *Pope* hath power
to depofe Soueraigne Princes, as D. *Schulckenius* doth
here colleft from thence, but the queftion was onely
concerning the authoritie of *S. Bernard.* And I
prooued clearely out of S. *Bernards* wordes, that although the *Pope*, as *Pope* hath power to command, or
forbid in fome cafes the vfe of the materiall fworde,
yet that he hath power, as he is *Pope*, to *vfe* it himfelfe,
or to depriue the *Emperour* of the *vfe* thereof, which
implyeth a power to vfe it himfelfe, this I faid could
not be proued, but rather the contrarie out of thofe
words of S. *Bernard*, who doh not only fay, that it is
not *fitting* for the *Pope* to vfe the materiall fword, as D.
Schulckenius would mince his words, but that it is *forbidden* the *Pope* to draw foorth, or vfe the materiall
fword.

fword. Now D. *Schulckenius* paffeth ouer S. *Bernard,*
and flyeth to the *Councell of Lateran* to proue, that if
the *Emperour* refufe at the *Popes* command to vfe the
materiall fword, he may by the Popes authoritie bee
depriued of the vfe thereof, whereas the prefent queftion was only concerning the opinion of S. *Bernard,*
and not what was the doctrine of the *Councell of Lateran* in this point, whofe authoritie I doe afmuch refpect either as Card. *Bellarmine,* or any other Catholike is bound to doe. But it is an eafie matter to wreft
the words of the *Councell* of *Lateran,* or any other to
their purpofe, contrary to the true meaning of the
Councell, and then to crie out, *ô the Councell of Lateran,
which is to be preferred before all* Barclaies, and Widdringtons &c. *whereas we doe afmuch refpect the authoritie* of the *Councell* of *Lateran,* or any other, as they do,
although we doe not fo much refpect their ouer wrefted collections, which they to ferue their owne turnes,
doe gather from any *Councel,* or text of holy *Scripture,*
contrarie to the plaine, proper, and true fenfe and meaning of the words. But to fuch fhiftings, and win-
dings euen learned men are fometimes brought, when
they will make their vncertaine opinions, and priuate
expofitions of holy *Scriptures,* or *Councells* to be *infallible* grounds of the *Catholike* faith.

29. Laftly, *but the foundation,* faith D. *Schulckenius,*
of Widdringtons *errour is, for that he thinketh, that the*
Pope *hath authoritie to conftraine the Emperour by reafon
of the faith, and free promife, which the* Emperour *gaue,
and made to the* Pope, *according to the fimilitude, which a
little before he put concerning one, who promifed an other
to fpend his life, and all his goods in defence of him. But
this foundation is falfe, becaufe the authoritie of the* Pope
ouer Chriftian Princes *doth not proceed from their onely
promife, or faith, which they haue giuen, but from the law
of God, by which law the* Pope *is made by* Chrift *the Paftour of all his flocke, the chiefe of all his familie, the head*
of

of all his body, and the Rector *of all his Church. Where-fore it is no maruaile, if from a false foundation he conclude a falshood, to wit, that* S. Bernards *words do not onely, not fauour the* Popes *temporall power, but are flat contrarie to it. What I beseech you, could be spoken more cleerely for the* Popes *temporall power, then that* which S. Bernard *said,* that the temporall sword is the *Popes,* and that both swords are the *Churches,* and that the temporall sword ought to be drawne foorth at the Popes becke? *And as for* Ioannes Parisiensis *there is no great reckoning to be made of him whatsoeuer he saith, both for that he is re-pugnant to the* Councell of Lateran, *and many others, and also that other his errours are condemned by the Church in the common Extrauagant,* Vas electionis, *and lastly, for that either he denieth only the* Popes *direct power in tem-poralls, or else he doth plainly contradict himselfe.*

30. But truely it is strange, that learned men, and who pretend to maintaine nothing but truth, dare ad-uenture to auouch so bouldly, and in such publike writings so manifest vntruths, and which they them-selues in their consciences can not but see to be plain, and palpable vntruths. I very often, and that of set purpose did affirme in my *Apologie,* and D. *Schulcke-nius* doth also set downe my words, *that the* Pope, *as* Pope, *hath power to command temporall Princes in tempo-rals in order to spirituall good,* and yet this man to make his Reader beleeue, that I doe teach flat *heresie,* blush-eth not to affirme in an other place, ⁿ that I deny, *that the* Pope, *as* Pope, *hath power to commaund temporall Princes in temporalls in order to spirituall good.* So like-wise, I did oftentimes in my *Apologie* affirme, º and D. *Schulckenius* doth also set downe my words, that the *Pope,* as *Pope* hath power by *the law of God, and for that he is appointed by* Christ *to be the supreme spirituall Pastour of the Catholike Church,* to constraine and pu-nish all disobedient Christians both Princes and peo-ple, with spirituall and Ecclesiasticall punishments;

and

n *Pag.* 256.

o *Num.* 90. 91. 181. 223. 341.

and yet now this man to perfwade his Reader, that
I teach heere a manifeft *errour*, is not afhamed to affirme, *that I am of opinon, that the Pope hath authoritie
to conftraine the Emperour in regard onely of the free promife, which the Emperour hath made to the Pope.* And
therefore D. *Schulckenius* neither dealeth truely nor
fincerely, and both deludeth his Reader, and alfo
wrongeth mee, in affirming that to bee my doctrine,
which I expreffely impugne, and that to be the foundation of my opinion (which hee is pleafed to call an
errour) which I in expreffe words, and that oftentimes haue denied.

21. For as I doe willingly grant, that although a
temporall Prince hath power to command, and with
temporall punifhments to compell, if neede require,
his temporall fubiects to make, and fweare an expreffe
promife of that true faith, loyaltie and temporall allegeance, which by the Law of God and nature they
doe owe to their lawfull Prince, yet I doe not affirme,
that a temporalll Prince hath power to conftraine his
rebellious fubiects by vertue onely of the promife,
which they haue made, but by vertue of his fupreme
temporall power which hee hath, as hee is a fupreme
temporall Prince by the Law of God and nature; So
alfo I do willingly grant, that although the *Pope* hath
power to command, and with fpirituall punifhments
to compell, if neede require, all Chriftian Princes and
people to make and fweare an expreffe promife of
that true faith, loyalty and fpirituall allegeance, which
as they are Chriftians and members of the myfticall
body of Chrift, they doe owe by the Law of God to
the fupreme fpirituall Paftour and, vifible head of this
myfticall bodie and Church of Chrift, and the Emperour at his coronation taketh fuch an oath, neuertheleffe I doe not affirme, that the *Pope* hath power to
conftraine and punifh difobedient *Princes*, and people by vertue onely of the promife, which they haue

made to the *Pope* of their ſpirituall obedience, but by vertue of his ſupreme ſpirituall power, which he hath by the Law of God, and his Paſtorall authority giuen to him by our Sauiour *Chriſt Ieſus*.

32. True it is, that the Reader might the better vnderſtand, that to command one to vſe a temporall thing, and to vſe it himſelfe, to command one to diſpoſe of temporals, and to diſpoſe of them himſelfe, are very different things, and that the one doth not neceſſarily follow from the other, I brought a familiar example of one, who either *by promiſe,* or *by ſome other obligation* (and yet D. *Schulckenius* taketh hold onely of the *promiſe,* and cleane omitteth *the other obligation*) is bound to diſpoſe, and giue his goods, or life at anthers command, who notwithſtanding this *promiſe,* or other obligation, doth ſtill keepe the property, dominion and right ouer his goods and life, in ſuch ſort, that the other cannot by vertue of his commanding power, which he hath ouer him and them, take them away and diſpoſe of them without his conſent, but if hee will not diſpoſe of his goods at the others command, according as by vertue either of his promiſe, or of ſome other obligation he is bound to doe, the other may complaine to the Magiſtrate, that hee will puniſh him for his offence, or cauſe him to performe his promiſe, ſo far forth as the coerciue power of the Magiſtrate doth extend. From which I concluded, that conſidering to haue a power to command the vſe of the temporall ſword, and to haue a power to vſe it, or to depriue of the vſe thereof, are two different things, neither doth one neceſſarily follow from the other, although the *Pope,* as *Pope,* hath according to S. *Bernard,* power to command the *Emperour* to vſe the temporall ſword, yet it doth not therefore follow that if the *Emperour* will not vſe the temporall ſword at the *Popes* command, the *Pope,* as *Pope,* can vſe it himſelfe, or depriue the *Emperour* of the vſe

thereof,

thereof, which implieth a power to vse the same, but
onely, that the *Pope,* being a spirituall Prince or Pastour, may punish the Emperor for his contempt with
spirituall punishments, which only doe belong to the
coerciue power of the supreme spirituall Prince & Pastor of the spirituall kingdome & Church of *Christ.*

33. Thus therefore you haue seen, that *S. Bernard*
doth nothing fauour, but it is rather flat contrarie to
the *Popes* power to vse the temporall sword, neither
could he scarse speake more cleerely against the same,
then he hath done. For although it be cleere, that the
temporall sword is, according to S. *Bernard,*the *Popes*
in some sort, and doth belong to the Church in *some*
sort (which words [*in some sort*] D. *Schulckenius* heere
cunningly omitteth) and that in some cases it must be
vsed at the *becke,* direction or declaratiue command
of the *Pope,* yet the aforesayd limitations of S.*Bernard*
that it is the Popes, and belongeth to the Pope in some sort,
that it is to be vsed for the Church, but not by the Church,
with the hand of the Souldier, and not of the Priest, at the
becke indeede of the Pope, *but at the command of the* Emperour, *and that our* Sauiour *commanded,*and not only
counselled *S. Peter to put vp his sword into the scabard,*
do plainly shew, that, according to S. *Bernard,*the *Pope*
as *Pope,*cannot vse the temporal sword, nor constrain
a temporall Prince by vsing temporall punishments,
which doth imply a power to vse the tempoṛall sword.

34. And for D. *Barclay,* and *Iohn* of *Paris* (to
omit our learned Country-man, *Alexander* of *Hales,*
whose words I related before) who doe giue the very
same answere, which I haue giuen to the aforesaid
words of S. *Bernard,* of whose authoritie although
Card. *Bellarmine,* heere doth make very small reckoning, yet I do plainly confesse, that in this controuersie
concerning the *Popes* authoritie to vse the temporall
sword, and to dispose of all temporals in order to spirituall good, I doe more regard their authoritie, then
I doe

p *Num.* 18.

I doe Card. *Bellarmines,* fpeaking with all dutifull refpect, for that in my opinion they haue handled this
queſtion more ſoundly, more cleerely, and more ſincerely then he hath done. Neither is their doctrine
repugnant to the *Councell* of *Laterane,* but onely to
the particular expoſition, which ſom few eſpecially of
late yeeres (who haue ſcraped together all the authorities of Fathers, Councells, Scriptures, facts, and
decrees of *Popes* which may ſeeme any way to fauour
the Popes temporall authoritie) haue wreſted out
the words of the ſaid *Councel,* contrarie to the plaine
ſenſe of the words, and the common vnderſtanding of all ancient Diuines, who neuer vrged this
authoritie of the *Councell* of *Laterane,* although it
hath beene ſo long publikely extant in the body of
the *Canon Law.* But it is now adaies a common fault
euen among Catholike Diuines, and thoſe alſo, who,
not perceiuing their owne errour, doe accuſe others
of the ſame, to alleadge, in confirmation of their
opinions, the holy Scriptures, and facred Councels
vnderſtood according to their owne priuate ſpirit and
meaning, and then to cry out againſt their brethren,
who miſlike their opinions, that they haue the holy
Sriptures, and facred Councels on their ſide, and that
therefore their doctrine is of *faith,* and the contrary
hereticall, and that their *Aduerſaries* doe oppoſe themſelues againſt the holy Scriptures, and decrees of the
Catholike Church, whereas wee doe regard, with all
dutifull reſpect the holy Scriptures, facred Councels,
and decrees of the Catholik Church (the authority of
which conſiſteth in the true and authenticall ſenſe, &
not in the letter, or in the expoſitió of any priuate Catholike Doctour, which expoſition others doe contradict) and do oppoſe our ſelues only againſt their vncertaine opinions, and expoſitions of holy Scriptures, or facred Councells, grounded vpon their priuate ſpirit and vnderſtanding, contrary to the true,

proper, and plaine meaning of the words.

35. And although this *Ioannes Parifienfis*, or rather another *Iohn* of *Paris* liuing at the fame time, and

q *Part.* 1. *ca.* 3.
nu. 7. *& feq.*

furnamed *de Poliaco,* as I faid before q, was copelled to recall in open Confiftory, at *Auinion* before *Pope Iohn* the 22. certain errors, which he maintained cocerning confeffion, and abfolution (of whofe authoritie neuerthelefle Card. *Bellarmine* in the latter Editions of his controuerfies ; notwithftanding thofe his errours, maketh fomerekoning, feeing he citeth him as a *Claf-*

r *Lib.* 5. *de Rō.*
Pont. cap. 1.

fically Doctour in fauour of his opinion r) yet this rather confirmeth mee in my opinion. For if his doctrine, which denieth that the *Pope*, as *Pope*, hath power to depriue iuridically, and by way of fentence, temporall Princes of their dominions, and to vfe the temporall fword, had beene thought in thofe daies to haue beene *hereticall,* or *erronious,* as now Card. *Bel-larmine,* and fome few other Iefuites will needes haue it to be, it is like, that he fhould alfo haue beene compelled to recall that doctrine, and that thofe learned Authors, who write of herefies, as *Alphonfus de Caftro, Prateolus, Genebrard,* D. *Sanders* ; and others would for the fame haue taxed him, and *Marfilius* of *Padua* (as alfo *Albericus ,* and thofe many Schoolemen and Doctours, related by *Trithemius* and *Al-maine,* who did defend the fame doctrine) with fome note of *herefie,* or *errour,* which feeing they haue not done, it is a manifeft figne, that they did not account that doctrine for *hereticall,* or *erronious,* & that the decree of the *Councel* of *Lateran,* which was long before any of thefe mens daies, and which was alfo fo publike and regiftred in the corps of the Canon Law, was not in thofe times vnderftood in that fenfe, as Card. *Bellarmine* now of late (for before in his controuerfies he made fmall reckoning of that authority, for that he cleane omitteth that decree : yet bringing many particular facts of Popes, yea & of Pope *Innocēt*

the

the third, in whose time, and by whose authoritie that *Councell* was held) and some few others without sufficient proofe, as I will shew beneath ſ, will needes haue that decree to be vnderstood.

36. Neither is that true, which D. *Schulckenius* affirmeth, that *Ioannes Parisiensis* (in acknowledging, *That when the Pope doth becken, the Emperour ought to exercise the iurisdiction of the secular power for the spirituall good. But if hee will not , or if it doth not seeme to him expedient, the Pope hath no other thing to do, because he hath not the materiall sword in command, but onely the Emperour, according to* S. Bernard) *dooth either speake of the direct power of the Pope to vse the materiall sword, or else contradict himselfe, when afterwards hee writeth, that the* Pope *may* per accidens, *depose the Emperour, by causing the people to depose him.* For *Ioannes Parisiensis* in that his *Treatise,* de potestate Regia & Papali , doth expresly impugne both the direct, and indirect coerciue power of the Pope to punish by way of sentence, and iuridically with temporall punishments, affirming, as D. *Schulckenius* also himselfe heere relateth, that *Excommunication, or some such like spirituall punishment is the last, which an Ecclesiasticall Iudge can inflict. For although it belongeth to an Ecclesiasticall Iudge, to bring men backe to God, and to withdraw them from sinne, yet he hath not this, but according to the way or meanes giuen him by God, which is by excluding from the Sacraments and the participation of the faithfull.*

37 Neither doth *Ioannes Parisiensis* therefore contradict himselfe in affirming , *that the Pope may depose* per accidens *by meanes of the people.* For although he be of opinion , as I shewed before t, that the people haue in some cases a coerciue power ouer their Prince and in some cases may depose him, and consequently the *Pope* may in those cases , if it be necessarie to the good of the Church, command the people, and with spirituall punishments compell them to vse their coerciue

ſ *Part.* 3. *ca.* 9.
& *seq.*

t *Part.* 1. *ca.* 2.

erciue power, and so the *Pope* may be said to depose a Prince *per accidens* by meanes of the people, with which philosophicall queſtion I will not at this time, as I often ſaid, intermeddle, yet concerning the *Popes* coerciue power to vſe him ſelfe the temporall ſword, or to depoſe the Emperour by way of iuridicall ſentence, (which is not repugnant to his authoritie to depoſe by meanes of the people, if the people haue any ſuch authoritie to depoſe, which many learned Diuines, to whoſe opinion the ancient Fathers ſeeme to aſſent as I haue ſignified heretofore doe denie,) [u] *Ioannes Pariſienſis* is cleane oppoſite to Card. *Bellarmines* opinion, and expreſſely affirmeth, that the *Pope* hath no power to depriue *iuridically*, or by way of ſentence, temporall Princes of their kingdomes, but only to inflict by way of *coercion* or conſtraint Eccleſiaſticall or ſpirituall Cenſures. And thus much both concerning my anſwer to *S. Bernards* authoritie, and alſo the *Reply*, which *D. Schulckenius* hath made therevnto.

u *in my* Apologie *nu*.411. and here part: 1. cap.3. nu.5.

38   Now to the authoritie of *Pope Boniface* the 8. I anſwer *firſt* that his words are to be vnderſtood in that ſenſe, as I expounded *S. Bernard*, whom hee, as Card: *Bellarmine* affirmeth, did imitate, to wit, that the temporall power is in order to ſpirituall good, or, which is all one, in ſpirituall things ſubiect to the command of the ſpirituall power, and that ſhee is to be inſtructed by the ſpirituall, not abſolutely in temporall gouernment, but in Chriſtian faith and religion, and that if ſhee goe out of the way, or erre in things belonging to Chriſtian faith and religion, ſhee is to bee iudged by the ſpiritual, but with ſpirituall not temporall puniſhments. And in this ſenſe it is very true, *that the ſword is vnder the ſword*, and *the temporall power is ſubiect to the ſpirituall*, but by this it is onely ſignified, that temporall Princes are in ſpiritualls, but not in meere temporals, ſubiect to the ſpirituall command,

mand, and fpirituall correction of fpirituall Paftours.

39 *Secondly*, although *Pope Boniface* fhould vnderftand thofe words in this fenfe, that temporall
Princes are, not onely in *fpiritualls*, but alfo in *temporalls* fubiect to the *Popes* power both to command,
and alfo to punifh temporally, yet his authoritie herein, as he is *Pope*, (for as he is a priuate Doctor, it is no
greater then of other Doctors) is not of any great
weight; confidering *firft*, that, as well obferueth
D. Duuall[x], a learned Schoole-Diuine, & one of the
Kings Readers in the Colledge of Sorbon, *although
Pope Boniface doth make mention both of the fpirituall,
and temporall fword, and in the progreffe of his Conftitution doth fay, that the temporall fword is vnder the fpirituall, yet in the definition or conclufion (which chiefely as
in the decrees of Councells is to be regarded, feeing that
this onely bindeth to beleeue) this onely hee pronounceth in
generall, but we declare, fay, define, and pronounce, that
it is neceffarie to the faluation of euery humane creature
to be fubiect to the Bifhop of Rome.* But in what manner all men muft be fubiect, it is not expreffed in this
definition; and therefore not to contradict this definition it is fufficient to affirme, that all men muft in
fpiritualls bee fubiect to the Popes power to command, and to punifh fpiritually.

40 *Secondly*, for that this *Extrauagant* was recalled by his Succeffour Pope *Clement* the fift, *in cap.
meruit, de priuilegijs*, wherein hee declareth, *that no
preiudice fhall arife to the King of France by that Extrauagant of Pope Boniface, but that all things fhall be vnderftood to be in the fame ftate, as they were before that
definition, as well concerning the Church, as concerning
the King, and Kingdome of France.* *Thirdly*, for that
all the authorities, which hee bringeth from holy
Scriptures to proue, that the Pope hath both the temporall and fpirituall fword, doe proue only, that the
Pope is the fpirituall Paftour of the Church, and hath

x *De fuprema
Rom. Pont.
poteft. part. 2
q.4. pag. 262.
263.*

spirituall power to binde, and loose, to iudge and punish spiritually, as, *whatsoeuer thou shalt binde on earth &c.* and *a spirituall man doth iudge all things, and he is iudged by none*, which place some Catholike writers expound of publike and authenticall iudgments : For all the other places of holy Scripture, which *Pope Boniface* alledgeth, are either taken in the mysticall, and not in the literall sense, as those, *behold two swords here, and put vp thy sword into the scabard,* but from the mysticall sense no forcible argument can bee drawne, as all Diuines doe grant, to proue any doctrine, vnlesse to haue that mysticall sense it be declared in other places of holy Scripture, or else they make nothing to the purpose, as are those words, which God spake to the Prophet Ieremie, *Behold I haue appointed thee this day ouer the Gentiles, and ouer Kingdomes, that thou maiest plucke vp and destroy, and waste and dissipate, and build and plant,* not to destroy nations, and kingdomes, and raise vp others, but by his preaching to plant virtues, and destroy vices; as *S. Hierome* expoundeth, and by foretelling the destruction of Kingdomes and Nations, if they doe not repent, and their increase and saluation if they will bee converted. Neither is the Pope *S. Ieremies* Successour in the spirit of prophesie, neither doe wee read, that *Ieremie* destroyed any kingdom, although he fulfilled all that, which he was appointed to do by Alm: God.

41. *It is the same,* saith *Andreas Capella* vpon this place, *to appoint him ouer the Gentiles, and to giue him a Prophet in the Gentiles; as he said before. I giue thee power and authoritie,* saith God, *to declare and foretell in my name, as my Prophet, the ruines and wastings of the Gentiles, and of Kingdomes. That thou threaten my enemies, whom in their Countries I haue planted, placed, confirmed, erected that I will abolish them with captiuities, vnlesse they will repent. And contrariwise, that I will build them, and plant them againe, that is, restore to their ancient state, them*

them whom I shall destroy and abollish if they will acknowledge their sinnes. And in these words all the charge of Ieremie is comprehended, and the matter of this whole booke
is declared. For it is a prophecie of the destruction of the
City, and temple, and of the captivitie of the people, and of
their returne from captivity, and of the reedifying of the
temple and City, and of the overthrow of other nations, and
kingdomes. Thus *Capella.* And the same expolition of
these words hath the *Glosse* vpon this place Besides
Pope *Boniface* in this *Extrauagant* alledgeth for Scripture that, which is no Scripture, to wit, for the truth
testifying the spirituall power hath to institute or instruct the
earthly power, and to iudge it if it shall not be good, which
words are not to be found in the holy Scripture.

42. *Lastly,* there is no more account to be made of
the authoritie of Pope *Boniface* the eight for this his
doctrine in this point, touching the Popes temporal
authoritie ouer temporall Princes, if we take him, as a
priuate Doctour deliuering his opinion, then of an o-
ther Doctour, as well learned as he was, who holdeth
with the *Canonists,* that the *Pope* is direct Lord & King
of the world not only spirituall, but also temporall;
for that *Pope Boniface* was of this opinion, that the
Pope hath direct power not only in spiritualls, but also
in temporalls. Whereupon he wrote to *Philip the faire,*
King of France, that he was subiect to him in spirituals and
temporalls, and that all those, who should hold the contrary
he reputed for heretikes: and that the kingdome of France
by reason of the Kings disobedience was falne to the Church
For which words Pope *Boniface* is taxed by *Ioannes Ti-*
lius [x] Bishop of Meldune, by *Robertus Guaguinus* [y], by
Platina [z], and others, of great pride, impudencie and arrogancie. Whereupon *Paulus Æmilius* (who doth o-
therwise greatly fauour Pope *Boniface*) writeth thus:
*Pope Boniface did add, at which all men did marmaile,
that the King of France ought to reuerence the Pope not
only in sacred manner, and by Episcopall right, as a Father

x *In Chron. ad
annum* 1302.
y *Lib.* 7. *in
Philippo Pulch.*
z *In vita* Boni-
facij octaui.
* *In Philippo
Pulchro.*

of our soules, but he ought also to acknowledge him , as his Prince by ciuill Iurisdiction, and in prophane matters and dominion. All this being confidered, as alfo , that all the words of that *Extrauagant* are fo generall , that they may be vnderftood as well, if not better, of the *Popes* direct dominion in temporalls, as of his indirect power to difpofe of temporals, which is only in order to fpirituall good, what great reckoning is to be made of this cóftitution of P. *Boniface,* it being withal reuerfed by P. *Clemens* the 5. who next but one fucceeded him, I remit to the cófideration of the iudicious *Reader*

Chap. 10. *Wherein the fimilitude of Pope* Innocent *the third, who compareth the fpirituall and temporall power to the* Sun *&* Moone, *is examined.*

1. THE *fixt,* and laft argument, which Card. *Bellarmine* bringth to proue the fubiection of the temporall power to the fpirituall, is taken from the authority of Pope *Innocent* the third, *who in cap.* Solite de maioritate & obedientia *doth wel,* faith he, [a] *compare the fpirituall & temporall power to the Sun & Moone. Therefore as the moone is fubiect to the Sun, for that fhe receiueth light from the Sun, & the Sun is not fubiect to the Moone, for that the Sun receiueth nothing from the Moon, fo also a king is fubiect to the Pope, & the Pope is not fubiect to a king*

2. But *firft* this fimilitude doth not proue, that the temporall power it felfe is fubiect to the fpirituall, or, which is all one, that a temporall *King* is fubiect to the *Pope* in refpect of his temporall power, which he doth not receiue from the *Pope,* but in refpect of the light of faith, which a temporall King receiueth from the fpirituall power. And therefore as the Moone, when fhe is eclypfed, & in oppofition to the Sun, doth not loofe that little light, which, according to the doctrin of the Philofophers and aftronomers , fhe hath of her owne nature, and not deriued from the Sunne, fo temporall Princes, when of Catholikes or Chriftians they become

a In tract. contra Barcl: c. 13. *in fine.*

come heretikes, or infidells, and are in oppofition to
the Pope, do not loofe their temporall power, and the
light of naturall reafon, which they receiue not from
the Pope, but only the light of faith and grace, which
they did receiue from the fpirituall power.

3. *Secondly,* that, which Card. *Bellarmine* affirmeth,
that the Pope *receiueth nothing from temporall Princes is
very vntrue,* and therefore in this point alfo that part of
the fimilitude is not fitly applyed. For the *Pope* hath
receiued from temporall Princes all his temporall dominion, iurifdiction, and temporall fword, and the
whole patrimonie of S. *Peter, wherein,* as the fame *Pope
Innocent* affirmeth, [b] *he doth* now *exercife the power of a
fupreme temporall Prince.* Neither is it only true, that
temporall Princes are in fpiritualls fubiect to the fpirituall power of fpirituall Paftours, from whom they receiue fpirituall light, and fupernaturall directions by
the holy Scriptures & Ecclefiafticall lawes, by which
they may fee how to liue like good Chriftians, and to
attaine to life euerlafting, but it is alfo true, that fpirituall Paftours, as inferiour Bifhops and Cleargie men
are in temporals fubiect to the temporall power of
temporall Princes, from whom they receiue the increafe of naturall light, and ciuill directions by ciuill
and temporall Lawes, by which they may fee, how
to conuerfe ciuilly among themfelues and other
men, and to attaine to temporall peace and quietneffe
in the ciuill common-wealth.

4. Whereupon well fayd S. *Ambrofe,* [c] *If thou wilt
not be fubiect to Cæfar, doe not haue wordly things, but if
thou haft riches, thou art fubiect to Cæfar.* For *all men,*
faith *Aftenfis,* [d] *are fubiect to the Emperour, Lay-men in
temporals, and Cleargie men, who doe receiue from him
temporals.* And *Gratian* the Compiler of the firft and
moft ancient part of the Canon Law, called the Decree, writeth thus : [e] *Cleargie men by their office are fubiect to the Bifhop, by the poffeffions of farmes or mannours*

[b] *In cap. per venerabilem qui filÿ fint legitimi.*

[c] *Lib. 10. in Lucä. cap. 20.*

[d] *In fumma lib. 2. tit. 39.*

[e] *Caufa 11. q. 1. c. p 11.*

they

they are subiect to the Emperour. From the Bishop they receiue vnction, tithes and first fruits, from the Emperour they receiue possessions of farmes or mannours. Therfore because by the Emperiall Law it is made, as he proo-ueth out of S. *Austin, that farmes be possessed, it is mani-*

f *Cap.6.nu.* 13. 14.15. *& cap.* 7. *nu.*12.13.
fest that Cleargie men by the possessions of farmes are sub-iect to the Emperour. See also aboue f many other Ca-tholike Authours who doe affirme that Cleargy men are subiect to the directiue power of temporall Prin-ces. Neither doth Pope *Innocent* in the aforesayd Chapter denie, but in expresse words affirme, that the *Emperour is superiour to those, who doe receiue from him temporals;* And therefore this similitude of the Sunne and Moone doth not prooue, that the temporall po-wer is subiect to the spirituall, or, which is all one, that temporall Princes are in temporals, or as they haue temporall power, subiect to spirituall Pastours, but it rather prooueth the flat contrarie.

g *Lib.2. de Ro. Pont.cap.29.* h *Lib.5.hierach Ecclef.cap.7.*
5. Yea and Card *Bellarmine* himselfe, g did for ma-ny years together hold with *Albertus Pighius,* h *that it is the more probable opinion, that S. Paul,* (& consequent-ly the rest of the Apostles) *was subiect in temporals to Ce-sar, not only* de facto, *but also de iure* : from whence sup-posing another true & vndoubted principle granted

i *Lib.2.de Rom. Pont.cap.29.& lib.5.cap.3.*
also by Card. *Bellarmine,* i *that the Law of Christ doth depriue no man of any his right or dominion,* it necessarily followeth, that if infidell Princes haue rightfull power and dominion, or iurisdiction ouer Cleargy men, there is no repugnance, but that they may keepe the same power, and iurisdiction ouer Cleargy men, al-though they become Christians. But Card. *Bellar-mine* hath now *forsooth* in his *Recognitions* recalled that opinion. *I doe not now approoue,* saith he, k *that which I*

k *Pag.*16.
said with Albertus Pighius, *that S. Paul did appeale to* Cæsar, *as to his lawfull Prince. And therefore I do persist in the former answer, that S.* Paul *was subiect to Cesar* de facto, *not* de iure, *and did appeale to him, not as his owne Superiour,*

Superiour, but as to the Superiour of the Preſident of Iew-
ry, and of the Iewes, by whom he was wronged. For other-
wiſe he could not free himſelfe from that vniuſt iudgement
and danger of a moſt vuiuſt death, but by hauing recourſe
to their Prince and Iudge, which hee himſelfe did ſigni-
fie Acts 28. *when he ſaith,* I am conſtrained to appeale
to *Caſar.*

    6 If Card. *Bellarmine* hath vpon ſufficient ground
recalled either this, or any other of his former opinions, he is truly therefore much to be commended, as
likewiſe is *S. Auſtin,* for making his booke of *Retracta-*
tions. But if he ſhould without ſufficient ground not
onely recall this opinion, which he for aboue twentie
yeeres together in publike print, and for many yeeres
before in publike writings had defended for the *more*
probable, but alſo condemne it for *improbable,* it being
alſo the common opinion of Diuines, any man might
iuſtly imagine, that affection, not reaſon moued him
thereunto. *I doe not approue,* ſaith he,[1] *in his* Recognitions, *that which I ſaid in that place with* Albertus Pighius, *that S. Paul did appeale to Caſar as to his lawfull*
Prince. But in his booke againſt D. *Barclay* hee goeth
much farther *I haue admoniſhed,* ſaith he,[m] *in the Re-*
cognition of my writings, that the opinion of Pighius, *which*
in times paſt I did follow, is improbable, *and that with*
better Doctours it is to be affirmed, that the Apoſtles were
exempted de iure from all ſubiection to earthly Princes.

    7. But truly I cannot but maruell, that Card. *Bell.*
could be ſo much ouerſeen, as to affirm, *that he did ad-*
moniſh in his Recognitions, that the opinion of Pighius *is*
improbable, ſeeing that he only ſaith there, *I doe not ap-*
proue the opinion of Pighius, *&c.* But he doth not ſay,
that it is improbable, vnleſſe, *forſooth,* what opinion C.
Bellarmine doth not *approue,* although it be *approued*
by other learned Catholikes, muſt forth with be accounted *improbable.* Beſides I wold gladly know, who
be thoſe *better Doctours,* whom Card. *Bellarmine* ſaith
are

l *Pag.* 16.

m *Cap.* 21. *pag.* 106.

are to be followed against the opinion of *Phighius*. For my owne part I doe not know what better Doctours there be (abstracting from the ancient Fathers, and Doctors of the Church) if we speake only of the Doctours themselues, and not of the doctrine which they teach; then among the Thomists, *Iohn* of *Paris*, *Dominicus Sotus*, *Victoria*, *Bartholomæus*, *Medina*, *Bannes*; among the Scotists, *Richardus de Mediavilla*, *Ioannes*, *Medina*, *Iofeph Angles*; and among the Iesuites, *Salmeron*, *Molina*, *Valentia*, *Richeome*, *Salas*, and many other Diuines, whom *Salas* citeth, who doe hold, that Clergie men are not by the law of God & nature, but only by the Ecclesiasticall Canons and priuileges of Princes exempted from the *coactiue* power of Secular Magistrates, and not at all from their *directiue* power, but that they are subiect to the *directiue* power of Secular Princes in those things, which doe not repugne to the Ecclesiasticall Canons, and their state, and confequently, that Cleargie men in the time of the Apostles, and long after were subiect to the *coactiue* power of temporall Princes. Yea and the ancient Fathers, especially *S. Chrysostome*, *Theophylact*, and *Oecumenius* doe in expresse words affirme, n *that whether hee be a Monke, a Priest, or an Apostle, hee is according to the doctrine of S. Paul subiect to Secular powers*. Only the Canonists (& yet not all of them, as Pope *Innoc:* *Nauar*, and *Coverruvias*) whom now Card: *Bellarm:* leauing the Diuines, & his ancient opinion vpon very weake grounds, as you shall see, doth follow, do vehemently defend, that Cleargie men are by the law of God and nature, exempted from all subiection to Secular Princes.

8 Now you shall see, for what reasons Card: *Bellarmine* was moued to recail his former opinion, and to condemne it as *improbable*. *For if the reason*, saith he o, *of the exemption of Clergie men be for that they are ministers of Christ, who is the Prince of the Kings*

of

n *Ad Rom.* 13.

o *In his Recognitions, pag.* 16.

of the Earth , and King of Kinges , truely they are ex-
empted de iure *not onely from the power of Chriftian*
Kinges , but alfo of Heathen Princes. If Card. *Bellar-*
mine meane , that the reafon , wherefore the Ecclefiafticall Canons , and Chriftian Princes haue exempted Cleargie men (I doe not fay from all fubiection ,
for notwithftanding their exemption they ftill remaine
fubiects to temporall Princes , but from paying of tributes , from the tribunall of Secular Magiftrates and
fuch like) be , *for that they are Minifters of Chrift* in
fpirituall , but not in Secular matters , I will not contradict this reafon , but from hence it doth not follow
that therefore Cleargie men in the time of the Apoftles , when there were no fuch pofitiue lawes of their
exemption , were not in temporall caufes fubiect *de iu-*
re to infidell Princes.

9. But if Card. *Bellarmine* meane , that the reafon ,
why Cleargie men are not onely by the Ecclefiafticall
Canons and lawes of Princes , but alfo by the law of
G o d and nature exempted from all fubiection to temporall Princes , is , *for that they are Minifters of Chrift,*
who is the King of Kings, this reafon doth not proue , but
fuppofe , that which is in queftion , to wit , that Cleargie men are by the law of G o d , and nature , exempted from all fubjection to temporall Princes , which
the common opinion of Diuines doth conftantly deny , whofe opinion to account *improbable,* or *temera-*
rious for fuch a weake reafon , which doth not *proue,*
but *fuppofe* the queftion , were in my iudgement to exceede the limits of Chriftian prudence , and modefty.
Neither is there any repugnance in naturall reafon ,
but that the *Minifters* of *Chrift,* who , as it is probable , was , according to his humanity , onely a fpirituall ,
and not a temporall King , (and although he was alfo
a temporall King , yet Secular Princes are his Minifters
in temporalls , and the Apoftles & their Succeffors are
his Minifters in fpiritualls) might in temporall caufes
　　　　　　　　P p　　　　　　　　be

be truely, and *de iure* fubject to temporall Princes, as the *Apoftles* them-felues, who are *Chrift* his chiefe *Minifters* jin his fpirituall kingdome, and Church, were, according to the expreffe doctrine of the ancient Fathers, as they are parts, members and cittizens of the temporall common-wealth fubiect to temporall Princes, in their temporal kingdomes, and in temporall affaires. Neither doe thofe words of Saint *Paul* ? *I am conftrained to appeale to* Cæfar, fignifie, that hee was fubject to *Cafar* onely *defacto*, and not *de iure*, more, then if a *Prieft*, being vniuftly oppreffed by his *Ordinary*, fhould appeale to the *Pope*, and fay, that he was conftrained, for that hee had fmall hope to finde iuftice at his *Ordinaries* hands, to appeale to the *Pope*, fignifie thereby, that hee was not fubject *de iure*, but onely *de facto* to the *Pope*.

p *Act.* 28.

10. An other reafon, which mooued *Card. Bellarmine* to recall his former opinion, and to affirme, *that Saint* Paul *did not appeale to* Cæfar, *as to his owne lawfull Iudge* but *as to the Iudge of the prefident of Iewrie and of the Iewes, who did vniuftly oppreffe him*, was faith he q, *for that the caufe of which they did accufe him being fpirituall, to wit, concerning the refurrection* of Chrift, *and the ceremonies of the law of* Moyfes, *could not by right appertaine to a Heathen Prince. See the Acts of the Apoftles* chap. 21. 22. 23. 24. & 25.

q *In tract. contra Bard. cap.* 3 *pag.* 51.

11. But truely it is ftrange, that Card. *Bellarmine* durft fo confidently remit his Reader to thofe *chapters* of the *Acts* of the *Apoftles*, to proue, that the caufe, whereof Saint *Paul* was accufed by the Iewes to the *Tribune*, and *Prefident* of *Iewrie*, and wherefore he appealed to *Cæfar*, was fpirituall, and not appertaining by right to a Heathen Prince, vnleffe hee will haue the raifing of fedition, and tumults, and the committing of a crime worthy of death, not to belong to a Heathen Prince. For it is cleere by thofe chapters, that the Iewes accufed him of *fedition*, and that he had *offended*

Cæfar

Cæsar, and endeauoured to haue him therefore *put to death. We haue found,* saith one *Tertullus* [t], who went to accuse S. *Paul* before the President *Felix, this man pestiferous, and raising seditions to all the Iewes in the world, &c.* And afterwards, [f] the *Iewes* before the President *Festus obiected against* S. Paul *many, and greuous crimes, which they could not proue,* but they might easily haue proued, that S. *Paul* did preach the Resurrection of *Christ,* for that hee confessed the same before both the *Presidents,* and King *Agrippa :* Wherevpon King *Agrippa* said to S. *Paul* [t], *A little thou perswadest me to become a Christian.* And before [u] S. *Paul* made answere to the President *Festus, that neither against the law of the Iewes, nor against the Temple, nor against* Cæsar, *haue I any thing offended;* which signifieth, that he was accused that he had offended against *Cæsar.* And a little after saith S. *Paul to Festus* [r], *The Iewes I haue not hurt as thou very well knowest. For if I haue hurt them, or done any thing worthy of death, I refuse not to dye, but if none of those thinges be, whereof they accuse me, no man can giue me to them, I appeale to* Cæsar.

12 By all which it is very cleare, that the *Iewes* sought to haue S. *Paul* put to death, and that all the crimes which they obiected against him, were false, and consequently that he was not accused merely for preaching the resurrection of *Christ,* which S. *Paul* would neuer haue denied, but for raising sedition and tumults in the people, and for doing wrong to *Cæsar.* Whereupon S. *Chrysostome* [x] commendeth S. *Paul, that he would be iudged before him whom he was accused to haue wronged.* And Card. *Bellarmine* himselfe, not agreeable to this his reason, did before in his *Controuersies* affirme [v], which as yet he hath not recalled, *that* S *Paul did for good and iust cause appeale to* Cæsar *when he was accused for raising sedition and tumults in the people.* And in that very place of his *Recognitions,* where

Pp 2   he

[t] *Act.* 24.

[f] *Act.* 25.

[t] *Act.* 26
[u] *Act.* 25.

[x] *Hom.* 51. *in Act.*

[v] *Lib.* 2. *de Rom Pont. cap.* 19.

he recalleth his opinion, he doth very plainely inſinuate, as you haue ſeene, that the cauſe whereof he was accuſed, was criminall, for which he was in danger ſaith Card. *Bellarmine*, of a moſt vniuſt death.

13   True it is that S. *Paul* did preach to the *Iewes* the reſurrection of *Chriſt*, according to the predictions of the holy Prophets, and for this cauſe they accuſed him of ſedition, and to be a man worthy of death, and therefore he appealed to the tribunall of *Cæſar*, not that *Cæſar* ſhould iudge, whether *Chriſt* was riſen from death to life, for this indeed had been a ſpirituall cauſe, but whether to preach to the *Iewes* the reſurrection of *Chriſt*, according to the predictions of the holy Prophets, were ſedition, and a crime worthy to be puniſhed with death by the Secular Magiſtrate. Wherefore *Feſtus* the Preſident of *Iewrie*, and King *Agrippa*, after that S. *Paul* had diſcourſed about the reſurrection of *Chriſt* [z], and King *Agrippa* had ſaid to S. *Paul*, *A little thou doſt perſwade me to become a Chriſtian*, they all roſe vp, *and going aſide they ſpake among themſelues, ſaying, that this man hath done nothing worthy of death, or bonds*; which anſwere alſo made *Lycias* the Tribune to the Preſident *Fælix* before in the 23. Chapter.

14   A *third* reaſon, which moued Card. *Bellarmine* to recall his former opinion, and that S *Paul* did not appeale to *Cæſar*, as to his lawfull Iudge, is, for that, ſaith he [a], *it doth ſeeme to be altogether repugnant to the Goſpell, that Chriſt did not free expreſly, and by name S. Peter, and the Apoſtles from the obligation, wherein they ſtood bound to Heathen Princes. For* Chriſt Mat. 17. *did pay the didrachmes for himſelfe and* Peter, *to auoide ſcandall. For that otherwiſe neither himſelfe, nor* Peter *were bound to pay that tribute, he did demonſtrate by thoſe words*: The Kinges of the earth, of whom doe they receiue tribute or cenſe? of their children, or of ſtrangers? And *Peter* anſwering, of ſtrangers, Ieſus

[z] Act. 26.

[a] *In tract. contra Barclaium. cap. 3. pag. 49.*

sus said vnto him, therefore the sonnes are free: *by which words he declared, that he was free from all tribute & cense, for that he was the sonne of the King of all Kings, and because when the sonne of a King is free, also his familie is reputed free, therefore* Peter, *and the Apostles, who by the gracious fauour of* Christ *did appertaine to his familie, ought also to be free.*

15   But this reason is neither sufficient, nor a-greeable to Card. *Bellarmines* owne principles. For *first* Card. *Baronius* affirmeth [b], *that this didrachme,* which was exacted from our Sauiour in this place, was not a tribute due to *Cæsar, but onely to God for the vse of the Temple, according to the law of God decreed in the* 30. *chapter of* Exodus: And therefore from this place no sufficient argument can be drawne, according to Card. *Baronius* doctrine, that the Apostles were exempted from paying of tributes, or any other temporall subiection, due to temporall Princes. Yea, and which is more, Card. *Bellarmine* himselfe in the latter Editions of his *Controuersies* approueth this *Exposition* for most true. *There be two interpretations,* saith he [c], *of this place:* Therefore sonnes are free. *The former is of* S. Hillarie, *who affirmeth, that this place is onely meant of the tribute, which God did impose vpon the Children of Israell,* Exodus 30. *to the vse of the temple, which tribute was properly called a* didrachme; *and according to this Exposition, which seemeth to vs to be most true, this is the force of the argument. The Kings of the earth, do not exact tribute of their sonnes but of strangers, therefore the King of heauen will not exact tribute of mee, who am his proper and naturall sonne. The second interpretation, which is of* S. Hierome, *who expoundeth those wordes of the tribute which was to bee paid to* Cæsar, *seemeth to bee the lesse probable, because the tribute which was to be paid to* Cæsar, *was not a* Didrachme, *but a penny, as it is plaine by* Math. 22. Shew me the tribute coyne: and they offered him a

penny

[b] *Ad ann. Christi* 33. *nu.* 31.

[c] *Lib.* 1. *de Clericis cap.* 28. *in propos.* 4.

penny. *Neither can it be demonstrated by any sound rea-*
son, that the tribute of the Didrachme *was wont to be paid*
to Cæsar, *but after the Ascension of Christ into heauen.*
For Iosephus *lib.* 7. *de bello Iudaico cap.* 26. *doth write*
that the tribute of the Didrachme, *which all the Iewes did*
pay to the temple euery yeare, should afterwards be brought
into the Capitole. Thus Card. *Bellarmine.*

16 Wherefore it is strange, that hee should now be
so forgetfull, as to bring this text of holy *Scripture* for
a reason, why hee changed his former opinion, and
which reason also hee saith doth *demonstrate, that*
Christ *our Sauiour did expresly, and by name free S.* Peter
and the Apostles from the obligation wherein they stood
bound to Cæsar, whereas Card. *Bellarmine* himselfe, as
you haue seene, expoundeth this place not of any tribute to bee paid to *Cæsar,* but onely due to *God* for the
vse of the temple. And therefore small reason had
Card. *Bellarmine* for the aforesaid reasons, which are
so weake, and repugnant to his owne doctrine, as you
haue seene, to recall his former opinion, which for so
long time hee had in publike Schooles, and writings,
with the common opinion of Diuines, taught and
maintained against the Canonists: but truely he had
no reason to condemne for such weak reasons the contrary opinion of the Schoole Diuines, of whose profession he himselfe also is, as *improbable.*

17 Far more agreeable to reason, and also to Card.
Bellarmines profession, hee being a Schoole Diuine,
were it for him in my iudgement to returne to his ancient opinion, which the Schoole Diuines doe generally maintaine, and rather to recall some other his o-
pinions, wherein hee plainely contradicteth his owne
doctrine, as I haue shewed before: As that *our Sauiour*
by those wordes, *therefore sonnes are free &c.* Math. 17.
did expresly, and by name free S. Peter and the Apostles
from the obligation, wherein they stood bound to Heathen
Princes, which is flatly repugnant to that, which hee
taught

taught in another place, *that these wordes are not meant of any tribute. which was to be paid to* Cæsar, *but onely of the tribute, which God did impose* Exod. 30. *vpon the children of Israell to the vse of the Temple.* And besides that *the cause whereof the Iewes did accuse S.* Paul, *and for which hee appealed to* Cæsar, *was spirituall,* [d] which is cleerely repugnant to that, which hee taught in another place, [e] *that S.* Pau' *did for good and iust cause appeale to* Cæsar, *and did acknowledge him for his Iudge, when he was accused of raysing sedition, and tumults in the people.* And moreouer, (to omit sundry other his contradictions) *that the Church of Christ is compounded* [f] *of spirituall and temporall power, as a man is compounded of soule and body, and that the temporall and spirituall Common-wealth doe make one totall body whereof the Pope is head, as a man is compounded of body and soule,* which is cleerely repugnant to that which hee taught in other places, *that the Church of* Christ *is compounded onely of spirituall power, and that the* Pope, *if wee will speake properly, hath onely spirituall and not temporall power.*

18 *But secondly* although wee should grant, that those words of our *Sauiour, therefore sonnes are free &c.* were meant of the tribute which was to bee paid to *Cæsar* and not to the temple. yet Card. *Bellarmine* himselfe did in the former Editions of his Controuersies giue therevnto a very sufficient answer, and which in his latter Editions he hath not confuted. For thus he writeth [g] : *I answer first that this place doth not conuince: for otherwise he should exempt from tributes all Christians, who are regenerate by Baptisme. Secondly I answer, that our Sauiour doth speake onely of himselfe. For he maketh this Argument: The sonnes of Kinges are free from tributes, because they neither pay tribute to their fathers, for that the goods of the parents and children are common, nor to other Kings, because they are not subiect to them, but I am the sonne of the first and chiefest King, therefore I owe*
tribute

[d] *In tract. contra* B. *rcl. cap.* 3 *pag* 51.
[e] *Lib.* 2. *de* Rom. *Pont. cap.* 29.
[f] *See aboue cap.* 2.
[g] *lib.* I *de clericis cap.* 28.

tribute to no man. Wherfore when our Sauiour *faith,* therefore Sonnes are free, *from thence hee meant onely to gather this, that he himselfe was not bound to pay tribute: of other men hee affirmed nothing.*

19 Thus answered Card. *Bellarmine* in times past, when he followed the opinion of the Diuines, concerning the exemption of Clergy men against the Canonists, who vrged this place of holy Scripture to proue, that Clergy men are exempted from paying of tributes by the law of God. But now, *forsooth,* he forsaketh the Diuines, and this very text, *therefore sonnes are free,* which then hee brought for an obiection against his opinion, and cleerely answered the same, he bringeth now for a chiefe ground to proue his new opinion, and (which is very remarkable) hee concealeth the answer which he then made to the said obiection: onely hee addeth this: *that when the sonnes of Kings are exempted from tribute, not onely their owne persons, but also their seruants and Ministers, and so their families are exempted from tributes. But it is certaine that all Clergie men do properly appertaine to the family of Christ, who is the sonne of the King of Kings. And this our Lord did seeme to signifie when hee said to S.* Peter, But that wee may not scandalize them, finding the stater take it, and giue it for me and thee. *As though he should say, that both hee, and his family, whereof S.* Peter *was a chiefe gouernour, ought to bee free from tributes. Which also S.* Hierome *doth seeme to haue vnderstood in his Commentary of that place, when hee saith,* that Clergy men doe not pay tributes for the honour of our Lord, and are as Kings children free from tributes: *and S.* Austin *lib. 1. qq. Euang. q. 23. where he writeth,* that in euery earthly Kingdome, the children of that Kingdome vnder which are all the Kingdomes of the earth, ought to be free, (*not are free,* as Card. *Bellarmine* affirmeth *S. Austin* to say,) from tributes.

20 Thus you see, how Card. *Bellarmine* runneth

vp and downe from the words of holy Scripture, *by which it is demonstrated*, saith he, *that S. Peter was not bound to pay tribute to Cæsar*, to the sense which he himselfe disproueth, and then from the sense to his priuate collections, and inferences, that if S. *Peter* was free, all the Apostles were free, and if all the Apostles, all Cleargie men. But if it had pleased him to haue also set downe the answere, which in the former Editions of his bookes he made to this obiection, the Reader would easily haue perceiued, that from this place of holy Scripture no sufficient reason could be gathered to cause him to recall his former opinion, although wee should grant, that those words of our *Sauiour* were meant of the tribute, which was to be paide to *Cæsar*, of which neuerthelesse Card. *Bellarmine* will not haue them to be vnderstood, but onely of the tribute which the children of Israell were by the law of God, *Exod.* 30. commanded to pay for their soules vnto the vse of the *tabernacle of testimonie*, for at that time the temple was not built. For *first*, saith he, *if this argument did conuince, not onely Cleargie men, but also all Christians, who being regenerate by baptisme are the children of Christ, and also doe properly appertaine to his spirituall familie, or Church, of which, S.* Peter *and the rest of the Apostles vnder him were chiefe gouernours, should be exempted from paying tributes.* Secondly, *our Sauiour*, saith he, *doth speake onely of himselfe, who was the sonne of the first and chiefest King, and that he himselfe was not bound to pay tribute: of other men he affirmeth nothing.*

21 *Thirdly*, to the authority of S. *Hierome*, he answereth, *that S. Hierome did not intend in that place, to proue out of the Gospell, that Cleargie men are free from tribute, but onely he doth bring a certaine congruence, wherefore they are freed by the decrees of Princes: for therefore he saith*, that they doe not pay tributes as the children of the Kingdome, *and he addeth an other*

ther cause, to *wit*, the honor of Chriſt: *for he ſaith, that for his honour Cleargie men doe not pay tributs. Therfore not the law of God*, *but the decrees of Princes made for the honour of Chriſt, haue exempted Cleargy men.* Thus *Card. Bellarmine.*

22 *Fourthly*, to the authority of S. *Auguſtine* he anſwereth, *that although* Ianſenius *(whom Salmeron* and *Suarez* doe follow*) doth affirme, that* S. Auſten *by the children of the ſupreme kingdome did vnderſtand the naturall children of God, and that he ſpake in the plurall number to obſerue the manner of our Sauiours ſpech*, ſo that the meaning of S. *Auſten* was, *that all the naturall ſonnes of God if it were poſſible that God could haue more naturall ſonnes then one, ſhould be exempted from paying of earthly tributes*: yet Card. *Bellarmine* doth not like well of this anſwere, and therefore he thinketh the anſwere of *Abulenſis* to be the more *probable, that* S. Auſten *did not vnderſtand naturall children, but Clergie men and Monkes, who, as alſo* S. Hierome *affirmeth, in Cap.* 17 Mat., *were and are free from tributes, as thoſe who appertaine to the familie of Chriſt. Neither doth it therefore from hence follow, that Cleargie men are by the law of God free from tributes. For firſt, that which* S. Auſten *ſaith, is not in the words of our* Sauiour, *but it is onely gathered by a probable conſequence, For our* Sauiour *doth onely ſpeake of the true and naturall children of* Kinges, *as* S. Chryſoſtome *doth expound that place. Secondly, our* Sauiour *himſelfe doth alſo properly command nothing in this place, that it may be called the law of God, but doth onely ſhew by the vſe and cuſtome of men, that the children of Kinges are free from tributes.* Thus Card. *Bellarmine* anſwered in his former Editions, which anſwere in his later editions he altogether concealeth, but for what cauſe I remit to the iudgement of the prudent Reader.

23 By all which it is apparant that our *Sauiour* did onely ſpeake of himſelfe, and of the naturall children

of Kings, when hee vfed thofe words, *therefore fonnes are free*; and of the feruants, or familie, either of Kings, or of the children of Kinges he faith nothing at all; and therefore from an other confequence drawne from the vfe, and cuftome of men, and not from the words of our Sauiour, can it be gathered, that thofe who are feruants, or of the familie of the children of Kings, are exempted either from fubiection to the inferiour magiftrates of the kingdome, or from the paying of tributs. But by no probable confequence it can be deduced, that thofe who are either feruants, and of the familie of Kinges children, or alfo feruants, and of the familie of the King himfelfe, are by the cuftome of any nation either exempted from fubiection to inferiour Magiftrates, and much leffe to the King himfelfe, or alfo from paying tributes, vnleffe the King vpon fome other fpeciall confideration doth grant to any of them fuch a priuiledge.

24 To thofe words of our *Sauiour*, *But that wee may not fcandalize them &c.* it is eafily anfwered according to the firft expofition of that *didrachme*, which Card. *Bellarmine* thinketh to be moft true, *that it was a tribute due to the temple or tabernacle, and not to Cæfar*: For I doe willingly grant, that S. *Peter*, who was appointed by *Chrift* to be the chiefe gouernour of his Church and temple, was exempted from paying tribute to the temple. But although we fhould admit, that the aforefaide *didrachme* was a tribute due to *Cæfar*, and not to the temple, yet from thofe words of our *Sauiour*, no fufficient argument can be drawne to proue, that S. *Peter*, and efpecially the reft of the Apoftles, were by the law of God exempted from paying tributes, and much leffe from temporall fubiection to Heathen Princes.

25 *Firft*, for that we may probably anfwere with *Ianfenius*, and *Abulenfis*, that Chrift did fpeake to S. *Peter* in the plurall number, [*but that wee may not fcan-*

dalize them] not for that S. *Peter* was bound to pay tribute onely by reafon of fcandall, but either becaufe our *Sauiour* did fpeake of his owne perfon, vfing the plurall number for the fingular, as it is vfuall, efpecially among great perfons; *we are wont*, faith S. *Epiphani-*

h In the herefie of the Manichies.

us [h], *to fpeake fingular thinges plurall, and plurall fingu-lar. For wee fay, wee haue tould you, and we haue feene you, and we come to you, and yet there be not two who fpeake, but one who is prefent* : or elfe becaufe the *fcan-dall*, which Chrift fhould haue giuen, would in fome fort haue redounded to S. *Peter*, as being a mediatour in that bufineffe. And therefore, as well affirmeth *Ian-*

i In Concord. Euang. cap. 69. in Mat. 17.

fenius [i], our Sauiour *did pay tribute for himfelfe onely to auoid fcandall & for S.*Peter *to honour him as with a cer-taine reward for his faith, obedience, and diligence,as a mediatour of this bufines, and an executor of the Miracle of finding the ftater in the fifhes mouth*, or as *Barradius* the Iefuite, and others doe affirme [k], *to honour him a-*

k In cap. 17. Mat. tom. 2. Lib. 10. cap. 32.

boue the reft, as the Prince of the Apoftles, and the head of the Church. See *Abulenfis*, q. 198. 199. and 200. in *cap*. 17. *Mat.* and *Barradius* vpon this place.

26 *Secondly*, although wee fhould grant, that our Sauiour did for fome fpeciall caufe exempt S. *Peter* from paying tribute to *Cæfar*, either by a perfonall pri-uiledge, or elfe reall, and defcending to his fucceffors, it doth not therefore follow, that he did exempt him from all ciuil fubiection to temporal Princes,as neither doth it follow, that becaufe the Children of Kinges, for that their goodes and their fathers are common, or any of the Kinges feruants are by fpeciall priuiledge exempted from paying tributes, they are therefore ex-empted from all ciuil fubiection and alleagiance to the King.

27 *Thirdly*, for that there is no probabilitie in my iudgment, that either *Chrift* did by thofe words in-tend to exempt the reft of the Apoftles, feeing that there is no mention at all made of them in that place,

or also that this priuiledg of exemption is extended to
S. *Peter* , and the rest of the Apostles , in regard onely
that they were of the spirituall familie , or Church of
Christ (I say of the *spirituall familie*, for, that I will
not deny, but that as they were of his corporall familie , and liued with him here on earth, and had no corporall goods but such as belonged to *Christ*, they were
exempted from paying tributes , but not from ciuill
subiection to Heathen *Princes*) because the exemption of seruants with their Maister, or of those, who
are of the familie of Kinges Children with the Kinges
Children themselues, is not grounded in the law of
nature, but onely in a certaine congruity, and custome of men, from which custome this argument to
exempt the Apostles , for that they were of *Christs* familie , is drawne : but there is no such custome among
nations, that the seruants or familie of Kinges Children
or of the King himselfe, are exempted from paying
tributes, although the children of Kinges hauing no o-
ther goodes , then which are their fathers, be exempted , as Card. *Bellarmine* a little aboue affirmed. But
howsoeuer, neither the seruants to Kinges children ,
nor the kinges children themselues, are exempted from
ciuill subiection, or from the *directiue*, or *coerciue* power of the King.

28   And therefore neither *Fa. Suarez*, who handleth this question at large, dare affirme , that from
those words of our Sauiour it can *certainely* , but onely
probably be gathered , that this exemption was extended to the rest of the Apostles. *I answere*, saith hee [1],
*that it is true , that Christ did not say plainly , that the fa-
milie is exempted with the children , neither doth it follow
by any euident , or necessary consequence , and therefore
the aforesaid opinion, for as much as belongeth to this part,
is neither of faith, nor altogether certaine. Neuerthelesse
it is most likely, that this extention to the rest of the Apostles is according to the intention of Christ,*

[1] *In defens. fid.
Catho.&c. lib.
4. cap. 8, in
fine.*

29. But truely, although there may be alleadged some *probable* congruities, wherefore our Sauiour might grant some speciall prerogatiue, and priuiledge of exemption to S. *Peter*, whom he had chosen to be the first and principall head and gouernour of his Church, rather then to the rest of the Apostles, as likewise the Diuines doe yeeld *probable* congruities, wherefore God almighty might giue to the B. Virgin *Mary*, whom he had chosen to be the mother of his immaculate Sonne, a speciall prerogatiue and priuiledge of exemption from originall sinne, but whether he did grant that priuiledge or no, it cannot certainely be proued, neuertheleffe for my owne part I doe not see any probable likelihood, that our *Sauiour* should giue to the rest of the Apostles, and much lesse to all Cleargie men, any speciall priuiledge of exemption from all ciuill subiection to temporall Princes. And therefore the most part of the Schoole Diuines, yea also and of the *Iesuites* themselues doe hould, that *Cleargie men are directly subiect to the ciuill lawes of temporall Princes, in all those thinges, which are not repugnant to their state, nor to the Ecclesiasticall Canons*, and consequently that they are not exempted from all subiection and obedience, and from the directiue or commanding power of Secular Princes, but that they are bound not onely by force of reason, but also by vertue of the law, and of their due obedience, to obserue such ciuill lawes.

30 A *fourth* reason which Card. *Bellarmine* bringeth ^m wherefore he recalled his former opinion, and why the Apostles were not *de iure* subiect to temporall Princes, is *because they are appointed by God Princes ouer all the earth*, as wee *read in the* 44. *Psalme*. For *although that principality was spirituall, not temporall, yet it was true principallity, and farre more noble then temporall principallitie.* But this reason is not sufficient, for as I obserued in my *Apologie*, ^n the same man being

ing confidered diuerfe waies may be fubiect, and fuperiour; fubiect in temporalls, and fupreame in fpirituals, and contrariwife; neither is temporall fubiection,
repugnant to fpirituall authority, nor temporall authority repugnant to fpiritual fubiection: neither from hence
doth it follow, that either temporall authority it felfe,
is fubiect to fpirituall power, or fpirituall power fubiect to temporall authority, but onely that the fame
man, who is fuperiour in temporalls, is fubiect in
fpiritualls, and who is fuperiour in fpiritualls is fubiect
in temporalls, as the fame man who is a Mufition may
be fubiect and feruant to a Phyfition, or contrariwife,
and yet it doth not from hence follow, that *Muficke* it felfe is fubiect to *Phyficke*, or contrariwife.

31 And if Card. *Bellarmine* doe anfwere, as he
doth in his *Schulckenius* [n], *that when the powers are e-
quall, it may perchance fall out, that the fame compared
diuerfe waies may be fubiect and fuperiour, but if the powers be vnequall, and one fubordained to an other, as are
fpirituall and ciuill power, it cannot fall out, that the fame
man be fubiect to him who is his fuperiour,* this anfwere
is alfo as infufficient as the former. *Firft,* for that the
temporall power it felfe is not fubordained to the fpirituall, as I haue fhewed before: for otherwife temporall *Princes* fhould not onely in fpiritualls, but alfo in
mere temporalls be fubiect to fpirituall *Paftours,* as if
Muficke it felfe be fubiect to *Phyficke,* a Mufition,
as he is a Mufition, and in all thinges belonging to
Muficke, fhould be fubiect to Phyficke, and confequently to a *Phyfition,* as he is a *Phyfition. Secondly,*
for that it is the common opinion of the Schoole Diuines, and alfo of the Iefuites, that *Cleargie* men are
fubiect to the directiue temporall power, or command
of temporall Princes.

32 *Thirdly,* for that there is no repugnance, but
rather a neceffary confequence, that fpirituall Princes,
not as they are fpirituall *Princes,* but as they are true

parts

[n] Pag. 172.

o *Lib. de Mo-
nachis. cap. 19.*

p *Lib. de Cle-
ricts. cap. 28.*

q *Pag. 339.*

r *Nauar. super
cap. non liceat
Papæ. 12. q. 2
55. 3°. nu. 6.*

parts and members of the temporall common wealth, should be subiect in temporall affaires to temporall Princes, for *euery member*, saith Card. *Bellarmine*, o *ought to be subiect to the head, and Cleargie men, besides that they are Cleargie men, are also citizens and parts of the ciuill common wealth*, as Card. *Bellarmine* affirmeth in an other place p, and *the King is head of the politike or ciuill body*, as also in his *Schulckenius*, he expresly affirmeth q. *Fourthly*, for that Card. *Bellarmine* is also now of opinion, at least wise he was when he wrote against D. *Barckley, that it is probable, that the Priests of the old law, who had true spirituall power, and were true spirituall Princes, were subiect to Kinges*, and therfore for this reason to recall his former opinion, and especially to condemne it as *improbable*, were both to contradict himselfe, and also to condemne of *temeritie* the learnedst Schoole Diuines of this age, and also of his Societie.

33 These be all the principall reasons, which I can finde in Card. *Bellarmine*, for which he was moued to recall his former opinion, and to condemne it as *improbable*, which how *probable* they be, or rather very insufficient to moue such a learned man, as Card. *Bellarmine* is, to forsake the Schole Diuines, and to fly to the Canonists, who as pope *Pius* the fift sincerely confessed, r *doe attribute to the Pope more authoritie then is fitting*, and to censure so rigorously, and rashly the learnedst Catholikes of this age, and also of his owne Societie, of *temeritie*, I remit to the iudgement of the discreete Reader, as also to consider, whether reason, or affection to aduance the *Popes* authoritie moued him not onely to recall his former opinion, but also to condemne it as *improbable*.

33 *Lastly*, that the Reader may haue some knowledge of the true state of the question concerning the authority of spirituall Pastors to exempt Clergy men from the power of Secular Princes, for that some Diuines

uines are of opinion, that from the exemption of Clergy men a strong Argument may bee drawne to proue that a spirituall Prince or Pastor hath power to depose or depriue a temporall Prince, who is subiect to him in spiritualls, of his temporall Kingdome and Dominions. *First* therefore the true state of the question betwixt *mee* and my *Aduersaries* is, not concerning the exemption of Cleargie men by way of *command*, for I doe willingly grant, that a spirituall Prince, or Pastor as hee is a spirituall Pastor, hath power to *command* a Christian Prince, who is subiect to him in spiritualls, not to exercise his temporall power in some cases, if the necessity of the Church, or Christian Religion doth require it, ouer the persons of Clergy men, who are his temporall Subiects: so that if a secular Prince should disobey the lawfull command of his spirituall Pastor, hee should offend against the vertue of Religion, for the which offence his spirituall Pastor might punish him with Ecclesiasticall censures : and of this manner of exemption by way of *command*, and spirituall *coercion*, all the Canons and Decrees of Popes and Councells, which doe signifie. imply, or suppose that Clergy men may by the authority of the Church without the consent of temporall Princes bee exempted from secular powers, either touching their persons or their goods, may bee very well vnderstood: I said *if the necessity of the Church doth require it*: for at this present I will not enter into particulars, what manner of necessity is required, that a spirituall Pastor may impose such a command vpon his temporall Prince.

34 But the controuersie betwixt *mee* and my *Aduersaries* betwixt those Catholikes who are so vehement for the Popes power to depose Princes, and those on the contrary side is, whether spirituall Pastors, as they are spirituall Pastors, or by vertue of their spirituall power, haue not onely by way of *command*, and spirituall *coercion*, but also by way of *sentence* authori-

ty to exempt without the conſent of Princes Clergy
men, who before were ſubiect to them in temporalls,
from the *directiue,* and *coerciue* power of ſecular Princes, in ſuch ſort, that after the *ſentence* of ſuch exemption bee giuen, Clergy men are no more the ſubiects
of that ſecular Prince, for that his ſpirituall Paſtor
doth depriue him of that ciuill power, which before
the ſentence hee had ouer Clergy men: And what
is ſaid of particular Biſhops, in reſpect of Princes who
are their ſpirituall children, is to bee vnderſtood of
the Supreme ſpirituall Paſtor in reſpect of all Chriſtian
Princes, who are ſubiect to him in ſpiritualls. This is the
true ſtate of the queſtion.

35 So that the Reader may clearely perceiue, that
although from the firſt manner of exemption, by way
of *command,* and ſpirituall *coercion,* no good argument
can be drawne, to proue, that the ſpirituall power
can depoſe Princes, and depriue them of their Regall
authoritie, by way of *ſentence,* yet there is great
coherence betwixt theſe two queſtions concerning
the power of ſpirituall Paſtors to depoſe Princes by
way of *ſentence,* and their power to exempt by way
of ſentence Cleargie men from all ſubiection to Secular Princes. For the *firſt* queſtion is whether the ſpirituall power can by way of *ſentence* depriue temporall
Princes of all their temporall power, and abſolue all
their Subiects from their temporall alleagiance: and
the *ſecond* is, whether it can depriue them of ſome
part of their temporall power, and abſolue ſome of
their ſubiects from their temporall allegiance. And
therefore thoſe Catholikes who doe grant the *ſecond,*
will eaſily grant the *firſt,* and who doe grant the *firſt,*
muſt of neceſſity grant the *ſecond,* for that there can
be no ſufficient reaſon alleadged, why the ſpirituall
power can in order to ſpirituall good depriue Princes
of ſome part of their Regall authoritie, and not of all,
and abſolue ſome ſubiects from their temporall allegiance

ance, and not all; and if it can depriue of all, it muſt needes follow that it can alſo of ſome part. And contrariwiſe thoſe Catholikes, who affirme, that the ſpirituall power cannot exempt, or abſolue Cleargie men from their temporall allegiance and ſubiection to temporall Princes, muſt conſequenily affirme, that it can not exempt or abſolue all ſubiects from their temporall allegiance: and who affirme, that it can not abſolue, or exempt all ſubiects from their temporall allegiance, nor depriue a temporall Prince of all his Regall authority, will eaſily affirme, that it cannot exempt or abſolue Cleargie men from their temporall alleagiance and ſubiection, nor depriue a temporall Prince of any part of his Regall authority.

36   But ſome doe greatly vrge this obiection: If the ſpirituall power can command temporall Princes not to exercife their temporall power ouer the perſons or goods of Cleargie men, without the conſent of their Eccleſiaſticall ſuperiour, it doth conſequently follow, that a temporall Prince doth offend, if he tranſgreſſe the iuſt and lawfull command of his ſpirituall Paſtour, and therefore it ſeemeth, that a temporall Prince hath no power ouer the perſons or goods of Cleargie men after ſuch a command, ſuppoſing it to be lawfull, vnleſſe wee will grant, that a temporall Prince hath power to commit ſinne, and to tranſgreſſe the lawfull command of his ſpirituall Paſtour.

37   To this obiection (wherewith I haue knowne diuers men of learning to bee ſomewhat perplexed) thoſe Catholikes, who deny that the ſpirituall power can depriue by way of *ſentence,* a temporall Prince of his Regall Authority, either wholly or in part, may eaſily anſwer in this manner: that if a temporall Prince doth excercife his temporall power ouer the perſons or goods of Clergy men againſt the lawfull command of his ſpirituall Paſtour, hee ſinneth indeed againſt Religion, and the generall vertue of obedience, in

that hee vseth his power contrary to the lawfull command of his spirituall Pastour, but hee doth not sinne againstthe speciall vertue of legall, ormorall iustice, in vsing his authority ouer them, who are not his subiects, and ouer whom hee hath no temporall power and Authority, in that manner as another man, who is not their Prince, should offend. Neither is it vnvsuall for a man to commit a sinne in doing that which in respect of iustice hee hath power and authority to doe.

38 As for example, it is a sinne against the vertue of liberality for one to giue away his goods prodigally, although if wee respect iustice hee hath true and full power to giue them away, for that he giueth nothing but that,which is his owne: and therefore that prodigall guift, although it be vnlawfull, yet is not vniust, as iustice is taken, not as it comprehendeth all vertues in generall, but in particular for a speciall vertue, and one of the foure Cardinall vertues. So also it is a sin again^t the vertue of temperance to giue money to commit an vnhonest act, and yet the gift is not vniust for that hee giueth nothing but his owne, and which according to iustice hee hath power to giue. So likewise if a Ghostly father command his penitent to giue a certaine part of his goods to the poore in satisfaction of his sinnes, if the penitent doe bestow them otherwise then hee was commanded, hee sinneth against the vertue of Religion and Sacrament of pennance, in transgressing his Ghostly fathers lawful command, but he committeth no iniustice, because hee giueth that which is his owne, and which, if wee regard the vertue of iustice, hee hath power to giue: neither doth the command of his Ghostly father depriue him of the right, dominion, property aud power, which he had before ouer those goods.

39 *Lastly*, if the *Pope* should vpon iust cause suspend a Priest from th eAltar, or a Bishop from his Episcopall

pall function, and confequently forbid the Prieft to confecrate, and the Bifhop to giue orders, if they fhould difobey the Popes lawfull command, they fhould finne againft the vertue of Religion, in vfing their power vnlawfully, but they fhould not finne for doing that which they haue no power to doe, as hee who is no Prieft or Bifhop fhould in confecrating or giuing orders offend, for that the power of a Prieft to confecrate and of a Bifhop to giue orders, cannot either wholly or in part bee taken away from them by the *Pope*. So likewife although a fpirituall Paftor fhould for iuft caufe forbid a temporall Prince, who is his fpirituall child, and fubiect, to excercife his Regall power and authority ouer Clergy men, if that temporall Prince fhould heerein tranfgreffe the command of his fpirituall Paftor, fuppofing it to bee lawfull, hee fhould indeed offend againft religion, in vfing his Regall power and authority contrary to the lawfull command of his fpirituall Paftor, which command was impofed for the motiue of Religion, neuerthelefle hee fhould not offend againft iuftice, in doing that which hee hath no power and authoriy to doe, in that manner as another man, who is not their Prince, fhould by depriuing them of their goods, or punifhing their perfons if they tranfgreffe the lawes, offend. For that it is not in the power of a fpirituall Paftor to depriue a temporall Prince either wholly or in part of his Regall power, and temporall Soueraignty.

40 Wherefore if wee refpect the power it felfe, and the vertue of legall or morall iuftice, a temporall Prince hath full, ample, and fupreme royall power and authority ouer Clergy men, notwithftanding that his fpirituall Paftor fhould for iuft caufe command him not to excercife his Regall power vpon the perfons of Clergie men, who doe offend his lawes: but if wee refpect the vfe and execution of the power, and the vertue of religion, the vfe indeed of his power in the

Rr 3   aforefaid

aforesaid case is so limited by the lawfull command of the spirituall Pastor, that the Prince vsing his power ouer Clergy men, sinneth against Religion, for that hee disobeyeth the lawfull command of his spirituall Superiour, which was imposed for the motiue of religion, but not against iustice for that hee doth not ex-cercise his Regall power but vpon those who are his Subiects, and doe owe vnto him true loyalty and temporall obedience.

41   And truely if the aforesaid obiection were of force, that the temporall Prince hath no power or authority ouer Clergie men, who are subiect to him in temporalls, against the lawfull command of his spirituall Pastour, because he hath no power to sinne, it would likewise follow, that a suspended Bishop, or Priest, haue no power to giue orders, or to consecrate, because they haue no power to sinne; and a penitent hath no lawfull right, or power to sell, or giue away his goods against the lawfull command of his Ghostly Father, because he hath no power to sinne; and a man hath no power, or right to giue money to a dishonest end, or to giue away his goods prodigally, and consequently they should be restored back againe, because he hath no power to sinne. I will say nothing at this time, how farre Cleargie men, either by the priuiledges of Christian Princes, or by the Ecclesiasticall Canons are *de facto* exempted both in their goods, and in their persons from ciuill powers, but onely I thought good at this time to set downe the true state of the question among Catholikes concerning the authority of spirituall Pastours to exempt Cleargie men from the temporall power of Christian Princes, that thereby they may clearely perceiue, what kinde of argument may be drawne from the exemption of Cleargie men, to proue the *Popes* power to depose Princes, and by way of sentence to depriue them wholy of their Regall authoritie.

42 Thus

42   Thus you haue feene in what manner temporall thinges are fubiect to fpirituall, temporall endes to
fpirituall endes, temporall power to the fpirituall power, the temporall fword to the fpirituall fword, the
flefh to the fpirit, the Moone to the Sunne, and temporall Princes to fpirituall Paftors; and that from the
fubiection and fubordination of the temporall power
to the fpirituall, no good argument can be brought to
proue, that the *Pope*, by vertue of his fpirituall powe r
can difpofe of temporalls, depofe temporall Princes,
or punifh temporally by way of *coercion*, but onely
that in order to fpirituall good he can command
temporalls, and punifh temporally by way of
command, but by way of *coercion* onely with fpirituall,
and not with temporall punifhments.   And by this
which hath bene faide, the Reader may eafily vnderftand the true fenfe and meaning of a certaine propofition, which Card. *Bellarmine* in his S*chulckenius* doth
often inculcate (as though there were fome great my-
ftery lye hidden therein)   to proue the Popes power to
depofe temporall Princes, to wit, *that a Chriſtian Prince
is a child of the Church, and fubiect to the Pope, not onely as he is a Chriſtian man, but alfo as he is a Chriſtian
Prince*; and the fame he affirmeth *of a Chriſtian Lawyer,
of a Chriſtian Souldier, of a Chriſtian Phyfitian*, and fo
of the reſt.

43   For all thefe three propofitions, A Chriftian
Prince, as he is a Chriftian Prince, is a child of the
Church, and fubiect to fpirituall Paftours : A Chriftian Prince as he is a Chriftian is a Child of the Church,
and fubiect to fpirituall Paftours : and a Prince as he is
a Chriftian, is a Childe of the Church and fubiect to
fpirituall Paftours ; haue one and the felfe fame fenfe ;
and fo likewife of a Chriftian Lawier, of a Chriftiar
Soldier, of a Chriftian Phyfitian &c. For the true meaning of them all is, that Chriftianitie, and not Regall
authority, or the knowledge of lawe, warfare, or
Phyfick

Phyſicke, is the cauſe why a Prince, a Lawier, a Soldier, a Phyſitian, and all other men of what trade ſoeuer they be, are Children of the Church, and ſubiect to ſpirituall Paſtours; and that therefore they are to be directed and inſtructed by ſpirituall Paſtours, not preciſely in the rules of ciuill gouernment, in the rules of lawe, warfare, or Phyſicke, but onely in the rules and principles of Chriſtian doctrine, and how they ought to gouerne ciuilly, and vſe their knowledge and trades according to the rules and precepts of Chriſtian Religion: which if they refuſe to doe, they may be corrected and puniſhed by ſpirituall Paſtours, with ſpirituall or Eccleſiaſticall puniſhments.

44   But from hence it doth not follow, that either temporall power, the knowledge of the lawe, warfare, or phyſicke, are among Chriſtians *per ſe* ſubiect to the ſpirituall power, but onely *per accidens*, as I haue often declared, and in thoſe thinges, which doe concerne or belong to Chriſtian Religion, or that ſpirituall Paſtours can by vertue of their ſpirituall power correct, or puniſh Chriſtian Princes, Lawiers, Soldiers, Phyſitians &c. by depriuing them by way of ſentence of their Regall authoritie, of their ſkill and knowledge in the lawes, in warfare, or Phyſicke, which they did not receiue from the ſpirituall power, but onely by depriuing them of the Sacramenis, and ſuch like ſpirituall benifites, of which they are made partakers by being Chriſtians, and by meanes of the ſpirituall power and authority of ſpirituall Paſtours. And thus much concerning the vnion and ſubiection of the temporall and ſpirituall power, and alſo of the ſecond part.

A N

AN ADIOINDER
to the firſt and ſecond Part,
wherein *Widdringtons* Interpretation of
that Clauſe of the Oath, wherein the Doctrine
(*that Princes, who are excommunicated or depri-*
ued by the Pope, may bee depoſed or murthered by
their Subiects) is abiured as *impious* and
hereticall, is prou ed to be found, and ſufficient,
and is cleared from all abſurdity or contradiction, euen by Mr. FITZ-HERBERTS
examples, and that it may without
any Periury be ſworne by any
CATHOLIKE.

(∵)

Ereciuing, Courteous Reader,
that this my *Anſwer* to Mr.
Fitzherberts Reply doth ariſe to
a greater bigneſſe, then at the
firſt I imagined : for that I am
compelled not onely to anſwer
him, but alſo D. *Schulckenius*,
to whom he remitteth his Reader for the confutation
of many of my Anſwers : I thought good for diuers
reaſons to diuide it into two Bookes, and to conclude
the firſt Booke with the firſt and ſecond Part; onely
adioy-

B

adioyning, by way of an Appendix, for thy better fatiffaction, the Anfwer which I made to Mr. *Fitzherberts* fourth Chapter, wherein hee excepteth againft thofe words of the Oath (*as impious and hereticall Doctrine*) for againft no other claufe of the Oath doth hee make any particular obiection, befides his generall difcourfe in fauour of the *Popes* power to depofe *Princes*, and to difpofe of all temporalls. Which his Doctrine, feeing that I haue already by extrinfecall grounds, and the authority of learned Catholikes (for to all the intrinfecall grounds which my *Aduerfary* bringeth, I will anfwer in the next booke, which, God willing, ere it be long thou fhalt receiue) proued not to bee fo certaine, but that the contrary hath euer beene, and is at this prefent approued by learned Catholikes, and confequently may without any danger of *herefie, error*, or *temerity*, be maintained by any Catholike : and confidering alfo that Mr. *Fitzherbert* taketh no particular exception againft any claufe of the Oath, but onely againft thofe words (*as impious and hereticall Doctrine*) it is euident that any man of iudgement may from that which I haue already faid and proued, eafily conclude, that the Oath may lawfully, and with a fafe Confcience bee taken, if my *Aduerfaries* obiections againft thofe words of the Oath (*as impious and hereticall Doctrine*) bee once cleerely confuted.

2 *Firft* therefore Mr. *Fitzherbert* in the beginning of his *fourth* Chapter, feemeth to take it very ill, *for that I fall*, faith he, *vppon him very foule, charging h m with flat falfity at the firft word*. But truely hee doth in this exaggerate the matter fomwhat more then is needfull, as alfo in that he faith, *that for a while I made my felfe merry with Fa. Leffius*. For befides that the word *flat* is added by himfelfe, I did neither *cogge, fcoffe, gibe, or make my felfe merry with Fa. Leffius* : but after I had brought thofe foure inftances to confute *Fa. Leffius* his antecedent propofition, whereon hee

grounded his confequence, I onely demanded, not
by way of *fcoffing, cogging, gibing, or making my felfe
merry*, as this man in this, and his former Chapter vntruely affirmeth, but rather out of pitty, compafsion,
and complaint, *whether thofe, and fuch like were not
trim Arguments to moue Englifh Catholicks prodigally
to caft away their goods, and to deny their allegiance
to their Prince.* And as for charging my Aduerfary with
flat falfity, my wordes were onely thefe: *Thirdly it is
falfe which this Author F. T. affirmeth, to wit, that the
Doctrine concerning the Popes power to depofe Princes,
is plainely abiured in this Oath, as impious and heretical,*
for this doctrine onely is abiured in this Oath as impious
and heretical, *that Princes being excommunicated or
depriued by the Pope, may bee depofed or murthered by
their fubiects or any other whatfoeuer: which pofition, as I
will declare beneath, hath this fenfe, that it is in the free
power of Subiects to depofe, or (if they will)to murther their
Prince, beeing excommunicated, or depriued by the
Pope.*

3 In the very firft beginning I affirmed, and Mr.
Fitzherbert in his firft Chapter related my words, *that
the fuppofition, which hee made, to wit, that the Popes
power to excommunicate Princes is denyed in this Oath,
is moft falfe,* and then he took no exception againft this
word, *moft falfe*: and now after he hath fo often fallen
very foule vpon mee, with charging mee with being
*abfurd, ridiculous, foolifh, malicious, impudent, im-
pious,* with *cogging, fcoffing, gibing, heretike, an d being no
good Child of the Catholike Church,* and vfing
many fuch like flanderous, and difgracefull termes a-
gainft mee, hee taketh it very ill for that I onely affirme
his affertion to bee *falfe*, which word neuerthelefe is
vfuall in Schooles among Difputers and Anfwerers, and
is not taken for any difgracefull tearme, being in fenfe
all one with *vntrue*, or *I deny the affertion or pofition.*
But becaufe I perceiue Mr. *Fitzherberts* patience can-

not brooke the very leaſt of thoſe ſo many foule, diſgracefull, and ſlanderous nicknames hee is pleaſed to
beſtow vpon me, and doth ſo eaſily *ſee a little mote in
my eye, not perceiuing the great beame in his owne:* I will
heereafter abſtaine from that word *falſe*, and in ſtead
thereof vſe *vntrue*, as in the Engliſh Edition I did tran-
ſlate it: neither can he haue any colour to bee diſtaſted
with this word *vntrue*, vnleſſe hee doe take it ill that I
doe not *forſooth* approue all his opinions, and applaud
whatſoeuer he ſhall ſay to be true.

4 But to the matter. Mr. *Fitzherbert* in his fourth
Chapter endeauoreth to proue two things : the *one*
that I haue falſly charged him with affirming, *that the
D octrine for the Popes power to depoſe Princes, is manifeſtly abiured in the Oath, as impious and hereticall*, which
hee denyeth to haue affirmed, although hee granteth withall, ʌhat i t is true if hee had affirmed it. The
*ſecond is, that my interpretation of that clauſe of the Oath,
wherein the aforeſaid Doctrine and Poſition*, That Princes being excommunicated or depriued by the Pope,
may be depoſed or murthered by their Subiects, *is abiured as* impious and hereticall, *is abſurd according to
my owne grounds*.

5. As touching the *firſt*. Mr. *Fitzherbert* affirmeth, [a]
*that he ſaith nothing at all touching his owne opinion,
whether the doctrine of depoſing Princes be abiured in the
Oath* as impious and hereticall *(and much leſſe that it is
manifeſtly abiured as I ſay he doth)* but *he affirmeth onely,
that the Oath is wholy repugnant to a Canon of the great
Councell of* Lateran *by reaſon of two clauſes therein*. And
for proofe thereof, he repeateth (*b*) the words of his
S upplement, which are theſe? *Fourthly, it appeareth alſo hereby, and by all the premiſes, that this Oath of pretended allegiance is an vnlawfull Oath, and not to be taken
by any Chriſtian man, ſeeing that it flatly contradicteth the
ſaid Councell, and Canon, not onely becauſe it denieth that
the Pope* hath any power or authority to depoſe his *Ma-*

ieſtie

iestie , or to difcharge any of his *Subiects* of their allegiance, and obedienceto his Maiefty, *but alfo becaufe it bindeth the takers of it in expreffe words to fweare thus. And I do further fweare, that from my hart I doe abhorre, deteft, & abiure, as impious and heretical, this damnable doctrin, and pofition,* that princesexcommunicated or depriued by the Pope may be depofed , *which pofition was by that Canon exprefly ordained to be practifed in fome cafes , yea and executed by the Councells order vpon* Reymond *Earle of Tolofa. Thus fay I in my Suppliment.*

6. *Now I report* [c] *me to the indifferent Reader, whether I affirme any more , then that thefe two claufes of the Oath are flatly againft the Councell of* Lateran *, becaufe the Popes power to depofe Princes (which the faid Councell acknowledgeth and approueth by an expreffe Canon) is denied therein ; and this is manifeft as well by all my precedent difcourfe , as by that which followeth; for all that which I amply debated before, touching the Councell of* Lateran *, concerned onely the Popes power to depofe Princes, without any one word whether the abiuration or deniall thereof be heretical; and my conclufion of the later claufe confirmeth the fame : for I add immediately thefe words ,* which pofition, (to wit, that Princes being excommunicated or depriued by the Pope may be depofed) was by that Canon exprefly ordained to be practifed in fome cafes;yea and was executed by the Councels order , vpon *Reymond* Earle of Tolofa.

c *Nu.* 3.

7. *Whereby it appeareth,* [d] *that whereas the claufe mentioneth two thinges; the one the doctrine and pofition ,* that Princes excommunicated, or depriued by the Pope may be depofed; *and the other, that the faid doctrine is abiured,* as impious and heretical; *I treat onely of the former, and fpeake not one word of the later. So as my Aduerfary* Widdrington *charging me to haue* falfly affirmed , that the Popes power to depofe Princes is manifeftly abiured in this Oath, *hath charged me falfely, and therefore may take his imputation of falfity to himfelfe.* Thus M.*Fitzherbert.*

d *Nu.* 4.

8. But in truth I cannot but wonder, where Mr. *Fitzherberts* memory was, when he wrote theſe words, that he could not perceiue, that he himſelfe here ſaith as much as I affirmed him to ſay: and therefore if he can finde no better a ſhift and euaſion, then to deny with ſo bould a face that very ſame thinge, which he himſelfe in this very place doth ſo plainly affirme, the *vntruth*, I dare not ſay *falſity*, wherewith I charged him, will ſtill remaine with him, and will not be taken from him by me, beſides the diſgrace for a man of his faſhion, quality, and profeſſion, to deny ſo bouldly that he affirmeth that thing, which euery Child who vnderſtandeth Engliſh, may perceiue that he doth affirme. For marke his words, *The Oath*, ſaith he, *bindeth the takers of it in expreſſe words to ſweare thus: And I doe further ſweare, that I doe from my heart abhorre, deteſt, and abiure*, as impious and hereticall, *this damnable doctrine and poſition, that Princes excommunicated or depriued by the Pope may be depoſed*. Now let any man iudge, whether he that affirmeth, that the Oath bindeth the takers of it in expreſſe words to ſweare, *that he doth abiure* as impious and hereticall *this doctrine, that Princes excommunicated or depriued by the Pope may be depoſed*, doth not affirme, *that the doctrine concerning the Papes power to depoſe Princes is plainely, manifeſtly, or in expreſſe words abiured in this oath as impious and hereticall*.

9. But obſerue how cunningly M. *Fitzherbert*, belike to returne the imputation of *falſity* vpon mee, would delude his Reader. *Whereas the clauſe of the oath*, ſaith he, *mentioneth two things; the one the doctrine and poſition*, that Princes excommunicated, or depriued by the Pope may be depoſed; *and the other, that the ſaid doctrine is abiured as impious and hereticall*, (Loe here againe hee granteth as much, as I ſaid hee did affirme, to wit, that the doctrine, which holdeth that Princes excommunicated or depriued by the Pope may be depoſed, is abiured in this oath as impious and hereticall)

I.

I treate onely of the former, and speake not one word of the later; and all that which I amply debated before touching the Councell of Lateran *concerned onely the Popes power to depose Princes, without any one word, whether the abiuration, or deniall thereof be hereticall.*

10. Belike this man would make his Reader beleeue, that I did say, that he had amply debated, treated, or made some discourse of this point, and that he had endeauoured to proue, that the oath is vnlawfull, nd against the Councell of *Lateran*, in regard it bindeth the takers of it to sweare, *that they doe from their heart abhorre, detest, and abiure* as impious and hereticall *this doctrine and position, that Princes excommunicated or deprined by the Pope may be deposed*; whereas I say no such thing, but onely that Master *Fitzherbert* doth barely affirme, *that the oath bindeth the takers to abiure, or, which is all one in sense, that in this oath is abiured as* impious and hereticall *this doctrine,* and categoricall *proposition,*ex parte prædicati, *that Princes excommunicated or deprined by the Pope may be deposed.* And thus much hee himselfe, as you haue seene in this very place, doth twice affirm: which his assertion I said is not true, for that it onely bindeth the takers to abiure as *impious, and hereticall,* this *doctrine* and hypotheticall *proposition* ex parte prædicati, *that Princes excommunicated or deprined by the Pope may be deposed or murthered by their subiects, or any other whatsoeuer,* which hath a farre different sense from the former, as I will shew beneath. So that he may still take to himselfe that imputation of *falsity,* or *vntruth,* wherewith I did truely charge him, and hereafter be more warie, if hee haue any care of his credit, not to maintaine such palpable vntruths, which euery Schoole-boy may easily perceiue so to be. And thus much for the first point. Now you shall see how learnedly he proueth the second.

11. *Neuerthelesse I would not,* saith he, e *haue* Widdring-

drington *to thinke, that becauſe I deny, that I haue ſaid
ſo in my* Supplement, *therefore I doe, or will deny, that it
is ſo: for it is euident in that clauſe, that the taker of the
oath abiureth this doctrine as* impious and hereticall, *to
wit, that Princes excommunicated or depriued by the
Pope may be depoſed, or murthered by their ſubiects, or any
other, whereby not onely the Popes power to depoſe Princes
is denyed, but alſo the doctrine thereof is abiured as* impious and hereticall: *And this, I ſay, is euident, notwithſtanding the friuolous euaſion, which my Aduerſary* Widdrington *ſeketh by his extrauagant interpretation of that
clauſe, when hee ſaith, as you haue heard, that the ſenſe
and meaning thereof is no other, but that it is* hereticall
*to affirme it to be in the free power of ſubiects or any other
to depoſe, or (if they liſt) to kill Princes that are excommunicated or depriued by the Pope.*

ᶠ *Nu.6.*   12. *Whereby* ᶠ *hee giueth to vnderſtand, that the
doctrine, and poſition abiured in that clauſe, containeth two
members, the one concerning the* depoſition *of Princes,
and the other concerning the* murther *of them; and that
it is abiured as* hereticall *in reſpect of the later onely: as
who would ſay, that it is an* hereticall *doctrine to teach,
or affirme,* that Princes excommunicated by the Pope
may be murthered. *So that albeit there be mention alſo of
the* depoſition *of Princes (as that they may be* depoſed
or murthered) *yet the doctrine of* depoſition *is not abiured in that clauſe as* hereticall, *except it be ioyned
with the* murther *of them; in ſuch ſort, that a man may
freely chooſe whether he will depoſe, or murther them.*

13. But that the Reader may more fully vnderſtand, whether Maſter *Fitzherberts* Reply be a *meere
ſhift,* or my anſwere an *abſurd, friuolous,* and *extrauagant euaſion,* and *contention de lana caprina* (ſuch foule
termes, and farre worſe it is not foule for him to vſe a-
gainſt mee, and yet if I doe onely ſay, *that hee affirmeth
that which is falſe,* or not true, *I fall very foule vpon him*)
I will ſet dovvne entirely, what I anſwered in my *Theologicall*

logicall Disputation, and not in that lame manner, as he relateth my answer. It was obiected by the *Author* of the *English Dialogue* betweene the two sisters *Pro teftancie and Puritanisme,* that this clause of the oath. (*And I do further sweare, that I do from my hart abhorre, deteft and abiure, as impiuos and hereticall, this damnable doctrine and pofition, That Princes which be excommuica- ted or depriued by the Pope, may be depofed or murthered by their fubiects, or any other whatfoeuer*) cannot be taken without periurie : And this was his argument.

14. *Whenfoeuer an affirmatiue propofition is* hereticall, *of neceffity it muft be either againft faith, and confequent- ly againft the expreffe word of God, or elfe the contra- dictorie negatiue muft be a pofition of faith, and contained in the expreffe word of God.*

But neither this affirmatiue pofition, That Princes which be excommunicated or depriued by the *Pope*, may be depofed or murthered by their Subiects, or a- ny other what foeuer, *is againft the expreffe word of God, neither the contradictorie negatiue, to wit,* that Princes being excommunicated or depriued by the *Pope*, **may** not be depofed or murthered by their fubiects, or any o- ther whatfoeuer, *is contained in the expreffe word of God.*

Therefore the former pofition, that Princes being ex- communicated or depriued by the *Pope*, may be de- pofed or murthered by their Subiects, or any other whatfoeuer, *is not hereticall.*

15 *And if perchance it fhould be anfwered, that where- as it is written in the 20. Chapter of* Exod. Thou fhalt not kill, *and* 1. Reg. 26. Deftroy him not, *for who fhall lay the hands on the Lords annointed, and be guiltleffe? One part of the aforefaid pofition, to wit,* that Princes may be murthered, *is hereticall and againft the expreffe Word of God, and therefore the whole pofition, in regard of this one part, may be abiured* as hereticall; *yet this an- fwer is not fufficient: For the pofition in hand, to wit,* That Princes being excommunicated or depriued by the

Pope may be depoſed, or murthered by their Subiects
or any other, *doth not abſolutely affirme*, that Princes,
after they be excommunicated or depriued by the
Pope, may be *murthered* by their ſubiects, or any other,
but with a diſiunction, to wit, may be depoſed, *or* murthered. *And therefore although the poſition were* hereticall, *if it did onely affirme they might be murthered, yet
not affirming this, but onely that they may be* depoſed,
or murdered, *there is no ſhewe of hereſie in it, in regard
of being contrary to the aforeſaid texts of Scripture, to
which it is nothing contrary at all.*

16. *For, according to the moſt true and approued rule of
the Logicians, to make a diſiunctiue propoſition, or any
thing affirmed vnder a diſiunction to be* falſe *and* hereticall, *it is neceſſary, that both parts of the diſiunction be alſo* falſe *and* hereticall; *neither is it ſufficient, that one onely part be* hereticall. *And therefore although that the ſecond part of the diſiunction to wit*, That Princes, being
excommunicated, or depriued by the Pope, may be
murthered, *be heretical and againſt the expreſſe word of
God; yet becauſe the firſt part of the diſiunction, to wit,
that ſuch* Princes may be depoſed by their Subiects,
or any other, *is not hereticall, nor contrary to the expreſſe
word of God, the whole diſiunctiue poſition cannot be in very deed* hereticall, *and therefore neither can it be abiured as* hereticall.

g *Cap. 5. ſec.
2. nu. 8. et
ſeq.*

17. To this obiection I gaue two anſwers. The *firſt*
" and *principall* anſwer was, g that albeit the aforeſaid
" propoſition, *Princes which be excommunicated or de-
" priued by the Pope, may be depoſed or murthered by their
" Subiects &c.* doth ſeeme by reaſon of that later con-
" iunction [*or*] to be a diſiunctiue propoſition, or rather
" a *Categoricall* propoſition of ſuch a *diſiunct predicate*,
" as the Logicians tearme it, which vertually doth
" imply, or may be reſolued into a diſiunctiue propoſi-
" tion (to the verity of which diſiunctiue propoſition, it
" is onely required, as it was ſaid in the obiection, that
                                                    one

" one part of the difiunction be true : and to make the
" whole difiunction falfe and *heretically*, both parts of
" the difiunction muft be falfe and *heretically* : nei-
" ther doth it fuffice, that one only part be falfe and
" *heretically*) Neuerthelefle according to the common
" fenfe and meaning of the words, it is in very deed,
" and according to our Engl fh phrafe, *equiualent* to
" a copulatiue propofition, or rather to a *Categoricall*
" propofition of fuch a *Copulate predicate*, which may
" be refolued into a copulatiue propofition, to the ve i-
" ty whereof, according to the Logicians rule, it is
" contrariwife required, that both parts of the copu-
" lation be true; and to make the whole propofition
" falfe and *heretically*, it is not required that both parts of
" the copulation be falfe and *heretically*, but it fufficeth
" that one onely part thereof be falfe and *heretically*.
" Neither is it vnufuall, that a coniunction difiunctiue
" be fometimes taken for a copulatiue, and a copula
" tiue for a difiunctiue, as we may fee in *Leg. fæpe. F.*
" *de verb. rum fignificat.* Whereof read *Fel nus* in Cap.
" *inter cæteras de refcriptis. Ioannes Azorius tom.* 1.
" *Inftit. Lib.* 5 *Cap.* 25. and *Salas, difp.* 21. *de Le-*
" *gibus,* fect. 3. regula 26.
"   18. But if any one will needes contend, that the
" aforefaid propofition, *Princes, which are excommuni-*
" *cated or depriued by the Pope &c.* by reafon of that
" difiunctiue coniunction [*or*] is altogither a difiunctiue
" propofition; this notwithftanding being granted,
" the obiection may eafily be anfwered. For albeit we
" admit it to be a difiunctiue propofition, neuerthelefle
" wee affirme, that it is not an *abfolute* difiunctiue,
" whereof the aforefaid rule of the Logicians, to wit,
" that both parts of the difiunction muft be *heretically*,
" to make the whole difiunction to be *heretical,* is to be
" vnderftood, but it is a *conditional* difiunctiue, which
" importeth a free choice, or election of the will, or
" which is all one, a free power to chofe whether part

"of the diſiunction we pleaſe, to the verity of which
"*conditionall* diſiunctiue is required, that you may
"chooſe whether part of the diſiunction you pleaſe;
"and if it be *hereticall* to affirme, that it is in the free
"power of the will to chooſe whether part of the diſ-
"iunction we pleaſe, the whole diſiunction, or diſ-
"iunctiue propoſition implying ſuch a *condition*, or free
"election, without doubt is *hereticall*.

"   19. Now that this diſiunction [*or*] being placed
"in the aforeſaid propoſition is in common ſenſe, ac-
"cording to our Engliſh phraſe, *equivalent* to [h] a copu-
"lation, or ſuch a diſiunction, which leaueth a free
"power in the Subjects to chooſe whether part they
"will, that is to depoſe the King, or if they pleaſe,
"to murther him, will moſt euidently appeare, if both
"in common ſpeech, and alſo in the lawes of the
"Realme, we diligently conſider the proper, and vſu-
"all ſignification of this word [*may*] when there fol-
"loweth the coniunction diſiunctiue [*or*]. And this
"may be ſhewed by almoſt innumerable examples,
"whereof ſome of them wee will here ſet downe. As
"for example : *you* may *ſtay here, or depart. You* may
"*eate or drinke. You* may *buy wine or oyle. You* may *goe*
"*to ſuch a place by land, or by water. You* may *buy that*
"*land in fee-farme, or by leaſe. The King by vertue of an*
"*Act of Parliament* may *take of conuicted Popiſh Recu-*
"*ſants twenty pounds for euery moneth, or the third part*
"*of all their lands. The Sheriefe* may *preſently hang a*
"*theiſe condemned to die, or delay his death for ſome ſmall*
"*time. If any perſon hold any lands of an other Lord, then*
"*of the King, by Knights ſeruice, hee* may *giue, diſpoſe,*
"*or aſſure by his laſt will, and teſtament, two parts of the*
"*ſaid lands holden by Knights ſeruice, or of as much there-*
"*of as ſhall amount to the full yearely valew of two parts.*
"*If a man by his laſt will and teſtament ordaine, that his*
"*Executors* may *beſtow twenty pounds vpon the poore, or*
"*repaire ſuch a bridge, it is in the free power of the Execu.*

                                        tors,

[h] The Latine word *æqui-pol-let* in this place of my *Theolog. Diſputation* is not well tranſlated into Engliſh *it doth import*, it ſhould be, it is equiualent.

" *tors, to chooſe whether of thoſe two they pleaſe. Finally*
" *in clauſes of reuocation , where the words are , that one*
" may *by any deed in his life time , or by his laſt will and*
" *teſtament renoke the ſaid vſes, and limit new, it is in his*
" *power and choice to doe it by the one , or by the other, as*
" *he ſhall pleaſe.* And in infinite ſuch like examples the
" verb [*may*] implieth a free power to chooſe either
" part of the diſiunction one pleaſeth , neither can
" there ſcarcely be alledged any one example, where-
" in the coniunction diſiunctiue [*or*] immediately fol-
" lowiug the verbe [*may*] is not ſo taken.
"　　20. Wherefore the plaine and vſuall meaning of
" the aforeſaid propoſition, *Princes, which be excom-*
" *municated, or depriued by the Prpe, may be depoſed, or*
" *murthered by their Subiects,* or, which is all one, *Sub-*
" *iects may depoſe, or murther their Princes being excom-*
" *municated, or depriued by the Pope (* for that in this laſt
" onely the *verbe paſſiue* is changed into the *actiue*) is,
" that it is in the free choice of the Subjects to *depoſe,*
" or if they will, to *murther* ſuch Princes.　So that if it
" be *hereticall* to affirme , as without doubt it is, that
" it is in the free power of Subjects to *depoſe,* or *mur-*
" *ther* ſuch Princes, becauſe it is *hereticall* and againſt
" the expreſſe word of God to affirme, that they may
" *murther* them, the aforeſaid poſition conſiſting of
" that diſiunction is *herepicall,* and therefore it may
" without any danger at all of periurie be abiured as
" *hereticall.*
"　　21. From hence it may be gathered firſt, that ac-
" cording to the common, and vſuall vnderſtan-
" ding of our Engliſh phraſe, there is a great diſtincti-
" on betwixt theſe two verbs [*may*] and [*can*].　For
" [*can*] doth vſually ſignifie a power in generall, whe-
" ther it be *naturall,* or *morall,* but [*may*] for the moſt
" part importeth a *morall* power , to wit, if it be vſed
" alone without any coniunction following it, moſt
" commonly it ſignifieth a lawfullnes to do the thing

" propoſed: As, I may doe this, ſignifieth, that it is
" lawfull for mee to doe this : but if there follow it a
" a *coniunction copulatiue* , ' or *diſiunctiue* , it implyeth a
" *choice , or free power, to chooſe whether part of the diſ-*
" *iunction, or copulation one will.*

"   Seeing therefore that the Latine verbe [*poſſum*]
" implyeth a power in generall, whether it bee natu-
" rall, or morall, and according to the thing affirmed
" or denyed, it is limited to a naturall or morall pow-
" er: as in this propoſition, *Ignis poteſt comburere,* *The*
" *fire hath power to burne,* it ſignifieth a naturall and ne-
" ceſſary power in the fire to burne: and in this, *poteſt*
" *homo eligere bonum , aut malum;* *A man hath power to*
" *chooſe good or euill,*it ſignifieth a morall and free pow-
" er: from hence it followeth , that this propoſition,
" *Subiects may depoſe or murther their Prince, being ex-*
" *communicated or depriued by the Pope ,* is not ſo pro-
" perly and ſignificantly tranſlated into Latine by the
" verbe [*poſſum*] *Sabditi poſſunt deponere aut occidere*
" *ſuum Principem excommunicatum &c.* as by the ſub-
" ſtantiue of [*poſſum*] or by the verbe [*permittitur*]
" to wit, *in poteſtate eſt ſubditorum, or permittitur ſub-*
" *ditis Principem ſuum excommunioatum , vel depri-*
" *uatum per Pontificem , deponere aut occidere.* *It*
" *is in the power of Subiects , or it is permitted to Sub-*
" *iects, to depoſe or murther their Prince being excom-*
" *municated or depriued by the Pope.* And therefore the
" Latine tranſlation of this Oath , doth not by the
" verbe [*poſſum*] ſignificantly expreſſe the proper and
" vſuall ſignification of the verbe [*may*] contained in
" the aforeſaid Poſition, vnleſſe either the coniunction
" copulatiue [*and*] be put in place of [*or*] to wit, *Prin-*
" *cipes per Papam excommunicati vel depriuati poſſun-*
" *per ſuos Subditos deponi & occidi, depoſed and murthe-*
" *red,* as Cardinall *Bellarmine,* and *Antonius Capellus*
" haue it in their bookes tranſlated , or elſe there bee
" vnderſtood a *condition* of the free-will to chooſe
                                                  whether

" whether part of the difiunction they pleafe, to wit,
" poffunt deponi per fuos Subditos, aut (fi velint,) occidi, bee
" depofed, or (if the Subiects will) be murthered.
" 23 Secondly from hence it is alfo gathered, that
" in a difiunctiue propofition, wherein is implyed a con-
" dition of the will to choofe freely either part of the
" difunction, it maketh all one fenfe, whether the con-
" iunction copulatiue [and] or the difiunctiue [or] bee
" vfed : For both of them doe fignifie a free power to
" choofe which part one pleafeth: and fo the coniunct-
" ion difiunctiue hath in fenfe the vertue and force of a
" copulatiue, & the copulatiue of a difiunctiue. Wher-
" fore when the ancient Fathers fpeak of our free-will,
" and doe affirme, that it is in our power to choofe
" good or euill, they vfe indifferently the coniunction
" difiunctiue [or] and the copulatiue [and] fometimes
" affirming that it is in our power to choofe good or
" euill; other times that it is in our power to choofe
" goood and euill. Yea Card. Bellarmine himfelfe pro-
" pounding in his Controuerfies the queftion concer-
" ning free-will, doth confound [or] with [and], and
" taketh them for all one. There is a controuerfie, faith
" he betwixt Catholikes and heretikes, whether a man in
" the ftate of corrupt nature hath free-will to choofe mo-
" rall good, [and] to auoid euill, or which is all one, to
" obferue [or] breake morall precepts.
" 24. Seeing therefore that in this propofition,
" Princes being excommunicated, or depriued by the Pope,
" may be depofed or murthered by their Subiects, or, which
" is all one, Subi cts may depofe or murther their Prince
" beeing excommunicated or depriued by the Pope, the
" verbe [may] doth import a free power in the Sub-
" iects to choofe which part of the difiunction they
" pleafe, that is, to depofe fuch Princes, or, if they
" pleafe, to murder them, it maketh all one fenfe, whe-
" ther it bee faid, Princes may be depofed or murthered,
" by their fubiects, or Princes may bee depofed and murthered

1 Tom. 4. Lib.
5, Chap, 13, in
prinoipio.

" thered by *their Subiects*, as Card. *Bellarmine*, and *An-*
" *tonius Cappellus*, putting the Coniunction copulatiue
" [*and*] do feeme to haue well obferued , and to be of
" opinion , that the aforefaid difiunctiue propofition
" is in very deed *equiualent* to a copulatiue , or fuch a
" *conditionall* difiunctiue , which vertually doth con-
" taine a copulatiue . And truely, if this pretended
" demonftration of this Author were fo euident an ar-
" gument, as hee imagineth it to be , to condemne
" this oath as facrilegious , without doubt it could
" not haue efcaped the moft quick vnderftandingo f
" Card. *Bellarmine*, who alfo would not haue neglect-
" ed to produce any reafon , which might clearly haue
" conuinced the oath to be apparantly vnlawfull.
"   Now from this which hath bene faid , it is eafie
" to anfwer in forme to the aforefaid obiection, whofe
" whole ftrength dependeth vpon the nature and qua-
" lity of a difiunctiue propofition.
"   Wherefore to the *minor* propofition it is anfwe-
" red , that it is *hereticall* and againft the expreffe word
" of God contayned in the aforefaid two texts of holy
" Scripture, to affirme , *That Princes , which be ex-*
" *communicated or depriued by the Pope may be depofed*
" *or murthered by their Subiects, or any other*, or, which
" is all one, *that Subiects, or any other may depofe or mur-*
" *ther fuch Princes*. For the plaine and common mea-
" ning of this propofition is , as I haue fhewed before,
" that it is in the free power of fubiects, or of any other,
" to depofe fuch Princes, or , if they will , to murther
" them , which propofition is flat *hereticall.*
"   26. And whereas it is obiected , that the afore-
" faid propofition , *Princes which be excommunicated*
" *&c.* is a *difiunctine* , but to the veritie of a *difiunctiue*
" propofition, it is fufficient , that one part of the dif-
" iunction be true, and to make the whole difiunct-
" iue propofition to be falfe and *hereticall*, it is necef-
" fary according to the moft certaine rule of the Logicians,

" gicians, that both parts of the difiunction be falfe
" and *hereticall*.

" It is anfwered firft to the *Minor*, that although
" in externall found the aforefaid propofition, *Princes*
" *which be excommunicated &c.* feeme to be a difiunct-
" *iue*, yet in very deede, and according to the plaine
" and common vnderftanding of our Englifh phrafe,
" it is, as I haue already fhewed, *equiualent* to a copu-
"latiue, to the veritie of which it is neceffary, that
" both parts of the *copulation* be true, and to make the
" whole copulatiue propofition to be falfe and *hereti-
" call*, it fufficeth, that one onely part of the copula-
" lation be falfe and *hereticall*. Now that one part of
" the aforefaid propofition, to wit, *that* Princes *which*
" *bee excommunicated or depriued by the Pope, may be*
" *murthered by their Subiects, or any other*, is flat *here-
" ticall*, it is too too manifeft.

" 27 But leaft we fhould feeme to contend about
" bare words, I anfwer *fecondly*, and grant, that the
" aforefaid propofition, *Princes, which be excommuni-
" cated, &c.* is a *difiunctiue*; But then the *Minor* propo-
" fition is to bee diftinguifhed. For when the Logi-
" cians affirme, that to the verity of a difiunctiue pro-
" pofition it is fufficient, that one part of the difiuncti-
" on be true, and to make the whole difiunctiue to be
" *hereticall*, it is neceffary that both parts of the dif-
" iunction be *hereticall*, that approued rule of the Lo-
" gicians is to be vnderftood of an *abfolute difiunctiue*,
" to wit, which doth not vertually containe in it a con-
" dition, or free power in the will to choofe whether
" part one pleafeth: For to the verity of this *conditio-
" nall* difiunctiue it is neceffary, that both parts of the
" difiunction may be chofen, and if it be *hereticall* to af-
" firme, that it is in the free choife of any man to chufe
" whether part of the difiunction he pleafeth, the
" whole difiunctiue propofition is *hereticall*. Now that
" it is *hereticall* to affirme, that it is in the free power

D   of

"of Subiects to depoſe, or if they will, to murther
"Princes being excommunicated or depriued by the
"Pope, no man can call in queſtion.

"   28. Neuertheleſſe the *Author* of this *Dialogue*
"doth ſeeme to deale ſomewhat cunningly, and en-
"deauoureth not ſo much to impugne *directly* the af-
"firmatiue propoſition, which is expreſly contained in
"the Oath, and to proue *directly*, that the aforeſaid
"poſition, *Princes being excommunicated &c. may be*
"*depoſed or murthered*, not to be *hereticall*, as the
"oath affirmeth it to be; but he flyeth from the affir-
"matiue to the negatiue, and indeauoureth to ſhew,
"that the contradictorie propoſition, to wit, *Princes*
"*being excommunicated &c. cannot be depoſed or mur-*
"*dered &c.* is not certaine of faith, nor contained in
"the expreſſe word of God; from whence he conclu-
"deth, that therefore the former affirmatiue propo-
"ſition, which is in expreſſe words contayned in the
"Oath, is not hereticall, *becauſe in what degree of falſ-*
"*hood any poſition is falſe, in the oppoſite degree of truth*
"*the contradictory muſt be true.*

"   29. But this *Author* by his manner of arguing ſee-
"meth deſirous to ſhun the difficulty, and to impugne
"a propoſition, which is more cleare and manifeſt, by
"an other more obſcure and equiuocall, which among
"Logicians is accounted a great defect in arguing,
"whoſe nature is *to proue one thing leſſe manifeſt by an o-*
"*ther more apparant.* For the falſhood of this affirma-
"tiue propoſition, *Princes, which be excommunicated*
"*or depriued by the Pope may be depoſed or murthered*
"*by their Subiects,* or which is all one, *Subiects may*
"*depoſe or murther ſuch* Princes, *who be excommunicated*
"*&c.* is more cleare and manifeſt in the common vn-
"derſtanding of our Engliſh phraſe, then is the truth
"of this negatiue, *Subiects may not depoſe or murther*
"*ſuch* Princes, *who be excommunicated &c.* by reaſon of
"the negatiue aduerb[*not*]which as the Logicians ſay, is

" of a *malignant nature*, for that it destroyeth, or deny-
" eth whatsoeuer followeth after it, making an af-
" firmatiue to be a negatiue, and a negatiue to be an
" affirmatiue, an vniuersall to be a particular, and a
" particular to be an vniuersall. *k*   So that the mea-
" ning of the aforesaid negatiue proposition, is by rea-
" son of that negatiue aduerbe [*not*] made ambiguous,
" and may haue this sense, that *Subiects may neither de-*
" *pose nor murther such Princes, who be excommunica-*
" *ted or depriued by the Pope* : which proposition so vn-
" derstood, is not of faith, , neither in very deed con-
" tradictory to the proper and vsuall meaning of the
" former affirmatiue, which is abiured in the Oath.
" And therefore no meruaile that this *Author* was de-
" sirous to fly from the affirmatiue to the negatiue.
"   30. Supposing therefore, that *contradiction*, ac-
" cording to the approued doctrine of *Aristotle*, *l* *is an*
" *affirming and denying of the selfe same thing, in the selfe*
" *same manner*, I answere, that this negatiue positi-
" on, *Princes which be excommunicated or depriued by*
" *the Pope, may not be deposed or murthered by their Sub-*
" *iects*, is contradictory to that affirmatiue position,
" which is abiured in the Oath, if the verbe [*may*] be
" taken in the same manner, or sense in the negatiue,
" as it is taken in the affirmatiue : And then as the *af-*
" *firmatiue* is *hereticall*, so the *negatiue* is of *Faith*. For
" as the sense of the affirmatiue is, as I haue shewed be-
" fore, *that it is in the free choise of Subiects either to*
" *depose such Princes who be excommunicated or depriued*
" *by the Pope, or if they will, to murther them*, which
" is false, *hereticall*, and against those expresse words
" of Scripture, *Thou shalt not kill, Kill him not &c.* So
" , the sense of the negatiue contradictory must be, *that*
" *it is not in the free choice of Subiects to depose such Prin-*
" *ces, or if they please, to murther them*; which propo-
" sition is most true, and contained in the expresse
" word of God, because it is not in their free power

D 2   to

k As this vni-
uersall affir-
matiue propo-
sition, *all men*
are sensible, is
by putting *not*
in the begin-
ing, *not all men*
are sensible,
made, a parti-
cular negatiue.

l Lib. 1. de
interpretat.
cap. 4.

" to *murther* them, as is manifeſt by the former places
" of holy Scripture.

31 And thus much concerning the *firſt* and *principall* Anſwer, which I thought good to ſet downe at
large, both for that the Reader may the better iudge
of my *Anſwer*, and alſo of M. *Fitzherberts Reply*, who
taketh no other particular exception againſt the Oath,
beſides the generall Doctrine concerning the Popes
power to depoſe Princes, which he will needs haue to
bee a poynt of faith, and therefore not to bee denyed
by any Catholike, and alſo for that there be ſome Catholikes, who although they be of opinion, as was the
Author of that Engliſh *Dialogue*, that there is nothing
againſt faith contained in the oath, and that the Doctrine for the Popes power to depoſe Princes is not a
poynt of faith, but in Controuerſie among Catholikes,
notwithſtanding the *Popes Breues*, or any other decree
of *Pope* or *Councell*, which are vrged to the contrary,
yet they can hardly be perſwaded, but that by reaſon
of that word [*hereticall*] that clauſe of the Oath is
vnlawfull and cannot bee taken without periury, as
the *Author* of that *Dialogue* did by the aforeſaid Argument pretend to demonſtrate.

m *nu.* 10.

32 Now you ſhall ſee what exceptions M. *Fitzherbert* taketh againſt this my Anſwer. *Firſt* hee ſaith,
ᵐ *that I contend de lana caprina, and labour in vaine to
proue, that the Engliſh word [may] in a diſiunctiue propoſition implyeth a freedome to chooſe whether part we liſt
of the diſiunction, wherein alſo by the way he ſaith, that I
abuſe ſtrangers in ſeeking to perſwade them, that the
Latine verbe [poſſunt] in the Latine Tranſlation of the
Oath, doth not ſufficiently expreſſe the nature of the Engliſh word [may] in this clauſe,* Principes per Papam
excommunicati vel depriuati poſſunt per ſuos ſubdi:os,
vel alios quoſcunque, deponi aut occidi: *Princes being
excommunicated or depriued by the Pope may be depoſed
or murthered by their Subiects, or any other whatſoeuer.*

33 But

33 But *first* who feeth not, that this queftion, to wit whether this propofition, *Princes which are excommunicated or depriued by the Pope, may bee depofed or murthered by their Subiects, or any other,* be fuch a *difiunctiue* propofition which implyeth a *free election* in the Subiects or others, to choofe whether they will *depofe* or *murther* fuch Princes, is both a queftion of great moment, and not *de lana caprina,* & alfo that I haue not laboured in vaine to proue, but by the common vnderftanding of the words in vfuall fpeech and in the lawes of our Realme, fufficiently proued that the verbe [*may*] in an affirmatiue difiunctiue propofition, when there followeth the coniunction difiunctiue [*or*] implyeth a freedome to choofe whether part of the difiunction wee lift, as by many examples both in common fpeech, and by the lawes of our Realme I haue cleerely conuinced; neither can there fcarcely be alleadged any one example, wherein the coniunction difiunctiue [*or*] immediatly following the verbe [*may*] in an affirmatiue propofition doth not imply a free election to choofe which part of the difiunction we pleafe.

34 *Secondly,* it is not true, that I haue abufed the Latine Reader in feeking to perfwade him, that the Latine verbe [*poffunt*] in the Latine Tranflation of the Oath, doth not fufficiently expreffe the proper and vfuall fignification of the verbe [*may*] contained in the aforefaid pofition, valeffe either the coniunction copulatiue [*et*] bee put in plaee of [*aut*], as Card. *Bellarmine, Anton. Capellus,* & now laftly F. *Suarez* haue it in their bookes tranflated, or elfe there be vnderftood a condition of the free will to choofe in that claufe [*depofed or murthered by their Subiects*] which part of the difiunction the Subiects pleafe: But M. *Fitzherbert* rather abufeth his Englifh Readers, who vnderftand not Latine in affirming the contrary. For the Latine verbe [*poffum*] doth by his proper fignification, as I haue faid, import a power in generall, whether it bee natu-

D 3   rall

rall or morall, and according to the matter it is limited to a naturall or morall power: but the verbe [*may*]
is by his proper ſignification limited onely to a morall
or *free* power: *free* I meane, not as *free* is all one with
morall, but if there follow the coniunction copulatiue
or diſiunctiue, to chooſe whether part of the diſiunction wee pleaſe: and if the verbe [*may*] doe ſometimes
ſignifie a naturall power, as in this, *the fire may burne*
wood or ſtraw, it is by reaſon of the matter, or of the
thing affirmed, or denyed, and not by vertue of the
proper and vſuall ſignification of the verbe [*may*]: And
howſoeuer, when the verbe [*may*] goeth before the
coniunction diſiunctiue [*or*] it doth properly and vſually
ſignifie a choice, freedome, or indifferency to take either part of the diſiunction.

  35. But marke here the cunning (I dare not ſay
fraude, and falſehood of my *Aduerſary*, for that hee
checked mee before for falling very foule vpon him in
ſaying that he affirmed that which was falſe, as though
forſooth all that hee affirmeth, I muſt take for true) in
abuſing both me and his Reader. *For whereas*, ſaith he,
the great myſterie of [may] *is no other, as* Widdrington
himſelfe expoundeth it, but that it ſignifieth in that clauſe
a morall or lawfull, and not a phyſicall, or naturall power,
who is ſo ſenſleſſe, if he be a Latiniſt, that doth not vnder-
ſtand ſo much by the word [poſſunt] *in the Latine tran-*
ſlation of that clauſe, I meane that it ſignifieth a morall
and not a naturall power? Yea and that according to the
axiome of the law, Hoc poſſumus quod iure poſſumus,
wee may doe that, which wee may lawfully doe? *To*
what purpoſe then doth hee abuſe his Latine Reader with
ſuch a long, and impertinent diſcourſe, as he maketh here,
touching the difference betwixt [poſſunt] *in Latine, and*
[may] *in Engliſh, as if in this caſe and queſtion there were*
ſome great diuerſitie.

  36. See now his ſleight. For when I did affirme,
that the difference betwixt the Engliſh word [*may*]
and

and the Latine [*poſſum*] was, that [*poſſum*] doth properly fignifie a power in generall, whether it be naturall or morall, and[*may*]doth properly fignifie a morall
and free power, I fpake of a morall power in generall,
and that briefly without any fuch long difcourfe, as
you haue feene, but when I fpake of this claufe of the
oath, [*may be depofed or murthered*] I did not fpeake
of a morall or lawfull power in generall, but in particular of fuch a morall or lawfull power, which implieth
a freedome to choofe which part of the difiunction we
pleafe. And therefore Mafter *Fitzherbert* faith vntruly abufing therein both me and his Reader, *that I doe*
make no other myſterie of [may] *in this claufe of the oath,*
but that it fignifieth a morall or lawfull, and not a phyſicall
or naturall power. For I make this *myſterie* of [*may*] that
whenfoeuer there followeth it the coniunction [*or*]
as it doth in this claufe of the oath, it doth fignifie not
onely a morall, or lawfull power in generall, but in particular fuch a morall, or lawfull power, which implieth
a free choice to take which part of the difiunction wee
lift. Which if my *Aduerfary* will likewife grant of the
Latine verbe [*poſſum*] we fhall quickly be at an agree-
ment concerning this claufe of the oath, to wit, that
I may truely and lawfully abiure as *hereticall* this damnable doctrine, and *conditionall difiunctiue* pofition, *That*
Princes, which be excommunicated, or depriued by the
Pope, may be depofed, or murthered by their Subiects, or
any other whatfoeuer, although one part onely of the
difiunction be *hereticall.*

   37. But the truth is, that Mafter *Fitzherbert* will not
feeme directly, and in expreffe words to admit, (although by thofe examples of propofitions which hee
himfelfe beneath doth bring it may cleerely be gathered)that the word [*may*] doth in this claufe of the
oath fignifie fuch a morall, or free power, which implyeth a free choice to take which part of the difiunction we pleafe: and therefore hee maketh a long difcourfe

courſe (I dare not ſay *impertinent*) and which hath bin
already anſweared by mee in my *Theologicall Diſputa-*
tion, whereby hee would ſeeme to ouerthrow my anſweare ; and therevpon hee called that diſtinction,
which I made betwixt a *conditionall diſiunctiue* propoſition, which implieth a freedome and condition of the
will to chooſe which part of the diſiunction we liſt, and
an *abſolute diſiunctiue*, which implieth no ſuch choice,
a friuolous euaſion, and *an extrauagant interpretation.*

38, Obſerue now, good Reader, how inſufficiently
this man doth impugne my anſweare. *But let vs ſee,*
ⁿ *Nu.11.*
ſaith hee, ⁿ *What* Widdrington *proueth by all this.*
Hee hath tould vs, that the coniunction [or] *is ſometimes*
taken for the copulatiue [and] *eſpecially when it follow-*
eth the verbe [may] *becauſe then the propoſition is not ab-*
ſolutely diſiunctiue, but conditionall, including a free elec-
tion of either part of the diſiunction, whereof hee alledgeth
ſome examples out of the Fathers, yea out of Card. Bellarmine *himſelfe. But what is this to the purpoſe ? Will*
hee ſay, that becauſe [or] *is vſed in thoſe places for* [and]
ergo it is alwaies ſo vſed? me thinkes hee ſhould be aſhamed
ſo to argue ; for beſides that his argument would be moſt
vicious, hee might be conuinced by infinite examples of
propoſitions , wherein the diſiunctiue coniunction [or] *is*
not taken for the copulatiue [and] *although the verbe*
[may] *goeth before it, yea though there be alſo freedome*
of election to chooſe either part of the diſiunction, as if wee
ſhould ſay, It is impious and hereticall to hold, that God
may be denied , or blaſphemed by his creatures. It is
not lawfull to teach , that a Prieſt may eate or drinke
before he ſay Maſſe. It is folly for a man to thinke, that
he may trauell by Sea or Land, without money. It is a
ſhame for a Souldier to ſay, that hee may yeeld or flie
vpon ſmall occaſion.

• *Nu.12.*
39 *In theſe and infinite other ſuch propoſitions* ᵒ *(which*
might be added if it were needfull) [or] *is not taken for*
[and] *but is* an abſolute diſiunctiue coniunction, *not-*
with-

withstanding that [may] *goe h before it , and that there is also free election to choose whether part of the disiuncti on a man will; yea(which is specially to be obserued for our purpose) whatsoeuer is affirmed of the one part, is also affirmed of the other ; as for example,* It is impious and hereticall , *whethersoeuer a man hold that* God may be denyed, or blasphemed; *It is* as vnlawfull to teach , *that a Priest may drinke , as that* he may eate *before hee say Masse ;* it is no lesse folly to thinke , *that a man may* trauell *by* Sea,*then by land without money*;*It is* no lesse shame for a Souldier to say, *that* he may yeeld , *then that* hee may fly vpon small occasion : *And the very like wee say also of the proposition now in question, to wit, that* [or] *in the words* depofed or murthered , *is no copulatiue, but a meere* difiunctiue coniunction, *and that the doctrine of* depofing *Princes is aiured therein* as impious and hereticall, *no lesse then the doctrine of* murthering *them , notwithstanding that the word* [may] *doth goe before* [or] *and that a man may choose whether part he will of the* difiunction.

40. *So as you see,* p *that neither his examples of propofitions , wherein the* difiunctiue *is taken for the copulatiue, nor his distinction of* absolute *difiunctiues,*and *conditionall doe proue any more, but that fometimes* [or] *is taken for* [and] *and that in fome* difiunctiue propofitions, *wherein the word* [may] *goeth before* [or] *the affirmation is not referred alike to both parts of the* difiunction : *and therefore against vs he hath proued nothing at all, vnlesse hee can make good this inference ,* It is fometimes fo, *ergo* it is alwaies fo, *which I am sure hee will not say for shame. And as for the Latine translation of the oath in* Card. Bellarmine *and* Capellus, *in the which wee reade* deponi et occidi,*where the coniunction* copulatiue[*and*] *is vfed for the* difiunctiue [or] *it little importeth,for that it was an error of him, that translated the same out of the English, which they vnderstood not, and therefore muft needs take it , as it was giuen them.* Thus M *Fitzherb* rt.

P *nu,* 13.

41. But what ſincerity can the *Reader* expect from this mans hands, when in a controuerſie of ſuch great moment, as is this concerning our obedience due to God and Cæſar, hee dealeth ſo corruptly? For *firſt* hee would make his *Reader* beleeue, that I affirme, *the con-iunction diſiunctiue* [or] *in this clauſe of the oath not to be a meere, and abſolute diſiunctiue coniunction, but a copulatiue,* and that the *coniunction* [or] *is taken for* [and] as though I ſhould affirme, that the propoſition is not in very deede a *diſiunctiue,* but a *pure copulatiue propoſition*; and that vnleſſe [or] be *taken* for [and] the ſaid propoſition, *Princes, which be excommunicated or depriued by the Pope, may be depoſed or murthered by their Subiects or any other,* would not be *hereticall* : Whereas I meane no ſuch thing ; neither did I euer ſay, *that* [or] *in this propoſition is taken for* [and] *or that this propoſition is not a true, and proper diſiunctiue propoſition.*

42. But that which I affirmed was, *that* [or] *in this propoſition is equiualent to* [and,] *and that although the propoſition by reaſon of that coniunction* [or] *may ſeeme to be ſuch a pure and abſolute diſiunctiue propoſition,* to the verity whereof, according to the Logicians rule, is onely required, that one part of the diſiunction be true, and to make the whole propoſition falſe and *hereticall* both parts of the diſiunction muſt be falſe and *hereticall, yet according to the common ſenſe and meaning of the words it is not in very deed, and according to our Engliſh phraſe ſuch a pure and abſolute diſiunctiue propoſition, but it is a conditionall diſiunctiue, which importeth a free choice to take which part of the* diſiunction *we pleaſe, which conditionall diſiunctiue propoſition is* equiualent *to a copulatiue, or which is all one, followeth the nature and conditions not of an abſolute and common* diſiunctiue propoſition, *whereof the Logicians treate, but of a copulatiue* propoſition, *to the verity whereof according to the Logicians rule, it is contrariwiſe required, that both parts of the copulatiue, or conditionall diſiunction, be true, and*

to make the whole propofition falfe and hereticall *it fuffi-ceth that one onely part be falfe and* hereticall : *And that therefore in this* conditionall difiunctiue *propofition it maketh all one fenfe,* for as much as concerneth the truth or falfehood of the propofition, *whether the con-iunction copulatiue* [and] *or the difiunctiue* [or] *be vfed,* although the force of the propofition be by the vulgar fort more eafily perceiued, if the coniunction copula-tiue [*and*] then if the difiunctiue [*or*] be vfed.

43. Wherefore I doe not affirme, that the coniunction *difiunctiue* [*or*] in this claufe of the oath is not an *ab-folute difiunctiue* coniunction (for I doe not make two forts of *difiunctiue coniunctions,* to wit, *abfolute* and *con-ditionall*) or that [*or*] in this claufe is *taken* for [*and*] as my *Aduerfary* would perfwade his Reader ; but that which I fay is, that the *propofition* is not an *abfolute difiunctiue propofition,* but a *conditionall difiunctiue,* and which implieth a free power to take which part of the *difiunction* we pleafe, and that therefore, for as much as concerneth the truth or falfhood of the propofition, it is *equiualent* to a *copulatiue propofition,* and followeth the nature and condition of a *copulatiue,* and that it hath the *fame fenfe,* whether the coniunction *copulatiue* [*and*] or the *difiunctiue* [*or*] be vfed.

44. *Secondly,* it is too too cleare, that I did not argue in that abfurd & childifh manner, as my *Adverfary* would make his Reader belieue I doe, *It is fometimes fo, there-fore it is alwaies fo* ; or thus, *the coniunction* difiunctiue [*or*] *is fometime taken for the copulatiue* [*and*] *therefore in this claufe of the Oath it is taken fo.* But I argued thus : The coniunction *difiunctiue* [*or*] when it followeth the verbe [*may*] is not onely *fometimes,* but *vfually* and *commonly* (I did not fay *taken*) but *equiualent* to the coniunction *copulatiue* [*and*] for that then the propofi-tion according to the common fenfe and vnderftan-ding of the words is not an *abfolute difiunctiue,* but a *conditionall difiunctiue propofition,* which includeth a

free condition of the will to chooſe either part of the
diſiunction, and therefore hath the ſame ſenſe, whether the coniunction *difiunctiue*, or the *co:u'atiue* be
vſed: therefore in this clauſe of the oath, *Princes may
be depoſed or murthered by their Subiects*, it ought ſo to
be taken, for that by an expreſſe clauſe wee are bound
to take the Oath and euery part thereof *plainly* and
ſincerely, according to the *common ſenſe and vnderſtanding* of the words. That it is in *common* ſenſe a *con-
d tionall difiunctiue propoſitio*, implying a free election
to take either part of the *d fiunction*, and conſequently *equiualent* to a *copulatiue* propoſition, I proued by
very many examples both in common ſpeech, and in
the lawes of this Realme : and in the end I added, *that
in infinite ſuch like examples the verb*[may]*implyeth a free
power to chuſe either part of the difiunction we pleaſe : neither can there be ſcarcely alleaged any one example* (ſpeaking of affirmatiue propoſitions)*wherein the coniunction*
[or]*immediately following the verbe* [may] *is not ſo taken*.

45   From whence I inferred, that in a *difiunctiue*
propoſition, wherein is implied a *condition* of the will
to chooſe freely either part of the *difiunction*,it maketh
the ſame ſenſe, whether the coniunction *copulatiue*,
[*and*] or the *difiunctiue* [*or*] be vſed: for both of them
doe import a free election to take which part one
pleaſeth, and ſo the coniunction *difiunctiue* hath in
ſenſe the vertue of a *copulatiue*, and the *copulatiue* the
vertue of a *difiunctiue*. And this I confirmed both by
the authority of the ancient Fathers, and alſo of Card.
Bellarmine himſelfe, who doe confound [*and*] with [*or*]
and [*or*] with [*and*] in propoſitions which doe imply a
free election to chooſe which part they will. What
good dealing then is this of my *Aduerſaries* to frame
my argument in that abſurd, and ridiculous manner,
it i ſometimes ſo, ergo it is alwaies ſo, and alſo to corrupt
my words and meaning, as you haue ſeene he hath
done?

46. And albeit I doe remit the Reader to *Felinus Azor*, and *Salas*, where they may see some examples, that a coniunction *disiunctiue*, euen in absolute *disiunctiue* propositions is sometimes *taken* for a *copulatiue*, and a *copulatiue* for a *disiunctiue*, it was not to draw an argument from thence, that therefore either alwaies, or in this clause of the Oath, it was so to be *taken*, but it was onely to shewe, that seeing it is not strange, e-uen in *absolute disiunctiue* propositions, whereof those Authors did chiefely treat, that [*and*] should not one-ly be *equiualent*, but be also taken for [*or*] and [*or*] for [*and*] therefore they ought not to meruaile, that in *conditionall disiunctiues* [*or*] should be, I doe not say *taken*, but *equiualent* to [*and*] and [*and*] to [*or*]. But the argument, which I brought to prooue, that in this clause of the Oath, the coniunction *disiunctiue* [*or*] is *equiualent* to the *copulatiue* [*and*] was taken from the plaine and vsuall sense of our English phrase, and from the common vnderstanding of our English lawes, wher-in the coniunction *disiunctiue* [*or*] following the verbe [*may*] doth commonly imply a free election to take which part of the *disiunction* we please, and which con-sequently is *equiualent* to a *copulatiue*, therefore in this clause of the Oath, which I am bound to take accor-ding to the *common sense* of the words, it ought so to be taken : This was my argument.

47 *Thirdly*, obserue how inconsiderately M. *Fitz-herbert* bringeth here foure examples of propositions to confute my answere, which neuer thelesse doe most clearely confirme the same. For in all of them the con-iunction [*or*] is *equiualent* to the *copulatiue* [*and*] and it maketh all one sense whether [*and*] or [*or*] be vsed. As for example, *God may be denyed or blasphemed by his Creatures. A Priest may eat or drinke before hee say Masse. A man may trauell by Sea or by land without mo-ny. A Soldier may yeeld or fly vpon small occasion.* In all these foure examples, wherein my *Aduersary* him-selfe

ſelfe granteth a freedome of election to chooſe whether part of th e diſiunction a man will, to be implyed,
the coniunction diſiunctiue [*or*] for as much as concerneth the truth or falſhood of the Propoſitions, is
equiualent to the copulatiue [*and*], and the propoſitions haue all one ſenſe: whether the coniunction [*and*],
or the coniunction [*or*] be vſed: And ſo it is all one ſenſe
whether we ſay that *God may bee denyed or blaſphemed
by his Creatures,* or that *God may be denyed and blaſphemed by his Creatures,* that *a Prieſt may eat or drinke before hee ſay Maſſe,* or that *a Prieſt may eat and drinke before hee ſay Maſſe,* and ſo of the reſt: For the ſenſe of
them all is, that they may chooſe this part or that part
of the *diſiunction,* or this part *and* that part of the *diſiunction,* as they will: And ſo the ſenſe of the firſt propoſition is, that it is in the free power and choice of
Creatures *to denie,* or *blaſpheme God,* or *to denie God*
and alſo *to blaſpheme him* if they will: and of the ſecond
that it is in the free power of a Prieſt *to eat* or *to drinke,*
or *to eat,* and, if he pleaſe, *to drinke before he ſay Maſſe,*
and ſo of the reſt. By which it is euident, that in all
of them it maketh the ſame ſenſe, whether the coniunction [*and*] or the coniunction [*or*] bee vſed: and ſo
in all of them the coniunction *diſiunctiue* is *equiualent*
to a *copulatiue,* and the *copulatiue* to a *diſiunctiue.*

    48 Laſtly albeit *that which* M. *Fitzherbert doth ſpe-
cially obſerue for his purpoſe,* be true, to wit, *that in all
thoſe foure examples, which he hath brought, whatſoeuer is
affirmed of the one part of the diſiunction is alſo affirmed
of the other, notwithſtanding that there be alſo free election to chooſe which part of the diſiunction a man will:* as
for example, *it is impious and hereticall whether ſoeuer
a man hold that God may bee denyed, or that hee may bee
blaſphemed by his Creatures,* it is as vnlawfull to teach
*that a Prieſt may drinke as that he may eat before hee ſay
Maſſe, and ſo of the reſt:* from whence he would inferre the like, that alſo in this clauſe of the Oath, the
                           doctrine

of the *Oath* as *impious and hereticall, &c.* are confuted.

31

doctrine of *depofing* Princes is no leffe abiured as *hereticall* then the doctrine of *murthering them:* neuerthelefle this his obferuation maketh nothing at all for *his purpofe*, vnlefic it be to bewray his owne ignorance, and want of Logick, whiles hee doth not perceiue what is truely affirmed of both parts of an *hypotheticall* propofition *by vertue of the forme*, and what by *vertue onely of the matter*. For although in all thofe foure propofitions, which he hath brought, it bee true that the fame *impiety, herefie, vnlawfulnes, folly* or *fhame*, which is affirmed of the one part of the difiunction, be alfo affirmed of the other, yet this is not true *by vertue of the forme of* the propofition confifting of a difiunctiue coniunction, which implyeth a choice to take which part of the *diftunction* a man will; but it is true *by reafon onely of the matter*, for that the fame thing which is affirmed of the *whole* or entire *difiunctiue* propofition, may bee alfo affirmed *feuerally* of either part of the *difiunction* : For it is *hereticall* to hold, *that God may be denyed by his Creatures*, and likewife it is alfo *hereticall* to hold, *that God may be blafphemed by his Creatures*, and fo of the reft.. But let him alter the *matter*, and keepe the fame *forme*, that is the fame difiunctiue coniunction, which implyeth a free choice to take which part of the *difiunction* a man will, and then hee will quickly perceiue how fowly hee is miftaken, and how infufficiently he hath confuted my *Anfwer*.

49 As for example, let vs alter the *matter* of his foure propofitions, and keepe the fame *forme*, that is keep the fame difiunctiue coniunction *implying a choice to take which part of the difiunction one wil*, & fay, *that it is impious and hereticall to hold, that God may be honoured or blafphemed by his creatures. It is not lawfull to teach that a Prieft may fleepe or eat before hee fay Maffe. It is folly for a man to thinke that hee may trauell by Sea or by Land with the like danger. It is a fhame for a Captaine to fay, that hee may fight or flye, when his Band is affaul-*

ted

ted by the Enemy. All theſe and infinite other ſuch propoſitions'(which might bee added if it were needfull)
are true by reaſon of one onely part of the *diſiunction*:
And the reaſon is generall and common to all *conditio-*
nall diſiunctiue propoſitions: for that a *diſiunctiue* propoſition which implyeth a free election to take which
part of the diſiunction one pleaſeth, is, I doe not ſay
ſometimes, but *alwaies equiualent to a copulatiue, and*
followeth the nature of a *copulatiue*, to the verity
whereof, as I haue ſhewed before, it is required that
both parts be true,and to make the *whole* or entire propoſition to bee falſe and *hereticall*, it ſufficeth,that one
onely part bee falſe and *hereticall*: and that therefore it
doth not follow by force of the *forme*,nature,and conditions of a *conditionall diſiunctiue propoſition*, but onely
by reaſon of the *matter*, that *whatſoeuer is affirmed of*
the one part of the diſiunction *is alſo affirmed of the other.*

50 Seeing therefore that this propoſition, *Subiects*
may depoſe or murther their Prince being excommunica-
ted or depriued by the Pope, implieth *a free election* to
chooſe which part of the *diſiunction* we pleaſe,and it is
hereticall to affirme, *that Subiects may murther ſuch a*
Prince, I may truely,lawfully, and without any periurie abiure that propoſition as *hereticall*, although the
doctrine onely of *murthering* ſuch Princes ſhould be
hereticall,and not the doctrine of *depoſing* them,where-
of neuertheleſſe wee will treat beneath q. So as you
ſee, that none of all M. *Fitzherberts* examples maketh
for him, but all are flat againſt him, and that it is not
true, that I doe argue in this ridiculous manner, *It is*
ſometimes ſo, therefore it is alwaies ſo, or *therefore it is*
now ſo, which were to argue *ex puris particularibus*,
from pure particular propoſitious, which kind of arguing
all Logicians account to be very vicious : But I argue
thus: *The words are commonly taken ſo*, ⬥*erefore I, who*
am bound to take the oath, and euery clauſe thereof accor-
ding to the common ſenſe of the words, am bound to take
this

q *Nu.*106.
& ſeq.

this clause of the oath so, which manner of arguing to be good, I am sure he will not deny for shame.

51. But my *Aduersary* little perceiueth, how hee himselfe falleth into that vice of arguing, whereof he vntruely accuseth me, to wit, *It is sometimes so, therefore it is alwaies so,* or *therefore it is now so.* For he pretendeth to proue, that because in those foure conditionall *disiunctiue* propositions, and many such like, *whatsoeuer is affirmed of the one part of the disiunction, is also affirmed of the other, notwithstanding that there be also free election to choose whether part of the disiunction a man will,* which is onely true in some particular propositions, and that onely by reason of the *matter* and not by *vertue* of the *forme* and quality of the *conditionall disiunctiue* proposition, *therefore in this clause of the oath,* because *hereticall* is affirmed of the doctrine to *murther* Princes, it must also be affirmed of the doctrine to *depose* them, which is to argue *ex puris particularibus, from pure particular propositions,* and is all one to say, *it is sometimes so, therefore it is now so.* But my manner of *arguing* is from a *vniuersall* proposition to inferre a *particular,* to wit, that because in *euery conditionall* disiunctiue proposition *implying* a choice, &c, by vertue of the *forme,* it is sufficient to make the whole proposition false and *hereticall,* that one onely part of the disiunction be false and *hereticall,* and consequently it is sufficient, that *hereticall* be affirmed of the one part, and not of the other, although sometimes by reason of the *matter* it may be affirmed of both, *therefore in this particular disiunctiue proposition,* Princes being excommunicated or depriued by the Pope may be deposed or murthered by their Subiects or any other, *it is sufficient to make the whole proposition hereticall, that one onely part of the disiunction be hereticall,* and that therefore the *doctrine* to *murther* such Princes may be abiured as *hereticall,* without abiuring as *hereticall* the doctrine to *depose* them.

F   52 And

52. And what man is there ſo ſimple, who may not preſently perceiue, that in the very ſame manner, and by the ſame foure examp'es which my Aduerſary bringeth to impugne my interpretation of thoſe words [*depoſed or murthered*] hee might argue, if the words were, [*depoſed and murthered*] and in thoſe his foure examples of propoſitions [*or*] were changed into [*and*] wherby they would be made *copulatiue*, and not *diſiun-* *ctiue* propoſitions ? For then alſo whatſoeuer is affirmed of the one part, would alſo be affirmed of the other : *As it is impious and hereticall to hold , that God may be denied and blaſphemed by his creatures . It is vnlawfull to teach, that a Prieſt may eate, and drinke before hee ſay Maſſe*, and ſo of the reſt : And yet if he haue any skill in Logike , as in truth I thinke hee hath but little, hee will be aſhamed to inferre from thence, that therefore in *copulatiue* propoſitions , *whatſoeuer is affirmed of the one part is alſo affirmed of the other* : for that in a falſe and *hereticall* copulatiue propoſition, it ſufficeth, accor-ding to the Logicians rule, that one onely part be falſe and *hereticall* : which plainly ſheweth how vicioully he confuteth my interpretation of thoſe words [*depoſed or murthered*] *ex puris particularibus , from ſome parti-cular examples of propoſitions* , which are onely true by reaſon of the *matter*, not regarding what is generally, and alwaies required by *vertue of the* forme, and nature of the *conditionall diſiunctiue* propoſition to make the whole propoſition true, or falſe, of faith or hereti call, howſoeuer truth, falſhood, or hereſie may be affirmed *ſeuerally* of one only, or of both parts of the *diſiunction*.

53. And whereas M. *Fitzherbert* affirmeth , that Card. *Bellarmine* , and *Capellus* were in the tranſlation of thoſe words [depoſed and murthered] deceiued by the error of him, who tranſlated the Oath out of Engliſh into Latin , I am content to take it at this time for an anſwere , for that I doe not relie vpon their au-thority in this poynt , but vpon the common vnder-ſtanding

ſtanding of all men, who in a *conditionall diſiunctiue*
propoſition make [*or*] *equiualent* to [*and*] and [*and*] to
[*or*]. Neuertheleſſe this I muſt needs ſay, that it might
be perchance an error of the *Printer*, which alſo if it had
bene, me thinkes that Card. *Bellarmine*, *Capellus*,
or *Fa. Suarez* would haue noted it among the errors,
if they had accounted it for any great errour, or to haue
cleane altered the ſenſe of the propoſition, as this
man would make it; but that it ſhould be an error of
the *Tranſlator* I can hardly be perſwaded, And my
reaſon is, becauſe it ſeemeth, that there was but one
onely *tranſlation* of the Oath out of Engliſh, which is
extant in publike writings, from which all thoſe writers, who haue ſet downe the oath in Latin, haue taken it, as *firſt* the *Pope* in his *Breue*, then Card. *Bellarmine*, *Fa. Gretzer*, *Capellus*, and now laſtly *Suarez*.
For that in none of all theſe Writers the tranſlation
of the Oath is in any point different, either ſo much as
in any one word, or the placing of a word, except in
thoſe words [*depoſed or murthered*] which is morally
impoſſible, if there had bene diuers tranſlations. Now
in the *Popes Breue*, and likewiſe in *Gretzer*, and in one
Edition of Card. *Bellarmines* booke againſt his *Maieſties Apologie*, we read [*depoſed or murthered*] but in
other Editions of the ſame booke, in *Capellus*, and now
laſtly in *Suarez*, we read [*depoſed and murthered*] which
is a ſigne, that is was an error rather of the *Printer*, then
of the *Tranſlator*, & alſo that the error was not great, &
much regarded by them, for that the ſenſe of the propoſition is all one whether wee read [*depoſed or murthered*] or [*depoſed and murthered*] it being a *conditionall diſiunctiue* propoſition, implyihg a free choiſe to
take both parts of the *diſiunction*, which therefore
for as much as concerneth the truth or falſhood of
the propoſition, hath the ſame ſenſe, whether the
coniunction copulatiue [*and*] or the diſiunctiue [*or*] be
vſed, as I haue ſhewed before.

F 2 54. But

54 But now *forsooth* M. *Fitzherbert* will cleare all this difficulty, and make it manifest out of my owne grounds, that the doctrine of the *d position* of Princes, is abiured in the Oath as *impious* and *hereticall*, no lesse then the doctrine of *murthering* them; for hitherto he hath so cleared the difficulty, as you haue seene, that I could not haue desired more cleare and fit *examples* of *propositions*, to confirme my interpretation of those words [*deposed or murthered*] then which he himselfe hath brought to impugne it. Thus therefore he writeth. r

r Nu. 14. 15 16,

·55. *But to cleare all this difficulty, and to make it manifest, that the doctrine of the* deposition *of Princes is abiured in the Oath* as impious and hereticall, *no lesse then the supposed doctrine of* murthering *them, I shall need no other testimony or proofe thereof, then such as may be taken from the Oath it selfe, considered euen according to those rules, which* Widdrington *himselfe hath laid downe for the interpretation of it in the very first chapter of his* Theological disputation, f *where he professeth to approue, & follow the doctrine of* Suarez t *in that point, as being conforme to the common opinion of Lawyers and Diuines. Now then he teacheth there out of* Suarez, *that if there be any doubt or question concerning the sense of a law, or any part thereof, three thinges are specially to be pondered for the exposition of it, to wit,* the words of the Law, the minde or intention of the Law-maker, and the reason or end of the Law; *and the same he saith are also to be considered for the clearing of any difficulty or doubt in the Oath.*

f Nu 7. t Lib. 6. de leg. cap. 1.

56. *As for the* words of the Law (*and consequently of the Oath*) *he saith, that they are to be vnderstood according to their proper, and vsuall signification; and the reason is, saith* Suarez, *because words are so to be vsed in common speech, and much more in Lawes, which ought to be cleare; but it is euident, that the words of the clause now in question, being taken in their vsuall and proper*
signification

signification, doe make clearely for vs, wherein I dare bouldly appeale to the iudgement of any discreet Reader; for albeit such a sense, as Widdrington imagineth, may be picked or rather wringed out of those words, yet no man at the first sight will, or can reasonably conceiue any thing else thereby, but that either part of the disiunctiue clause is abiured alike.

57. For although the coniunction [or] is sometimes taken for a copulatiue, yet it is commonly a disiunctiue, and hath that signification diuers times euen in this oath; as any man may see, that list to obserue it: As for example (to omit all the rest which might be vrged to this purpose) the very next words before deposed or murthered, are excomunicated or depriued, wherein it is cleare, that [or] hath the ordinarie and proper signification of a disiunctiue, giuing to vnderstand, that whether Princes be onely excommunicated, or depriued also of their right to their States by the Pope, it is impious and hereticall doctrine to teach, that they may be either deposed or murthered. Also the same is to be noted in the words immediatly following, to wit, by their Subiects or any other, wherein it is signified, that neither Subiects, nor yet any other may depose or murther Princes excommunicated or depriued by the Pope: and the like may bee exemplified in the other clauses of the Oath, at least thirty times, for so often I doe find the coniunction [or] therein, and alwaies vsed properly for a disiunctiue, as also I dare say it is vsed in like maner, and in the same sense, aboue a hundred times in the same Statute. Thus M. Fitzherbert.

58 Now you shall see how well he hath cleered this difficulty. His Argument if it bee reduced to a syllogisticall forme is this. The words of euery law (and consequently of this Oath) are according to Suarez, whose doctrine I approue heerein, to bee taken in their proper and vsuall signification, but those words, [deposed or murthered, &c.] according to their proper and vsuall signification doe signifie, that the supposed Doctrine of murthe-

F 3   ring

ring Princes , *and of* depoſing them , *is abiured alike*, *therefore in the aforeſaid clauſe* , *I abhorre* , *deteſt and abiure,&c. the doctrine of* depoſing, *and of* murthering *Princes which bee excommunicated,&c. are both abiured as hereticall.* The *Minor* hee proueth two wayes , *firſt* by appealing to the iudgement of euery diſcreet man, who at the *firſt fight* can reaſonably conceiue nothing elſe, but that either part of that *diſiunctiue* clauſe is abiured alike . *Secondly* for that although the Coniunction [*or*] bee ſometimes taken for a *copulatiue* , yet it is commonly a *diſiunctiue* , and hath the ordinary and proper ſignification of a *diſiunctiue*, and in this oath , wherein it is found at leaſt thirty times , and in the ſame ſtatute aboue a hundred times , it is alwaies vſed properly for a *diſiunctiue coniunction.*

59 But firſt obſerue , good Reader, thoſe words of my Aduerſary,[*the ſuppoſed doctrine of murthering Princes:*] For a little beneath ᵘ hee affirmeth, *that murder implyeth alwaies an vnlawfull act, yea and a mortall ſinne,* whereby hee doth ſeeme to inſinuate , that the *Oath* ſpeaketh onely of *murther* in this ſenſe, and *ſuppoſeth* that ſome Catholikes doe teach, that it is lawfull to *murther* Princes, as *murther implyeth an vnlawfull act,* whereas no Catholike can bee ſo ignorant as to imagine, much leſſe to teach , that it is lawfull to doe an vnlawfull act, or to commit a mortall ſinne,ſeeing that *God* himſelfe cannot giue authority to *murther* any man, as *murther implyeth an vnlawfull act , or a mortall ſinne:* Neither did his *Maieſty,*and the *Parliament* take *murther* only in this ſenſe, but by the word [*murthered*] they vnderſtood,that all killing of Princes excommunicated or depriued by the Pope, was directly and abſolutely an vnlawfull act,and they did ſuppoſe, that ſome Catholikes taught this doctrine,that the Pope,in order to ſpirituall good, might giue leaue to take away the liues of wicked and hereticall Princes by all thoſe waies either publike, or ſecret and vnawares, by which
temporall

temporall Princes, in order to temporall good, haue authority to take away the liues of rebellious subiects, who either cannot at all, or at least cannot without great preiudice to the publike good of the State, bee publikely apprehended or condemned.

60 And I would to God that this doctrine, were onely a *supposed doctrine*, and had neuer beene taught or approued by any Catholike. But alas it cleerely followeth from the doctrine and grounds for the Pop's power to depriue Princes of all their temporall right and authority, as I most euidently did demonstrate in my *Apologie* [x], to which my Argument D. *Schulckenius* [y] onely answereth with *a transeat*, or *let it passe as impertinent to the matter*; and the same is sufficiently confirmed by the same D. *Schulckenius* [z] in other places of his booke, and before him by *Gregorius de Valentia* [a], *Schioppius* [b], and now lately by *Suarez* [c], for which cause principally his book was by a sollemne decree of the *Parliament* publikely *condemned and burnt at Paris by the hangman*, as containing *damnable, pernicious, scandalous and seditious propositions, tending to the subuersion of States, and to induce the subiects of Kings and Soueraigne Princes, and others, to attempt against their sacred persons*; neither is that Decree which was publ shed and printed by the *Kings authority*, as yet recalled, or *Suarez* booke permitted by authority to be sold at *Paris*, howsoeuer some fauourers of the *Iesuits* doe not sticke to affirme heere among the common people. Yea and M. *Fitzherbert* himselfe, although *hee will not (forsooth) meddle with the liues of Princes*, yet boldly affirmeth, [d] *that the Pope hath power to take away my life, and hath power ouer the goods and liues of all Christians*, which wordes beeing generall, and including all Christians, and consequently Christian Princes, according to his doctrine, as you shall see beneath, [e] doe cleerely shew what his opin on and iudgement is in this poynt, touching the *killing* also

x *nu.* 43. & *seq.*
y *Pag.* 144. *I arswer* (saith hee) *that so ma_ny wordes are needtesse, for whither al these doe tend euery man seeth, nei_ther is it hard to solue the Ar_guments, let them passe as not making to the matter.*
z *Pag.* 413. 450.
a *Secunda se_cundæ* Disp. 1. q 12. punc. 2. *assertio secuda_*
b *In his Ecclesi_asticus cap.* 42. pag 140.
c *In defens.fidei lib.* 6. *cap.* 4. *nu.* 18. 20.
d *Cap.* 2. nu. 15. 16. 17.
e *Part.* 3. *cap.* 9. 10.

alſo, or murdering of Chriſtian Princes.

61. Now to his argument. Firſt therefore his *Maior*
propoſition I doe wi'lingly grant, to wit, that if there
be any doubt or queſtion concerning the ſenſe of any
law, or any part thereof, (and conſequently for the
cleering of any difficulty, or doubt in this oath) three
things are ſpecial'y to be pondered for the expoſition
of it, *the words of the law*, *the mind or intention of the*
law-maker, and the reaſon or end of the law; and that the
words of the law, and conſequently of this oath, are
to be vnderſtood in their *proper and vſuall ſignification*,
as alſo by a peculiar clauſe it is expreſsly ordained
therein; And of this his *Maior* propoſition no man
maketh doubt.

62. But his *Minor* propoſition I vtterly deny: and
to his firſt proofe thereof, I anſwere as eaſily, but more
fully with the like words, which hee himſelfe vſeth.
For I affirme, that the contrary is euident, and that the
words of this clauſe now in queſtion do make clearely
for vs, wherein I dare boldly appeale to the iudgement
of any learned and diſcreet Reader, for that no man of
any learning or iudgement, who knoweth the difference betwixt an *abſolute* and *conditionall diſiunctiue*
propoſition, which implieth a free choice to take either
part of the diſiunction, I doe not ſay, *at the firſt ſight*,
but after mature diliberation, and a diligent examination of all the words of this clauſe, and of the natures
of an *abſolute* and *conditionall diſiunctiue* propoſition
will, or can reaſonably conceiue, that in a *conditionall*
diſiunctiue propoſition, which implyeth a freedome to
chooſe which part of the *diſiunction* one will, as is the
propoſition which is now in queſtion, both parts of the
diſiunction muſt be abiured alike, for that to make the
whole *conditionall diſiunctiue* propoſition to be *hereti-*
call, or to be abiured as *hereticall*, it ſufficeth that one
onely part of the *diſiunction* be *hereticall*: as I may tru
ly and lawfully abiure this propoſition as *hereticall*,

God

God may be honoured or blasphemed by his creatures, or, which is all one, *it is in the free choice of creatures, to honour or to blaspheme God,* wherein one onely part of the *disiunction* is *hereticall,* and the other of faith, and so both parts of the *disiunction* are not abiured as *hereticall,* although the *whole,* and entire proposition be *hereticall,* and may therefore be truely abiured as *hereticall.*

63. What any learned man, but especially the vulgar sort of Catholikes (considering the different grounds of *Catholikes,* and *Protestants* in points of Religion, and that the oath was made by a *Protestant Parliament,* and that the *title* of the *Act,* wherein the taking thereof is commanded, *is for the better discouering and repressing of Popish Recusants,* and such like reasons) may *at the first sight* conceiue of the lawfulnesse thereof, as also what they may *at the first sight* conceiue of the sense of this clause, which is now in question (considering that the coniunction *disiunctiue* [*or*] doth more vsually make an *absolute disiunctiue,* then a *conditionall disiunctiue* proposition, for that where once it followeth the verbe [*may*] and consequently maketh a *conditionall disiunctiue* proposition, which is *equiualent* to a *copulatiue,* aboue a hundred times at least it doth not follow the verbe [*may*] but maketh an *absolute disiunctiue* proposition, and withall not examining the difference betwixt an *absolute* and a *conditionall disiunctiue* proposition) may, I say, *at the first sight* conceiue of the esens and meaning of this clause of the Oath, is no sufficient Argument to proue that this clause or any other of the Oath, is, according to the true, proper, and vsuall vnderstanding of the wordes in very deed vnlawfull. For many things may seeme to bee so *at the first sight,* which after a second reuiew, and a more diligent examination of the matter do seeme to be far otherwise.

64 My *Aduersary* following therein Card, *Bellarmine,*

G   *Gretzer,*

Gretzer, Leſſius & *Suarez*, did *at the firſt ſight* conceiue,
that the *Popes* power to *excommunicate* the *King* was
denyed in this Oath, but *at the ſecond ſight* , and vpon
better conſideration, hee hath, as it ſeemes, perceiued
his error and ouer ſight, for that being charged therewith by me, hee hath paſſed it ouer altogether with
ſilence. Many alſo of our Engliſh Catholikes did *at
the firſt ſight* conceiue, that the Popes power to abſolue from ſinnes, to grant Pardons and indulgences,
and to diſpenſe in oathes, was denyed in this oath, taking ſome colour or pretence from thoſe words, *abſolue* , *pardons* and *diſpenſations* , but after the *ſecond
ſight* they ſaw that there was no ſuch thing , as *at the
firſt ſight* they conceiued. Many ſuch like exceptions
I could alleadge, which *at the firſt ſight* ſome conceiued againſt the Oath, which vpon the ſecond review,
and after a more diligent conſideration appeared to
haue no firme ground to rely vpon.

65 But if any learned or diſcreet Catholick man
will make a ſecond review, and a more diligent examination of the Oath, and of all the clauſes and wordes
contained therein, and wil alſo duly conſider (which
I obſerued in my *Theologicall diſputation* f) the difference betwixt the opinion, and the intention of his
Maieſty, and that although his *Maieſty* , and the
Parliament be of opinion , that the Pope hath no power to excommunicate his *Maieſty* , yet they did not intend to binde Catholiks to acknowledge ſo much in
this Oath , and that although the title of that Act,
wherein many lawes were enacted againſt Catholiques touching points of Religion , for the which it
might well be called an *Act for the better diſcouering
and repreſſing of* Popiſh *Recuſants,* euen for points of
Religion, yet the *Preamble* or *Title* to the particular
Act , wherein the *Oath* is eſtabliſhed, is, *to make a better triall how his* Maieſties *Subiects ſtand affected towards his* Maieſtie *concerning points of their loyalty,* and
due

f *Cap.* 4. *ſec.* 3

due obedience : And that his *Maiesty* and the *Parliament*
did also publikly declare, that they onely intended to
exact of Catholiques by this oath a profeffion of that
temporall allegiance, and ciuill obedience, which all
Subiects doe by the Law of God and nature owe to
their temporall Prince : And to make a diftinction, not
betwixt *Catholiques,* and *Proteftants,* touching points of
Religion, but betwixt *Catholiques* & *Catholiques* touching points of opinion; and betwixt *ciuilly obedient Catho-*
likes and of quiet difpofition, and in all other thinges good
Subiects, and fuch other Catholikes, as in their hearts
maintained the like bloody maximes, that the Powder
Traitors did: And that therefore the particular *Act*
concerning the *Oath* it felfe, might very well haue
beene intituled, although it was not, *An Act for the*
better difcouering and repreffing of Popifh Recufants, not
in generall, but of fuch, *as were caried away with the*
like fanaticall zeale, and bloody maximes that the powder
Traitors were. If any man, I fay, will duely confider
thefe thinges, and the other obiections and anfwers,
which I propounded in my *Theologicall difputation,*
and in my *Appendix* to *Suarez*, I dare boldly appeale
to his iudgment herein, for that no man will, or can
reafonably (the premifes confidered) conceiue any
forcible or conuincing reafon, for which Englifh Catholiques are bound in confcience to refufe the Oath.

66 And as for this claufe which is now in queftion,
it is euident (the difference betwixt an *abfolute dif-*
iunctiue, and a *conditionall difiunctiue* propofition being duely confidered) that the words being taken in
their proper and vfuall fignification, doe make clearly
for me, wherein I dare bouldly appeale to the iudgement of any difcreet Reader. For albeit fuch a fenfe
as this man imagineth, may be conceiued at *the firft*
fight, for the reafon aforefaid, yet no man after due
confideration, and who obferueth the difference betwixt an *abfolute*, and a *conditionall difiunctiue* propofi-

G 2

tion, and perceiueth, that to make a *conditionall diſ-iunctiue* propoſition, which followeth the nature of a *copulatiue*, to be *hereticall*, and to be abiured as *he eti-call*, it is ſufficient that one onely part thereof be *h re-ticall*, and that therefore both parts of the *diſiunction* are not of neceſſity to be abiured alike, will or can rea-ſonably conceiue, that both parts of that *conditionall diſ-iunctiue* clauſe [*may be depoſed or murthered*] are by ver-tue of the *diſiunctiue* coniunction [*or*] to be abiured alike.

57 To the ſecond proofe of his *Minor* propoſition I anſwere, that he contendeth, to vſe his owne words, *de lana caprina*, and laboureth in vaine to prooue that, which I doe not deny. For I make no queſtion, but that [*or*] in this clauſe of the Oath [*depoſed or murthered*] is a *diſiunctiue coniunction*, and hath the ordinary and proper ſignification of a *diſiunctiue coniunction*, But that which I affirme is, that although in this clauſe of the oath it be truely and properly a *diſiunctiue coniunct-ion*, yet becauſe it immediately followeth the verbe [*may*] it maketh ſuch a *diſiunctiue propoſition*, which implyeth a free choice to take either part of the *diſ-iunction*, and which conſequently being not an *abſo-lute*, but a *conditionall diſiunctiue* propoſition, is *equi-ualent* to a *copulatiue*, and not to an *ordinary*, or *abſo-lute diſiunctiue* propoſition.

68 And although the coniunction *diſiunctiue* [*or*] doth alſo more commonly, as I obſerued before, make an *abſolute diſiunctiue*, then a *conditionall diſiunctiue* propoſition, for that where you ſhall finde it once to follow the verbe [*may*] and ſo to make a *conditionall diſiunctiue* propoſition, you ſhall finde it aboue a hun-dred times not to follow the verbe [*may*] and ſo not to make a *conditionall*, but an *abſolute* diſiunctiue pro-poſition, and in this very Oath, where the coniunction [*or*] is found to be taken affirmatiuely about ſixeteene times, and not to follow the verbe [*may*] (for almoſt in

all

all other places of the oath it is taken negatiuely, and is all one with [*nor*] or [*neither*] yet once onely or twice at the moſt it followeth the verbe [*may*] and maketh a *conditionall* diſiunctiue propoſition : Neuertheleſſe this I ſay is certaine and not to be called in queſtion, that *whenſoeuer* the coniunction diſiunctiue [*or*] doth make a conditionall diſiunctiue propoſition, which im-plyeth a free choiſe to take which part of the diſiunct-ion we pleaſe, as it doth in this clauſe of the oath, neither doth my *Aduerſarie* deny, but rather as you haue ſeene, ſuppoſeth the ſame, it is *equiualent* to a *copulatiue* propoſition, and followeth the nature of a *copulatiue*, to the verity whereof, according to the ap-proued rule of the Logicians, it is required that both parts be true, and to make the whole propoſition to be falſe and *hereticall*, it ſufficeth that one onely part be falſe and *hereticall*, which contrariwiſe falleth out in an *abſolute*, or *ordinarie diſiunctiue* propoſition.

69. Vnleſſe therefore my *Aduerſary* can proue, either that the coniunction [*or*] when it immediatly followeth the verbe [*may*] doth not commonly and v-ſually make a *conditionall diſiunctiue* propoſition, im-plying a free choiſe to take which part of the diſtunct-ion one pleaſe, which hitherto he hath not proued, but rather ſuppoſed both by thoſe foure examples of propoſitions, and alſo in this clauſe of the oath, as you haue ſeene, that the coniunction [*or*] implyeth ſuch a choiſe, or elſe that a *conditionall diſiunctiue* propoſition which implieth ſuch a choiſe, doth not *alwaies* follow the nature and condition of a *copulatiue* propoſition, for as much as concerneth the truth or falſhood there-of, which he will neuer be able to proue, for that a *conditionall diſiunctiue* propoſition, implyeth a free choiſe to take, if we pleaſe, both parts of the *diſiunct-ion*, and euery Logician knoweth, that the word [*v-terque, both*] ſuppoſeth *diſtributiuely*, and is reſolued by the coniunction *copulatiue*, as, *to take both*, ſignifi-

G 3   eth

eth *to take this and that*, and not onely *this or that*; it is
euident that he ſaith nothing to the purpoſe, neither
doth he impugne my anſwere, but fighteth in vaine
with his owne ſhadow.

70. Wherefore M. *Fitzherbert* perceiuing at laſt,
that this ſecond proofe of his *Minor* propoſition was
little to the purpoſe, and did not confute my anſwer:
concerning the *conditionall diſiunctiue* propoſition,
he would now ſeeme to ſay ſomething to the purpoſe,
(but in very deed ſaith nothing as you ſhall ſee) and to
cleane ouerthrowe that *diſtinction*, which before he
called a *friuolous euaſion*, and an *extrauagant interpre-*
tation, and now he calleth it a *ſhift*, which neuertheleſſe by his former diſcourſe, and examples of propoſitions, as you haue ſeene, and now againe he doth

g Nu. 17.

clearly confirme. For thus he writeth. g *And if* Widdrington *doth flye here to his former ſhift, and ſay, that*
in the other clauſes [or] *is an abſolute diſiunctiue,* and
that in the words [depoſed or murthered] *it is a conditi-*
onall, becauſe the verbe [may] *going before it, doth de-*
note or ſignifie a free election to chooſe either part, he is
to vnderſtand, that the ſame may alſo be ſaid of other
clauſes in the Oath, wherein neuertheleſſe it is manifeſt.
that [or] *is a pure diſiunctiue, and that whatſoeuer is af-*
firmed of one part of the diſiunction, is alſo affirmed of the
other: As for example &c.

71. But obſerue *good Reader, firſt* how this man ſtill
harpeth vpon the ſame ſtring, to make thee belieue
that I affirme the coniunction *diſiunctiue* [or] in the
words [may be depoſed or murthered] not to be a *pure*,
or *abſolute*, but a *conditionall diſiunctiue coniunction*,
whereas I doe make no ſuch diſtinction of an *abſolute*,
and conditionall diſiunctiue coniunction, but onely of an
abſolute, and *conditionall diſiunctiue propoſition*. For that
which I affirme is, that although the coniunction [or]
in thoſe words [may be depoſed or murthered] be a *pure*,
true, and if we may call it ſo, an *abſolute diſiunctiue*

coniunction, yet in them, and *whenfoeuer* elfe it immediately followeth the verbe [*may*] it maketh, as I haue
often faid, according to the common and vfuall fignification of our Englifh phrafe, fuch a *difiunctiue propofition*, which implyeth a free choife to take both parts,
or either part of the difiunction if we pleafe, for which
caufe I call it a *conditionall difiunctiue propofition*, which
in very deede, for as much as concerneth the truth or
falfhood of the propofition, followeth the nature of
a *copulatiue* propofition, and not of the *common difiunctiue* propofition, whereof the Logicians treate, which
therefore I call an *abfolute difiunctiue* propofition, for
that it implyeth no fuch freedome of election, or condition of the will, to choofe, if we pleafe, either part
of the difiunction: the nature and condition of which
abfolute, or common *difiunctiue* propofition, is fuch,
that to the truth thereof, according to the receiued
doctrine of the Logicians, it is fufficient, that one onely part of the *difiunction* be true, although the other
be moft falfe and *hereticall*, and to make fuch an *abfolute difiunctiue* propofition to be falfe and *hereticall*, it
is neceffarie that both parts be falfe and *hereticall*: As
for example, this *difiunctiue* propofition, *God is iuft*, *or
vniuft*, is a moft true and certaine propofition, although
the former part of the *difiunction* only be true, and of
faith, and the fecond part be falfe and *hereticall*.

72 But contrarywife it hapneth in a *copulatiue* propofition, for to make it true, both parts muft be true,
but to make it falfe and *hereticall*, it fufficeth that one
onely part be falfe and *hereticall*; and therefore this
propofition, *God is iuft*, *and vniuft*, is a moft falfe and
hereticall propofition, although the former part of the
propofition be moft true, and of faith. And if perchance both parts of the *copulatiue* propofition be falfe
and *hereticall*, as in this, *God is vniuft, and vnmercifull*,
this is not by reafon of the *forme*, or by *vertue* of the
coniunction, vniting both parts in one entire propofition

on, but by reason onely of the *matter*, for that both
parts of the proposition being taken *seuerally* by themselues in two *entyre* propositions are false and *hereticall*,
as this proposition being taken it by it selfe, *God is vniust*, is an *hereticall* proposition, and so likewise is this,
God is vnmercifull.

73 Now, as I haue often said, a *conditionall difiunctiue* proposition, whch implyeth a free choice to
take both parts of the disiunction, if wee please, although it be a true *disiunctiue* proposition, by reason of
the *disiunctiue* coniunction [*or*] yet, for as much as
concerneth the truth or falshood of the proposition, it
followeth the nature & quality of a *copulatiue*, and not
of a *common disiunctiue* proposition, for which reason, I
affirmed that although it was a *disiunctiue* proposition,
yet by reason of the choice, freedome, or indifferency
to take either part of the *disiunction*, it was *equiual nt*
to a *copulatiue* proposition. And therefore this proposition, *God may be iust or vniust*, speaking of externall
iustice, or iniustice, or which is all one, *it is in the power of
God*, or *God hath free power to doe externall acts of iustice
or iniustice*, is a most false and *hereticall* proposition,
although the former part of the *disiunction* bee true.
And if perchance it happen that both parts of the
disiunction be false and *hereticall*, as in this, *God may
be vniust cr vnmercifull*, this is not by vertue of the
forme, and by *force* of the *disiunctiue coniunction* implying an indifferency to both parts of the *disiunction*, but
by *vertue* of the *matter*, for that both parts of the *disiunction* beeing taken *seuerally* by themselues in two
entire propositions, are false and *hereticall*. So that you
may see a manifest difference betwixt an *absolute*, and
conditionall disiunctiue proposition, and betwixt these
two *disiunctiue* propositions, *God doth workes of iustice
or iniustice*, and *God may doe workes of iustice or iniustice*:
for the *first* is true, and the *second* false, the first is an
absolute disiunctiue, and the second a *conditionall*, and
　　　　　　　　　　　　　　　　　　　followeth

of the Oath as *impious and hereticall, &c.* are confuted.

49

followeth the nature and condition of a *copulatiue,* and not of a pure or common *difiunctiue* popofition.

74 *Secondly* obferue how vnlearnedly M. *Fitzherbert* doth infinuate, that in a *pure difiunctiue* propofition *whatfoeuer is affirmed of the one part of the difiunction is alfo affirmed of the other.* For if hee had but any fmall fkill in Logicke, he would quickly haue perceiued how groffely he is miftaken, and that according to the common and approued rule of the Logicians, the moft true and neceffary *difiunctiue* propofition is, when the one part of the *difiunction* is contradictory to the other, as this propofition, *God is iuft, or not iuft,* is a moft true and neceffary propofition, and yet the firft part of the difiunction is of faith, and the *fecond hereticall.* And if perchance hee doe fay, that hee meant onely of fuch *difiunctiue* propofitions, in which both parts of the *difiunction* are falfe, and confequently the whole difiunctiue propofition is falfe, this alfo is manifeftly vntrue.

75 For although to make a *pure, abfolute,* and *ordinary difiunctiue* propofition to be falfe, it is neceffary, that both parts of the *difiunction* bee falfe, yet it is not neceffary, that both parts bee falfe in the fame degree, or with the fame kind of *falfhood;* as in thefe examples, *either God is vniuft, or Card.* Bellarmine *is vnlearned,* both parts of the *difiunction* are falfe, and yet the firft is *hereticall* and *impoffible,* the fecond not *hereticall,* nor *impoffible,* but *contingent :* either London *is not,* or Hierufalem *was not,* both be falfe, yet the *firft* is onely repugnant to humane truth, and the fecond alfo to diuine. Likewife *either S. Peter was not head of the Apoftles, or hee was a direct temporall King of the whole Chriftian world,* both are falfe, but not in the fame degree of falfhood. So that in thefe, and infinite others which might bee alleadged, it is not true, *that whatfoeuer is affirmed of the one part of the difiunction, is alfo affirmed of the other.* And therefore no meruaile, that

in *conditionall diſiunctiue* propoſitions, which follow the nature of *copulatiues*, and not of *pure*, or *abſolute ciſinctiue* propoſitions, whatſoeuer is affirmed of the one part, is not by vertue of the *coniunction* affirmed of the other; I ſay *by vertue of the coniunction*, for that both in abſolute, and alſo in *conditionall diſunctiues*, as likewiſe in *copulatiue* propoſitions, it may fall out, that by reaſon of the *matter* or of the *thing affirmed or denyed*, the ſame falſhood which is affirmed of the one part, is affirmed alſo of the other: but this is not, to vſe the Logicians phraſe, *vi forma*, or *vi coniunctionis*, *by vertue of the forme*, or *by force of the coniunction*, but *vi materia, by reaſon or vertue of the matter*, as I declared before. So that you ſee the more M. *Fitzherbert* meddleth with thᵉſe *Dialecticall* queſtions, which are cleane out of the ſpheare of his knowledge, the more hee diſcouereth his vnskilfulnes.

76 But yet hee will ſtill goe on to bewray his ignorance, and want of Logike. For marke how vnlearnedly hee goeth about to proue, that what I ſaid of that clauſe of the Oath, [*depoſed or murthered*] to wit, *that it is a conditionall diſiunctiue* propoſition, and *did ſignifie a free election to take either part of the diſiunction, may alſo bee ſaid of other clauſes of the Oath, wherein neuertheleſſe it is manifeſt*, that [or] *is a pure diſiunctiue, and that whatſeuer is affirmed of the one part of the diſiunction, is alſo affirmed of the other*: As for example, *the Oath bindeth the takᵉrs thereof to ſweare*, that the Pope hath no power or authority to depoſe the King: *which is as much in effect*, *as that the Pope may not lawfully doe it*: *Therefore let vs make the propoſition ſo, and lay it downe with the other diſiunctiue clauſes, which follow immediately*; *and to make the whole like to that clauſe that is now in queſtion, let vs conceiue it thus.*

ʰ *nu.* 18.

77. I abiure ʰ this doctrine as falſe, that the *Pope* may depoſe the *King*, or diſpoſe of any his *Maieſties* kingdomes, or dominions; Or authorize any forraigne

P:ince

Prince to inuade, or annoy him; Or difcharge any of his fubjects of their allegiance to his *Maieſtie*; Or giue licence to any of them to beare armes, raiſe tumults, or to offer any violence to his *Maieſties* Royall perſon, &c.

78. *Here now* i *it cannot be denyed that* [or] *is diſiunctiue in all theſe ſeuerall ſentences in ſuch ſort, that which of them ſoeuer any man doth teash, hee teacheth (according to the intent of this oath) a falſe doctrine, notwithſtanding that the word* [may] *goeth before* [or] *and mplieth a free election to chooſe any one of them; in ſo much that if a man ſhould ſay onely, that the Pope may authorize a forraine Prince to inuade* his Maieſtie, *he is condemned by the oath, to ſpeake no liſſe vntruely, then if hee ſhould ſay, that the* Pope *may depoſe his* Maieſtie ; *or giue licence to any to offer violence to his perſon.*

79. *Therefore* k *if* Widdrington *apply the words* [impious and hereticall] *in the other clauſe to the doctrine of* murthering *onely, and not alſo to the doctrine of* depoſing *Princes, why may not he, or any man elſe doe the like in the foreſaid example, and offirme, that the laſt member, and part thereof (which denieth the Popes power to giue licence to offer violence to his* Maieſties *perſon) is onely abiured as falſe, whereby the former parts, or clauſes concerning* the Popes power to depoſe his Maieſtie, *or,* to diſpoſe of his kingdomes, *or* to giue licence to forraigne Princes to inuade, or annoy him (*which are principall points of the oath*) *would be ſuperfluous, and to no purpoſe. So as it is manifeſt, that the words of the* oath [depoſed, or murthered] *being conſidered according to their proper, and vſuall ſignification in the clauſe where they are, and compared alſo with the other clauſes, parts, and circumſtances of the oath, cannot admit* Widdringtons *interpretation, who applieth the note of* hereſie *to the* Murther, *and not alſo to the* depoſition *of Princes. Thus much concerning the words of the law, or oath.*

80. Behold now, how vnlearnedly Mr. *Fitzherbert* (and yet his ignorance is the leſſe excuſable, for that he

i *Nu.* 19.

k *Nu* 20.

he might haue ſeene the weakeneſſe of his argument
in my *Theologicall Diſputation*, where the *Authour* of
the aforeſaid *Engliſh Dialogue* obiecteth the like argument, but in a contrary manner) argueth from the
truth of a *conditionall diſiunctiue* propoſition, which is
negatiue de dicto, to the falſhood of a *conditionall diſiunctiue*, which is *affirmatiue de modo*, and frameth an
oath of his owne inuention far different in ſenſe from
the oath preſcribed by his Maieſtie, which neuertheleſſe hee pretendeth to haue the ſame ſenſe and ſignification with his new deuiſed oath. For the oath preſcribed by his *Maieſty* is a *negatiue* propoſition *de dicto*,
to wit, *that the* Pope *hath not any power or authoritie to
depoſe the King*, *or to diſpoſe of any his Maiſties Kingdomes or Dominions*, *or to authorize any forraine
Prince to inuade or annoy him*, *or to diſcharge any of his
Subiects of their allegiance and obedience to his* Maieſtie,
or to giue licence to any of them to beare armes, *raiſe tumults*, *or to offer any violence to his* Maieſties *Royall perſon*,*&c.* And all this I muſt acknowledge to be true,
and therefore I called this whole propoſition, *negatiue
de dicto*, and *affirmatiue de modo.* And the ſenſe of this
oath is cleere, to wit, that the *Pope* hath not any lawfull power to doe any one of theſe things, ſo that if the
Pope hath power to doe any one of them, the *whole*,
and entire *diſiunctiue* propoſition conſiſting of thoſe
particular clauſes is by *vertue* of the *forme* of words,
and of the *coniunction* diſiunctiue [*or*] or rather [*nor*]
not true, but falſe. I ſay by vertue of the *forme of words*,
for that the negation [*not*] going before, and hauing
a power to *diſtribute*, to vſe the Logicians phraſe, or to
deny all that followeth it, maketh all thoſe *diſiunctiue*
coniunctions [*or*] which follow, to be *equiualent* to
[*nor*] or [*neither*,] which, as I ſay, being a *diſtributiue*
ſigne, is to be reſolued, as euery Logician knoweth, by
the coniunction *copulatiue* [*and*] and not by the *diſiunctiue* [*or*] for which cauſe ſome *Grammarians* doe alſo

fo hould; that the coniunction [*nor*] or [*neither*] is
not a *difiunctiue*, but a *copulatiue* coniunction.

81. But the oath, which Mr. *Fitzherbert* hath framed, is a propofition *negatiue de modo*, and *affirmatiue
de dicto*, to wit, *that the* Pope *may, or, which according
to his owne expofition, is all one, that it is in the* Popes
free and lawfull power to depofe the King, *or to difpofe any
of his* Maiefties *Kingdomes, or dominions, or to authorize
any forraine Prince to inuade or annoy him;or to difcharge
any of his fubiects of their allegiance and obedience to his*
Maieftie; *or to giue licence to any of them to beare armes,
raife tumults, or to offer any violence to his* Maiefties *Royall perfon, &c.* and this *whole*, or entire *difiunctiue* propofition confifting of all thefe particular branches M.
Fitzherbert will haue to be abiured as *falfe*. Now hee
that hath but any fmall fkill in Logicke may eafily perceiue a great difference betwixt the fenfe and meaning
of thefe two oaths, or propofitions. For in the oath
prefcribed by his *Maieftie* wee may *by vertue of the
words*, and from the *force* and fignification of the *difiunctiue* coniunction [*or*] which, as I haue fhewed
before, is by reafon of the precedent negation [*not*]
equiualent to [*nor*] neceffarily inferre, that the *Pope*
hath *neither* power to depofe the *King*, nor to *difpofe of
any his* Maiefties *Kingdomes or Dominions, nor to doe
any other of thofe things there mentioned*; and therefore
he that grarteth,that the Pope hath power to doe any
one of thofe things there mentioned,muft confequently graunt, that the whole, or entire oath,or propofition confifting of all thofe particular claufes is *falfe*.

82 But in the oath inuented by my *Aduerfary*, although indeed *by vertue of the matter*,we may well conclude, that the *Pope* hath *neither* power to depofe the
Kinge, nor to difpofe of any his Maiefties kingdomes
or dominions, nor to doe any other of thofe thinges
there mentioned, for that all and euery one of thofe
thinges which are denied to the Pope in that *totall*

H 3   oath

oath, or propoſition, may alſo be denied to him in *ſe-*
uerall oaths, or propoſitions, *yet by vertue of the words*,
and from the *force* and ſignification of the *diſunctiue*
coniunction [*or*] which, as M. *Fitzherbert* himſelfe
doth grant, maketh there a *conditionall diſiumctiue*
propoſition, implying a free choiſe to take which part
of the *diſiunction* we pleaſe, we cannot rightly conclude, that the Pope hath *neither* power to depoſe the
King, nor to diſpoſe of any his *Maieſties* kingdomes or
dominions &c.

83 For what man can be ſo ignorant, as to imagine,
that theſe two propoſitions make the ſame ſenſe, or
that the firſt doth rightly inferre the ſecond. *It is falſe,*
that it is in my free and lawfull power to doe this or that,
therefore it is true, that I may lawfully neither doe this
nor that. My *Aduerſary* cannot deny, but that it is
falſe. that he had lawfull freedome to deale ſincerely,
or corrnptly in this his Reply, therefore by his owne
manner of arguing he muſt grant, that it is true, that
he had lawfull freedome neither to deale ſincerely nor
corruptly in his Reply. Likewiſe he cannot deny, but
that it is falſe, that it is in the free and lawfull power
of creatures to honour or blaſpheme God, of Prieſts to
eate or ſleepe before they ſay Maſſe, of Souldiers to
fight or fly when their Country is inuaded by the ene-
mie, and (to exemplifie in our owne matter) of the
Pope to depoſe or murther Princes, *as murther is taken*
for an vnlawfull Act : Will he therefore inferre from
thence in that manner as he argueth here, that it is
therefore true, that creatures may lawfully neither honour nor blaſpheme God, that Prieſts may lawfully
neither eate nor ſleepe before they ſay Maſſe, that
Soldiers may lawfully neither fight nor flye, when
their Country is inuaded, and that the Pope may lawfully neither depoſe Princes nor murther them, *as mur-*
ther is taken for an vnlawful act? Wherfore if my *Aduer-*
ſary will but keepe ſtill the ſame *forme*, and the ſame

diſiunctiue

disiunctiue coniunction [*or*] aud alter but a little the *matter*, by adding onely to the end of the affirmatiue oath, framed by himselfe, this clause, [*or to murther his* Maiesty] he will quickly perceiue his error, and he will uot deny, but that the oath with that addition is very false; and neuerthelesse he dare not from thence conclude the truth of the *negatiue*, or that therefore it is true, that the Pope hath not any power neither to depose the King, nor to dispose &c. for that he granteth, that the Pope hath lawfull power to depose the King, and to dispose &c. onely he denyeth, that the Pope hath power to *murther him*, as *murther is taken for an vnlawfull act.*

84. But the causes of M. *Fitzherberts* errour are manifest. *First*, for that he for want of Logike doth not, as it seemes, consider the difference betwixt the *forme*, and the *matter* of an *hypothiticall* proposition, and what is required to the truth or falshood of a *disiunctiue*, or *copulatiue* proposition, as well *by vertue of the forme*, as *of the matter*. For to make a *pure*, or *absolute disiunctiue* proposition to be true, it is sufficient, *by vertue of the forme*, that one part of the disiunction be true, but to make it false, both parts must be false. Contrariwise it falleth out in a *copulatiue* proposition, for to make it true, both parts of the copulation must be true, and to make it false, it sufficeth *by vertue of the forme*, or *by force of the copulatiue coniunction*, that one onely part be false, although by *reason of the matter* both parts also may be false, but this is impertinent to the forme. *Secondly*, he doth not consider, that a *conditionall disiunctiue* proposition, which implyeth a free choise to take which part of the *disiunction* we please, followeth the nature of a *copulatiue*, and not of a *pure*, *common*, or *absolute disiunctiue* proposition. *Thirdly* he doth not consider, that whatsoeuer is taken, or to vse the Logicians phrase, *supposeth distributiuely*, as euery negation doth *distribute*, and *deny* whatsoeuer followeth

followeth that negation, is to be reſolued by a *copula-tiue*, and not by a *diſtinctiue* coniunction.

85. *Fourthly*, he doth not conſider, that to make a *copulatiue* propoſition, or ſuch a *diſiunctiue*, which is *equiualent* to a *copulatiue* to be *hereticall*, it ſufficeth that one onely part be *hereticall*. *Fiftly*,he doth not conſider, that although to make a *pure*, *common*, or *abſolute diſiunctiue* propoſition to be *falſe*, it is neceſſary that both parts of the *diſiunction* be falſe, yet it is not neceſſary that both parts be *falſe* in the ſame degree of *falſhood*, for that the one part may be impoſſible, the other not, the one part *hereticall*, and the other not, and that therefore the ſame kinde of *falſhood* which is affirmed of the one part, is not neceſſarily affirmed of the other. *Laſtly*, he doth not conſider, how vicious a kinde of arguing it is, from the *falſhood* of an affirmatiue *conditionall diſiunctiue* propoſition to conclude the *truth* of a *negatiue*, whereby he would make his *affirmatiue* oath, inuented by himſelfe, to haue the ſame ſenſe with the *negatiue* oath preſcribed by his *Maieſty*. And his ignorance herein is the leſſe excuſable, for that the inſufficiencie of this his argument he might haue ſeene declared in my *Theologicall diſputation*, where I clearely ſhewed, as you haue ſeene before, how vnſoundly the *Author* of that Engliſh *Dialogue* vrged the like argument, which my anſwere to that argument is alſo here altogether concealed by M. *Fitzherbert*. And therefore I will giue him this charitable aduiſe, that if he haue any care of his credit and reputation, he doe not hereafter ſo bouldly aduenture to meddle with theſe queſtions belonging to Logike, except he haue the helpe and furtherance of ſome of his company more skilfull herein then himſelfe, leaſt that by granting one inconuenience, he fall, according to the ancient prouerbe, into a thouſand abſurdities.

86. By this it is euident *firſt*, that although the

Oat!

Oath ordained by his *Maiesty*, and the *Oath* framed by M. *Fitzherbert* containe the same *disiunctiue* clauses, and so they doe both agree in the *matter*, yet they differ greatly in the *forme*, and in the *sense* and vnderstanding of the *disiunctiue* coniunction [*or*.] For in the *Oath*, prescribed by his *Maiestie*, that which *by vertue of the forme*, and by *force* of the coniunction [*or*] which in all those particular sentences is *equiualent* to [*nor*] I doe acknowledge to be true, is, *that the* Pope *hath not power to doe any one of all those thinges mentioned in those disiunctiue clauses*, and that which I acknowledge to be *false*, is, *that the* Pope *hath power to doe any one of all those thinges*, as *either to depose the* King *or to dispose of his Dominions*, and so forth: And therefore although to those clauses were added also this clause [*or to murther his Maiesty*] yet my *Aduersary* cannot affirme, that it would change at all the *truth*, or *falshood* of the *whole oath*, or *entyre proposition*, but if the *oath* were *true* before, it would also be *true* now, and if it were *false* before, it would also be *false* now.

87   But if the *oath*, which M. *Fitzherbert* hath framed, that which *by vertue of the forme*, and by *force* of the coniunction [*or*] which as he himselfe confesseth, *implyeth a free election to chose any one of those seuerall sentences* or *clauses*, I acknowledge to be *true*, is, *that the* Pope *hath not power to doe all those thinges mentioned in those clauses*, or, which is all one, *to doe which of all those thinges he shall please*, and that which I acknowledge to be *false*, is, *that the* Pope *hath power to doe all those thinges mentioned in those clauses* or which is all one, *to doe which of all those thinges he shall please.* And therefore if to those clauses of M. *Fitzherberts* new deuised *oath*, should be added also this clause [*or to murther his Maiesty*] he cannot denie, but that his *oath*, or *entyre disiunctiue proposition*, which before in his opinion was *false*, is now by adding that clause made *true*, and

I   therefore

therefore that it is *false*, *that the Pope hath power to
murther his M iestie.* I he adding of which clause
doth clearely shew the manifest difference betwixt the
forme of these two *oaths*, and the different signification of the coniunction [*or*] in both of them, albeit
in the *matter* of all the particular clauses, and propositions, they doe both agree.

88 *Secondly*, by this also it is easie to answere the
demand, which M. *Fitzherbert* propoundeth, to wit,
wherefore the word [hereticall] *in the doctrine and position of his* Maiesties oath, *may be referred to the doctrine
of* murthering *Princes*, *and not of* deposing *them*, *and
the word* [false] *may not with the like reason in the* oath
or intire disiunctiue propo[s]ition, *which my* Aduersary
hath framed, *be referred to the last member*, *and part
thereof*, *which denyeth the* Popes *power to offer violence
to his* Maiesties *person*, *and not to the former concerning
the* Popes *power to depose his Maiesty.* For if wee regard the *forme* of both propositions, and the *vertue*, or
force of the disiunctiue coniunction [*or*] which implyeth a free choise to take which part of the *disiunction* we please, and therefore to make the whole
disiunctiue proposition to be *false and hereticall*, it
sufficeth, that one onely part thereof be *false and
hereticall*, as they both agree in the *forme*, and in
the sense of the *disiunctiue* coniunction [*or*] as it is sufficient by *vertue of the forme*, to make that *affirmatiue*
position, *Princes being excommunicated or depriued by
the Pope may be deposed or murthered by their Subiects*,
or any other, to be *hereticall*, so also to make this *affirmatiue* proposition, which my *Aduersary* hath framed,
The Pope may, or which is all one, *it is in the Popes free
and lawfull power to depose the Kinges Maiesty*, *or to offer violence to his Royall person*, to be *false*, it sufficeth,
by vertue of the forme, and by *force* of the *disiunctiue*
coniunction [*or*] that one onely part of the *disiunction*
be *false*: But the onely difference is *in the matter.* And
there-

therefore if the doctrine of *deposing* Princes, be not
so clearely and properly *hereticall*, as is the doctrine
of *murthering* them, the word [*hereticall*] may with
better reason be referred to the doctrine of *murthering*, then of *deposing*: But because the doctrine
which teacheth, that the *Pope* may *depose* his *Maiesty*, as also that he *may offer violence to his Royall person*, are *false*, (although perchance the latter be false
in a more high and manifest degree of *falshood*, then is
the former) therefore the word [*false*] may, *by vertue
of the matter*, but not *by force of the coniunction* disiunctiue [*or*] in the *oath*, framed by my *Aduersary*, be referred to both.

89. I say, in the oath framed by my *Aduersary*, for
as these two particular propositions are set downe in
the *oath* ordained by his *Maiestie*, both of them are,
not onely, *by vertue of the matter*, but also by *reason of
the forme*, and by *force* of the *coniunction* [*or*] which is
equiualent to [*nor*] affirmed to be *false*, as I declared
before. So that it is manifest, that these words of the
oath [*may be deposed, or murthered*] being considered
according to their proper and vsuall signification in the
conditionall disiunctiue clause where they are, and compared also with the other clauses, parts, and circumstances of the oath, may very well admit the interpretation, which I haue made; and the application of *heresie*
(taking *heresie* in a strict sense) may be applyed onely
to the *murther*, and not also to the *deposition* of Princes,
although it may also in a *proper sense*, and wherein
many learned Catholikes doe take the word *heresie*,
be applyed to both, as I will shewe beneath. [1] And
thus much concerning the wordes of the law, and
oath.

90   Now for his *Maiesties* meaning, or intention
in that clause (which was the second rule assigned
for the interpretation of the oath) *the same*, saith M.
Fitzherbert, [m] *according to the doctrine of* Suarez, *which*

[1] *Nu.* 106. *et
sq.*

[m] *Nu.* 12.

Widdrington approoueth, is to be gathered principally by the words, and which, as you haue ſeene, being to be taken in their proper and common ſenſe, doe ſhew, that his Maieſties *meaning was no other, but to ordaine the abiuration of both parts of that clauſe alike, that is to ſay, as truely impious and hereticall.*

91 But contrariwiſe I haue cleerely ſhewed beʼore, that according to the *proper* and vſuall ſignification of the words, the common vnderſtanding of men, and the receiued doctrine of the Logicians, to make a *copulatiue* propoſition, or a *conditionall diſiunctiue*, which followeth the nature of a *copulatiue*, to bee *hereticall*, it ſufficeth that one onely part thereof bee *hereticall.* Seeing therefore that his *Maieſties* meaning onely was to bind his *Catholike* Subiects, to take this clauſe of the *Oath* in that ſenſe, which the words according to their *true, proper*, and *vſuall ſignification* doe beare, and that according to the *true* and *common ſenſe of the wordes*, it ſufficeth to abiure this clauſe of the Oath, as *hereticall*, if one onely part thereof bee *hereticall*, it is manifeſt that his *Maieſties* meaning was not to ordaine that both parts of this clauſe ſhould bee abiured alike, vnleſſe from the *common ſenſe and vnderſtanding of the wordes* it can be rightly gathered, as I haue proued it cannot, that both parts muſt of neceſſity be abiured alike.

n *nu.* 21.

92 *But if it be wel conſidered,* ſaith M. *Fitzherbert* n , *what reaſon* Widdrington *hath to condemne the aforeſaid doctrine,* as truely hereticall, *in reſpect of one part of the clauſe (to wit, that part which concerneth violent attempts vpon the perſons of Princes) it will eaſily appeare, that his* Maieſty *pretendeth as much, if not more reaſon, to condemne it in like maner in regard of the other part, which concerneth the* depoſition *of Princes. For whereas* Widdrington *hath no other reaſon for his conceipt, but becauſe hee thinketh that all doctrine preiudiciall to the liues of Princes is repugnant to the holy Scriptures (whereby hee*

con-

consequently holdeth it for hereticall) his Maiesty *is perswaded also that he hath the same reason to condemne the doctrine of the Popes power to depose Princes for hereticall, as it may euidently appeare by the manifold places, and texts of Scripture, which hee alleadgeth for the proofe of his owne Ecclesiasticall Primacy, and the obligation of his Subiects to yeeld him ciuil obedience, whereon he groundeth the lawfulnes of the Oath, and the abiuration of the doctrine condemned therein.*

93. *And therefore omitting* ° *to examine, how well the Scriptures alledged by his* Maiestie, *serue for the proofe of the matter in question, as also to note, how impertinently* Widdrington *applyeth the precept,* non Occides, *to his purpose, by occasion of the word* murther *in the oath (which precept being indeed vnderstood of* murther, *and consequently implying alwaies an vnlawfull act, yea a mortall sinne, was neuer held by any to be lawfull, and therefore doth not in that sort and sense belong to our question, as* Widdrington *knoweth well enough) but omitting, I say, to speake further of this, that which here I affirme is, that his* Maiestie *alledgeth much more Scripture to condemne the doctrine touching the depofition of Princes, then* Widdrington *doth for the condemnation of* violent *attempts against their persons; whereby it is manifest, that hee hath no reason to say, that his* Maiestie *meant, that the latter part of that clause should be abiured,* as hereticall, *and not the former, especially seeing that the expresse words of the* oath, *(according to their most vsuall, and proper signification) together with the circumstances thereof, doe proue both alike, as it appeareth by the premisses. And this I hope may suffice for the confutation of his first, and best answeare.*

94. But *first*, as it appeareth alfo by the *premisses,* the expreffe words of this claufe (according to their moft vfuall, and proper fignification) together with all other circumftances, doe cleerely proue, that both parts of that *disiunctiue* propofition are not of neceffi-

tie to be abiured alike , for that to make a *conditionall*
diſiunctiue propoſition , as is the *doctrine* , and *poſition*
abiured in this clauſe , to be *hereticall* , it is ſufficient,
that one part of the *diſiunction* be *hereticall* , and that
therefore both parts of the *diſiunction* are not of neceſſity to bee abiured alike , as by the *forme* of my
Aduerſaries owne examples I haue euidently conuinced: and therefore his premiſſes doe no way proue his
concluſion in this point.

94 *Secondly*, that his *Maieſty* had far greater reaſon
to bee more vehement againſt the practiſe of *murthe-*
ring Princes being excommunicated, or depriued by
the *Pope*, then of *depoſing*, or thruſting them out of the
poſſeſſion of their kingdomes, and to haue the former
being the more *heinous, impious, damnable* and *deteſta-*
ble crime, and more plainely and expreſly forbidden in
holy Scriptures, to bee abiured in a more high and
eminent degree,then the latter,it is plainely conuinced
by the great and manifeſt inequality of the crimes, by
the irrecuperable , and not recompenſable damage,
which proceedeth from the *former* , and not from the
later, and yet the *former* being the more eaſily and
ſuddainely to bee performed then the *latter*, (for that
the *latter* cannot bee accompliſhed but by a mighty
power, which alſo may faile, the euent of warre being
vncertaine, but the *former* by the aduenturous bold-
neſſe onely of one villaine may bee effected) together
with the knowne practiſes of the late *murthers* of the
moſt Chriſtian Kings of France , and the execrable
conſpiracy of the *Pouder-Traytors* , which was the
chiefe occaſion of the ordaining of this Oath. And
therefore his *Maieſty* hath neither *more reaſon* , nor *as*
much reaſon to condemne that part of this clauſe ,
which concerneth the *depoſing* of Princes being excommunicated,or depriued by the Pope, for *hereticall,*
taking *hereticall* for that which importeth a plaine,
manifeſt, and confeſſed *hereſie*,or falſhood cleerely re-

pugnant to holy Scriptures, as either he himselfe, or I, or
any man else may haue to condemne that part for *hereti-*
call, which concerneth the *murthering* of such Princes.

95. But to reduce Mr. *Fitzherberts* whole discourse
to a compendious forme of arguing ; That, which hee
chiefely laboureth to proue against me in this chapter,
is, that this position , *Princes which be excommunicated*
or depriued by the Pope may be deposed or murthered by
their Subiects or ary other whatsoeuer, is by the *oath* condemned for *hereticall,* in regard as well of the *deposition*
of such Princes , as of the *murthering* of them. And
this hee endeauoureth to proue by two waies : *first* by
the common sense, and vnderstanding of the words,
which doe *signifie* , saith hee , *that both parts a e abiured*
alike , to which purpose hee bringeth *foure examples*
of propositions, which, as you haue seene, make nothing for him, but are flat against him, and hee frameth
an *oath* of his owne inuention, to paralell it with the
oath ordained by his *Maiestie* , which neuerthelesse
is far different from it in sense, as I haue shewed before.

96. Secondly, hee pretendeth to proue the same by
his *Maiesties* meaning, or intention, *which was,* saith
hee, *that both parts should be abiured as hereticall.* And
this also hee pretendeth to prove by two waies. *First,*
by the proper and common sense of the words , by which his
Maiesties *intenti n is principally to be gathered.* But this
proofe is all one with the former, and therefore with
the same facility it is denied, as it is affirmed ; for that
the proper and vsuall sense of the words doe not import, that both parts of the disiunction are of necessity
to be abiured alike, by reason of the *conditionall disiun-*
ctiue proposition, as I haue often repeated before. Se-
condly , hee would seeme to proue the same by this argument. *His* Maiestie *is perswaded, hat the doctrine, not*
only which alloweth the practise of deposing *Princes being*
excommunicated or depriued by the Pope , *but also which*
speculatiuely maintaineth, that the Pope *hath power to de-*
                                                      pos

poſe Princes,is hereticall,*and repugnant to the holy Scrip-tures, as may euidently appeare by the manifold places,and texts of Scripture, which he alledgeth,* &c. yea, *and hee t alledgeth much more Scripture , to condemne the doctrine touching the* depoſition *of Princes, then* Widdring:on *doth for violent attempts againſt their perſons,therefore it is manifeſt that according to his* Maieſties *intention both parts of that clauſe ſhould be abiured as* hereticall.

97 But *firſt*, this conſequence of my *Aduerſary* : (His Maieſtie *is perſwaded , that not onely the doctrine which teacheth , that the* Pope *hath power to* murther *Princes , but alſo to* depoſe *them, is* hereticall, *therefore his* Maieſties *meaning , or intention was , that in the a-foreſaid clauſe of the oath, both parts ſhould be abiured , as hereticall*, taking *hereticall* in that ſtrict ſenſe , whereof I will ſpeake beneath P) M. *Fitzherbert* might haue ſeene, if it had pleaſed him , in my *Theologicall diſpu-tation* q, to be very inſufficient ; where I did clearly ſhewe , that there is a great difference to be made be-twixt his *Maieſties* perſwaſion or opinion, and his mea-ning or intention. For his *Maieſty* doth, according to the grounds of the *Proteſtant Religion* , defend diuers opinions , which neuertheleſſe he doth not intend to binde his Catholike Subiects by this *oath* to defend and profeſſe.

98 As for example. His *Maieſty* is perſwaded , that he is the *ſupreame Lord and Gouernour,in all cauſes, as well Eccleſiaſticall, as temporall* , and yet he doth not intend that his Catholike Subiects ſhall by thoſe words of this oath [*our Soueraigne Lord King Iames*] profeſſe and maintaine the ſame. Neither doth he *ground the lawfulnes of this oath , and the abiuration of the doctrine condemned therein ,vpon his Eccleſiaſticall Prim cie*, as my *Aduerſary* here ſeemeth to inſinuate , for that the *Oath* of his *Eccleſiaſticall Supremacie*, as his *Maieſty* himſelfe affirmeth, r *was deuiſed for putting a difference betwene* Papiſts,*and Proteſtants , but this oath was or-dained*

dained for making a difference betweene the ciuilly obedi-
ent Papists, and the peruerſe diſciples of the Powder-
treaſon.

99 Alſo his *Maieſty* is perſwaded, that the Pope
hath not power to *excommunicate* his *Maieſty,* and yet
he doth intend by thoſe words of the oath [*notwith-*
ſtanding any ſentence of excommunication &c.] to binde
Engliſh Catholikes to profeſſe the ſame; ᶠ howſoeuer Card. *Bellarmine, Gretzer, Leſſius,* and *Suarez*
without ſufficient proofe, and M. *Fitzherbert* without any proofe at all, doe affirme, *that the Popes power*
to excommunicate is denied in this oath. For although
the lower houſe of Parliament, as his *Maieſty* alſo affirmeth ᵗ, *at the firſt framing of this oath made it to con-*
taine, that the Pope *had no power to excommunicate his*
Maieſty, *yet his* Maieſtie *did purpoſely decline that poi·t,*
ᵘ *and forced them to reforme it, onely making it to con-*
clude, that no excommunication of the Popes *can war-*
rant his Subieĉts to practiſe againſt his perſon, or ſtate, as
indeed *taking any ſuch temporall violence to be farre*
without the limits of ſuch a ſpirituall Cenſure, as *Excom-*
munication is.

100 Likewiſe his *Maieſty* is perſwaded, that all
reconcilings of his Subieĉts to the *Pope,* and all retur-
nings of Engliſh Prieſts made by the *Popes* authority,
into this Realme &c, are truely and properly *treaſons,*
although not *naturally,* and forbidden by the lawe of
nature, vnleſſe they be repugnant to true, naturall,
and ciuill alleagiance, yet *poſitiue* and forbidden by the
lawes of the Realme, neuertheleſſe by thoſe words of
the oath [*to diſcloſe all treaſons &c.*] he did not intend
to binde his Catholike Subieĉts to reueale and diſcloſe
ſuch kinde of treaſons, vnleſſe they be truely and properly vnnaturall treaſons, and repugnant to naturall
alleagiance. For that his *Maieſty was carefull,* as he
himſelfe alſo writeth ˣ, *that nothing ſhould be contai-*
ned in this oath, except the profeſſion of naturall allegiance,

K *and*

ᶠ See my *Th.*
Diſp. cap. 4.
ſec. 1.

ᵗ In his *Pre-*
monition pag
9.

ᵘ In the Cata-
logue of the
lyes of *Tor-*
tus. nu. 1.

ˣ In his *Pre-*
monition pag.
9.
naturall.

*and ciuill, and temporall obedience, with a promiſe to
reſiſt all contrarie, vnnaturall,* and *vnciuill violence.*

101 Wherefore ſeeing that his *Maieſtie* doth binde
the ſwearer to take his *oath according to the plaine
and common ſenſe and vnderſtanding of the words,* although his *Maieſty* be perſwaded, that it is *hereticall*
to hould, *that the* Pope *hath power to depoſe princes,* yet
from thence it cannot rightly be concluded, that therfore by this *oath* he intended to bind his Catholike
Subiects to acknowledge and profeſſe the ſame, vnleſſe
the words of the *oath, according to their proper and vſuall ſignification* doe imply the ſame. Conſidering
therefore, that as I haue clearly conuinced, to make
that propoſition , *Princes which be excommunicated or
depriued by the Pope may be depoſed or murthered by their
Subiects, or any other,* to be *hereticall,* it is ſufficient,
according to the common ſenſe of the words, and
the approued doctrine of Logicians, that one onely part of the *diſiunction* be *hereticall,* as without doubt
the latter part of this *diſiunction* is, it is euident, that
his *Maieſties* meaning was no other, then to binde the
ſwearer to that ſenſe, to which the words being taken
in their proper and vſuall ſignification doe binde. And
thus much concerning the conſequence.

102 Now touching the *antecedent* propoſition, although it be true, that his *Maieſty* is perſwaded, that
not onely the doctrine, which alloweth the practiſe of
depoſing Princes, which be excommunicated or depriued by the Pope, but alſo the *ſpeculatiue* doctrine, which
teacheth, that the Pope hath power to depriue Princes,
is a falſe doctrine, and repugnant to holy Scriptures,
and conſequently *hereticall,* taking *hereticall* for that
which implyeth an vntruth, contrary to the word of
God reuealed in holy Scriptures, in which ſenſe alſo
all thoſe Catholikes, who doe hould this doctrine of
the *Popes* power to depriue Princes of their kingdomes,
to be falſe, doe hould alſo, that it is contrary to the
word

word of God, and confequently alfo *hereticall* ; yet if
hereticall be taken for that which importeth a knowne
and manifeft vntruth repugnant to holy Scriptures,
and fo acknowledged alfo to be by the common confent alfo of Catholikes, my *Aduerfarie* will hardly
proue, that his *Maiefty* is perfwaded, that the *fpecu-*
latiue doctrine, which holdeth, that the *Pope* hath
power to depriue Princes, or to depofe them by a iuridicall fentence, is *hereticall* in this fenfe, or repugnant
to holy Scriptures in the opinion of all, or of the moft
part of Catholikes, albeit he be perfwaded that the
fpeculatiue doctrine, which approueth the *Popes* power to *murther* or to take away the liues of Princes, be
in this fenfe *hereticall*, as in very deed it is : And therfore all thofe Priefts, who then were Prifoners in
Newgate, and the *Gate-houfe*, and now are in *Wif-*
beech, being examined by his *Maieftses Commiffioners*
vpon certaine articles, and did directly anfwere to the
queftions which were propounded, did agree in this,
that it was directly and abfolutely murther for any man to
take away the life of his Maiefty, and that the Church
could not define it to be lawfull for any man to kill his Ma-
iefty, although for the point of *depofing*, fome of them
anfwered othei wife, fome others declined the queftion, and many of them did infinuate, that as yet this
point touching the Popes power to depofe Princes is
not defined by the Church.

103 And although his *Maiefty* doth alleage much
more Scripture to condemn the doctrine touching the
depofition of Princes, then I doe for the condemnation of violent attempts againft their perfons, yet it cannot be denied, both that his *Maiefty* might haue
brought more plaine and pregnant places, againft the
doctine of *murthering* Princes, if he had thought it
needefull, and not fuppofed it to be a manifeft vntruth,
and condemned by the common confent alfo of Catholikes, and alfo that all thofe places, which his *Ma-*

ieſty bringeth to proue, that Subiects owe ciuill obedience to temporall Princes, and againſt the *Popes*
Eccleſiaſticall power to depriue Princes of their temporall kingdomes, doe more forcibly conclude aga nſt
violent attempts againſt their ſacred perſons, and a-
gainſt the Popes Eccleſiaſticall or ſpirituall power to
murther *kill*, or depriue them of their liues, which
*bloody puniſhments Eccleſiaſticall mildnes doth ſo much
abhorre.*

104. Neither doe I take the word [*murthered*] in
that clauſe of the *oath*, as it doth *formally* ſignifie *an
vnlawfull act, and a mortall ſinne*, and in that ſenſe
apply the precept, *Thou ſhalt not kill*, to this clauſe of
the oath, as my *Aduerſary* would perſwade the Reader, but I take *murthered* in that clauſe, as it doth denote *materially* the *killing* of Princes, which be excommunicated or depriued by the Pope: And I affirme,
that the *killing* of ſuch Princes is *directly and abſolutely
a mortall ſinne*, and is that *murther*, or *killing*, which
is forbidden by the law of God, and nature, reuealed
to vs in the holy Scriptures, and eſpecially in thoſe
two places which the *Author* of the Engliſh *Dialogue*,
whoſe obiection againſt that clauſe of the oath I tooke
vpon mee to anſwere, did alleadge. The *firſt* place
1, *Reg.* 26. *Kill him not, for who ſhall extend his hand
againſt the Lords annointed, and be innocent?* doth more
particularly belong to Princes. The *ſecond* place *Exod.*
20. *Thou ſhalt not kill*, is common alſo to priuate men,
and therefore much more to be ayplyed to the *killing*
of Princes.

105. Neither is it neceſſary as I obſerued in my *Appendix* y againſt *Suarez*, to make that poſition
contained in the *Oath* to be *hereticall*, and repugnant
to Gods commandement, that the Scripture ſhould
haue added, *Thou ſhalt not kill Princes which be excommunicated or depriued by the Pope.* It is ſufficient that
all *killing* both of priuate men, and much more alſo of
temporal

y part 2. ſec. 5
nu. 4.

temporall Princes, (who haue in their handes the materiall sword it selfe, and supreme power to kill or saue) is vnlawfull and forbidden by this precept, which is not warrantable either by other places of holy Scripture, or declared by the Church to bee lawfull, and to haue sufficient warrant, Now it is manifest, that neither the Church, nor any one Catholike Doctour euer taught, that the Popes sentence of *excommunication* or *depriuation*, although wee should grant, that the *Pope* hath power to *depriue* Princes by way of *sentence*, doth giue sufficient warrant or authority to Subiects to *kill* their Prince, for that the Popes sentence of *depriuation* doth at the most by the consent of all Catholicks, depriue a Prince of his *right* to *reigne*, but not of his corporall life, or of his *right* to *liue*. And thus much concerning the antecedent proposition.

106 *Lastly* to say something also concerning the consequent, although as you haue seene, I do vtterly deny, that to *abiure* this *doctrine* and position as *hereticall, That Princes which bee excommunicated or depriued by the Pope may be depofed or murthered by their Subiects or any other*, it is necessary by *vertue of the forme* of words being taken in their proper and vsuall signification, and by *force* of the coniunction disiunctiue [*or*], that both parts of the *disiunction* bee *abiured* as *hereticall*, neuertheleffe I doe willingly grant, that by *vertue of the mater* both parts of that *disiunctiue* proposition may bee truely *abiured* as *hereticall*, if wee take the word *hereticall*, as by many learned Catholickes it is taken in a true, proper, and vsuall signification. For the better vnderstanding whereof wee must obserue out of *Alphonsus de Castro* [z] *Didacus Couerruuias* [a], and others, *that although the Catholike Church can determine of* herefie, *yet an affertion is not therefore* herefie, *becaufe the Church hath defined it, but becaufe it is repugnant to Catholike faith, or which is all one, to that which is reuealed by God. For the Church by her de-*

z Lib. 1. aduerf-herefes cap. 8.
a Lib. 4. variar. refolut. cap. 14.

K 3   *finition*

finition doth not make ſuch a poſition to be hereſie , *ſeeing that it would be* hereſie, *although ſhe ſhould not define it; but the Church cauſeth this , that by her cenſure ſhe maketh knowne, and manifeſt to vs, that to bee* hereſie, *which before was not certainly knowne, whether it might iuſtly be called* hereſie, *or no.*

107. *For the whole* Church (*excluding* Chriſt *her principall head*) *hath not power to make a new Article of faith which neuertheleſſe ſhee might doe if ſhe could make an aſſertion to be* hereticall: *But that the Church hath not power to make a new Article of faith, it is conuinced by manifeſt reaſon. For euery aſſertion is therefore called* Catholike, *for that it is reuealed by God : Seing therefore that diuine reuelation doth not depend vpon the approbation, or declaration of the Church, the declaration of the Church doth not make that* Catholike, *which is reuealed by God. The Chnrch* therefore *doth determine that this is reueaſed by God, but ſhee doth not make that which is reuealed by God to be true: for if ſuch a verity be called* Catholike, *for that it is contained in holy Scripture, ſeeing that ſuch a verity to bee contained in holy Scripture doth not depend vpon any humane will, but vpon God alone, the Author of thoſe Scriptures, it is manifeſt by this reaſon, that the Church can doe nothing at all, that ſuch a truth doth belong to faith: For the holy Scriptures haue this of themſelues that wee are bound to beleeue them in all things. Wherefore the Church defining any thing to be of faith, although ſhe doth certainly define, and cannot erre, yet by her definition ſhe doth not make that truth to bee* Catholike *faith. For ſhee did therefore define that truth to be* Catholike, *becauſe that truth was* Catholike, *and if it had not beene* Catholike, *the Church defining it to bee* Catholike *ſhould haue erred, therefore it was* Catholike *and reuealed by God before the Church defined it. Wherefore the Church cannot make a new Article of faith, but that which before was true faith, but not certainely knowne to vs, the Church by her definition maketh*

keth it knowne to vs.

108 *In like maner wee haue this from the Church, to know certainly which is diuine Scripture, and we are bound to account that to be diuine Scripture, which the Church hath defined to be diuine.* And *although shee doth certainely define, and cannot erre, yet shee doth not make by her definition, that Scripture to bee diuine: for therefore shee hath declared it to be diuine, becanse it was truely diuine, and if it had not beene before diuine Scripture, the Church would not haue declared it to be diuine. Wherefore although that assertion which is condemned by the Catholike Church to be contrary to* Catholike faith, *and to bee accounted* herefie, *was also* herefie *before the definition of the Church, yet before the Church did define it, the maintainers of that opinion were not called* heretickes, *becanse it was not knowne, whether that opinion was contrary to* Catholike faith: *but now after the definition of the Church they shall bee called* hereticks, *whosoeuer shall approue and maintaine that opinion, not for that their opinion was not before false, contrary to Catholike faith, and* herefie, *but becanse this name of* hereickes *beeing infamous, and appertaining to that most heinous crime, doth require a certaine pertinacy, and rebellion departing from the definitions of the Catholike Church, which could not truely be accounted at that time, when it was doubtfull and disputable, and the Church had not defined, whether that opinion was repugnant to Religion and faith.*

109. *In this sense therefore it may be said, that the Church hath power to declare an assertion to be* Catholike, *and to appertaine to* Catholike faith, *to this effect, that after the definition of the Church, the said assertion is so manifestly of faith, that he is to be accounted an obstinate* hereticke, *who defending the contrary shall depart from that definition, although before the definition of the Church, the said assertion albeit was most true and Catholike, yet by reason of the doubt, and controuersie touching that point*

h.,

hee could not iuſtly be called an heretick *, who ſhould allow, and follow the contrary poſition.* And what hath bene ſaid, if there be any doubt, or controuerſie touching any text of holy Scripture, and the true ſenſe thereof, is proportionally to be vnderſtood, if there be any doubt, or controruerſie touching any definition of the Church, and the true ſenſe thereof; as wee ſee there is now a controuerſie betwixt the *Diuines* of *Rome,* and *Paris,* touching the definition of the *Councell of Conſtance* concerning the Superiority of the *Church* , or a Generall *Councell* aboue the Pope , and among many other Catholikes touching the decrees and declarations of diuerſe other *Generall Councells,* and now lately touching the ſenſe of thoſe words of the *Councell of Lateran, Si vero Dominus temporalis, &c. But if the temporall Lord, &c.* Which ſome *Catholikes* of late haue greatly vrged to proue the *Popes* power to depoſe Princes, whereof *beneath* b we will diſcourſe at large.

b *Part.* 3 *.cap.* 9. *& ſeq.*

110. From this doctrine, which neither Mr. *Fitzherbert*, nor any other can proue to be *improbable* , it cleerely followeth, that *hereſie* being a falſhood repugnant to holy Scriptures, or diuine reuelation, with the ſame *certainty* , or *probability,* wherewith one is perſwaded, that ſuch a doctrine, or poſition, is falſe, and *repugnant* to *holy Scriptures,* or *diuine* reuelation, with the ſame *certainty,* or probabilitie hee may *abhorre, deteſt,* and *abiure* that doctrine for *hereticall*; And conſequently it followeth, that if it be lawfull to *abhorre, deteſt,* and *abiure* for *impious, damnable,* and *falſe* doctrine *repugnant* to *truth* contained in the *word of God,* this Doctrine and poſition , *That Princes which be excommunicated or depriued by the Pope may be depoſed or murthered by their Subiects or any other,* (which *poſition* for that it concerneth *practiſe,* and not onely *ſpeculation,* is in very deed *falſe, impious, damnable,* and *repugnant* to *truth* contained in *holy Scriptures,* and ought ſo to be accounted, not onely by thoſe, who are of opinion

on that the *Pope* hath not power to *depriue* Princes, but
alfo, fo long as this queftion remaineth vndecided and
in controuerfie, by thofe who doe *fpeculatiuely* thinke
that hee hath authority to depriue them) it is lawfull
alfo to abiure it for *hereticall*. And this I hope may fuffice for the defence of my firft, and principall anfweare,
and for the confutation of M. *Fitzherberts Reply* therevnto.

111. The *Second* anfwere, which I haue heard
many Catholikes giue to the aforefaid obiection of the
Authour of that Englifh *Dialogue* againft the word
[*hereticall*] contained in this claufe of the oath, and
which *Anfweare* Mr. *Fitzherbert* laboureth in vaine to
ouerthrow, I related ᶜ in thefe words. *The fecond prin-* ᶜ *Cap.* 5. *Sec.*
cipall anfweare, which fome of our Countrimen doe 2. *nu.* 28. 29
make to the aforefaid obiection, is gathered from the
doctrine of Card. *Bellarmine*, who expounding ᵈ that ᵈ *Lib.* 2. *de Con-*
fentence of *Pope Gregory* the firft ᵉ *I confeffe, that I* *cil. cap.* 12.
doe receiue the foure firft Councells, as the foure bookes of
the Gofpell, affirmeth, *that the aduerbe* [as] *doth import* ᵉ *Lib.* 1. *epift.*
a fimilitude, and not an equality, as that of Matth. 5. *Be* 24.
you perfect, as your heauenly Father is perfect. For in like
manner thefe Catholiks doe anfweare, that thofe
words, *I doe abhorre, deteft, and abiure as heretical, &c.*
doe not import an *equality*, but a *fimilitude*, and that
in common fpeech they doe onely fignifie, that I doe
exceedingly deteft that doctrine. And fo wee vfually
fay, *I hate him as the diuel, I loue him as my brother,* not
intending thereby to affirme, that the *one* is in truth a
Diuel, or the *other* my *brother*.

112 Now to omit the word [*murthered*] as though
there were no mention at all made in the oath, concerning the *murthering* of Princes, and to fpeake onely of *depofing* them; thefe men affirme, that the aforefaid pofition, *Princes, which be excommunicated or*
depriued by the Pope, may be depofed by their Subiects,
or any other, fuppofing that this queftion concerning

L   the

the *Popes* power to depofe Princes , is not yet decided, is in their iudgments a falfe , and feditious propofition, and that it hath fome fimilitude with *herefie* , not for that they thinke it to be in very deed *heretic:ll* (taking *heretkall* in that ftrictfenfe, as fome Catholikes doe take it) but for that they doe conftintly hold it to be of fuch a nature , that it may be condemned by the Church for an *hereticall* propofition(and then the maintainers thereof to be p operly *heretikes*) if *depofing* be taken in that fenfe, as it is in this branch of the oath diftin guifhed from *depriuing*. For to *depriue* a Prince, is to take away by lawfull fentence his Regall authority, and in this branch is referred to the *Pope*, but to *depofe* a Prince is to thruft him out of the poffeffion of his kingdome , and in this branch is referred to *Subiects*, or *any other whatfoeuer*.

113. The *falfhood* therefore of the aforefaid pofition, may be gathered partly from holy Scripture , f *Render to Cæfar the thinges which are Cæfars* : which precept is plainly vnderftood , not onely of *rendring* to *Cæfar* that which is *Cæfars*, but alfo of not *taking* away from him that which is his , and which he lawfully poffeffeth : as alfo contrarywife the plaine meaning of that precept of the *Decalogue*, *Thou fhalt not fteale*, g is not onely that wee muft not *take* away vniuftly , that thing which is our neighbours, but alfo that we muft *render* to him that which is his owne. And partly it may be gathered from the moft true principles of the Diuines, and Lawyers, to wit , *that no man is to be put out of his lawfull poffeffions , vntill the right of the aduerfe part be fufficiently decided.*

114 Seeing therefore that this queftion concerning the *Popes* power to depriue Princes is not as yet fufficiently decided , for that *as yet the Iudge hath not determined the controuerfie*, as *Trithemius* h well affirmed, and we alfo aboue i haue fhewed, fo long as it is in queftion among Catholikes, and *probably* difputed

---

Marginal notes:

f *Mat.* 22.

g *Exod.* 20.

h *In Chron. Monaft. Hirfa. ad annum* 1105.
i *Cap.* 3. *fec.* 3

ted on both fides, whether the *Pope* hath fuch authority to *depriue* Princes or no, they cannot by vertue of
any *Excommunication*, or *fentence* of *depriuation*, made
by the *Pope* againft them, be *depofed* by their *Subiects*,
or any other whatfoeuer, or, which is all one, be *violently* by their Subiects, or any other, *thruft out* from
their Kingdomes which they doe *rightfully poffeffe*. By
this therefore which hath bene faid it is manifeft e-
nough, that according to both thefe anfwers, although
many doe like beft the former, that the aforefaid pofition, *Princes which be excommunicated or de riued by
the Pope, may be depofed by their Subiects, or any other
whatfoeuer*, may truely, lawfully, and without any
danger of periury be abiured as *impious* and *hereti all*
doctrine. Thus I anfwered in my *Theol. Difputation*.

115   Now againft this *Anfwere* M. *Fitzherbert* obiecteth thus: *Th s fecond anfwere* faith he [k], *is fufficiently
confuted by the words of the law or oath,which as I haue fignified ought to be taken,& vnderftood in th ir moft proper
& cleare fenfe; in which refpect the aduerbe* [as] *being ioyned to* impious and hereticall, *muft needs denote and fig-
rifie, not a fimilitude, nor yet an equalitie, (by the way of
comparifon) but a realitie of impiety, and herefie in that
doctrine, for fo,no doubt ,doth euery man take it that readeth the faid claufe.*

k *Cap.* 4. *nu.*
25.

116.   But to this it is anfwered, *firft*, that M. *Fitzherbert* abufeth his Reader in corrupting and concealing thofe rules, which I related out of *Suarez*, and
others, for the vnderftanding of the words of euery
law, and confequently of this oath. For neither did
thofe Authors affirme, that the words of euery law
ought to be taken, and vnderftood in their *moft* proper, and *moft* vfuall fenfe, but onely in their *proper* and
vfuall fenfe, taking *proper*, as it is oppofed to *improper*, or *metaphoricall*, and not to that which is fomewhat the *leffe proper* ,and *vfuall*, as it is oppofed to *vnufuall*, and not to that which is fomewhat the *leffe vfu-*

L 2   *all*

all: Neither did they alſo affirme, that the words of
euery law, are *alwaies* to be vnderſtood in their *proper*
and *vſuall* ſignification : but the *matter* alſo of the law,
the *will* of the law-maker, and other *circumſtances* are
to be regarded. *Wherefore if at any time*, ſaith Suarez [1],
*the words taken in their proper ſignification ſhould argue
any iniuſtice, or like abſurditie in the minde of the Law*;
*maker, they muſt be drawne to a ſenſe although improper,
wherein the law may be iuſt and reaſonable, becauſe this is
preſumed to be the will of the Law-maker, as it hath bene
declared by many lawes in ff.* tit. de legibus. *For in a
doubtfull word of the Law*, ſaith the Law, *that ſenſe is
rather to be choſen, which is void of all default, eſpecially
ſeeing that by this the will alſo of the Law-maker may be
gathered. For it ought not to be preſumed, that the Law-
maker did intend to commaund any abſurd or inconuenient
thing, vnleſſe the contrarie doe euidently appeare.*

117   *But if it chance*, ſaith *Suarez* [m], *that any words
of the Law haue together many proper and vſuall ſignifica-
tions, then we muſt obſerue that rule, which in all ambiguous and equiuocall ſpeeches, is wont prudently to be obſerued, to wit that the matter of the Law with other circumſtances be diligently conſidered, for by them the meaning of the words will be eaſily determined. For the words
muſt eſpecially be agreable to the matter, according to that
rule of the law*, [o] whenſoeuer the ſame ſpech hath two
ſenſes, let that eſpecially be taken, which is more agreable to the matter. And therefore if the words be *ambiguous or doubtfull*, they muſt be drawne to that ſenſe,
as I ſaid before, which containeth no *iniuſtice* or *abſurdity: And a benigne and fauourable interpretation, if
there be no other let, is alwaies to be preferred, according to that approued rule of the law*, [p] Lawes are to be in-
terpreted in the more fauourable ſenſe, that thereby
their will and meaning might be conſerued: *and doubtfull ſpeeches*, as *Emanuell Sa.* affirmeth, [q] *are to be taken
in the better ſenſe, and which is more profitable to the ſpea-
ker*

[1] *Lib. 6. de
Leg. cap. 1, nu.
17.*

[m] *Cap. 1. nu.
11.*

[o] *Leg. Quoti-
es ff. de regulis
Iuris.*

[p] *Leg. Benig-
nius ff. de legi-
bus.*
[q] *Verbo Inter-
pretatio
nu. 17.*

ker. This, and much more to the fame purpofe did I there at large relate, which my *Aduerfary* here concealeth, and which if he had fet downe, would plainly haue fatiffied his chiefeft exception, by which, contrary to the aforefaid rule, he laboureth to drawe the wordes of this oath, which hee may *fauorably*, and *commodioufly* expound, to containe in his opinion, an *vnlawfull*, and *inconuenient fenfe.*

118. And from this, which I haue now related, it is anfwered *fecondly*, that the Aduerbe [*as*] being an Aduerbe of *fimilitude*, doth *moft properly, moft commonly*, and *moft vfually* denote a *fimilitude*, or fome *equality* by way of *comparifon*, and not an *identitie*, or *reality*: and it *fometimes* it doth fignifie an *identitie*, or *reality*, as *many times* it doth, although *feldome* in *comparifon* of the other, this is *by reafon of the matter*, & not *by vertue of the word*, or by force of the *Aduerbe* of fimilitude [*as*]. Wherefore to know, when the Aduerbe [*as*] doth fignifie a *fimilitude*, and when a *reality*, or *identity*, we muft regard the matter, to which it is applied. Seing therfore that this *doctrine* or *pofition*, *That Princes which be excommunicated or depriued by the Pope, may be depofed, orthruft out of the poffeffion of their kingdomes by their fubiects or any other*, fo long as this *doctrine* concerning the *Popes* power to *depriue* Princes remaineth queftionable, and not decided, is *truely impious*, and although it be not *truely hereticall*, taking *hereticall* for that, which to maintaine maketh one a *formall hereticke*, yet it hath a great *affinity*, and *fimilitude* with this *heretical*, for that it is a *falfe, impious*, and *damnable* doctrine, *repugnant* to morall iuftice, *iniurious* to Soueraigne Princes in a moft high degree, and *contrary* alfo to the word of G o d reuealed in holy Scriptures, which therefore may by an *authenticall definition* of the Church be declared to be *properly* and *ftrictly heretical*, for this caufe it may well be faid, that according to the aforefaid rule, that doubtfull or ambiguous words of a law

L 3　　　　　are

are to be taken in the more *fauorable* ſenſe and wherein they containe no *iniuſtice*, or *vntruth*, the Aduerbe
[*as*] being, according to his moſt *proper*, and moſt
vſual ſignification, an *Aduerbe* of *ſimilitude*, may in
the word [*impious*] by *reaſon* of the *matter*, and not by
force of the *word*, denote, and ſignifie an *identitie*, or
reality of *impiety*, and in the word [*heretical*] onely a
ſimilitude, or ſome *equality* of *hereſie* by the way of
compariſon', taking *hereſie* in the aforeſaid rigorous manner : Neither ought any man that readeth
the ſaid clauſe, the aforeſaid rules being obſerued, vnderſtand the Aduerbe [*as*] in any other ſenſe, eſpecially which is thought to be *falſe*, or *inconuenient*.

119. *But beſides that this difference may be noted,*
ſaith Mr. *Fitzherbert* ᵣ, *betwixt the examples, which*
Widdrington *giueth, and this clauſe of the oath, that in*
the examples, to wit, I loue him as my brother, *and*, I
hate him as the Diuell,*and ſuch like, the word* [As] *hath*
relation to two diuerſe ſubiects, and therefore muſt needes
be vnderſtood comparatiuely, *whereas in the clauſe of the*
oath, *there is ſpeech onely of one ſubiect, to wit, of the*
doctrine,*and* heretical *being an* adiective *is affirmed alſo*
of the ſaid doctrine, *as* prædicatum de ſubjecto, *and*
therefore the word [as] *being referred to* here icall,
which is affirmed of the doctrine *onely, cannot be vnder-*
ſtood comparatiuely *(as it is in the examples where there*
are two different ſubiects) but muſt needs denote a reality
of hereſie *in the doctrine.*

120. But *firſt* it is vntrue, that in the examples,
which I brought, the Aduerbe [*as*] muſt of neceſſity
haue relation to two diuerſe *ſubiects*, or *perſons* : for it
may be referred to one and the ſame ſubiect or perſon;
as if one ſhould be blamed for not louing his brother,
or for not hating the Diuell, hee might very well anſweare, and ſay, in truth *I loue him as my brother*, or *I*
hate him as the Diuell : where the Aduerbe [*as*] by
reaſon of the *matter* doth ſignifie a *reality* of *brother-*
hood

hood, and a *true Diuel*, and not onely a *similitude*, or an *equality* by the way of comparison. And therefore to know when the Aduerbe [*as*] doth denote a *reality*, and not a *similitude*, wee must regard the *matter*, to which it hath relation, for that *most commonly*, and according to the *most proper* signification, and *force* of the *word*, it being an *Aduerbe* of *similitude*, doth denote onely a *similitude*, and if perchance it doth signifie a *reality*, it is not *by force of the word*, and by the *most common* signification thereof, but *by reason of the matter*, to which it is applyed.

121. *Secondly*, it is also vntrue, that the Aduerbe [*as*] when it connecteth the *predicate* with the *subiect*, or the *adiectiue* with the *substantiue*, doth alwaies denote a *realitie*, and not onely a *similitude*, or an *equality* by the way of comparison, as by infinite examples contained in the holy Scriptures I could conuince. As Psal. 37. *Ego autem tanquam surdus non audiebam, &c.* and *I as deafe did not heare*, and *as dumbe opened not my mouth*. Isa. 53. *Et nos putauimus eum quasi leprosum*. And *we accounted him as leprous*. Isa. 57. *quia tacens et quasi non videns*. For *I houlding my peace*, said almighty GOD, *and as not seeing*. Isa. 59. *palpauimus sicut caeci parietem*. *Wee as blind groped the wall*. Iob.12. *errare eos faciet quasi ebrios*, *hee will cause them to erre as being drunken*. Mat.28. *Et facti sunt velut mortui*. And *they became as dead*. Mar. 9. *Factus est sicut mortuus*. *He became as dead*. 1 Cor. 15. *tanquam abortiuo visus est et mihi*. And *hee appeared to me also as an abortiue*. 2 Cor.11. *ne quis me putet insipientem, alioquin velut insipientem accipite me*, *Let no man thinke mee to be foolish*, *otherwise take mee as foolish* Apocalyp. 1. *Cecidi ad pedes eius tanquam mortuus*. *I fell at his feet as dead*.

122. In these, and infinite other examples, which might bee alleadged, there is speech onely of *one subiect*, and the Aduerbe [*as*] doth connect the *adiectiue* or *predicate*, with the *substantiue* or *subiect*, and yet it doth

doth not denote a *reality*, but onely a *ſimilitude.* And
if perchance any one ſhould reply, and ſay, that in
thoſe examples, although one onely *ſubſtantiue* or *ſub-*
iect bee expreſſed, yet there may bee vnderſtood not
the ſame *ſubſtantiue* or *ſubiect*, but an other : as *I fell*
at his feet as a dead man , *take me as a fooliſh man* , and
ſo of the reſt: ſo likewiſe we may ſay that in this clauſe
of the Oath there may bee alſo vnderſtood an other
ſubſtantiue or *ſubiect*, as, *I abhorre, deteſt and abiure as*
impious and hereticall *doctrine, this doctrine and poſi-*
tion &c. Wherefore whether there bee one *ſubiect* or
two, whether the *adiectiue* bee affirmed of the *ſub-*
ſtantiue, as *predicatum de ſubiecto*, or no, the Aduerbe
[*as*] by the *proper* ſignification, and *force* of the word
being an *Aduerbe* of *ſimilitude*, doth *moſt commonly*,
and vſually denote a *ſimilitude*, and if at any time it ſignifie a *reality*, or *identitie*, it is not ſo much *by force of*
the word, as *by vertue of the matter*, to which it is referred.

123 And this is the reaſon, why the Aduerbe [*as*]
being referred to *impious* in this clauſe of the Oath,
doth denote a *reality*, and truth of *impiety* , and being
referred to *hereticall* doth onely denote a *ſimilitude* of
hereſie , taking *hereſie* in that ſtrict ſenſe before declared: becauſe although it being an *Aduerbe* of *ſimili-*
tude, doth *by vertue* and *force* of the *word* onely denote a *ſimilitude*, both in the word *hereticall*, and alſo
in the word *impious* , yet *by reaſon of the matter*, to
which it is referred, for that the *doctrine* contained
in this clauſe is *truely impious*, and it is *hereticall* onely
by *ſimili ude* and *compariſon* , taking *hereticall* in that
rigorous ſenſe before mentioned, therefore according
to the aforeſaid rule, *that the ſenſe of the wordes of euery*
law is to bee vnderſtood according to the matter, and that
the *ſenſe* and *meaning of the wordes of euery law*, (and
conſequently of this *oath* eſtabliſhed by a publike law)
ought to bee drawne to that ſenſe, if there be no other let,

which

which *containeth no vntruth, iniuſtice, or abſurdity,* and
that the Aduerbe [*as*] in *common ſenſe,* and vnderſtanding of men, to which *common and vſuall ſenſe* his
Maieſty doth in expreſſe wordes bind the takers of
this *oath,* doth onely denote a *ſimilitude* and not a *reality,* vnleſſe the *matter* which is treated of doth enforce
vs therevnto, there is great reaſon, that the Aduerbe
[*as*] ſhould in the word *impious, by vertue of the matter,*
and not *by force of the word,* being taken in his *moſt
proper* and vſuall ſignification, ſignifie a *reality,* and in
the word *hereticall,* taking *hereticall* in that rigorous
manner ſo often repeated, ſhould denote onely a
ſimilitude, or ſome *equality* by the way of *compariſon.*

    124 And by this which hath beene ſaid, that alſo
which M. *Fitzherbert* laſtly addeth, is eaſily anſwered.
Furthermore, ſaith hee [f], *it is euident, that the Aduerbe* [as] *being conſidered as it is ioyned with the word*
[impious] *doth clerely imply the reality whereof I ſpeake,
ſignifying that the ſaid doctrine is* truely impious, *and
wicked, and not onely to be eſteemed ſo by the way of ſimilitude, or compariſon, as it is manifeſt by the wordes before and after, which are,* I doe from my heart abhorre,
deteſt, and abiure, as impious and hereticall, this damnable doctrine, &c. *Whereby it is cleare, that his* Maieſties *meaning was to cauſe the takers of this* oath *to
condemne that doctrine to bee* truely impious, *ſeeing that
hee will haue them to ſweare, that they abhorre and deteſt it from their heart, and calleth it alſo a damnable
doctrine.*

    125 *And this being ſo, I would gladly know of* Wid-
drington, *what reaſon hee can haue to take the Aduerbe*
[as] *in one ſenſe as it is referred to* hereticall, *and in an
other, as it is ioyned with* impious, *ſeeing that is referred
to both alike with a copulatiue coniunction, the one immediately following the other: will hee ſay that it is to bee taken* properly *in the one, and* improperly *in the other? How*

[f] *n. 27. 28.*

can that *ſtand with his former rules out of* Suarez. *touching the cleare and perſpicuous ſenſe*, *which is required in Lawes and Oaths (eſpecially in this oath, wherein there is an expreſſe clauſe afterwards to exclude all equiuocation?)therefore hee muſt needs grant, that if the doctrine be abiured as* truely impious, *it is alſo abiured as* truely heretically, *or elſe hee muſt make ſuch a* Gallimaufrey, *as was neuer made in any law or oath, within the compaſſe of foure wordes onely.*

126. But this is eaſily anſwered by that which I haue already ſaide. For *firſt*, if the word [*hereticall*] be taken in that ſenſe, as *Alphonſus de Caſtro*, *Couerruuias*, and many other learned Catholikes doe take it, *for euery falſe doctrine, which is repugnant to the word of God, or diuine reuelation*, which is a *proper*, and *vſuall* ſignification of the word [*hereticall*] and in which ſe ſe alſo, as I conceiue, his *Maieſty*, and other *Proteſtants* doe take that word, and not *for that doctrine which is made hereticall by the definition or declaration of the Catholike Romane Church*, then the aduerbe [*as*] both in the word *impious*, and alſo in the word *hereticall* doth *by vertue of the matter*, and other circumſtances, denote a *reality* of *impiety*, and *hereſie*, although not *by force of the word* being taken in the *moſt proper* and vſuall ſignification, which being an aduerbe of *ſimilitude*, would onely denote a *ſimilitude* both of *hereſie*, and alſo *impiety*, vnleſſe the *matter*, with other circumſtances, did imply the contrary.

127. But if the word [*hereticall*] be taken for that doctrine, which is made *hereticall* by the Church, and which before the declaration, or definition of the Church is not accounted *hereticall*, although it be in very deede a *falſe doctrine*, and *contrary to the word of God*, reuealed to vs in the holy Scriptures (which ſignification of the word, *hereticall*, whether it be the more *proper*, and the more vſuall then the *former*, or no, I will not now contend, it being ſufficient, and ouer
ſufficient

fufficient for my purpofe, that the *former* fenfe is *pro-*
per and *vfuall* among Catholikes, and not *metaphoricall*
and *vnufuall*) then the reafon, which a little aboue
I alleaged, is very fufficient, and my *Aduerfarie's* de-
maund is clearly fatisfied, to wit, why the aduerbe [*as*]
fhould *by vertue of the matter*, and *by the approued rules*
of Diuines and Lawyers, for the interpretation of the
words of euery Law, being referred to *impious*, fignifie a *realitie* of *impiety*, and being referred to *hereti-*
call, fhould onely denote a *fimilitude* of *herefie*, taking
herefie in that rigorous fenfe (although *by vertue of the*
word, and proper fignification of the aduerbe [*as*] it
being an aduerbe of *fimilitude*, both in the word *im-*
pious, and alfo in the word *hereticall*, doth onely fignifie, as I haue faide, a *fimilitude* of *impiety*, and *here-*
fie) either then fhould the aduerbe [*as*] be taken
properly in one, and *improperly* in the other, as my
Aduerfary would feeme to inferre, but it is taken *pro-*
perly in both, for that the aduerbe [*as*] doth *properly*,
and vfually, *by reafon of the matter* fometimes denote
a *realitie*, and fometimes a *fimilitude*, although moft
properly and *moft vfually*, it being an aduerbe of *fimi-*
litude, doth *by force of the word* denote onely a *fimi-*
litude.

128 *Secondly*, to that which M. *Fitzherbert* obiecteth
touching *equinocatiõ*, which by an expreffe claufe is excluded in this oath, I anfwered alfo in my *Theological*
Difputation[t], that his *Maiefty* by thofe words [*with-*
out any equinocation] did not vnderftand and meane,
that in the *oath*, no *equinocall* word, or fentence was
contained, for this is almoft impoffible, feeing that
moft words are *equinocall*, and haue *diuerfe*, yea and
fometimes alfo *proper* and *vfuall* fignifications: But
his *Maiefties* meaning was, that the fwearer fhould
not *equinocate*, that is, *deale vnfincerely*, but he fhould
deale *plainely*, and *fincerely*, without any fraude or
guile, nor take the words in an other fenfe, then the

t *Cap. 8. fec*
2.

common meaning and vnderstanding of them doe
beare. And so those words [*without any equiuocati-*
on &c.] are onely a declaration of those former words
[*And all these thinges I doe plainely and sincerely acknow-*
ledge and sweare &c.] For it is one thing to vse *equiuo-*
call words, which may be called a *materiall equiuoca-*
tion , and an other thing to *equiuocate* , or to vse *for-*
mall equiuocation. For to *equiuocate* properly, or to
vse *formall equiuocation* , as it is commonly vnderstood
in this Kingdome , is to vse *equiuocall* words, or some
secret reseruation of purpose to *delude* the hearer, so
that he, who heareth the words, vnderstandeth them
in an other sense, then he who vttereth them , and it
importeth an *vnsincere manner of dealing.* If therefore in this *oath* there be perchance *many common sen-*
ses of the same word, sentence, or proposition , all
circumstances duely considered , we ought to take it
in that *common sense* , wherein we are perswaded his
Maiestie would haue vs to take it, for this is his principall meaning and intention, that we should deale
plainely and sincerely with him , without any fraude,
guile, mentall euasion, or secret reseruation whatsoeuer.

129   And if it should so fall out that we cannot be
assured of his *Maiesties* meaning and intention, when
any difficulty concerning the sense of any word or sentence contained in the oath shall arise, then we must re-
curre to those generall rules, which *Diuines* & *Lawiers*
assigne for the interpreting of the wordes of euery
law, for this wee may with iust reason presume to bee
the generall intention of his *Maiesty* , as also of euery
lawmaker. And if perchance there bee any Catholike
so scrupulous, that by applying the aforesaid generall
rules to any ambiguous and doubtfull word, or sentence in the *oath*, he cannot yet quiet his conscience,
yet he may auoid all danger of equiuocating, by publikely declaring in what sense he taketh that word or
sentence

sentence, which hath diuers *proper* and *vsuall* significations: as by declaring in what sense hee taketh the Aduerbe [*as*] both in the word *impious* and also in the word *hereticall*. and likewise in what sense he taketh the word *hereticall*, and so of others, and this declaration will both auoid all danger of *equiuocating*, and also without doubt satisfie the *Magistrate*, so that his *declaration* be not knowne to be against his *Maiesties meaning and intention*.

130 And truely it is strange, that whereas the oath is by his *Maiesty*, and the *Parliament* propounded, and expressed in such maner of wordes, that according to the approued rules assigned by *Catholike* Diuines and Lawyers for the interpreting of lawes, it may bee expounded in a *true*, *lawfull*, and *commodious* sense to the swearer, which sense also is agreeable to the *proper* and vsuall signification of the words, yet M *Fitzherbert*, and other impugners of the oath, (for which English Catholikes are to giue them little thankes) will needs haue them, *contrary to the aforesaid rules*, vnderstand in that sense, which they account to be *false*, *vnlawfull*, and to bee an *vtter ruine to the refusers* of the oath, whereas, according to the aforesaid rules, *they ought to draw the wordes, to a metaphoricall and improper sense, if the proper sense should argue in the law*, (and consequently in the oath ordained by a publike law) *any falshood, iniustice, absurdity, or other inconuenience*.

131 Seeing therefore it cannot be denyed, that the *proper* and *vsuall* signification of the Aduerbe [*as*] it being an Aduerbe of *similitude*, is to signifie a *similitude*, and often times also *by reason of the matter*, but not *by force of the word*, being taken in the *most proper and most vsuall signification*, a *reality*: and of the word [*hereticall*] as it is taken by many Catholike Diuines, for *euery falshood repugnant to diuine reuelation*, it is manifest, that whether we affirme, that the Aduerbe

[*as*] doth ſignifie onely a *ſimilitude*, or alſo a *reality* both in the word *impious*, and alſo in the word, *hereticall*, or a *reality* in the *firſt*, and a *ſimilitude* in the *ſecond* in the maner before declared, it is no *gallimaufre*, but a *true*, and *plaine* declaring of the *common* ſenſe, and vnderſtanding of the wordes according to the approued rules preſcribed by Catholike Diuines and Lawyers for the interpreting of doubtfull and ambiguous wordes in euery Law. And thus much concerning the *ſecond Anſwer*, and M. *Fitzherberts Reply* againſt the ſame.

132 Now then to make an end of this Chapter, vpon theſe *premiſes* I will draw foure concluſions contrary to thoſe which M. *Fitzherbert* heere collecteth. *Firſt*, ſaith hee [u] , *whereas* Widdrington *chargeth mee to haue affirmed falſly, that the doctrine of the Popes power to depoſe Princes, is manifeſtly abiured in the oath, as* impious and hereticall. *hee chargeth me* falſly *in two reſpects, the one becauſe I affirmed no ſuch thing, and the other for that albeit I had ſaid ſo, yet I had ſaid truely, as it euidently appeareth, not onely by the plaine wordes, ſubſtance and circumſtances of the oath, but alſo by his Maieſties meaning and intention therein.*

133 But contrariwiſe I conclude, that whereas I charged him *to haue falſly* or vntruely *affirmed, that the doctrine of the Popes power to depoſe Princes is manifeſtly* abiured in this *oath, as* impious & hereticall, I charged him truly in two reſpects: the one becauſe it is true, that he affirmeth ſo much as I haue cleerly conuinced by his owne wordes, and I wonder that hee is not aſhamed to affirme ſuch a palpable vntruth: the other for that this aſſertion of his is falſe, as euidently appeareth both by the plaine words, ſubſtance, and circumſtances of the oath, and alſo by his *Maieſties* meaning and intention therein, which is to bee gathered principally by the words, which, as you haue ſeene, being taken in their *proper* and *common* ſenſe, doe cleerly ſhew

u *nu.* 29.

shew that both parts of that *disiunctiue* propofition, *Princes which bee excommunicated or depriued by the Pope may bee depofed or murthered by their fubiects*, are not of neceffity to bee abiured as *hereticall*, although *by vertue of the matter*, if *hereticall* bee taken for euery falfe doctrine which is repugnant to truth, contained in holy Scriptures, whether the Church haue declared, or not declared it to bee fo, both parts of that pofi.ition, which alloweth the practife of *depofing* or *murthering* Princes which bee excommunicated or depriued by the *Pope*, may bee truely abiured as *hereticall*, as I haue aboundantly shewed before.

134 *Secondly, it appeareth*, faith M. *Fitzherbert* ˣ, *how different* Widdringtons *doctrine & belief concerning the Popes power to depofe Princes, i from his* Maiefties, *yea from the whole fubftance of the oath, feeing that acc ording to* Widdringtons *opinion, the faid doctrine is probable, (and confequently may bee held, taught, and fworne) whereas his* Maiefty *by this oath condemneth it for deteftable, damnable, impious, and* hereticall, *whereby it may appeare alfo what good feruice he doth to his* Maiefty *with this his probable doctrine, as I haue noted before in the Preface.*

x *nu* 30.

See Preface nu. 25. 26, & 27.

135. But whether my *doctrine*, and *beleife* concerning the *Popes* power to depofe Princes be different from his *Maiefties*, or no, (which my *Aduerfary*, if hee had beene pleafed to haue diligently perufed my writings, might quickly haue perceiued) it is *impertinent* to the prefent queftion conncerning the lawfulneffe, or vnlawfulneffe of the oath; and therefore I neede not at this time to fpeake more expreffely thereof, for not giuing my *Aduerfary* occafion to wrangle about *impertinent* queftions, and to decline the chiefe point, which is controuerfie about the lawfulneffe of the oath. For to proue the oath to be *lawfull*, or *vnlawfull*, wee muft not fo much regard what his *Maiefties* beliefe, or opinion is, touching any point of controuerfie, which may
            feeme

ſeeme to be any way inſinuated in the oath, as it appeareth by his *opinion* concerning his Primacie in ſpiritualls, and the *Popes* power to *excommunicate* him, and
ſuch like, which neuertheleſſe he doth not intend, that
his Subjects ſhall be bound to affirme or deny in this
oath; wee muſt not I ſay, ſo much regard his *opinion*, as
his *intention*, and what is the true *ſenſe*, and *meaning*
of the *oath according to the plain and common vnderſtan-*
ding of the words, to which his *Maieſty* doth bind the
taker, and what *by vertue of the words* we muſt *acknow-*
ledge, profeſſe, deteſt, and *abiure* in this *oath* : Now it is
euident, as I haue ſhewed before, that my opinion is
not different from the ſubſtance of the oath, nor from
that which his *Maieſty* intendeth to bind the ſwearer to
acknowledge, or *abiure* in this oath.

136. For I affirme two things, which are the whole
ſubſtance of the oath ; The *firſt*, is that any Catholike
may *lawfully*, and with a *ſafe conſcience declare, teſtiſie,*
and acknowledge, before God, and in his conſcience, that
the Pope hath no power to depoſe his Maieſty, *nor to diſpoſe*
of any his kingdomes, or Dominions, and ſo of the other
clauſes, which doe follow from this doctrine. And my
reaſon is, for that the doctrine for the *Popes* power to
depoſe Princes, I will not ſay at this preſent, is a *falſe*
doctrine, and *repugnant* to the holy Scriptures,
and to the ancient Fathers, but it is not *certaine*,
and a point of faith, (as Maiſter *Fitzherbert*, and
ſome others of his companie will needs haue it to be)
and the *contrary* is *probable* and conſequently may
with a *ſafe* and *probable* conſcience be acknowledged
and maintained by any Catholike. But whether it be
probable, that the Pope hath power to depoſe Princes
or no, I doe not at this preſent diſpute, neither doe I
either grant it, or deny it, or meddle at all therewith,
as being vnneceſſary to proue the *oath* to be lawfull.
That which I affirme at this time is, that it is *probable*,
that the *Pope* hath no ſuch power. Let vs firſt agree
about

about this point, that it is *probable*, that the Pope hath
no such power, and then we will dispute, how *probable*
it is, that he hath such a power. In the meane time all
Mr. *Fitzherberts* cunning, turning, and winding shall
not draw mee to so great a disaduantage, as to take vpon mee to proue that to be *certaine*, which he, and the
rest of my *Aduersaries* will not grant to be so much
as *probable*.

137. The *second* thing, which touching *practise* I
doe affirme, is, that this doctrine and position, *That
Princes, which be excommunicated or depriued by the
Pope, may be deposed by their Subiects or any other*, to o-
mit now the word [*murthered*] is an *impious* and *damnable* doctrine, and in what sense it may be called *hereticall*, as also whether *by vertue of the words* both parts
of that *disiunctiue* position contained in the oath are
abiured alike, and whether there be the same reason,
that the *deposing*, and *murthering* of Princes should be
abiured *alike*, I haue sufficiently declared before.
Whereby it may also appeare, that my doctrine bringeth no danger at all to his *Maiestie*, as that of my *Aduersaries* doth, but giueth great security both to his
Maiesties person and State, as also I haue noted before
in the Preface y, which the Reader would quickly
haue perceaued, if Mr. *Fitzherbert* had not guilfully,
to disgrace mee with his *Maiestie*, concealed the chiefest part of my answeare and doctrine touching the
security, which it gaue to his *Maiestie*, for which
cause hee hath laboured so much to haue my bookes
forbidden, that the *Reader* may not see my answeares
and doctrine, but after that mangled, and lame manner, as hee is pleased to curtoll and diffigure them.

138. *Thirdly, it is euident*, saith Mr. Fitzherbert, z
that neither Widdrington, *nor any man that followeth
his doctrine, can lawfully sweare this clause of the oath,
whereof wee treat : for no man can with safe conscience
abiure, as* impious and hereticall, *any opinion, which
hee*

y *nu.* 61. & *seq.*

z *nu.* 31.

N

hee *houldeth to be* probable, *as* Widdrington *granteth our opinion to be.*

139. But on the contrary part I fay, that it is euident, that any man who followeth my doctrine, may lawfully fweare this claufe of the oath, whereof wee treat : for any man may with fafe confcience *abiure,* as *impious and hereticall,* that doctrine and pofition, which is truely as *impious and hereticall:* Neither doe I grant, that the doctrine and pofition contained in this claufe of the oath, which, as you fee, belongeth to *practife,* is *probable,* as my Aduerfary vntruely affirmeth, but I acknowledge, that it is a *falfe, damnable, impious,* and *hereticall* doctrine, and that therefore it ought by all Catholikes to be *abhorred. detefled, and abiur d fo from their hearts,* as I haue cleerely proued before: and as for the fpeculatiue doctrine of *depofing* Princes, I neither grant, nor deny it to be *probable,* nor medle at all therewith, as being *impertinen ,*as I haue often faid, to proue that the *oath* may lawfully be taken.

* *nn. 32.*

140 *Laftly, I conclude,* faith M.*Fitzherbert* [2], *that albeit there were no o her thing in the oath to make it vnlawfull, yet this onely claufe might fuffice to doe it, yea and ought to moue all Catholikes to refufe it. For furely he muft be a Catholike of a ftrange confcience, that can perfwade himfelfe to deteft, abiure, and abhorre from his heart, a doctrine that is taught by the beft Catholike wri-'ers, ancient and moderne, and confirmed by the practife of the* Catholike Church, *and the authority of diuers* Generall and Prouinciall Councells, *as experience hath fhewed for many hundreds of yeares. So as thou feeft,* good Reader, *what* Widdrington *gaineth by his wrangling, feeing that the further he goeth, the further he intangleth himfelfe ftill in an inextricable labyrinth of abfurdities, whiles he feeketh to intangle the confciences of* Catholikes *in the fnares of his pretended probabilities. And this fhall fuffice for this point.*

141. But contrariwife I conclude, that this claufe

is

is not sufficient to make the *oath* vnlawfull, or to moue
any Catholike to refuse the same. For surely he must
be a Catholike of a strange conscience, and *caried a-*
way with the like fanaticall zeale and bloody maximes
*that the Powder-Traitors were,*that can perswade himselfe, that the *murthering* of Princes,being excommunicated or depriued by the Pope, and the doctrine
thereof, which is a part of that *conditionall disiunctiue*
proposition, abiured in this clause of the oath, ought
not to be *detested, abhorred and abiured from his heart:*
Neither was this doctrine euer taught before in the
Church of God by any Catholike writer, ancient or
moderne, or confirmed by the practise of the Catholike Church, or authority of any Generall or Prouinciall Councell.

142. And although the doctrine for the Popes
power to depose Princes by way of *sentence* hath bene
taught by many Catholike writers, and also *practised*
by diuers Popes, onely since the time of Pope *Gregory*
the seauenth, who was the *first Pope*, saith *Onuphrius,*
that *contrary to the custome of his ancestors, durst, I doe*
not say excommunicate, but also depriue Cæsar *himselfe*
(by whom if he was not chosen, he was at least confirmed)
of his Kingdome and Empire: A thing not heard of before
those times [b], yet considering that this doctrine hath
not as yet bene *defined* by the Church,and consequently is not a *certaine* and decided point of faith, but hath
euer bene, and is euen to this day vehemently impugned by many learned Catholikes, truely that Catholike must be a man either of a strange conscience, or
of a weake vnderstanding, who considering the question touching the Popes power to depose Princes,to be
disputable, and as yet not *decided* by the Church, *for*
that there hath euer bene, saith *Azor* [c], *a great contro-*
uersie betwixt Emperours and Kinges *on the one part,*
and the Bishops of Rome *on the other, touching this point)*
can perswade himselfe, that it is lawfull to depose, or

N 2　　　　　　　　　thrust

*See aboue
part 1. cap. 6.
nu. 24.*

c *Azor.*

thrust a King out of his Kingdome, which he lawfully possesseth, so long as the controuersie betwixt the
Pope, and temporall Princes, touching this point remaineth vndecided.

143, For it is manifest, according to the knowne,
and approued rule of the law, which is also grounded
vpon the light of reason, that no man can lawfully be
thrust out from the possession of that thing, which
he rightfully and lawfully possesseth, vntill the controuersie betwixt him and his *Aduersary* touching that
thing be decided by the Iudge. And for this reason,
as I coniecture, Card. *Bellarmine*, and some fewe o-
thers of his *Society* haue of late yeares bene so vehement to make this doctrine for the *Popes* power to depose Princes to be a *Point of faith*, and not to be called
in question by any Catholike; foreseing belike that if
they granted it to be *disputable*, and a thing in controuersie among Catholikes, they must consequently
grant, that the *Popes* power to depose Princes, is onely *titulus sine re*, and can neuer be lawfully put in *practise*, much like to the *title* which one hath to a faire Pal-
lace, whereof an other man is in possession, which neuerthelesse he shall neuer by *dispossessing* the other lawfully enioy, vntill the Iudge hath *decided* his *title*. And
therefore the *practise* not onely touching the *murthering* of Princes excommunicated or depriued by the
Pope, but also touching the *deposing* them, or *thrust-
ing* them out of the possession of their kingdomes, and
the doctrine thereof, may and ought by all good Catholikes to be *detested, abhorred, and abiured from their
hearts*, although *by vertue of the words, and by force of
the disiunctiue* coniunction [*or*] following the verbe
[*may*] it sufficeth, as I shewed before, to abiure the
whole *disiunctiue* position, *as hereticall*, that one onely
part of the *disiunction* be abiured *as hereticall*.

144. So as thou seest, good Reader, both that the
probabilitie, which I maintaine, is not onely pretended

ded, but true and reall, and alfo to render backe Mr.
Fitzherberts words, what he gaineth by his *wrangling*, and *concealing* the chiefe points of my opinion and
doctrine, feeing that the further hee goeth, the further
hee bewrayeth his want both of learning and fincerity,
& *intangleth* himfelfe ftill in an inextricable labyrinth
of abfurdities, whiles hee feeketh to intangle the confciences of Catholikes in the fnares of his *pretended new Catholike faith*; which for that it is, end euer
hath beene euen from the very firft broaching thereof,
impugned by learned Catholikes, as a new inuented
doctrine, preiudiciall to the Soueraigntie of temporal
Princes, and not acknowledged by any one of the ancient Fathers, cleerely conuinceth, that it is not *Catholike.* Neither can that man be accounted a true *Catholike*, who with *Catholike* faith, which cannot be fubiect to errour, beleeueth that doctrine, which is doubtfull, difputable, vncertaine, and not *Catholike*, as is
this, which teacheth that the Pope hath power to depofe Princes. And truely if I fhould perceiue my *Catholike* faith to rely and depend vpon fo weak a ground
and foundation, as is the Popes authority to depofe
Princes, or any other fuch like difputable queftion, I
fhould fcarce thinke my felfe to be a *true Catholike*, and
to haue a *true Catholike* and fupernaturall, but onely a
pretended Catholike, and fupernaturall faith.

145. By which alfo the iudicious Reader may eafily coniecture, what manner of exceptions Mr. *Fitzherbert* can take againft the other claufes of the oath, feeing that thefe obiections, which he hath made againft
this claufe, which he only impugneth, notwithftanding
that he vaunted in the beginning of this chapter, that
he would proue my explication of this claufe, to be a *friuolous euafion*, an *extrauagant interpretation*, and *alfo abfurd euen by my own grounds*, I haue euidently conuinced
to be weake and vnfound, and *himfelfe* by handling the
matter fo infufficiently, guilfully, & bitterly, as he hath

done(but farre more ſpitefully in the former chapters, charging me with *cogging, ſcoffing,* & *gibing,* for being *abſurd, ridiculous, fooliſh, malicious, impious, impudent, heretike* and *no good child of the Catholike Church,* and vſing ſuch like ſlaunderous and diſgracefull tearmes) to be *void of learning, ſincerity, charity,* and alſo *Chriſtian modeſty.* And this may ſuffice alſo for this point.

FINIS.

Faults escaped.

IN the *Epistle*, num. 9. l. 20. *there.* p. 14. l. 37. *I confesse* p. 19 l. 24. *write.* p. 20. l. 23. *reasons.* p. 39. l 4. *Parisioners.* p. 55. l. 20. *Secular.* & l. 34. *the cause.* p. 67. l 9. *lawes.* p. 78. l. 12. *to none.* p 80. l. 34 *S. Dominick.* p 9. l. 4. *Eisengrenius.* p 100. l. *fift.* p. 140. l. 5, *had had.* p, 144. l. 25, *although.* p. 145. l. 31. put out the *comma.* p. 148. l. 13. adde in the margent ᵐ *cap. 6.* p. 158 l. 22. *that Christian.* p. 164. l. 25. *intention.* p. 175. l. 14. *subiect to the.* p. 179. lin. 10. 11. *the spirituall power.*

In the *Adioynder* p. 13. l. 26. *hereticall.* p. 38. *against* the 18. line, adde in the margent. ᵘ *num.* 23. p. 41. l. 29. *sense.* p. 57. l. 21. *but in the.* p. 76. l. 35. *may bee.*

COurteous Reader, *In the* Appendix *to my* Supplication *to the* Popes Holinesse. *Pag* 123. *L.* 15. *I affirmed* M. Wilson, *who made the English* Martyrologe, *wherein Fa.* Garnet, *and Fa.* Holdcorne, *are put for Martyrs, to bee a* Iesuit: *for that I was so informed by two credible persons. But because I haue heard since that one confidently auerre, that although he doth wholly depend vpon the* Iesuits, *and is directed by them, yet he is not as yet a* Iesuite *in habit, I desire that the word* [Iesuite] *in that place thou wilt account for not written, and I haue caused it to be blotted out in the Booke which I sent to his* Holinesse. *But wherefore the* Iesuites *are desirous to haue certaine persons, who either by vow, or promise doe wholly depend on them, and are at their dispose, not to take their habit for a time, but to liue in the world like* Lay-men, *or* Secular Priests, *I shall perchance haue occasion to declare hereafter.*